How to Apply for

Department of Veterans Affairs Benefits for Recent and Senior Veterans and Their Survivors

SENIOR VETERANS SERVICE ALLIANCE 2016 EDITION

Published by the Senior Veterans Service Alliance – May 2016

www.seniorvets.org

Printing: DMT Publishing, North Salt Lake, Utah

How to Apply for

Department of Veterans Affairs Benefits for Recent and Senior Veterans and Their Survivors

Written by: Thomas Day

Cover Design: Roxanne Pope

This book uses VA's "Fully Developed Claims" process for faster and successful decisions

- Claims for Pension and Death Pension with Aid and Attendance or Housebound
- Claims for Compensation and Dependency and Indemnity Compensation (DIC)
- Compensation, SMC and DIC with Aid and Attendance or Housebound Allowance
- Enrolling in Veterans Health Care
- Applying for a State Veterans Home
- Applying for Burial and Accrued Benefits
- Applying for Home Improvement Grants

TABLE OF CONTENTS

APPENDIX 289

GETTING STARTED
Applying for the Right Benefit

Thank you for purchasing our book. It will help you apply for benefits available from the Department of Veterans Affairs (DVA / VA / VBA). We are excited for you and hope the information presented here will help you prepare a strong claim. We encourage you to utilize the checklists and forms on the accompanying DVD disk to ensure your claim is fully developed and properly submitted.

Where to Submit Claims – Claims Intake Center
In order to improve timeliness and lessen the cost of scanning claims into the Veterans Benefits Management System (VBMS), VA has implemented Centralized Mail Processing (CMP). Under these new procedures, claimants and beneficiaries should now send all mail directly to the scanning vendor (Jainesville, Wisconsin Intake Center), eliminating the need for Regional Office (RO) or Pension Management Center (PMC) mail processing. The vendor will scan and upload the digital images for processing. Please refer to the data disk for the appropriate PO Box for your claim.

Benefits for Living Veterans

If you are a veteran or helping a veteran, it is important to know if the application will involve a service-connected disability before you apply. VA describes a service-connected disability as an injury or disease incurred while on active duty or an injury or disease worsened by active military service. Certain veterans may also be classified as having a service-connected disability if the disability was caused by VA Healthcare. There are benefits available for veterans with and without service-connected disabilities.

Service-connected Benefits for Veterans
Shown below are benefits available for living veterans with service-connected issues and the corresponding chapters in this book which will help you prepare that type of claim:

- *Disability Compensation*, a tax-free benefit paid to a veteran for a service-connected disability. See Chapters 3 and 4.
- *Special Monthly Compensation (SMC)*, additional allowances for a service-connected veteran with special circumstances such as the need of aid and attendance by another person. See Chapter 3, Section B and Chapter 4, Section B.
- *VA Healthcare*, see Chapter 6.
- *Housing Grants*, home modifications and other allowances, see Chapter 4, Section B, #21.
- *State Veterans Homes and Benefits*, see Chapter 5.

Non-Service-connected Benefits for Veterans
Shown below are benefits available for living veterans with no service-connected issues and the corresponding chapters which will help you prepare that type of claim:

- *Pension*, commonly called "*Aid and Attendance*," is a tax-free monthly benefit for low income veterans or for veterans who are incurring significant home care, assisted living or nursing home expenses. See Chapter 2
- *VA Healthcare*, see Chapter 6.
- *Housing Grants*, for home modifications and other allowances, see Chapter 4, Section B, #21.
- *State Veterans Homes and Benefits*, see Chapter 5.

Benefits for Surviving Spouses (and in some cases dependent children)

If you are the surviving spouse of a veteran or are assisting a surviving spouse, it is important to know if the application will involve a service-connected disability of the deceased veteran before you apply. VA describes a service-connected disability as an injury or disease incurred while on active duty or an injury or disease worsened by active military service. Certain veterans may also be classified as having a service-connected disability if the disability was caused by VA Healthcare. There are benefits available for surviving spouses of veterans who had service-connected disabilities and who did not.

Shown below are benefits available for surviving spouses of veterans. Pay careful attention to whether or not the benefit is tied to a service-connected issue. <u>If you have questions about your eligibility or status as an entitled surviving spouse based on circumstances like divorce or remarriage, please see Chapter 1</u>, page 9.

- *Dependency and Indemnity Compensation (DIC)* is payable to eligible survivors of a military service member who died on active duty or whose death after service resulted from a service-connected injury or disease. It is also available due to improper treatment of the deceased veteran from VA healthcare or rehabilitation services. DIC is automatically granted to a surviving spouse for a veteran who was permanently and totally disabled for 10 years or more. See Chapters 3 and 4.
- *Survivors (Death) Pension*, commonly called "*Aid and Attendance*," is a tax-free monthly benefit for low income surviving spouses or for surviving spouses who are incurring significant home care, assisted living or nursing home expenses. This benefit is available to widows of veterans with and without service-connected issues. See Chapter 2.
- *CHAMP VA*, a health care benefits program that provides coverage to the spouse or widow(er) and to dependent children of a qualifying sponsor. See Chapter 6.
- *State Veterans Homes and Benefits*, available under certain conditions for any spouse. See Chapter 5
- *Accrued Benefits*, available under certain conditions to survivors or those who have paid for the final expense of a deceased veteran. See Chapter 2.
- *Burial Benefits*, partial reimbursements. See Chapter 7 for rates and instructions.

About the Author
Thomas Day

I am passionate about helping seniors with their issues. This passion, in particular, spills over to my helping veterans and their survivors deal with their elder years and eldercare issues. This (because I am a veteran and because I am disabled myself and most importantly), thanks to the VA healthcare system, I am able to help other veterans become aware of their benefits.

Salt Lake VA Medical Center

My health was going downhill. Vital nerves in my body were gradually deteriorating which would have eventually resulted in an early death. The treatments I received from VA health care saved my life from this rare, wasting disorder. Private-sector doctors couldn't figure it out, but VA doctors did figure it out and stopped the disease process. Unfortunately they could do nothing about the residual nerve damage which has left me mostly disabled. Despite the physical limitations, this great gift from VA has allowed me to become actively involved in helping veterans and other folks in the community plan for their final years of life and obtain needed government benefits.

University of Utah Campus

After graduating high school in 1962, I pursued a year of study at the University of Utah. The next 2 1/2 years were spent in the European country of Austria for my church where I learned to speak German and serve the Austrian people. I reenrolled at the University of Utah in studies with the Department of Physics in the spring of 1966. I graduated with a BA in physics and math in the winter of 1969. My sweetheart, Susan and I met and married in the spring of 1967.

During my college years, the Vietnam War was in full swing and knowing I would be called up, I decided to enlist in the Air Force ROTC program. I subsequently received a commission as a second lieutenant when I graduated from college. I spent the next year -- from June 1969 through June 1970 -- completing basic pilot training at Webb Air Force Base in west Texas. Additional advanced flight training was completed by November of 1970 and I was then assigned as an Instructor Pilot for T-38 advanced jet training at Moody Air Force Base in Georgia. I left the service as a captain with an

Tom as an Air Force Pilot

honorable discharge in the winter of 1973 having completed a little under 4 1/2 years as an Air Force pilot.

The years from 1973 through 1985 were spent in a variety of business pursuits. In 1985, I joined a large insurance company as a registered representative and agent. One aspect or another of financial services has been my profession ever since. In 1997, I struck out on my own as an independent registered investment advisor and fee-based financial planner. Because I no longer had group health insurance for my family, I obtained individual insurance for them and I enrolled in the VA healthcare system. At that time VA was still taking Priority Group 7 veterans into the health care system. As it turned out, enrolling in VA health care was one of the most important events in my life because it prolonged my life and allowed me to pursue the goal of helping other people with aging issues.

During the intervening years I have not only been grateful for veterans health care, but I was able to use the VA loan guarantee for purchasing several homes and the veterans educational benefit for completing an MBA at the University of Utah School of Business. And most recently, I was particularly grateful to receive a 10% disability rating for hearing loss associated with ear infections and with my years on the flight line and exposure to afterburners and other jet noise. This helps me stay in the healthcare system as a Priority Group 3.

My disability and lack of activity had caused me over many years to experience significant weight gain. My primary care physician at VA challenged me to become more involved with my health and helped me enroll in VA MOVE – a weight loss program. The VA MOVE! Program inspired me to do something about my weight and lack of exercise and is continuing to inspire me to fulfill the goals of its program.

Tom's Educational Background, Credentials and Certifications

- Accredited Claims Agent with the Department of Veterans Affairs
- BA in physics and math, University of Utah, 1969
- USAF pilot training, Webb AFB, Texas, June 1969 to June 1970
- USAF Survival School, Fairchild AFB, Washington, July 1970
- USAF Pilot Instructor School, Tyndall AFB, Florida, August 1970 to November 1970
- MBA, University of Utah, 1983
- Series 6 Exam, 1985 / Series 7 Exam, 1990
- CLU, American College, 1992
- Series 65 Exam, Registered Investment Advisor, 1996
- Author of over 120 web published articles
- Author of 6 print published books about eldercare issues and veterans benefits
- Author of 6 print published training manuals and marketing booklets
- Editor - Study guide and manual for the VA accredited agents exam
- Director of the National Care Planning Council, longtermcarelink.net
- Board Member of the Senior Veterans Service Alliance and Chief Training Officer, seniorvets.org

INTRODUCTION
Overview to Benefits for Senior Veterans & Their Survivors

According to Department of Veterans Affairs (VA) census estimates, there are approximately 13 million veterans and their single surviving spouses age 65 and older. Comparing this to a total of 41 million Americans (65 and older), veterans and their single surviving spouses represent about 1/3 of the senior population. According to VA about 42% of all veterans are 65 and older. This number will grow as most Vietnam veterans – the largest cohort – are still younger than age 65.

Putting Things in Perspective

Senior veterans are typically in receipt of four cash income programs from VA. Two of these programs – Pension and Death Pension – are paid to veterans and their surviving spouses who are non-service-connected disabled. The other two of these programs – Compensation and DIC – are paid to veterans or surviving spouses due to disability or death from service connection. These programs are covered in detail in this book. For now let's look at some statistics.

The table below represents the number of beneficiaries of these four benefit types of income that VA paid in 2014. VA handled about 4,697,600 cases in 2014, and of those about 39% or 1,853,200 beneficiaries were age 65 and older. Of those 1.85 million beneficiaries 65 and older, only about 26% or 496,000 beneficiaries received Pension and Death Pension.

Why are these observations important? Because those practitioners who focus on educating seniors about veterans benefits almost always direct their attention exclusively to Pension or Death Pension – only about 11% of all VA beneficiaries. In contrast, those receiving service-connected payments represent 82% of all beneficiaries. Those seniors who could benefit from knowing more about Compensation and DIC and the aid and attendance allowances available.

Number of Beneficiaries – 2014	Younger than 65	Age 65 & Older	Total all Ages	% of Total	% of 65 & +
Disability Compensation	2,780,200	1,065,800	3,846,000	81.9%	57.5%
DIC for Spouse	55,300	300,300	355,600	7.6%	16.2%
Pension	5,500	309,200	314,800	6.7%	16.7%
Death Pension for Spouse	3,300	177,900	181,200	3.9%	9.6%
100% Disabled	121,800	203,700	325,500	6.9%	11.0%
Tinnitus / Hearing Loss Claims			1,070,000	22.8%	
Healthcare System			9,000,000+		

Source: National Care Planning Council and VA statistical data

Understanding Benefits for Veterans and Their Dependents

Pension and Death Pension

Commonly called "aid and attendance," these twin benefits provide monthly tax-free payments to veterans who served during a period of war or to their single surviving spouses. Pension can help cover the cost of home care, assisted living and nursing home services. Pension is also available to veterans or surviving spouses with very low income who do not have long-term care costs. Cash income payments from Pension range from about $719 a month to around $2,120 a month depending on the type of claim and the medical rating involved. Most people don't even know of the existence of this benefit. VA does not advertise well and as such many eligible people never apply.

It is unfortunate that Pension has been misnamed "aid and attendance." "Aid and attendance" and "housebound" are actually additional monetary allowances provided with Pension if the recipient of Pension monies needs the regular aid and attendance of another person or is considered housebound. The misnomer creates confusion because aid and attendance assistance allowances are also available for service-connected disabilities (Disability Compensation) and to a spouse of a service connected disabled veteran and also an aid and attendance allowance is available to a surviving spouse of a veteran if the surviving spouse is receiving DIC (Dependents Indemnity Compensation). There are about 16 different monetary levels of aid and attendance or housebound allowances available with non-service-connected and service-connected disability programs for veterans or their surviving spouses. **Approximately 309,200 senior veterans received Pension in 2014 and 177,900 of senior veteran survivors received Death Pension.**

Disability Compensation

Disability Compensation is a tax-free benefit paid to a veteran for a service-connected disability that happened as a result of active duty, active duty for training, inactive duty training or injury from VA healthcare. Cash income payments for Compensation range from a low of about $133 a month to a high of about $8,500 a month in 2015-16. Special benefits like grants for new automobiles or modifying existing automobiles, grants for constructing or modifying homes, clothing allowances and so on are payable for severe service-connected disabilities. A veteran cannot receive Pension and Compensation at the same time and a surviving spouse cannot receive Death Pension and DIC at the same time. A choice must be made which benefit the beneficiary wants to receive.

An aid and attendance or housebound assistance allowance in the form of Special Monthly Compensation (SMC) is available to the veteran who is 100% disabled. A single veteran rated for 100% disability will receive a check for about $2,907 a month in 2015-16 and if the veteran has a spouse the amount is $3,069 a month. A 100% disabled veteran meeting the SMC Schedule (l) aid and attendance criteria can receive $3,617 a month and if that veteran has a spouse, the amount can be $3,779 a month. Higher amounts are possible if the aid and attendance involves certain severe disabilities. Additional disabilities also add $103 per month per disability to SMC under Schedule (j).

This aid and attendance allowance is not an automatic benefit and most veterans don't even know about this special assistance and never apply for it. If the veteran receiving Compensation is not 100% disabled, it may be possible to get a higher rating up to 100%. Most veterans receiving Compensation don't have a clue as to their eligibility for this special benefit.

Also, an aid and attendance allowance is available due to the need for these services to a disabled spouse of a veteran where the veteran is 30% or more disabled. The amount goes up as the disability rating goes up. For example, a 30% disabled veteran can generate a $44 a month benefit as a result of his or her disabled spouse. A 100% disabled veteran can generate $149 a month. Again, it is not common knowledge these additional allowances are available and VA does not normally notify people of their existence.

Of particular note for Disability Compensation are Agent Orange claims for each and every veteran who was stationed in Vietnam and who has developed presumptive health conditions such as certain forms of cancer, type II diabetes, ischemic heart disease (lack of proper blood flow to the heart), B cell leukemia and Parkinson's disease. Veterans with service-connected hearing loss can also make claims and receive free hearing aids. This hearing disability rating will also get them into the health care system. Many veterans don't know of the existence of Agent Orange claims or the fact that they might be eligible for service-connected disability for hearing loss. **Approximately 3,846,000 beneficiaries received Compensation in 2014 and of those approximately 1,065,800 were 65 and older. Of all beneficiaries, approximately 325,500 are 100% disabled and about 203,700 of those are age 65 and older.**

Health Care Benefits

The VA health care system is the largest single provider of health care in the United States. It has also been recognized by numerous surveys as being one of the best providers of health care as well. Not all veterans can receive care in the system. Eligibility requires either service-connected disability, receipt of Pension, special service recognition such as prisoner of war or Purple Heart or low income and less than $80,000 in assets. For all beneficiaries – not to include those who are means tested – all services are free and medications are $8.00 per month per medication regardless of what it is. Means tested veterans must pay a co-pay for services. There are no other out-of-pocket costs such as health care premiums. Help can also be provided with disability-required home renovation grants of $2,000 or $6,800, orthotics, prosthetics and in certain cases hearing aids. VA outpatient clinics are available in most communities. **Over 9 million individuals are enrolled in the health care system.**

DIC

Dependents Indemnity Compensation (DIC) – also called Dependency and Indemnity Compensation – is payable to eligible survivors of a military service member who died on active duty or whose death after service resulted from a service-connected injury or disease. It is also available due to improper treatment of the deceased veteran from VA healthcare or rehabilitation services. DIC is automatically granted to a surviving spouse for a veteran who was permanently and totally disabled for 10 years or more. DIC pays $1,254.19 a month in 2015-16 to a surviving spouse. Additional amounts are available if there are dependent children. A dependent child is one who is 18 years old or younger or 23 years old or younger and enrolled full-time in school or is an adult who became totally dependent prior to the age of 18. If the veteran was 100% continuously disabled at least 8 years immediately preceding death, the amount is $1,520.51.

If the surviving spouse needs the aid and attendance of another person such as home care, assisted living or nursing home care, an additional $310.71 a month assistance benefit will be paid. This DIC with aid and attendance benefit is about $310 more a month than a surviving spouse can receive from Death Pension. This additional benefit is not automatic and most individuals receiving DIC do not even know it is available. An additional monthly benefit for being housebound is also available. **Approximately 355,600 spouse survivors received DIC in 2014 and of those approximately 300,300 are age 65 and older. The majority of these are surviving spouses of veterans from the Vietnam era.**

Burial Benefits

Money is available for burial costs for veterans who were service disabled, receiving Pension or died under VA care. If the death was a result of service-connected disability, $2,000 is available. If the death was non-service related, and the veteran was receiving Pension or Compensation or was entitled to either of these, up to $722 is available for plot allowance and burial and $309 in funeral expense allowances. All veterans also receive free burial in State and Federal VA cemeteries. Under certain conditions, spouses and other family members can receive free burial in State and Federal VA cemeteries. All veterans are eligible for a grave marker (or equivalent monetary allowance), a flag for the coffin, a graveside honor guard and a letter from the President of the United States.

State Veteran Benefits

All states offer various additional benefits to veterans to include special recognition, property tax reduction, free hunting and fishing and state parks admission as well as a whole host of other benefits. Some states are more generous than others and in some states veterans can receive a one-time cash stipend. All states have at least one or more veterans homes that are available to various classes of veterans depending on the rules of the home. Some homes require the veteran to have been a war veteran and others do not. Federal rules require that at least 25% of all beds in state veterans homes be reserved for the spouses of veterans if those beds are available.

Where to Submit Claims – Claims Intake Center

In order to improve timeliness and costliness of scanning claims into the Veterans Benefits Management System (VBMS), VA has implemented Centralized Mail Processing (CMP). Under these new procedures, claimants and beneficiaries should now send all mail directly to the scanning vendor (Jainesville, Wisconsin Intake Center), eliminating the need for Regional Office (RO) or Pension Management Center (PMC) mail processing. The vendor will scan and upload the digital images for processing. Please refer to the data disk for a full list of appropriate PO Box for your claim.

CHAPTER 1
Important Information

Please read the information in this chapter before you attempt to submit any application for benefits!!

Submitting Claims and Communicating with VA

Claimants and beneficiaries for Compensation, Pension, Survivor Benefits and other benefits should now send all mail directly to VA's Intake Center in Jainesville, Wisconsin. Any material mailed directly to Regional Offices (RO) or Pension Management Centers (PMC) will automatically be re-directed by the U.S. Postal Service (USPS) to the intake center for scanning and processing. Jainsville, Wisconsin will scan and upload the digital images for processing. Please refer to the data disk for the appropriate PO Box in Jainesville for your claim.

VA's Duty to Assist

Under federal law, the Department of Veterans Affairs is required to find certain documents for you if you adequately identify the existence of those documents in your initial application. For disability claims, VA is also required to assemble medical information necessary to make a decision on a claim. This so-called "duty to assist" comes into play when your application for benefits appears to have merit. In other words, if you submit an application that in VA's opinion is not a valid application for benefits, whether you think so or not, VA has no obligation to assist you in locating records or producing medical information. Your initial application must contain enough information to have VA reasonably believe you are entitled to a certain benefit. Then VA is required to assist you.

For example, there should be no requirement for you to submit an original or a certified copy of your discharge – typically DD 214. VA says it will not accept any applications without this original or certified copy. The department's reasoning is, you have to prove that you are a veteran before the agency will crank in its duty to assist. Technically, you shouldn't have to do this. As long as you provide enough evidence that you are a veteran, without producing your discharge, VA should proceed. If you were to press the issue and assert your right for duty to assist, VA could easily get its own certified copy from its record center in St. Louis. That's where you will probably have to go to get your own copy. Try and assert yourself and see how far you get. Veterans Affairs does not think you have a valid claim until you can provide positive evidence that you were in the service.

Unfortunately, as great as the duty to assist sounds – in practice, VA is not very reliable in helping you find evidence for your claim. Because of the huge backlog of claims already in the system, it is simply not feasible for veteran service representatives in the regional office to assist you in any timely fashion. You can certainly submit an application without any corroborating evidence and the staff may get around to helping you assemble the evidence for your claim in a year or two or more. Or more likely, you will be asked to help locate information or identify issues that are not clear, and over time you either don't provide the information they are requesting or you don't provide it in the form they are requesting. Once you stop responding, they will take what they have and no longer apply their duty to assist. When this happens, you will be sent a notice that they are making a decision within the next 30 days based on the information they have. If there is not enough information for a favorable decision, you will likely receive a denial. This is not a wise way to approach a claim for benefits.

The reason for the agency having a backlog of so many claims is due to individuals submitting applications and relying on VA to build their case for them. By submitting such a claim, you are only adding to the backlog. There is a better way.

The Fully Developed Claim Concept

In recent years, the Department of Veterans Affairs has developed a system called the "fully developed claim." Fully developed claims treatment is now available for applications for Pension, Death Pension, DIC and Compensation. By using the fully developed claim system, you sign a statement that in essence waives your right to the duty to assist. You are basically telling the regional office, with a fully developed claim, to take the information you give to the agency and make a decision on it. This speeds up the approval process immensely, but it also puts a great deal more burden on you. If you don't provide the information up front that VA is looking for, you will likely receive a denial.

In order to get a decision on most claims we cover in this book, a great deal of medical and supportive information must be provided. If you are going to take away VA's duty to help you collect that information, you must provide it yourself. What this means is that it may take quite a while for you to get all of the information together in order to give the agency enough material to make a decision. But this is exactly what you have to do.

In the meantime, you have made a decision to go after a benefit to which you think you are entitled. If it takes you months to assemble all of the information for a claim, you have lost the opportunity for several months of benefit. We will discuss how to retroactively protect your benefit in the "Intent to File" section below.

Requirement for Service

For benefits purposes, a veteran is a person who has served in the armed forces of the United States. Not only does this include the Army, the Navy, the Marines and the Air Force but it also includes the Coast Guard, the Army Corps of Engineers and seagoing service during World War II as a Merchant Marine up to August 15, 1945. Merchant Marines after that date are not considered veterans for purposes of Pension or Compensation. Service may also include officers of the United States Public Health Service for certain benefits. In addition, full-time cadets in service academies are also considered for certain benefits. There are also about 40 other categories of individuals who were in the line of combat during World War II who are also considered veterans for benefits purposes.

Members of the National Guard or the Reserves are not considered veterans unless they were called to active duty by an order of the President of the United States and have honorably served for the period of service for which they were called. A great majority of the Gulf War and Middle East Conflict soldiers since 1990, have been called up from their reserve or guard units for active duty and do qualify for veterans benefits. For Compensation benefits, National Guard and Reserves can receive benefits based on injury or illness incurred during the initial active duty training or inactive duty training for their service or while traveling to or from initial basic training on orders.

Benefits are only available to individuals who were performing in the line of duty while they were in service. Willful misconduct is not considered in the line of duty, and any resulting claim not covered for benefits. Authorized leave is considered in the line of duty. Absent without leave (AWOL) is not generally considered in the line of duty, but there may be extenuating circumstances for which benefits are available. Likewise, the veteran must have a discharge from the service other than dishonorable to be eligible for benefits.

VA requires an original or certified copy of the discharge paper in order to verify an individual is a veteran. Since 1950, this discharge is called Form DD 214. Reserve and Guard who are called up to active service are also going to receive a DD 214 at discharge. Many of the services provide documents that claim to be separation or discharge documents, but often these are used for purposes of awarding medals or putting history on a wall. VA will not accept a copy of any of these documents – only a DD 214 or its pre-1950 equivalent. Prior to 1950, each service had its own discharge document and there is no standard numbering system.

Your first step in starting a claim is to get the original or a certified copy of the discharge. If you have an original copy and send it in with the claim, veteran service representatives will treat it in a respected manner and return it to you as quickly as possible. If you do not want to send the original copy, you can get it copied and certified as a copy from a veterans service organization, your state VA regional office or in many states, the veteran himself carrying the document to the county recorder, should be entitled to a certified copy for free. Many states have archives of discharge papers that they maintain on behalf of their veterans. If the veteran is living in the state where he was considered a resident when he or she was discharged, contact the state Department of Veterans Affairs to see if the state does have an archive. If this is the case, a certified copy will be furnished to you.

A certified copy of the discharge as well as copies of service medical records and service personnel records can be obtained from the Records Center in St. Louis. Use form SF 180 – which we provide you – to request a certified discharge copy and/or the personnel or medical records. Some records of veterans were destroyed due to water damage from a fire in the Records Center in 1973. If your claim needs one of these records, the center will try and reconstruct the discharge to the best of its ability using other sources.

Effective Date of Your Claim

Establishing an effective date for your claim is an extremely important part of the claim. The effective date determines when VA will start paying you when a claim is approved. As a general rule, benefits are paid from the first day of the month following the month of the effective date. If the applicant did not meet the qualification criteria for the benefit at the effective date but met those criteria at a later date, benefits will be paid from the first day of the month following that later date. For veterans who died and for their survivors' benefits, the benefit will start the first day of the month following the month of death.

For example, an application for Compensation is made but the veteran is not currently experiencing any disabling condition. The effective date is the date that the application was received and stamped in the regional office. At a later date, when the disabling condition manifests itself, additional information is submitted as additional evidence to show the disabling condition. This is the point at which qualification criteria along with other criteria for granting a benefit would occur and this would be the defining date for payment of benefits.

Another example might be an application for Pension where the veteran did not meet the income test at the point of application. Later the veteran enters an assisted living and is experiencing significant medical costs which offset the income and allow the veteran to qualify. In the month in which the income qualifies on a prospective basis for 12 months, that is the month that determines when payments will be made.

For any application where qualification for benefit is otherwise assumed – unlike the examples above – you should always establish an effective date at the earliest possible date. This can be done through a process called an "Intent to File," formerly known as an "Informal Claim." Submitting an "Intent to File" (generally via VA Form 21-0966) allows the applicant to notify VA that the applicant (or claimant) will be turning in a formal claim for a benefit at a future date. VA recognizes an "Intent to File" for establishing an effective date for back-pay purposes.

For example, the veteran is assembling a rather complicated application for Compensation that may take three or four months to get all of the medical information as well as lay testimonies. The veteran should at the earliest possible point in the current month submit an "Intent to File" to establish an effective date so when the benefit is approved, payment will start from the first day of the month following the month of the effective date. Failure to do this could result in the loss of many months of payment.

An "Intent to File," at the least, should provide the name of the claimant, the name of the veteran if different, the benefit being applied for and a service number, VA case number or Social Security number of the veteran and the claimant if they are different persons. It is not necessary to provide a brief description of why the claimant thinks he or she is entitled to the benefit. It is, however, helpful to submit a copy of the veterans discharge along with the "Intent to File." We provide you the "Intent to File" VBA Form 21-0966 for various benefits on the Claim Support Data Disk provided with this book.

Do not submit an "Intent to File" if you do not qualify for the benefit at the time of filing. This could result in a denial and mess up your claim until you can prove to VA that you did qualify for the benefit at a later date. When you think you are qualified, file the "Intent to File" even if your formal claim is not yet completed. VA must receive the "Intent to File" in the pension center or regional office and it must be physically date-stamped by a member of the staff for the date to be effective. This can be a problem for "Intent to Files" mailed in near the end of the month. Sometimes these claims have to be hand carried to the regional office, or overnight delivery is sometimes possible or some regional offices have a fax number where the "Intent to File" can be sent in.

There is another decided advantage to filing an "Intent to File". You have an entire year after the effective date of the "Intent to File" to provide all of the information to VA in the form of a fully developed claim but still keep the benefit payment stream as if you had filed a formal claim at the time you filed the "Intent to File". In other words, when the benefit is approved, you will receive a sizable retroactive benefit to the first day of the month following the month in which you filed the "Intent to File" and received the effective date stamp.

Why is this an advantage? Because if you file an incomplete formal claim and leave out important information that could later be provided, VA may not know this fact and you could end up getting a denial. Your haste in filing a formal claim without preparation, could end up in a permanent denial or in extending the period of time necessary for VA to grant a proper approval. Your haste has also cut short the full year for your submitting the claim information, because VA can make a decision based on information you have submitted – other than an "Intent to File" – at any time. The formal claim does not enjoy the extension of 12 months to submit information.

Under some scenarios for veterans, it may be possible to establish an effective date 12 months prior to your date of filing an "Intent to File". If VA suspects that you would have qualified for certain benefits, such as Pension (under the Liberalizing Law), 12 months prior to your application, VA will notify you in your award letter of this possible additional award. You can then take the proper action to see if you qualify for an additional 12 months worth of benefits.

Signatures and Power Of Attorney

Deciding who is to sign an application and/or other documents associated with an application is one of the most confusing parts of filing a claim. No one can sign an application for benefits other than the claimant or a court appointed guardian for the claimant. A state recognized power of attorney does not authorize that power of attorney agent to sign for the claimant. The claimant is either the veteran or if the veteran is deceased, the surviving dependent or spouse of the veteran who is entitled to that particular benefit.

There is no mental competency test for the claimant for signing the original application. If the person can move his or her hand, that is all that is necessary. Obviously if the person is not conscious or not capable of making a mark, then the only other person who can sign is a court-appointed guardian. Most families figure out how to get the claimant to sign the application. Any other documents pertaining to a claim where the VA form indicates the signature of the veteran or the claimant is required, must be signed by that person. A power of attorney cannot sign this document for the veteran or the claimant. Other documents pertaining to an application can be signed by representatives for the claimant or by other individuals providing information on behalf of the claimant. Any direct statements in writing made by the claimant must be signed by the claimant.

VA will also recognize another individual representing the interest of the claimant with an application before the agency for benefits. The department calls this individual a "VA power of attorney." This can be any individual on a once-in-a-lifetime basis, or it can be any accredited claims agent, or accredited attorney or accredited service officer on an unlimited basis. VA will not recognize a state law power of attorney for this purpose. VA will only recognize a power of attorney for approval by submitting the appropriate signed document (VBA Form 21-22a) furnished by the department. The claimant must sign the VA power of attorney. The person acting as power of attorney can be any individual such as a family member, friend or an accredited agent or an accredited attorney. The VA power of attorney can act on behalf of the veteran in responding to inquiries from the regional office. The POA does not have authority to answer questions on the application pertaining to facts known by the claimant. The claimant must answer these missing facts and sign the correspondence.

How VA Makes Decisions Approving or Denying Benefits

For most claims covered in this book a so-called Rating Veterans Service Representative makes the final decision concerning an award. Rating decisions require an evaluation of medical conditions, interpretation of VA regulations pertaining to disability, assets and income tests for some benefits and other judgment calls made by the RVSR. A decision made by this person is called a "rating." RVSR's have received a great deal of training and have acquired a great deal of experience before they are given this responsibility. Even so, they often make mistakes or misjudgments because many of their decisions are subjective and often times the evidence is not conclusive. You cannot expect to have the rating service representative go out of his or her way to build your case for you. That is not their job. Their job is to determine whether there is enough evidence to make a decision and at that point to make the decision.

You must do everything you can in preparing your claim in order to help the rating service representative make the most informed decision. The more information and evidence you can provide, that is pertinent to your claim, the better the chance for the right decision on your case. It is understandable, that a weakly supported claim is likely going to receive a denial. What other choice does the RVSR have?

VA's Principle of Reasonable Doubt

This principle is an important issue when a decision is made concerning an approval or a denial for senior veterans. With many Compensation claims for older veterans, and DIC claims, there is often very little evidence substantiating the link between service and the actual disability. In many cases, the rating service officer must make a decision based on weighing inconclusive evidence and then deciding which way to go – either denial or award. A number of claims for older veterans are often made using this principle. Here is the regulation that governs it.

38 CFR § 3.102 Reasonable doubt.

It is the defined and consistently applied policy of the Department of Veterans Affairs to administer the law under a broad interpretation, consistent, however, with the facts shown in every case. When, after careful consideration of all procurable and assembled data, a reasonable doubt arises regarding service origin, the degree of disability, or any other point, such doubt will be resolved in favor of the claimant. By reasonable doubt is meant one which exists because of an approximate balance of positive and negative evidence which does not satisfactorily prove or disprove the claim. It is a substantial doubt and one within the range of probability as distinguished from pure speculation or remote possibility. It is not a means of reconciling actual conflict or a contradiction in the evidence. Mere suspicion or doubt as to the truth of any statements submitted, as distinguished from impeachment or contradiction by evidence or known facts, is not justifiable basis for denying the application of the reasonable doubt doctrine if the entire, complete record otherwise warrants invoking this doctrine. The reasonable doubt doctrine is also applicable even in the absence of official records, particularly if the basic incident allegedly arose under combat, or similarly strenuous conditions, and is consistent with the probable results of such known hardships.

(Authority: 38 U.S.C. 501)

This principle is extremely important when you are preparing your claim. You must provide enough positive evidence for your claim in order to offset any suspicions from the rating service representative that you do not deserve the claim. Here are the instructions to The Rating Veteran Service Representative on how to apply this principle. This is found in Adjudication Manual M21 –1MR

12. Weighing the Evidence

a. Assigning Weight to the Evidence After assigning weight to the evidence

- review the evidence in its totality, and
- determine the balancing of scales.

Note: Do not assign weight unjustly or arbitrarily.

b. Questions to Ask When Weighing Evidence

Ask the questions listed below when weighing evidence.

- Did the evidence originate in service or in close proximity to service?
- Is the medical opinion supported by clinical data?
- How detailed is the opinion?
- Is the opinion based on personal knowledge or on history provided by another person?

c. Handling Imbalanced Evidence

If the evidence shows an overwhelming imbalance, then the evidence requires a decision in that direction, either for or against.

Note: The claim must be granted if all of the evidence is favorable.

d. Handling Evidence in Equipoise
Resolve reasonable doubt in favor of the claimant if all procurable evidence, after being weighed, is found in approximate balance or equipoise. 38 CFR 3.102 dictates that the veteran prevails when the evidence neither satisfactorily proves nor disproves an issue.

Reference: For more information on applying reasonable doubt, see Alemany v. Brown, 9 Vet. App. 518 (1996).

e. Considering Reasonable Doubt
Consider reasonable doubt only when the evidence is in equipoise, not when the evidence weighs either in favor or against the claimant.

f. Example of Evidence in Equipoise
In the following example there is no compelling justification to side with either expert:

"Evidence supportive of the claim includes the July 1991 opinion of Dr. T., who treated the veteran for several years prior to his death, that PTSD had been the major factor in the veteran's suicide. Evidence against the claim includes the January 1992 opinion of the VA physician that the evidence did not point to PTSD as the actual cause of suicide and that the veteran's suicide had occurred in the setting of alcohol dependence, family breakdown, and depression."

g. Reaching a Conclusion
When weighing the evidence to reach a conclusion

- discuss the evidence in favor of the claim
- discuss the evidence against the claim, and
- explain that
    - one set of evidence outweighs the other set, or
    - the evidence is in equal balance for and against the claim.

Responding to Denials

Many claimants respond to a denial by making a new application or by initiating an appeal or by requesting an SRO (service review officer). Before you take these actions, it is often better to take a step back and read your denial letter from the VA and decide exactly what the service representative is saying. Unfortunately, VA-speak is not always translatable into human-speak. Not to say that the language is convoluted or particularly laden with technical words, but what the words are conveying often portrays a different understanding based on how VA understands these words from what you think the intent is. If you don't understand exactly what the letter is saying, you must find someone who can interpret it for you. In many cases the denial is simply a result of lacking evidence regarding a certain issue or of not meeting certain requirements at the time of application.

It has been our experience that individuals not really understanding what meaning a denial letter is conveying, often go to a great deal of time and effort to find more detail of the same kind of evidence and submit it thinking that the agency didn't have enough information for that particular issue. They are surprised that they are again denied. What they didn't know is that particular issue was not what service representative was addressing even though it seemed to be the issue that the veteran service representative was addressing. Letters from VA can be very confusing.

Almost all denials can be overturned simply by responding with what the regulations call "new and material evidence." Do this first – if possible – instead of appealing! If it is something new that VA has not seen before in another form and it is material to your claim – as long as you submit this evidence before a year from the denial has elapsed – VA will typically reopen your case and give you a new decision.

It is extremely important that this information is indeed new and material information. Otherwise, the adjudicator will stick to his or her original decision after taking months and months and sitting on your information.

Marriage

Applications for benefits almost always require information on marriages – both current and previous. If marriage information is difficult to come by, all is not lost. Here are the rules that VA applies pertaining to marriage dates and the place of marriage or whether individuals were considered marriage or not.

Marriage Deemed Valid
A claimant filing for death benefits as the surviving spouse of a veteran must establish that the claimant and the veteran had a valid marriage. In most cases, this is accomplished by proving the existence of a legal marriage under State law. However, it is also possible under certain circumstances to "deem valid" for Department of Veterans Affairs (VA) purposes a marriage which is not valid under State law.

The fact that benefits were paid for a person as the spouse of the veteran during the veteran's lifetime does not automatically establish that person's status as the surviving spouse after the veteran's death.

The surviving spouse claimant must submit satisfactory evidence of his/her status as the surviving spouse of the veteran based on a marriage that is either legal or deemed valid and must meet the other requirements set forth in this topic.

Remarriage
Generally, remarriage of the surviving spouse after the death of the veteran will void any benefits that were available to the surviving spouse including Death Pension and DIC. Here are some exceptions to this rule

38 CFR § 3.55 Marriage void, terminated or annulled

Marriage Was Void or Annulled
Remarriage of a surviving spouse shall not bar the furnishing of benefits to such surviving spouse if the marriage:

- Was void, or
- Has been annulled by a court having basic authority to render annulment decrees, unless it is determined by the Department of Veterans Affairs that the annulment was obtained through fraud by either party or by collusion.

Marriage Terminated Prior to November 1, 1990
On or after January 1, 1971, remarriage of a surviving spouse terminated prior to November 1, 1990, or terminated by legal proceedings commenced prior to November 1, 1990, by an individual who, but for the remarriage, would be considered the surviving spouse, shall not bar the furnishing of benefits to such surviving spouse provided that the marriage:

- Has been terminated by death, or
- Has been dissolved by a court with basic authority to render divorce decrees unless the Department of Veterans Affairs determines that the divorce was secured through fraud by the surviving spouse or by collusion.

DIC Benefits for Terminated Remarriage
On or after October 1, 1998, remarriage of a surviving spouse terminated by death, divorce, or annulment, will not bar the furnishing of dependency and indemnity Compensation (DIC), unless the Secretary determines that the divorce or annulment was secured through fraud or collusion.

Non--Married Relationship

- On or after January 1, 1971, the fact that a surviving spouse has lived with another person and has held himself or herself out openly to the public as the spouse of such other person shall not bar the furnishing of benefits to him or her after he or she terminates the relationship, if the relationship terminated prior to November 1, 1990.

- On or after October 1, 1998, the fact that a surviving spouse has lived with another person and has held himself or herself out openly to the public as the spouse of such other person will not bar the furnishing of dependency and indemnity Compensation (DIC) to the surviving spouse if he or she ceases living with such other person and holding himself or herself out openly to the public as such other person's spouse.

Benefits for a surviving spouse who remarries after age 57 (presumed currently married)
On or after January 1, 2004, the remarriage of a surviving spouse after the age of 57 shall not bar the furnishing of benefits relating to

- DIC -- dependency and indemnity Compensation under 38 U.S.C. 1311,
- medical care for survivors and dependents under 38 U.S.C. 1781,
- educational assistance under 38 U.S.C. chapter 35, or
- housing loans under 38 U.S.C. chapter 37, subject to the limitation in paragraph (a)(10)(ii) of this section.

Divorce or Annulment
Documentary proof of dissolution of all prior marriages of both parties is required if dissolution of prior marriages cannot be established based on the claimant's certified statement. This means that the statement in the application attesting to the dates and places of the divorces or annulments will be sufficient evidence for proof unless those facts are not furnished.

Acceptable documentary evidence for termination of a prior marriage through annulment is a copy or abstract of the annulment decree.

The only acceptable documentary evidence for termination of a prior marriage through divorce (other than the original divorce decree) is a copy or abstract of a final decree of divorce.

Some jurisdictions provide a two-step process for dissolving a marriage:

- first: an interlocutory decree of divorce is granted, and
- second: after a passage of a specified period of time, a final divorce decree is entered.

Notes:
- The parties continue to be married until the final divorce decree is granted.
- An interlocutory decree of divorce does not dissolve a marriage.

Certain "marriages" have no legal effect even though the parties may have gone through a marriage ceremony, and registered the marriage. Such marriages are legally void because the parties did not satisfy the legal requirements for entering into a marriage at the time of the alleged marriage. Not all legally defective marriages are void. For example, in most jurisdictions marriage by underage individuals is not automatically void.

Generally, a marriage is considered void only if the defect is fundamental. Grounds for voiding a marriage vary from state to state, but in most States a marriage is void if either party is already married at the time of the marriage, or if the parties are closely related.

If a marriage is determined to have been void, there is no need to dissolve it through divorce or annulment before entering into a subsequent marriage. Likewise, a remarried surviving spouse whose subsequent marriage is annulled or declared void may reestablish entitlement as a surviving spouse.

When a claimant who was divorced from the veteran at the time of the veteran's death attempts to establish entitlement as the veteran's surviving spouse based on a court decree setting aside or vacating the divorce, obtain all relevant documents, such as the court decree that set aside the divorce, and refer the case to Regional Counsel for an opinion on the issue of the validity of the order setting aside the divorce.

A determination by Regional Counsel that the decree setting aside the divorce is valid means that the claimant was the legal surviving spouse of the veteran (assuming the marriage can be established in the first place).

38 CFR § 3.53 Continuous cohabitation.
(a) General. The requirement that there must be continuous cohabitation from the date of marriage to the date of death of the veteran will be considered as having been met when the evidence shows that any separation was due to the misconduct of, or procured by, the veteran without the fault of the surviving spouse. Temporary separations which ordinarily occur, including those caused for the time being through fault of either party, will not break the continuity of the cohabitation.

(b) Findings of fact. The statement of the surviving spouse as to the reason for the separation will be accepted in the absence of contradictory information. If the evidence establishes that the separation was by mutual consent and that the parties lived apart for purposes of convenience, health, business, or any other reason which did not show an intent on the part of the surviving spouse to desert the veteran, the continuity of the cohabitation will not be considered as having been broken. State laws will not control in determining questions of desertion; however, due weight will be given to findings of fact in court decisions made during the life of the veteran on issues subsequently involved in the application of this section.

The claimant must meet the continuous cohabitation requirement of 38 CFR 3.50(b)(1) to qualify as the surviving spouse of a veteran for VA purposes. This requirement is most commonly met by virtue of the surviving spouse having lived continuously with the veteran from the date of marriage to the date of the veteran's death; however, the requirement is also met in any of the following occurred.

1. The veteran and claimant were living apart at the time of the veteran's death due to marital discord, but the claimant was not materially at fault for the separation, or any fault on the part of the claimant was insignificant.

2. Fault or the absence of fault is determined based on an analysis of conduct at the time of the separation. This means that the conduct of the spouse after the separation is not a factor in determining continuous cohabitation and may not be used as a basis for denying benefits.

Separations occurring during the course of the marriage, regardless of fault, are irrelevant if the parties are no longer estranged at the time of the veteran's death.

The spouse of a deceased veteran who was separated from the veteran due to the fault of the veteran has no affirmative obligation to attempt to reconcile with the veteran. As long as the spouse is not materially at fault in the separation, the continuous cohabitation requirement is met. Note: It is irrelevant that the parties lived apart for many years prior to the veteran's death, as long as the spouse was not at fault for the separation.

Evidence for the Marriage
Successful development of a marital relationship for VA purposes requires knowledge of where the claimed marriage took place, and the requirements for establishing a legal marriage in the jurisdiction where the marriage took place.

VA accepts the oral, written, or faxed statement of a claimant as proof of marriage provided the statement contains the

1. date of marriage (month and year), and
2. location of the event (city and state.)

Before a marriage may be established for VA purposes, it is always necessary to have the claimant's statement of marital history. The statement of marital history must

1. show all prior marriages of both parties, and
2. include the following information:
    a. the first and last name of prior marriage partners
    b. the current spouse's Social Security number (SSN)
    c. how the prior marriages terminated (death, divorce, annulment)
    d. the date the prior marriages terminated (month and year, at a minimum), and
    e. the place where the prior marriages terminated (city and state).

Documentary evidence of marriage is required if

- the claimant does not reside within a State (outside of the United States)
- the claimant's statement raises a question as to its validity
- the claimant's statement conflicts with other evidence of record, or
- there is a reasonable indication of fraud or misrepresentation.

In all jurisdictions in the U.S. and most other places in the world, a marriage cannot be contracted if either party is already married. Establishment of a legal marriage always implies a finding that the parties to the marriage were free to marry at the time of the alleged marriage. If either party was married previously, the current marriage may not be established unless the prior marriage is

1. terminated by
    a. death
    b. divorce
    c. annulment, or
2. determined to be void under State law.

Documentary proof of dissolution of all prior marriages of both parties is required if dissolution of prior marriages cannot be established based on the claimant's certified statement.

Request documentary evidence of a marriage when the claimant's statement is not sufficient to establish the marriage.

Primary evidence consists of a copy or abstract of the public record of a marriage, or a copy of the church record of marriage, containing sufficient data to identify the

1. parties involved
2. date and place of the marriage, and
3. number of prior marriages, if shown on the official record.

Note: Telephone the claimant, use the MARRIAGE CERTIFICATE field on the BDN 204 screen, or send a locally-generated letter via MAP-D to request a marriage certificate.

If primary evidence is unavailable, the marriage may still be established by submission of the following evidence in the order of preference listed:

- an official report from the service department as to a marriage that occurred while the veteran was in service
- an affidavit of the clergyman or magistrate who officiated
- the original certificate of marriage, if VA is satisfied that it is genuine and free from alteration
- affidavits or certified statements signed by two or more witnesses to the ceremony, or
- any other secondary evidence that reasonably supports a belief by the adjudicating activity that a valid marriage actually occurred.

Evidence for Death
The fact of death may be established on the basis of any one of the following forms of primary evidence:

- an official death certificate
- a copy of a coroner's report of death or a verdict of a coroner's jury
- a death certificate signed by a medical officer if death occurred in a hospital or institution under the control of the U.S. Government
- a clinical summary or other report showing the fact and date of death signed by a medical officer if death occurred in a hospital or institution under the control of the U.S. Government
- an official report of death of a member of a uniformed service from the Secretary of the department concerned if death occurred while the deceased was
    - on the retired list
    - in an inactive duty status, or
    - on active duty
- a U.S. consular report of death bearing the signature and seal of the U.S. consul if death occurred abroad, or
- an official report of death from the head of the department concerned if the
    - deceased was, at the time of death, a civilian employee of a U.S. Government agency, and
    - death occurred abroad.

When primary evidence cannot be furnished, the claimant must state the reason why. Once the claimant explains the reason for the lack of primary evidence, the fact of death may be established on the basis of the following secondary evidence:

- a finding of the fact of death made by another Federal agency in the absence of evidence to the contrary, or
- affidavits from persons who have
    - personal knowledge of the fact of death, and

- viewed the body and know it to be the body of the person whose death is being established

Note: Affidavits must set forth all the facts and circumstances concerning the death such as the date, place, time, and cause thereof.

In the absence of the primary or secondary evidence outlined in M21-1MR, Part III, Subpart iii, 5.B.8. b and c, VA may make a finding of death if the fact of death is shown by a preponderance of competent evidence. An administrative decision is required.

Death Determined by a Seven-Year Absence
No State law providing for presumption of death shall be applicable to claims for benefits under laws administered by VA. If evidence is submitted, establishing the continued and unexplained absence of any individual from home and family for a 7-year period, death shall be considered sufficiently proved. Except in a suit brought pursuant to section 784, Government insurance, the finding of death by VA shall be final and conclusive. See VA Form 21-1775, Statement of Disappearance.

Accrued Benefits (benefits due at the death of the claimant)

Accrued benefits are those that could have been obtained but the claimant died during the application or fiduciary appointment process. Essentially, when a claimant dies, VA must have all of the pertinent information in its possession in order to make a decision to grant benefits. If information is missing, the claim is generally denied. This rule was often called "the claim dies with the claimant rule." Fortunately, the retroactive payment or withholdings due to incompetency proposals can be paid to certain living individuals. These individuals are exclusively a surviving spouse, dependent children or dependent parents. These individuals may apply for a *Substitution of Claimant* using VBA Form 21-0847. These monies generally cannot be paid to the claimant's estate. See chapter 2 for more detail.

If there is no one to pay benefits to, VA will pay the out-of-pocket cost incurred by <u>any person</u> for *final expenses* such as hospital, hospice, funeral or burial. This does not include payments owed to care providers such as assisted living or nursing homes. This accrued benefit for final expenses cannot exceed the retroactive benefit or other withholdings that would have been paid had the claimant not died. We provide a form (VBA Form 21-601) for applying for this on the data disc provided with this book. See chapter 2 for more detail.

A new law enacted in 2010 allows an individual to step in and take over the claim or an appeal for the claimant thus eliminating the need for VA needing all the information to make a favorable decision at the time of death. This so-called substitution rule allows the substitute for the claimant to continue to provide the regional office with continued information until the claim is fully adjudicated.

Appeals

Any claimant receiving a denial or a decision that the claimant considered unfair such as a lesser disability rating, can appeal the decision through the regional office where the claim was submitted. The process is lengthy and complicated and can often take years. Generally, unfavorable decisions can be reversed without appealing.

If a development or denial letter is sent to you, it is generally not necessary to initiate an appeal. We warn you to consider an appeal cautiously and only as a last resort. Generally, a response with new information and evidence clarifying an issue will satisfy an inquiry or give VA enough reason to re-open a denied claim without having to appeal. In your response, refrain from using the word "appeal" and "disagree." Also, remember to write something like "with this new and material evidence and information I have enclosed, I am requesting that you continue (or re-open and reconsider) processing my application."

The Importance of Submitting a Fully Developed Claim

If you have read most or all of the preceding information, it must now be clear to you that you must provide as much relevant information as possible in order to receive a favorable decision. This information must provide evidence that the service representative in the regional office is looking for to make a decision. You cannot simply submit an application not knowing what VA really wants and expect to get either a timely or a favorable decision. This book will help you assemble the evidence that we know that the adjudicators in the regional office are looking for.

The balance of this book is devoted to helping you understand how to put together a fully developed claim which will help you receive a timely decision and a favorable one as well. Naturally, even a fully developed claim is not a guarantee against a denial. We cannot assure you that following all of the techniques and strategies and checklists we provide in this book will always result in approval of benefits.

CHAPTER 2
Pension and Death Pension (Commonly Called Aid and Attendance)

Defining What Pension Is

Pension and Death Pension are disability income programs available to veterans or to the single surviving spouses of deceased veterans. These programs provide tax-free income which can range from $719/month to $2,837/month. For younger totally disabled veterans, the benefit can also be available to dependent children. The veteran had to have served on active duty at least 90 days with one of those days during a period of war. Service in combat is not required, only that the veteran was in the service during wartime and was discharged with a discharge that was not classified as dishonorable. For veterans of the Gulf War, the service requirement is 24 months or completing the requirement for active duty service, whichever comes first. Charts showing the available amount of income and the dates for wartime service are included below.

There is a sister benefit to Pension called Disability Compensation. This is for veterans who are disabled because of injuries or illnesses incurred while on active duty. Compensation is sometimes the more desirable benefit for a number of reasons we will not go into here. A veteran household cannot receive Pension and Compensation at the same time. A decision must be made as to which benefit is better and the veteran must choose only that benefit.

Period of War	Beginning and Ending Dates
World War II	December 7, 1941 through December 31, 1946
Korean Conflict	June 27, 1950 through January 31, 1955
Vietnam Era	August 5, 1964 through May 7, 1975; for veterans who served "in country" before August 5, 1964, February 28, 1961 through May 7, 1975
Gulf War	August 2, 1990 through a date to be set by law or Presidential Proclamation

The Disability and Medical Needs Tests

If the veteran is younger than age 65, he or she must be totally disabled to receive Pension. Medical evidence must be submitted for these types of applications to prove total disability. Being on Social Security disability is generally adequate proof of total disability prior to age 65. At age 65 and older there is no requirement for disability. For a single surviving spouse applying for a Death Pension benefit, the deceased veteran did not have to meet any disability or age requirements nor does the surviving spouse need to meet any disability requirements, regardless of his or her age. The surviving spouse had to have been married to the veteran, they had to be living together at the veteran's death and the surviving spouse must be single at the time of application and cannot have remarried after November 1, 1990.

VA will also provide additional income in the form of an allowance to the basic Pension or Death Pension benefit if the veteran or the surviving spouse has a regular medical need for assistance or a need for supervision due to disability. If the non-veteran spouse of a living veteran has a regular medical need for assistance or supervision, a lesser benefit without the additional income allowance is available. These allowances are granted for the regular need for "aid and attendance" or if the beneficiary is "housebound."

A medical need for assistance or supervision due to disability is in most cases crucial to getting the Pension benefit or not getting it. A so-called "rating" from VA recognizes either the regular need for aid and attendance from another entity or the condition of being housebound. This rating then allows certain medical expenses and ancillary non-medical expenses to be annualized and subtracted from future annual income in order to meet the income test. Except for very poor veteran households, most veteran households could not get the Pension benefit without this special rating provision for the deduction of annualized medical and medical-related expenses.

The high cost of medical and medical-related expenses associated with long term care such as home care, assisted living or nursing home care are usually the trigger that allows for a rating, The resulting medical deductions allow a claimant household to qualify for Pension. That is why only about 5% of all eligible individuals are actually receiving Pension. Most don't know about this special deduction. It is unfortunate that many seniors, who might be eligible, miss out because they don't know about this special provision allowing them to meet the income test.

The Income Test

Pension is based on a maximum yearly income amount called the "Maximum Annual Pension Rate" (MAPR). A claimant household – both husband and wife where that constitutes a household – must be making less than this amount in order to qualify for a benefit. The benefit is the difference between this MAPR and the combined gross household income reduced for medical costs and adjusted by a 5% deductible. This adjusted income is called by VA "Income for VA Purposes" or IVAP. If the veteran or spouse has a need for the aid and attendance of another person the MAPR is much higher. If the veteran has no need of the aid and attendance of another person, the veteran's income must be very small in order to meet the income test.

Claimants, qualifying on income alone, without a rating for aid and attendance or housebound, typically need to make such little money that they are below the poverty level. It is still worthwhile, however, to make an application for these very low income applicants even though the benefit might only be a few hundred dollars.

As mentioned above, combined household income of the claimant – combined income of husband and wife and dependent residents where applicable – cannot exceed the Maximum Annual Pension Rate (MAPR) for that category of application. (We list 9 categories of Pension income amounts in the section on how Pension is calculated.) As an example, using rates for

2015-16, a husband and spouse with no medical rating cannot have a combined income of more than $1,404 a month or $16,851 a year from all sources. As another example, a single surviving spouse with an "aid and attendance" medical rating cannot make more than $1,150 a month or $13,794 a year from all sources. However, the household income can be reduced by future predictable monthly medical costs to meet the income test under certain special conditions. Thus households earning $2,000 to $6,000 a month or more might still qualify even though their current income does not meet the income test.

VA considers income to be anything that comes through the door that is cash or the equivalent of cash in a given year. For example, a gift of stock would be considered income. Winnings from gambling, an inheritance or receiving a gift of property would be considered income. Withdrawals from IRAs, 401(k)s and other retirement accounts are considered income. The cash left in the IRA or other retirement account is considered an asset. Social Security income and Social Security disability income are considered income. Generally, income that is not consumed and carried over to the next month becomes an asset.

Income from VA Compensation is not considered income for Pension purposes. However, if a claimant is switching from Compensation to Pension, they should notify VA of their intention to switch benefits as part of their application for pension. Income from DIC is also not considered income for death pension purposes. A beneficiary may not receive both Compensation and Pension at the same time. It is wise to evaluate which benefit will pay more. A widow of a veteran may not receive both DIC and death pension at the same time. DIC pays more and is the preferred benefit. See Chapter 3 on how to receive DIC and the Aid and Attendance Allowance.

Some forms of receipt are not considered income. Most importantly, ongoing income from Pension itself or retroactive benefits paid for Pension applications are not considered income for purposes of Pension, nor is the retroactive amount considered an asset for purposes of Pension. It is very important to understand that existing Pension payments do not need to be counted as income if an increase in Pension benefits is requested at a future date.

Payments from welfare programs such as Medicaid or SSI are also not considered income. Certain types of government grants and awards are not considered income. Life insurance proceeds are not considered income; nor are improvements of property. However the improvement would make the property more valuable as an asset under the asset rule.

The sale of property through a private installment contract where the contract is owned by the veteran or surviving spouse is a unique situation that is neither income nor asset until the principal amount of the loan has been repaid. Sometimes applicants set up these sales in order to convert assets into non-counting assets for qualifying for Pension or Death Pension.

The Asset Test

As a general rule household assets cannot exceed $80,000. But there is no specific amount in the regulations. Veterans service representatives in the regional office are required to file paperwork justifying their decision if they allow assets greater than $80,000. No service representative is going to stick his or her neck out to get the regional office director to sign off on allowing assets greater than $80,000 and thus this amount has become a traditional ceiling. Concerning the asset test, the service representative is encouraged to analyze the veteran's household needs for maintenance and weigh those needs against assets that can be readily converted to cash and whether the income from that cash will cover the difference in the household income and the cost of medical care over the care recipient's remaining life span. However, this rule is only a suggestion and the final decision is left to the rating representative.

In the end, the decision as to allowable assets is a subjective decision made by a service representative. In certain cases a benefit award could be denied unless assets are below $20,000 or even $10,000. Over the years, we have found that a reasonable rule of thumb for allowable assets for a couple is about $40,000 and for a single individual about $20,000. This amount can be nudged up for younger claimants. This does not mean that applications with higher assets have been denied. We have seen applications with assets in the neighborhood of $50,000-$70,000 approved. The more assets on an application, the more likely the denial.

A personal residence, a reasonable amount of land on which it sits, personal property and automobiles for personal use are exempted from the asset test. In recent years, VA has taken the position that if the home is not occupied by the veteran or the veteran's spouse it is no longer an exempt IF it is being rented. This can have a devastating effect on the Pension recipient and could disqualify them. At this point, VA will seek to count the residence as an asset which will likely cause the recipient to be over assets. The rent will count as new income as well.

If VA finds out about the house being lived in by individuals other than the veteran or the spouse and the equity value of the home is a significant amount, the regional office will notify the beneficiary of this issue and request more information. In most cases, the VA will send a follow-up letter cancelling the benefit or demanding repayment of all the benefit money from the point at which the beneficiary no longer qualified.

A bigger problem to deal with is when the home sells. Usually the agency will learn the house is sold when a 1099S is issued by the IRS (showing the veteran or spouse on the title at the time of sale). VA has a tight relationship with the IRS for individuals who are on claim. The agency receives all 1099 notices for beneficiaries from the IRS during computer crosschecks to match up with reported assets and income. Any changes that could disqualify a beneficiary are red flagged and investigated.

If this problem with the home is going to end up being your situation when you apply – even if the house is currently being lived in by the claimants and is therefore exempt – you must contact someone who can give you advice with this issue. You do not want to get a letter, a year or two from qualifying for the benefit, demanding an amount of $30,000-$70,000 in overpaid Pension monies that must be repaid to the Department of Veterans Affairs. VA is not very nice in the way it goes about collecting these overpayments.

Currently, as of December 2015, there is no penalty for gifting assets in order to qualify to receive Pension or Death Pension nor is there any federal law that prohibits it. However, VA and Congress certainly do not like it. It is not our position to condone or condemn the gifting of assets in order to receive Pension. We understand that some individuals also convert assets into income in various ways to qualify. Again, we have no position on this other than we do know it is happening. Congress does recognize that assets could have been gifted prior to applying for Pension. Provisions for this are included in the regulations and rules pertaining to what is considered a gift and what is considered retained assets. As of 2016, VA is working with law makers to implement regulations similar to Medicaid which will employ a 3 year look back period and penalties associated with asset transfers.

If assets are gifted or converted to income, this could create a penalty if the veteran or surviving spouse wishes to apply for Medicaid in the future. In fact, gifting to qualify could unknowingly create a disaster for a future Medicaid application. Assets should never be gifted or converted to income unless an expert is consulted who understands the implications of these actions on Medicaid qualification or on federal taxes. In some cases, actions taken to qualify for Pension should never be undertaken if a Medicaid application is imminent.

Here are the rules from Title 38 Code of Federal Regulations regarding assets (typically referred to as "net worth" in the regulations).

38 CFR § 3.274 Relationship of net worth to Pension entitlement.
(a) *Veteran.* Pension shall be denied or discontinued when the corpus of the estate of the veteran, and of the veteran's spouse, are such that under all the circumstances, including consideration of the annual income of the veteran, the veteran's spouse, and the veteran's children, it is reasonable that some part of the corpus of such estates be consumed for the veteran's maintenance.
(b) *Increased Pension payable to a veteran for a child.* Increased Pension payable to a veteran on account of a child shall be denied or discontinued when the corpus of the estate of the child is such that under all the circumstances including consideration of the veteran's and spouse's income and the income of the veteran's child or children, it is reasonable that some part of the corpus of such child's estate be consumed for the child's maintenance.
(c) *Surviving spouse.* Pension payable to a surviving spouse shall be denied or discontinued when the corpus of the estate of the surviving spouse is such that under all the circumstances, including consideration of the surviving spouse's income and the income of any child for whom the surviving spouse is receiving Pension, it is reasonable that some part of the corpus of the surviving spouse's estate be consumed for the surviving spouse's maintenance.
(d) *Increased Pension payable to a surviving spouse for a child.* Increased Pension payable to a surviving spouse on account of a child shall be denied or discontinued when the corpus of the estate of the child is such that under all the circumstances, including consideration of the income of the surviving spouse and child and the income of any other child for whom the surviving spouse is receiving increased Pension, it is reasonable that some part of the corpus of the child's estate be consumed for the maintenance of the child.
(e) *Child.* Pension payable to a child shall be denied or discontinued when the corpus of the estate of the child is such that under all the circumstances, including consideration of the income of the child, the income of any person with whom the child is residing who is legally responsible for such child's support, and the corpus of estate of such person, it is reasonable that some part of the corpus of such estates be consumed for the child's maintenance.

38 CFR § 3.275 Criteria for evaluating net worth.

(a) *General.* The following rules are for application in determining the corpus of estate or net worth of a veteran, surviving spouse or child under §3.274.

(b) *Definition.* The terms *corpus of estate* and *net worth* mean the market value, less mortgages or other encumbrances, of all real and personal property owned by the claimant, except the claimant's dwelling (single family unit), including a reasonable lot area, and personal effects suitable to and consistent with the claimant's reasonable mode of life.

(c) *Ownership.* See §3.271(d).

(d) *Evaluation.* In determining whether some part of the claimant's estate (or combined estates under §3.274 (a) and (e)) should be consumed for the claimant's maintenance, consideration will be given to the amount of the claimant's income together with the following: Whether the property can be readily converted into cash at no substantial sacrifice; life expectancy; number of dependents who meet the definition of *member of the family* (the definition contained in §3.250(b)(2) is applicable to the improved Pension program); potential rate of depletion, including unusual medical expenses under the principles outlined in §3.272(g) for the claimant and the claimant's dependents.

(e) *Educational expenses.* There shall be excluded from the corpus of estate or net worth of a child reasonable amounts for actual or prospective educational or vocational expenses. The amount so excluded shall not be such as to provide for education or training beyond age 23.

(f) *Agent Orange settlement payments.* There shall be excluded from the corpus of the estate or net worth of a claimant any payment made from the Agent Orange Settlement Fund or any other fund established pursuant to the settlement in the In re Agent Orange product liability litigation, M.D.L. No. 381 (E.D.N.Y.). (January 1, 1989)

(g) *Restitution to individuals of Japanese ancestry.* There shall be excluded from the corpus of estate or net worth of a claimant any payment made as restitution under Public Law 100–383 to individuals of Japanese ancestry who were interned, evacuated, or relocated during the period December 7, 1941, through June 30, 1946, pursuant to any law, Executive order, Presidential proclamation, directive, or other official action respecting these individuals. (August 10, 1988)

(h) *Radiation Exposure Compensation Act.* There shall be excluded from the corpus of estate or net worth of a claimant any payment made under Section 6 of the Radiation Exposure Compensation Act of 1990.

(i) *Monetary allowance under 38 U.S.C. chapter 18 for certain individuals who are children of Vietnam veterans.* There shall be excluded from the corpus of estate or net worth of a claimant any allowance paid under the provisions of 38 U.S.C. chapter 18 to or for an individual who is a child of a Vietnam veteran.

(j) *Victims of Crime Act.* There shall be excluded from the corpus of estate or net worth of a claimant any amounts received as Compensation under the Victims of Crime Act of 1984 unless the total amount of assistance received from all federally funded programs is sufficient to fully compensate the claimant for losses suffered as a result of the crime.

(k) *Medicare Prescription Drug Discount Card and Transitional Assistance Program.* There shall be excluded from the corpus of estate or net worth of a claimant payments received under the Medicare transitional assistance program and any savings associated with the Medicare prescription drug discount card.

38 CFR § 3.276 Certain transfers or waivers disregarded.
(a) *Waiver of receipt of income.* Potential income, not excludable under §3.272 and whose receipt has been waived by an individual, shall be included as countable income of that individual for Department of Veterans Affairs Pension purposes.
(b) *Transfer of assets.* For Pension purposes, a gift of property made by an individual to a relative residing in the same household shall not be recognized as reducing the corpus of the grantor's estate. A sale of property to such a relative shall not be recognized as reducing the corpus of the seller's estate if the purchase price, or other consideration for the sale, is so low as to be tantamount to a gift. A gift of property to someone other than a relative residing in the grantor's household will not be recognized as reducing the corpus of the grantor's estate unless it is clear that the grantor has relinquished all rights of ownership, including the right of control of the property.

Death (Survivors) Pension for a Single Surviving Spouse

The rules pertaining to application for Death (Survivors) Pension for a single surviving spouse – who was married to a veteran – are very much the same as the rules pertaining to application for Pension from the veteran himself. There are, however, some minor but very important differences.

The single surviving spouse can be any age and does not have to be permanently and totally disabled prior to age 65. The veteran who died did not have to be totally disabled if death occurred before age 65. The veteran who died did have to qualify based on active duty service days as well as serving during a period of war.

Application for Death Pension should not be made unless it is certain that the surviving spouse meets the rules to be a surviving spouse. All of these following conditions must apply or the surviving spouse is not eligible for Death Pension.

1. The surviving spouse must have met the conditions to be married under VA rules. Generally this means a marriage lasting at least a year or a child as a result of the marriage regardless of the length of time married. Under certain conditions, VA will also accept common-law marriages or marriages where the couple held themselves out to be married and can prove that that was their intent.

2. The surviving spouse must have lived continuously with the veteran while they were married unless they were separated due to the fault of the veteran. Evidence regarding such a separation will be required.

3. The surviving spouse must have been married to the veteran when the veteran died.

4. The surviving spouse cannot have remarried after the veteran's death even if the surviving spouse is currently single. There is one exception to this rule. If the surviving spouse married after the veteran's death and that marriage has been terminated either

through death or divorce prior to November 1 of 1990 and the surviving spouse has remained single, that person can still receive the benefit.

It should be noted that if a surviving spouse married more than one veteran, any one of those veteran marriages would qualify the surviving spouse if the surviving spouse meets all of the rules above.

Reducing Income through Medical Expenses

The following excerpt is from the National Care Planning Council.

> "What if 25% of all seniors in this country could receive up to $2,120 a month in additional income from the government to cover their long term care costs? They can! Under the right circumstances, Pension or Death Pension could pay additional income to cover long term care costs for at least 1/4 of all US senior households at some time during those people's lives. But the provisions of this program are such a well-kept secret that only about 5% of eligible seniors are actually receiving the benefit. The exciting news about this program is that this new-found money can be used to pay members of the family, friends or just about anyone else to provide care in the home.
>
> According to VA, there are approximately 6,250,000 living veterans of foreign wars, age 65 and older. Extrapolation of government data also provides estimates of approximately 3,900,000 surviving single spouses or other surviving dependents of these veterans. These 10,150,000 eligible individuals represent about 25% of all 40,230,000 US seniors age 65 and older. Under the right circumstances, these households can qualify for a little-known veterans' disability income called "Pension."

If a potential applicant were to call a local regional office, the veterans service representative on the phone would typically ask whether the inquiry is for a veteran or survivor, the marital status, the amount of household income, the amount of assets and the medical status. The VSR would check his or her table and if the household income exceeds the MAPR for that particular type of application category, the person calling the office would probably be told there is no benefit. In many cases this is not true. Keep in mind, however, some VSR's are aware of the special medical deduction and may not discourage callers in cases such as these, but in many cases we are told of this untrue response by service officers and in these cases the callers – due to untrue information – are discouraged or prevented from applying for a benefit that they could have received.

There are two issues that are crucial in receiving a successful award for covering the cost of home care, assisted living, adult day care or nursing home care. The first crucial element is understanding that VA will accept and total up certain recurring medical expenses for a period of 12 months in advance. Unfortunately, this is not common knowledge. The application form only has provision for reporting medical costs incurred in the month of application. Someone filling out the form, without knowing of the special provision for deducting expenses, has no clue that future costs for home care, assisted living or nursing home can count towards future recurring medical costs. Since the award is based on subtracting 12 months of future unreimbursed medical cost from 12 months of future income, having VA recognize medical costs in advance means the difference between receiving an award and receiving a denial.

The second crucial issue is understanding what type of evidence is necessary to submit with an application in order to receive the credit for medical expenses prospectively over the 12 month period into the future from the effective date of the application.

The Importance of a Rating

Having a Rating Veterans Service Representative determine (via VBA Form 21-2680) the need for aid and attendance or being housebound is called a "rating." A rating is not only important in producing a larger Pension income – due to the larger rating allowance MAPR – but also in receiving credit for unreimbursed medical expenses. For example, someone in assisted living who is there primarily for retirement and not because of the need for assistance could not apply any future room and board costs towards reduction of his income. VA would not allow these expenses. On the other hand, with either of the disability ratings, the cost of assisted living, including room and board, will count as a medical expense.

Another example might be someone receiving care at home. Without the additional disability ratings, the only recurring medical costs that are allowed as unreimbursed medical expenses are those paid to licensed health professionals providing care in the home.

Here is another example of the importance of a rating. In 2012, VA began denying claims for independent living based on the fact that independent living is not licensed to provide aid and attendance services – under VA's definition – to its community residents. This made the room and board in independent living nondeductible from income due to the fact that a rating was not forthcoming. This issue was resolved in October 2012 with a special letter from the Department that clarified under what conditions the department could issue a rating and make the room and board in independent living a deductible medical expense. We will discuss this in greater detail further on.

Here is how a rating applies to home care services. If the disabled person has been rated housebound or in need of aid and attendance, VA will allow deduction of all fees paid to a non-licensed in-home attendant as long as the attendant provides some so-called "medical" or "nursing" services for the disabled person. As an example, helping the care recipients shower would be considered a "nursing" service. Another might be help with ambulating.

With either rating, the attendant does not have to be a licensed health professional. All reasonable fees paid to this service provider for personal care of the disabled person and maintenance of the disabled person's immediate environment may be allowed. This includes such services as cooking and housecleaning for the person receiving Pension or Death Pension. It is not necessary to distinguish between "medical" and "nonmedical" services for allowing medical expense deductions.

With the ratings, VA will also allow members of the family, friends, church members or neighbors to provide care and they do not have to be licensed. The spouse cannot be an in-home attendant. A family member or other person may be considered an in-home attendant only if he or she is actually being paid. Documentation must be submitted.

<u>In most Pension cases that involve long term care, there would be no benefit without the additional income deductions allowed by a rating for aid and attendance or housebound.</u>

Understanding an Original Application for Pension

A Pension award is dependent upon three things: 1) income, 2) assets and 3) medical expenses. An original application for Pension is simply an estimate of these three factors that, if the proper conditions are met, starts a benefit flowing. The actual benefit is determined, retroactively at the beginning of each year, when the actual income, actual assets and actual medical expenses are determined from the previous year. If these three factors are not the same as estimated with the original application, the benefit will be adjusted.

Additional Pension benefit income can be provided from the previous year if household income and medical expenses allow for a greater benefit. Additional Pension benefit income can also be provided in the future to adjust for new household income and medical expenses. Or future benefits might be reduced based on failure to meet the three means testing factors. The occurrence of unforeseen disqualifying assets, unforeseen additional disqualifying income or overestimating previous medical expenses can also result in a termination of benefits going forward or a demand from VA for repayment of all previous benefits. It is extremely important to maintain this means testing for Pension on an ongoing basis and to notify the department of any changes when they occur. Failure to do so could be disastrous.

Applying Income, Assets and Medical Expenses to 12 Month Prospective Period

Understanding how the department applies income and medical expenses and assets in estimating and paying benefits for the first year is perhaps one of the most confusing aspects of applying for Pension.

Remember, an initial or original application for Pension is generally based on income estimates, asset estimates and medical expense estimates as of the month of application and extending 12 months into the future. There may be some exceptions to this, but let's keep it simple at this point. Income prior to the application, assets prior to the application and medical expenses prior to the application are not pertinent and are disregarded. Many people make the mistake of listing medical expenses for previous months. Or they may list some sort of extraordinary income receipt prior to application. Or they may list assets that they no longer have that were in place prior to application. Providing this information just confuses the veteran service representative and could result in a denial.

The application is an estimate of the three factors for the future 12 months generally starting from the month following the month of application. Assets listed on the application are those that would apply to this period of time. Likewise, even though previous income is listed on the application, only that income which can be verified as recurring each month, will be used by VA as an income estimate for the coming 12 months. Finally, medical expenses that can be applied to offset income are only those that can be certified by the applicant to recur each month for the future 12 month period from the date of the application going forward.

Most medical expenses that occur on a one-time basis are deductible, but for the initial application you cannot use them. This principle of all medical expenses applying means, after the first year estimate, you can go back and apply additional one-time costs. If you are not getting the full benefit, the VA will retroactively make up that full benefit.

General Medical Costs Eligible for the 12 Month Prospective Deduction

Because of the rule outlined above, only certain recurring, out-of-pocket – UNREIMBURSED – medical expenses will be used as an estimate for the initial 12 months of benefit. Here are the ones most commonly used. Combined household medical expenses are used, not just those of the claimant.

1. The monthly recurring out-of-pocket cost of long term care services for home care provided by professionals or family, independent living, assisted living, adult day services and nursing home services when VA determines that the services are deductible.

2. The recurring out-of-pocket cost for health insurance premiums such as Medicare Part B, Medicare supplements, Medicare advantage plans, supplemental health insurance plans and long-term care insurance but not to include reimbursement policies such as AFLAC.

3. The out-of-pocket cost for possible visits for medical treatment that can be proven that need to be performed on a regular basis. An example might be dialysis. Another example might be ongoing chiropractic treatments.

4. The out-of-pocket cost for renting medical equipment on a monthly basis such as health monitoring equipment, hospital beds and so on.

If you can come up with any other recurring costs that are not reimbursed and are out-of-pocket – as long as you can prove that they will exist month to month – VA will probably accept that.

Medical Costs Eligible for Ongoing Receipt of Pension after Initial Application

After receiving the benefit for at least five months, you should submit to the Department, evidence of medical expenses that are not recurring as well as actual evidence of all of the expenses that were used to estimate the benefit initially. This is important for several reasons.

1. Often the recurring medical expenses that you estimated for the initial application were actually less than those you estimated. Unless you can come up with additional expenses that are allowable after the initial award, you may have a reduction in future benefits.

2. Often the income that you estimate for the initial application may be less than your actual income for the period. Again, without offsetting medical expenses, you may see a reduction in future benefits.

3. If your initial award is less than the maximum that was available, evidence of additional medical expenses will allow VA to give you a catch-up payment for those benefits that you missed.

You will use VA Form 21-8416 Medical Expense Report which we include on the Claim Support Data Disk with this book. The form will be accompanied by VA Form 21-4138 "Statement in Support of Claim," which is the standard communication form used with VA. All forms are available on the Data Disk. Details on how to do this reporting are outlined in a section below.

Here is a list of medical expenses that are deductible – typically only after receiving an initial award for benefits. The list below shows many of the common allowable medical expenses, but this list is not all-inclusive. Any expenses are allowable that are directly related to medical care. These must be unreimbursed expenses paid out-of-pocket by the beneficiary and spouse. Remember, all household medical expenses are deductible, not just those incurred by the beneficiary.

- Abdominal supports
- Acupuncture service
- Ambulance hire
- Anesthetist
- Arch supports
- Artificial limbs and teeth
- Back supports
- Braces
- Cardiographs
- Chiropodist
- Chiropractor
- Convalescent home (for medical treatment only)
- Crutches
- Dental service, for example, cleaning, x- ray, filling teeth
- Dentures
- Dermatologist
- Drugs, prescription and nonprescription
- Gynecologist
- Hearing aids and batteries
- Home health services
- Hospital expenses
- Insulin treatment
- Insurance premiums, for medical insurance only
- Invalid chair
- Lab tests
- Lip reading lessons designed to overcome a disability
- Lodging incurred in conjunction with out-of-town travel for treatment (to be determined on a facts-found basis)

- Medicare Part B premiums
- Neurologist
- Nursing services for medical care, including nurse's board paid by claimant
- Occupational therapist
- Ophthalmologist
- Optician
- Optometrist
- Oral surgery
- Osteopath, licensed
- Pediatrician
- Physical examinations
- Physician
- Physical therapy
- Podiatrist
- Psychiatrist
- Psychoanalyst
- Psychologist
- Psychotherapy
- Radium therapy
- Sacroiliac belt
- Seeing-Eye dog and maintenance
- Speech therapist
- Splints
- Surgeon
- Telephone/teletype special communications equipment for the deaf
- Transportation expenses for medical purposes (41.5 cents per mile effective January 1, 2009, plus parking and tolls or actual fares for taxi, buses)
- Vaccines
- Wheelchairs
- Whirlpool baths for medical purposes
- X-rays

Note: The deductible transportation expense for medical purposes was 28.5 cents per mile from January 1, 2008, through December 31, 2008. Prior to January 1, 2008, the deductible transportation expense was 20 cents per mile. There is no change for 2014.

Denial of Pension Benefits after an Initial Award

Pension is not an entitlement like Social Security. An award for pension is dependent upon the veteran or surviving spouse meeting marital requirements as well as means-tested requirements of income, assets and medical expenses on an ongoing basis. If VA discovers that a pension recipient (beneficiary) does not meet any one of these requirements, the pension recipient could become ineligible at that point. Recipients of pension are required to report any changes immediately to VA. Very few of them do.

Unfortunately, ineligibility can be created even from the initial application. We have seen numerous instances where VA has determined the recipient of Pension monies was ineligible from the beginning and had to repay amounts of $20,000 or more to VA. Sometimes this happens because information was withheld by the applicant. Sometimes this happens when the person helping with the filing of a claim does it wrong or also withholds information in order to get the claim approved. Oftentimes this happens when an exempt asset such as the home is no longer exempt (e.g. the house is sold) and counts as a disqualifying asset.

The Importance of Keeping VA Informed

Ultimately, it is the responsibility of the claimant to make full monthly payments for care as long as they are receiving monthly payments from VA. Furthermore, it is the claimant's responsibility to notify VA if their living situation, marital status, care costs, income, or assets change. Other parties like the claimant's representative should remind and assist the claimant or beneficiary with these notifications.

The forms below were used in the past for the Eligibility Verification Report (EVR) which was due every calendar year between June and the end of February. These reports are no longer being used as VA will now rely primarily on computer matching with Social Security and the IRS to track assets and income. Unfortunately, for many beneficiaries, VA will not know about changes in a timely manner nor will they know solely through computer matching with other federal agencies.

It is therefore extremely important for you to report any changes in residence, marital status, costs, income or assets immediately to the Pension management office were your claim originated. It is not necessary to use the forms that were originally used for the EVR unless VA asks for these forms in a letter. The forms listed below can be found on the Data Disk. The least you should ever do is provide VA with a statement regarding a change on VBA Form 21-4138.

VBA-21-4138-ARE – Statement in Support of Claim
VBA-21-0510-ARE – Eligibility Verification Report Instructions
VBA-21-8049-ARE – Request for Details of Expenses
VBA-21-0518-1-ARE – Improved Pension Eligibility Verification Report, Surviving Spouse
VBA-21-0516-1-ARE – Improved Pension Eligibility Verification Report, Veteran with No Children
***See the Claims Support Data Disc for submitting to VA's Claims Intake Center

Criteria for Receiving a Rating for Aid and Attendance

Almost without exception, ratings received in conjunction with long term care services in the home or in a care facility are ratings for aid and attendance. This must be obvious because these are the type of services that these care providers offer. They provide professional help with activities of daily living and incidental activities of daily living. Assistance with ADLs and IADL's involves the services of a person to provide the regular aid and attendance to a resident or a client receiving this care. It may be possible that a claimant residing in one of these care

settings is housebound and does not need any assistance but it is not usually the case. About the only situation where a housebound rating would be useful is to allow deduction for room and board in assisted living or independent living. Anywhere else and a rating for aid and attendance would be needed to generate the necessary medical deductions.
Here are the regulations governing how a veteran service representative in the regional office should make a decision concerning the need for the aid and attendance of another person or concerning whether a veteran or surviving spouse is housebound.

38 CFR § 3.351 Special monthly dependency and indemnity Compensation, death Compensation, Pension and spouse's Compensation ratings.

(b) Aid and attendance; need. Need for aid and attendance means helplessness or being so nearly helpless as to require the regular aid and attendance of another person. The criteria set forth in paragraph (c) of this section will be applied in determining whether such need exists.

(c) Aid and attendance; criteria. The veteran, spouse, surviving spouse or parent will be considered in need of regular aid and attendance if he or she:
(1) Is blind or so nearly blind as to have corrected visual acuity of 5/200 or less, in both eyes, or concentric contraction of the visual field to 5 degrees or less; or
(2) Is a patient in a nursing home because of mental or physical incapacity; or
(3) Establishes a factual need for aid and attendance under the criteria set forth in §3.352(a).

Housebound; improved Pension; death.

The annual rate of Death Pension payable to a surviving spouse who does not qualify for an annual rate of Death Pension payable under §3.23(a)(6) based on need for aid and attendance shall be as set forth in §3.23(a)(7) if the surviving spouse is permanently housebound by reason of disability. The "permanently housebound" requirement is met when the surviving spouse is substantially confined to his or her home (ward or clinical areas, if institutionalized) or immediate premises by reason of disability or disabilities which it is reasonably certain will remain throughout the surviving spouse's lifetime.

§ 3.352 Criteria for determining need for aid and attendance and "permanently bedridden."

(a) Basic criteria for regular aid and attendance and permanently bedridden. The following will be accorded consideration in determining the need for regular aid and attendance (§3.351(c)(3):

- inability of claimant to dress or undress himself (herself), or to keep himself (herself) ordinarily clean and presentable;
- frequent need of adjustment of any special prosthetic or orthopedic appliances which by reason of the particular disability cannot be done without aid (this will not include the adjustment of appliances which normal persons would be unable to adjust without aid, such as supports, belts, lacing at the back, etc.);
- inability of claimant to feed himself (herself) through loss of coordination of upper extremities or through extreme weakness;

- inability to attend to the wants of nature;
- or incapacity, physical or mental, which requires care or assistance on a regular basis to protect the claimant from hazards or dangers incident to his or her daily environment.
- "Bedridden" will be a proper basis for the determination (need for aid and attendance). For the purpose of this paragraph "bedridden" will be that condition which, through its essential character, actually requires that the claimant remain in bed. The fact that claimant has voluntarily taken to bed or that a physician has prescribed rest in bed for the greater or lesser part of the day to promote convalescence or cure will not suffice.

It is not required that all of the disabling conditions enumerated in this paragraph be found to exist before a favorable rating may be made. The particular personal functions which the veteran is unable to perform should be considered in connection with his or her condition as a whole. It is only necessary that the evidence establish that the veteran is so helpless as to need regular aid and attendance, not that there be a constant need.

Determinations that the veteran is so helpless, as to be in need of regular aid and attendance will not be based solely upon an opinion that the claimant's condition is such as would require him or her to be in bed. They must be based on the actual requirement of personal assistance.

Interpreting the Regulations for the Requirement for Aid and Attendance

We have taken the rules above and applied them to more modern terminology of providing assistance. Here is our list based on the regulations above.

1. Assistance with bathing/showering
2. Assistance with toileting
3. Assistance with feeding
4. Assistance with dressing/undressing
5. Assistance with transferring in/out of bed/chair
6. Assistance with incontinence
7. Assistance with ambulating (walking)
8. Assistance with keeping oneself ordinarily clean and presentable
9. Assistance with frequent need of adjustment of special prosthetic or orthopedic devices which cannot be done without aid
10. Having an incapacity (physical or mental) requiring care/assistance on a regular basis to protect patient from hazards or dangers incident to his/her daily environment
11. Is blind or so nearly blind as to have corrected visual acuity of 5/200 or less, in both eyes, or concentric contraction of the visual field to 5 degrees or less
12. Is a patient in a nursing home because of mental or physical incapacity
13. Meets the criteria of being totally bedridden as defined above

As is mentioned in the regulation, there does not need to be a certain number of these incapacities in order to determine a rating for aid and attendance. The rating service representative simply must determine from the evidence whether the claimant is so helpless as to require the regular aid and attendance of another person based on one or more of these conditions.

From our experience with the rating authority, the person who is applying or the spouse of the veteran who is applying should exhibit the need for and be receiving at least two or more of the services from #1 through #8 above and from #9 through #13, only one of these need apply.

Medical Deduction Rules for Personal Care Arrangements

A personal care arrangement is the necessary requirement that needs to be taken in order to qualify a child, another member of the family or a friend to be paid through the Pension benefit. VA does not care who provides long term care services as long as it is a legitimate arrangement and money changes hands and under the right conditions family, friends or volunteers can provide the care. It does not work for a spouse living in the home to be a caregiver. The spouse could definitely be paid but must turn around and count that income towards the income test for pension. It just doesn't work.

In order to initiate a claim for services provided to a veteran household by a member of the family or others, evidence of payment to a member of the family must be produced with the original application. Also there must be a rating for aid and attendance or the paid services of a member of the family or others are not deductible from the veteran household income. The only exception to this would be if the member of the family is a licensed health professional. Beyond that, VA does not really require any further evidence. The personal-care attendant must be providing at least two or more of the services #1 through #8 or at least one of the services listed #9 through #13 in the section entitled "**Interpreting the Regulations for the Requirement for Aid and Attendance**" above. A combination of services from the first part of the list and the second part of the list could also be provided. Your doctor must also report that you have a medical need for these services.

There is a problem with these care arrangements. On average, VA will audit about 4% of Pension claims. This audit will require additional documentation to verify the actual costs and services provided. In the event of an audit, we believe that to protect the family members providing care as well as the professional providing the advice to the veteran family, there should be an appropriate care contract in place. In addition, members of the family or other informal caregivers being paid for care fall under the IRS domestic employee rules -- the so-called "nanny tax." Taxes need to be withheld and paid and a W-2 needs to be issued. This also creates a paper trail to verify to VA that money is exchanging hands and that legitimate services are being provided.

Establishing a formal paper trail has another advantage. Often, after these personal care arrangements are set up initially, the veteran or the surviving spouse fails to pay the caregiver each month thereafter because money is coming in from the Department of Veterans Affairs. Why continue to pay when money flows in every month? This failure to pay could lead to a retroactive denial of benefits and a demand from VA to repay all of the benefits from a certain previous date. By setting up a formal arrangement with the taxes being accounted for, the money must be paid every month. A formal arrangement creates the continuity of month-to-month payments that ensures the deduction for medical care can be claimed consistently. Without a proper paper trail, it may be difficult to prove that services were paid for. This could result in the benefit being denied retroactively and a demand for repayment.

If the contract also meets Medicaid rules in those states that allow personal care contracts for transferring assets to children in anticipation of Medicaid or for spend down for Medicaid, this is an additional benefit to setting up these personal care arrangements. In fact if the arrangement set up for receiving the Pension benefit does not meet the contract requirements under the Medicaid rules in your state and an application for Medicaid is made at some future date, Medicaid will likely declare the money paid to the children a transfer for less than value. This will create a penalty for Medicaid because Medicaid will argue that the parents transferred the money to the children in a deliberate attempt to get rid of their assets to qualify for Medicaid.

This transfer for less than value problem would only present itself if excess income were being held over to future months. Money received and spent in the same month is not an asset for Medicaid purposes and the transfer for less than value rule would not apply. In the event money is being held over to the next month, you must be sure that you have the proper kind of contract in place in case you have to apply for Medicaid.

Giving the money back to the parents to pay their bills constitutes a gift under Veterans Department rules. Gifts are considered income under the rules. If you are ever audited and these gifts show up in their checking accounts, VA will count that as income and could come back and disqualify them for all benefits as well as demanding repayment.

You can pay their bills for them but you can't put the money in their account. Put the money into an account with only your name or someone else's name on it and not the name of the veteran or the veteran spouse on the account. Use this account to pay bills if necessary. By the way, if VA assigns a fiduciary for the benefit award, the fiduciary service representative will require you to set up accounts according to the way Fiduciary Services requires it. This may be in contradiction to what we are telling you here. Don't come back and blame us if VA Fiduciary Services wants a different arrangement and a different contract. This might also become a dilemma for you under Medicaid. In fact, it might be better for you with the initial application to try and avoid the appointment of a fiduciary altogether. We will give you some ideas concerning this later on.

As far as a personal care attendant being a contractor and receiving a 1099 as opposed to being a domestic employee, caregivers are domestic employees. On the other hand if the caregiver is indeed in the personal-care business and has other clients that the caregiver is servicing with care services, then the attendant can receive a 1099. Otherwise, if the caregiver only has the parent or relative as a client, that is considered a domestic employee under IRS rules and social security and unemployment taxes need to be withheld. We don't care what their CPA says. We have dozens and dozens of articles from respected tax experts to back this up. Hiring a caregiver is the same as hiring a nanny. Come on guys, how many prominent politicians have been nailed by the IRS for not taking care of the taxes on the Nannies they hire? On the other hand if your CPA wants to take responsibility for saying otherwise, rely on the CPA and let the CPA assume the liability.

Medical Deduction Rules for Licensed Personal Care Services

The licensed personal care or private duty home care service company must be providing one or more of the services listed in the section entitled "**Interpreting the Regulations for the Requirement for Aid and Attendance**" above. The same rules apply as for the in-home attendant above. There must be at least two or more services from the list from #1 through #8 and if any services are being furnished from #9 through #13, you only need one of them. Your doctor must also report that you have a medical need for these services. As long as services are being provided from the aid and attendance criteria list, all reasonable fees paid to the licensed health professional for personal care of the disabled person and maintenance of the disabled person's immediate environment may be allowed. This includes such services as cooking and housecleaning for the disabled person.

It is not necessary to distinguish between medical and nonmedical services. However, services that are beyond the scope of personal care of the disabled person and maintenance of the disabled person's immediate environment may not be allowed. Example: A veteran, who is not rated for A&A or Housebound benefits, hires an LVN (who is licensed by the State) as an in-home attendant. The LVN administers medication and provides for the veteran's personal needs. The LVN also cooks for the veteran, handles the veteran's financial affairs (pays bills, files tax returns, and so on), and drives the veteran's child to school each day.

The bookkeeper and chauffeur services are beyond the scope of the medical expense deduction. The Veterans Service Representative (VSR) must apportion the value of these services and the value of the services that may be considered for purposes of the medical expense deduction. If it is determined that 50 percent of the LVN's time is spent on activities that are beyond the scope of the medical expense deduction, allow 50 percent of the fees paid to the attendant.

For the purposes of the medical expense deduction, a licensed health professional refers to an individual licensed to furnish health services by the state in which the services are provided. Licensed health professionals may include, but are not limited to

- registered nurses
- physician's assistants
- licensed vocational nurses (LVNs)
- licensed practical nurses (LPNs), and
- certified nursing assistants (CNAs).

Medical Deduction Rules for Independent Living

Over the past few years, especially during 2011 through 2013, VA has been struggling with allowing a deduction for room and board in independent living (ILF) and at the same time justifying a rating for aid and attendance. Rating service representatives in the regional office have had a hard time interpreting the rules and the granting of benefits has not been consistent – some being awarded under the same conditions that others were denied.

The manual M21-1MR does cover the situation where an individual can be in a facility that does not necessarily offer assistance to the extent that a beneficiary needs the regular aid and attendance of another person but still needs to be in a protected environment because that person cannot take care of himself or herself without this protected environment. In December 2012, VA clarified the rules pertaining to independent living and under what conditions room and board could become deductible as it is with assisted living.

If there is a need for aid and attendance in independent living, we have designed forms and a procedure for you to follow in order to get an award in compliance with the new rules. If there is not a need for aid and attendance in independent living, do not bother to make application as VA will not accept such things as medication management, pull cords, availability of staff, preparation and serving of meals and other services provided by independent living as triggering a rating for aid and attendance. It won't happen.

A third-party provider must be providing two or more of the activities of daily living services listed in the section entitled "**Interpreting the Regulations for the Requirement for Aid and Attendance**" above. Furthermore, your doctor must prescribe, in writing, that the claimant must reside in that certain facility to separately contract for custodial care with the specific third-party provider in order for ILF room and board expenses to be deductable. We will discuss this in greater detail below.

Medical Deduction Rules for Assisted Living

It is generally accepted by the Department that an assisted living facility – or whatever it might be called in your state – that is licensed to provide assistance with the aid and attendance criteria in the section above, is eligible for the deduction for the room and board portion from income in order to meet the income test.

As with independent living, if there is no medical need for the aid and attendance of another person and the applicant is not receiving one or more of the services listed in the section entitled "**Interpreting the Regulations for the Requirement for Aid and Attendance**" above, do not bother to apply. Without these services, as far as VA is concerned, the assisted living is just another retirement living arrangement and is not eligible for the special medical deduction. There must be at least two or more services from the list from #1 through #8 and if any services are being furnished from #9 through #13, you only need one of them. In order to receive a successful award, your assisted living must produce evidence that it is providing one or more of the services in the criteria list. Your doctor must also report that you have a medical need for these services.

Medical Deduction Rules for Nursing Homes

If a claimant for Pension or Death Pension is in a nursing home for a medical need as a patient as opposed to being a resident, then the out-of-pocket cost of the nursing home is always deductible from income and a rating for aid and attendance is generally automatic. It may seem surprising that we should have to differentiate between a patient in a nursing home as opposed to being a resident. Under certain conditions, a nursing home might be the only alternative for an individual who is so poor as to be unable to live in any other situation. Medicaid would be paying the bill. In this case, the individual might not need the services of the nursing home, but needs a place to live. It is rare this happens as Medicaid does have certain medical requirements for eligibility, but it could happen.

Medical Deductions for the Unhealthy Spouse of a Healthy Living Veteran

A rating for aid and attendance or housebound is only available to a veteran making application for Pension or to a surviving spouse making application for Death Pension. However, household long term care costs for home care, assisted living, independent living and nursing homes are deductible from household income for a married couple. If the non-veteran spouse of a healthy veteran is generating these costs, there is no provision for providing a rating for aid and attendance to the healthy veteran. Remember, for a married veteran, the application is submitted by the veteran, not by the non-veteran spouse creating the long term care costs. This creates a dilemma, because the non-veteran spouse should deserve the deduction for room and board or for non-licensed home attendants as well as the veteran. In addition, without a rating, the benefit for a couple is not as large and instead of being $2,120 a month it is only $1,404 a month.

VA recognizes this inequity and allows a special provision for granting the deduction for room and board or for non-licensed personal care attendants. If the doctor of the non-veteran spouse, who is generating the long term care costs, certifies in writing that the care recipient must be maintained in a "protected environment" because of that person's medical needs, VA will allow the special deductions. Unfortunately, this will result in a smaller award.

The non-veteran spouse must also demonstrate a need for aid and attendance even though there is no rating for aid and attendance. This means the doctor must certify the medical condition of the non-veteran spouse which will justify the need for aid and attendance and a licensed or non-licensed provider needs to certify that the services are being offered as listed in the section entitled "**Interpreting the Regulations for the Requirement for Aid and Attendance**" above. There must be at least two or more services from the list from #1 through #8 and if any services are being furnished from #9 through #13, you only need one of them. In addition, as with all claims for the special medical deduction, evidence must be provided for the out-of-pocket cost of long term care services provided under the aid and attendance criteria section above.

Examples of How Pension is Calculated

Now that you understand the special rules that make Pension awards possible for folks with income above the poverty level, let's look at some examples of how it works. On the next page are the maximum annual Pension rates for 2015-16 for veterans or surviving spouses for dependency conditions.

Before we go on, let's look at the basics of calculating a Pension award. VA adds up all of the anticipated annual gross household income. Next, VA adds up all eligible medical expenses, which for an initial benefit, are those that can be proven to be recurring over the coming 12 months. From these medical expenses is subtracted a 5% deduction required by law. This deduction is calculated by multiplying the basic MAPR (without rating allowances) for a given category. This deduction is subtracted from the annual anticipated medical costs. The newly adjusted medical cost is then subtracted from the annual gross income. This new adjusted income is called by VA "IVAP" or "Income for VA Purposes." If the adjusted income is less than zero, IVAP is zero. The benefit is determined by subtracting IVAP from the MAPR for that particular category of application. For example the MAPR for a couple with a rating for aid and attendance is $25,022 per year. This difference between MAPR and IVAP becomes the Pension benefit which is then divided by 12 and rounded down and paid on a monthly basis.

2015-16 Maximum Annual Pension Rates (MAPR) Effective December 1, 2014 – 1.7% Annual Increase		
If you are a veteran...	**Annual**	**Monthly**
Without Spouse or Child	$12,868	$1,072
No dependents, medical expenses must exceed 5% of MAPR	$643	$54
With One Dependent	$16,851	$1,404
With dependents, medical expenses must exceed 5% of MAPR	$842	$70
Housebound Without Dependents	$15,725	$1,310
Housebound With One Dependent	$19,710	$1,642
A&A Without Dependents	$21,466	$1,788
A&A With One Dependent	$25,448	$2,120
Two Vets Married to Each Other	$16,851	$1,404
Two Vets Married to Each Other One H/B	$19,710	$1,642
Two Vets Married to Each Other Both H/B	$22,566	$1,880
Two Vets Married to Each Other One A/A	$25,448	$2,120
Two Vets Married to Each Other One A/A One H/B	$28,300	$2,358
Two Vets Married to Each Other Both A/A	$34,050	$2,837
Add for Mexican Border Period or WW1 to any category above	$2,923	$243
Add for Each Additional Child to any category above	$2,198	$183

2015-16 Maximum Annual Death Pension Rates (MAPR) Effective December 1, 2014 – 1.7% Annual Increase		
If you are a surviving spouse...	**Annual**	**Monthly**
MAPR Without Dependent Child	$8,630	$719
No dependents, medical expenses must exceed 5% of MAPR	$431	$36
MAPR With One Dependent Child	$11,296	$941
With dependents, medical expenses must exceed 5% of MAPR	$564	$47
Housebound Without Dependents	$10,548	$879
Housebound With One Dependent	$13,209	$1,100
A&A Without Dependents	$13,794	$1,149
A&A Without Dependents (SAW Veteran's Surviving Spouse)	$14,353	$1,196
A&A With One Dependent	$16,456	$1,371
A&A With One Dependent (SAW Veteran's Surviving Spouse)	$16,954	$1,412
SBP/MIW Annuity Limitation	$8,629	$719
Add for Each Additional Child	$2,198	$183
MAPR FOR CHILD ALONE	$2,198	$183
Child Earned Income Exclusion effective 1/1/2000	$7,322	$610

Pension offers 9 different maximum annual benefit amounts based on whether the award is for a veteran with a spouse, a single veteran or the single surviving spouse of a veteran. There are also additional rates associated with additional dependent children. The only time an older veteran household will have dependent children is if they have one or more totally disabled or mentally retarded adult children living in the home. In addition, these adult children can only be counted as dependents if they were totally dependent prior to age 18.

The calculation of each of these different categories of Pension income will allow for a benefit from zero dollars all the way up to the maximum annual Pension rate or MAPR for that category. We have listed those categories below along with the minimum and maximum monthly Pension income for that category.

Husband and spouse with no rating allowances -- $0 to $1,404 per month
Husband and spouse with housebound allowance -- $0 to $1,642 per month
Husband and spouse with aid and attendance allowance -- $0 to $2,120 per month
Single veteran with no rating allowances -- $0 to $1,072 per month
Single veteran with housebound allowance -- $0 to $1,310 per month
Single veteran with aid and attendance allowance -- $0 to $1,788 per month
Surviving single spouse of a veteran with no rating allowances -- $0 to $719 per month
Surviving single spouse of a veteran with housebound allowance -- $0 to $879 per month
Surviving single spouse of a veteran with aid and attendance allowance -- $0 to $1,149/m

Our sample cases are designed to illustrate at least five of the Pension income categories above. In addition our cases also illustrate how Pension dovetails with the long term care costs of the following care services:

- Home care or adult day care
- Residential care or assisted living
- Nursing home care

Sample Case #1 Veteran and Spouse - Veteran Receiving Paid Long Term Care at Home

This case illustrates a partial Pension benefit for a couple with a housebound allowance. It shows how Pension can be used to pay for home care aides. The case also illustrates that with John receiving Pension he will automatically qualify for free VA medical care and possibly a grant of up to $2,000 to help him renovate his home to accommodate his disability. These are additional and valuable benefits available because he is receiving Pension. We also discuss using a reverse mortgage because we feel this is a very valuable planning tool for providing additional funds for long term care costs in the home.

John is 93 years old and is a veteran of World War II. He did not serve in a combat zone. Mary, his wife, is 83 years old. John takes a variety of expensive prescription drugs and due to his weight generally remains seated in a chair all day and watches television. John also suffers from mild dementia and is often confused and Mary is concerned about leaving him alone. It is difficult for John to leave his home and walk any more than a block without tiring. For his own safety he cannot drive.

John and Mary have a combined income of $3,125 a month which consists of Social Security for both, a small Pension and interest income. They have $66,000 in retirement savings and own a house and a car. They also have $120,000 available to them as a reverse mortgage equity line of credit if they choose to exercise this option. They are not required to pay anything other than the closing costs for this line of credit as long as one or both of them is alive and living in the home. In other words, there are no monthly loan payments. The potential line of credit will grow by earning 5% interest as well.

Mary has found it necessary to hire a non-medical home care agency which costs her $2,000 a month. The agency helps John with his some of his physical needs but primarily allows Mary to leave the home and still have John supervised. She is paying for this out of their income and savings. Their other recurring unreimbursed medical expenses amount to $342 a month. The home health agency has also recommended installing grab bars, a walk-in tub shower and other modifications such as handrails to help John navigate inside his home. These aides are primarily to prevent John from falling. Mary has received estimates for the cost of this to be about $3,000.

John applies for and is awarded a VA Pension with a "Housebound Allowance". Based on his continuing need for home care, VA will allow him to count 12 months of future home care costs towards the calculation of his benefit. He may also be eligible for a VA home renovation grant of $2,000 to help cover the cost of the recommended home modifications. An estimate of his Pension benefit is included below.

Estimates from the table below show that John and Mary now have an additional $789 per month with the Pension benefit to apply to their medical costs each month. As an example, the home care now costs $1,211 instead of $2,000 when they receive the Pension benefit.

John is also eligible for a priority group #5 application for medical benefits from his regional Veterans Administration Medical Center. This is because he is receiving the Pension. The medical center is 350 miles away but has a local outpatient clinic in their town that is conveniently close. John applies and is accepted. All of his medical costs are now free. His expensive medications will also be capped at $960 a year and he will not have to pay any more than that. This is a decided advantage over his old drug plan.

Veteran and Spouse - Veteran Receiving Paid Long Term Care at Home

Total 12-month, future family income from all sources	$37,500
Less 12 months-worth, prospective, unreimbursed medical expenses	$28,100
Subtract 5% of basic MAPR for this category	$842
Medical Expenses Adjusted for Deduction	$27,258
IVAP (Income for VA Purposes) (Future income less future medical costs)	$10,242
Couples Pension MAPR with Housebound	$19,710
Less IVAP	$10,241
Calculated Yearly Pension Amount	$9,466
Monthly Pension Award (yearly divided by 12 and rounded down)	$788

Sample Case #2   Single Veteran - Veteran in Assisted Living

This case illustrates the maximum veteran Pension benefit available with an aid and attendance allowance. As a general rule, anyone using residential care or assisted living is likely to receive the aid and attendance allowance as opposed to a housebound allowance. And as we will learn in Chapter 5, without the allowance rating there would be no Pension benefit in this example.

Jim is 92 years old and is a veteran of World War II. He did not serve in a combat zone. Christine, his daughter, takes care of him in her home. Jim is a large man and has many medical problems. He has difficulty attending to his own needs without help. Christine has difficulty helping him get out of bed, dress, bathe and move about. Jim also suffers from dementia and is often confused and Christine is concerned about leaving him alone.

Jim has income of $2,017 a month which consists of Social Security, a small Pension and interest income. He also has $20,300 in retirement savings and a car.

Christine can no longer handle Jim in the home and she has decided that he needs to go to an assisted living facility which will cost $3,200 a month. Additional out-of-pocket recurring, unreimbursed medical costs are $200 a month.

Jim qualifies for the Improved Pension Benefit with an "Aid and Attendance Allowance". The estimate is below.

Single Veteran - Veteran in Assisted Living

Total 12-month, future family income from all sources	$24,200
Less 12 months-worth, prospective, unreimbursed medical expenses	$40,800
Subtract 5% of basic MAPR for this category	$643
Medical Expenses Adjusted for Deduction	$40,157
IVAP (Income for VA Purposes) (Future income less future medical costs)	$0
Single Veteran Pension MAPR with Aid and Attendance	$21,466
Less IVAP	$0
Calculated Yearly Pension Amount	$21,466
Monthly Pension Award (yearly divided by 12 and rounded down)	$1,788

Sample Case #3   Veteran and Spouse - Veteran in a Nursing Home

This case illustrates the maximum benefit available to a single veteran with aid and attendance allowance. Residency in a nursing home automatically includes the aid and attendance allowance. The case was specifically designed to illustrate how Medicaid and veterans Pension could dovetail in providing more income. As a general rule, VA Pension does not work well with Medicaid unless there is a spend down as in this case or the nursing home has no Medicaid beds. If Medicaid is available, it is unlikely that VA Pension would be needed.

Same case as example #1 except John cannot remain at home. John is 93 years old and is a veteran of World War II. He did not serve in a combat zone. Mary, his wife, is 83 years old. John is a large man and has many medical problems. He takes a variety of expensive prescription drugs and has difficulty attending to his own needs without help. Mary is a frail woman and has difficulty helping him get out of bed, dress, bathe and move about. John also suffers from mild dementia and is often confused and Mary is concerned about leaving him alone. It is difficult for John to leave his home without using a walker and an aide to help him.

John and Mary have a combined income of $3,125 a month which consists of Social Security for both, a small Pension and interest income. They have $66,000 in retirement savings and own a house and a car. They also have $120,000 available to them as a reverse mortgage equity line of credit if they choose to exercise this option. They are not required to pay anything other than the closing costs for this line of credit as long as one or both of them is alive and living in the home. In other words, there are no monthly loan payments. The potential line of credit will grow by earning 5% interest as well.

John has a nasty fall and breaks his hip. After surgery, a hospital stay and a 20 day stay in a nursing home rehab facility, John's health deteriorates even further. Mary decides she cannot care for him at home and after being told by several assisted living facilities they cannot take him, she finds she must place John in a nursing home.

Because of the differential in cost between the nursing home and their income, John will qualify for the improved Pension benefit with an aid and attendance allowance but in the state in which they live, he will also qualify for Medicaid. Based on a previous analysis in example #2 we know that the VA will not pay more than $2,121 a month in Pension that could be applied to John's nursing home cost. <u>On the other hand, Medicaid will pay the much higher cost between the nursing home and John's income in lieu of the VA Pension benefit.</u> Should Mary worry about applying for the Pension benefit knowing that Medicaid may cover the entire cost of the nursing home and allow a guaranteed spousal income as well?

In this particular example Mary could come away with more money for her personal needs by using both the VA benefit and Medicaid.

To understand why the combination of the two benefits is better we need to understand how Medicaid works.

Suppose John and Mary do not have the VA benefit. Medicaid will not start paying for John's nursing home costs until he has spent his portion of the family assets down to less than $2,000. In the state in which he resides, John is responsible for spending $33,000 of their $66,000 in retirement savings. He can spend this on anything he wants but in this case the money needs to go towards the nursing home or he won't have a place to live. (Assume no Medicaid planning is done.)

John's income is $2,375 a month and Mary's income is $800 a month. The cost of the nursing home is $6,000 a month. John must pay $3,625 a month out of his spend down savings allowance money to the nursing home. After 10 months John will be below $2,000 and Medicaid will take over paying the $3,200 a month. Or Mary could take whatever income she needs, perhaps the full $2,400 a month, and let John spend the $33,000 for the nursing home in which case he would qualify for Medicaid in about 6 months. <u>After Medicaid takes over, John's income must go towards the nursing home unless Mary will be impoverished by that, which will be the case.</u>

In addition to $800 a month, Mary has her own $33,000 and she also has access to $120,000 in the reverse mortgage , if left in the line of credit, will not prevent John qualifying for Medicaid.

Medicaid will also not impoverish Mary completely and in the state where Mary resides, Medicaid will give her back $1,600 a month from John's income to bring her income to $2,400 a month. This is called the minimum monthly needs allowance. But this is only after John has spent down his $33,000 and qualifies for Medicaid. Mary has to live on something else in the meantime. Now let's suppose that Mary helps John apply for the VA Pension with aid and attendance and Medicaid at the same time. John must go through his spend down but the VA will also provide additional money for this period of time. The benefit estimate is below.

Veteran and Spouse - Veteran in a Nursing Home

Total 12-month, future family income from all sources	$37,500
Less 12 months-worth, prospective, unreimbursed medical expenses	$61,920
Subtract 5% of basic MAPR for this category	$842
Medical Expenses Adjusted for Deduction	$61,078
IVAP (Income for VA Purposes) (Future income less future medical costs)	$0
Couples Pension MAPR with Aid and Attendance	$25,448
Less IVAP	$0
Calculated Yearly Pension Amount	$25,448
Monthly Pension Award (yearly divided by 12 and rounded down)	$2,120

They now have an additional $2,120 a month to use for income or to apply to the nursing home while John is going through his spend down. Over the period of months where John is applying his spend down money, this is an additional $10,800 to $18,000 (depending on the spend down period) that they have that wouldn't be there without the VA benefit. If nothing else, this simply sustains their standard of living for an additional number of months.

VA continues paying $2,120 a month when John becomes eligible for Medicaid as long as Mary is alive. If Mary dies, the amount goes to $90 a month. The extra money for John goes towards his nursing home cost and reduces his future Medicaid liability.

Sample Case #4 Single Surviving Spouse with Paid Home Care Services
This case illustrates the maximum Pension benefit with aid and attendance allowance available to a single veteran who is receiving help from home care aides in his home.

George is the surviving spouse of a World War II veteran. His wife did not die while in the service. His income from Social Security is $1,200 a month. He receives care in his home which costs $9,600 a year. His other unreimbursed, annualized medical expenses are about $800 a year. Currently his family is paying for the home care costs. George is eligible for the Death Pension benefit with aid and attendance allowance and annualization of his yearly home care costs. An estimate of his benefit is found below.

Single Surviving Spouse with Paid Home Care Services

Total 12-month, future family income from all sources	$14,600
Less 12 months-worth, prospective, unreimbursed medical expenses	$10,400
Subtract 5% of basic MAPR for this category	$431
Medical Expenses Adjusted for Deduction	$9,969
IVAP (Income for VA Purposes) (Future income less future medical costs)	$4,631
Single Survivor Death Pension MAPR with Aid and Attendance	$13,794
Less IVAP	$4,631
Calculated Yearly Pension Amount	$9,163
Monthly Pension Award (yearly divided by 12 and rounded down)	$764

Sample Case #5 Surviving Spouse of a Veteran - No Large Offsetting Medical Cost

This case was designed to illustrate that Pension whether for a couple or a surviving spouse is totally dependent upon income where there are no large offsetting and recurring medical costs such as home care, assisted living or nursing care. It is precisely these types of cases that represent the majority of people receiving VA Pension. In other words most of those receiving VA Pension receive it because of low income and not because of recurring medical expenses. In fact that is the secret that VA keeps hidden with the claims process. VA provides no information that helps an applicant understand that the recurring costs mentioned above can be annualized for the future 12 month period and subtracted from income to allow a successful Pension award. Even though Beverly has a low income it is above the Pension threshold and without offsetting recurring medical costs, she will not receive a Death Pension. The case goes on to illustrate the power of using recurring medical costs that now allow Beverly to qualify

Beverly is the surviving spouse of a Korean veteran who died recently. Her husband had been receiving help for his nursing home costs through the improved Pension benefit with aid and attendance allowance. Because she is the surviving spouse of a qualifying veteran, Beverly is eligible for a death benefit Pension. Her income is $1,300 a month and her unreimbursed, annualized medical expenses are $1,800 a year.

Surviving Spouse of a Veteran - No Large Offsetting Medical Costs

Total 12-month, future family income from all sources	$15,600
Less 12 months-worth, prospective, unreimbursed medical expenses	$1,800
Subtract 5% of basic MAPR for this category	$431
Medical Expenses Adjusted for Deduction	$1,369
IVAP (Income for VA Purposes) (Future income less future medical costs)	$14,231
Single Survivor Death Pension MAPR with Aid and Attendance	$13,794
Less IVAP	$14,231
Calculated Yearly Pension Amount	$0
Monthly Pension Award (yearly divided by 12 and rounded down)	$0

Based on her total income and IVAP she would not be granted a death benefit Pension. On the other hand, if she needs home care on a regular basis and it can be proven that that home care provided by a licensed health professional costs her more than about $1,200 a month, she would now qualify for a benefit based on the actual cost of care. Beverly files for a death benefit and is declined the award based on income.

After a year of being a widow, Beverly has decided to move into a residential care home that provides assisted living. She needs help with dressing and supervision with her medications and she also desires the social stimulation of being around other people her own age. She finds a home in a residential neighborhood that will charge her $1,850 a month. Her unreimbursed, annualized medical expenses with the additional cost of residential care now amount to a total of $24,300 a year. She re-files for a death benefit Pension with an aid and attendance allowance. The estimate is found below. This time, she does qualify for the benefit which pays her an additional $1,150 a month and brings her total income to $2,450 a month. She now has enough money to cover the cost of her new living arrangement.

Surviving Spouse of a Veteran - With Large Offsetting Medical Costs

Total 12-month, future family income from all sources	$15,600
Less 12 months-worth, prospective, unreimbursed medical expenses	$24,300
Subtract 5% of basic MAPR for this category	$431
Medical Expenses Adjusted for Deduction	$23,869
IVAP (Income for VA Purposes) (Future income less future medical costs)	$0
Single Survivor Death Pension MAPR with Aid and Attendance	$13,794
Less IVAP	$0
Calculated Yearly Pension Amount	$13,794
Monthly Pension Award (yearly divided by 12 and rounded down)	$1,149

Sample Case #6 Healthy Veteran with Non-Veteran Spouse Generating the Medical Costs
Non-veteran spouse of a living veteran receiving paid home care. Under VA rules she does not qualify for a rating but she does meet the special medical needs test because her medical costs are deductible and count toward the household medical expenses. In this case, the doctor produces a letter for her that indicates she needs the care at home and she needs to be in a "protected environment." The home care providers are not licensed, but the letter from the doctor, a medical need and the need for aid and attendance allow all costs to be deductible. The application is made through the veteran but because he is healthy there is no rating. Income and care costs are listed below. Family meets the asset test.

Healthy Veteran with Non-Veteran Spouse Generating the Medical Costs

Total 12 month, future family income from all sources	$32,000
Less 12 months-worth, prospective, unreimbursed medical expenses	$33,250
Subtract 5% of basic MAPR for this category	$842
Medical Expenses Adjusted for Deduction	$32,408
IVAP (Income for VA Purposes) (Future income less future medical costs)	$0
Couples Pension MAPR with No Rating	$16,851
Less IVAP	$0
Calculated Yearly Pension Amount	$16,851
Monthly Pension Award (yearly divided by 12 and rounded down)	$1,404

Making Application for Pension or Death Pension on Your Own

***See the Claims Support Data Disc for submitting to VA's Claims Intake Center

The purpose of this book is to assist you in making your own application for Pension or Death Pension. There are three types of applications for this benefit. The first of these is an application based on income only where the veteran or surviving spouse cannot have an adjusted income greater than the maximum allowable Pension rate for that category. Here are those limits.

1. Veteran with One Dependent – cannot have more than $1,404 a month in combined adjusted gross household income (IVAP) – veteran and spouse
2. Single Veteran – cannot have more than $1,072 a month adjusted gross income (IVAP)
3. Single Surviving Spouse – cannot have more than $719 a month adjusted gross income

The veteran must be age 65 and older or totally disabled prior to 65. There is no such requirement for the surviving spouse. The benefit will be the difference between the Maximum Annual Pension Rate listed above and the IVAP. About the only medical expenses that can be used to produce an IVAP less than the actual household gross income are the out-of-pocket cost of Medicare Part B, other health insurance premiums and ongoing out-of-pocket prescription drug costs. Very rarely will this be enough to reduce the income to produce more than a few hundred dollars of benefit per month. But even that extra income is welcomed for veterans or surviving spouses currently experiencing the poverty-level income listed above. As you can see, only those at poverty level could really qualify for an income-only-based benefit.

Three Types of Application for Pension

The **first type** is an application for income only as covered in the section above – without significant medical deductions or a rating. An application for income-only-based benefit simply requires having a certified copy or the original of the discharge and filling out form VBA-527EZ for the veteran or VBA-534EZ for the surviving spouse. Evidence of paying Medicare Part B is not necessary; however, evidence of paying other insurance or ongoing out-of-pocket prescription drug is necessary. That's it. We provide you the forms on the Claim Support Data Disk for this type of application. This type of application would not include a rating and thus would only provide the Maximum Annual Pension Rate without a rating minus the gross income adjusted for medical costs. It wouldn't be a lot of money.

The **second type** of income-only-based benefit involves meeting the definition of housebound. There are typically no deductible assistance medical costs with a housebound rating as there would be with a rating for aid and attendance. It is the cost of the aid and attendance of another person that helps generate the additional deductible medical expenses. There is, however, a deduction for the room and board for independent living or assisted living. For a rating for housebound, the monthly cost of the assisted living or independent living would be reduced by the amount of money or equivalent amount of money that is going towards assistance in these communities. This portion would not be deductible. On the other hand, obtaining a rating for housebound with this type of application adds an additional amount of money onto the basic

MAPR which in turn yields a greater difference between the MAPR with a rating for housebound and the income adjusted for medical costs and deductible – the IVAP. This application does require going through the process outlined below.

The **third type** of application involves all of the complicated issues revolving around long term care costs and the need for aid and attendance (custodial care). With this type of application, the claimant can really have any income level so long as he or she can reduce that income with costs associated with long term care – which can usually be done. The resulting benefit is more likely going to be the MAPR with a rating for aid and attendance, which can be as high as $1,788 a month for a single veteran, $1,149 for a surviving spouse applying for death pension, or $2,837 for 2 married veterans each with a rating for aid and attendance. The complexity of these types of claims is considerably more challenging than the simple income-only-based claim.

<u>The majority of this chapter is devoted to helping you file Pension and Death Pension Claims for those who are unhealthy enough to earn a medical rating for Aid and Attendance and are in immediate or near immediate need of personal care</u>. This may include home care, assisted living, or nursing home care (see claim type 3 in the table below). These types of claims may involve hours your time as well as 7 to 10 different documents from perhaps 5 to 7 different sources. Our goal is to help you avoid a variety of pitfalls inherent in these types of applications and to produce fully developed claims. <u>Using our process and our experience, your approval times will be fast (2-5 months) and your chances of receiving an award will be greatly enhanced</u>.

The Claim Support Data Disk

This disk is a valuable asset. Forms associated with Pension, Death Pension, and the aid and attendance allowance can all be found on the disk. The Data Disk also contains checklists and instructions on how to prepare a fully developed claim and gather supporting evidence to strengthen a claim. Some of these documents are standard VBA forms; however, there are a great number of valuable forms that we have designed based on our experience that we have found to produce more efficient and timely results. One unique advantage of the disk is that you can print any mix of forms and documents you need at your leisure. Or if you choose not to print and fill them out by hand, most of these forms are PDF fillable (you can complete them on your computer or email them across the country for someone else to complete on their computer, print, then sign with a pen). Whichever you prefer, remember that VA likes wet signatures and clean faxes. Copies of copies of copies mixed with bad hand writing can ruin a claim.

When you examine the Claim Support Data Disk you will see that there are 4 major folders on the disk. These folders are devoted to application for Pension, Compensation and DIC, health care benefits and burial benefits. At this point we are interested in application for Pension.

1 Application for Pension and Death Pension
2 Application for Compensation and DIC
3 Application for Health Care Benefits
4 Application for Burial Benefits
CENTRALIZED MAIL PROCESSING - Where to Send Claims, PDF

Under the title "1 Application for Pension and Death Pension" you will find the following subfolders.

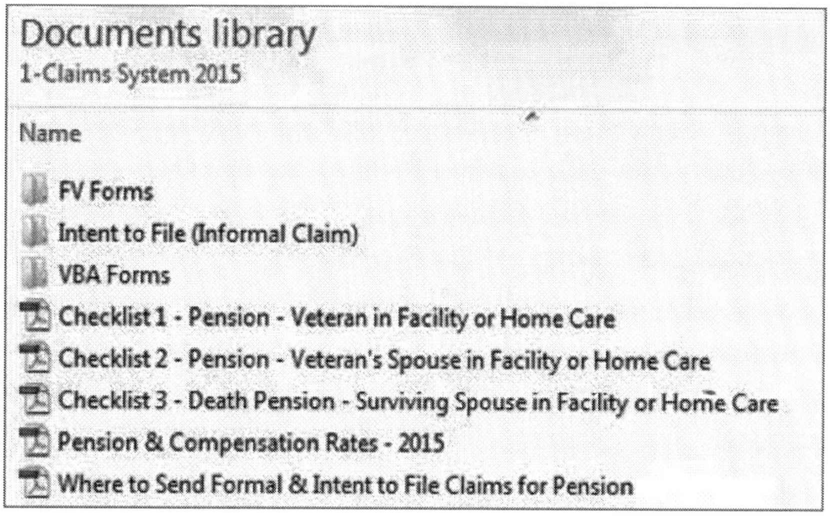

Note that with Checklist 2, the veteran is alive and reasonably healthy. In this case the veteran would not earn any type of medical rating. Rather it is the unhealthy spouse who requires the aid and attendance of another person. The veteran in this case <u>is still the claimant</u> but the couple is seeking pension based off the spouse's needs and costs.

Under the folder titled "VBA Forms" you will find several different forms. You will never use all of these forms for an initial application. Many are support or ancillary documents that might be used but very seldom come into play. Here is a list of each form in this folder:

Form Used to Obtain DD 214*
SF 180 – Request Pertaining to Military Records
* order military records online (archives.gov/veterans/military-service-records/) or (aardvarkresearchgroup.com)

Initial Application Forms
VBA-21-534EZ – Application for DIC, Death Pension, and/or Accrued Benefits
VBA-21-527EZ – Application for Pension

Forms Used with Initial Application
VBA-21-22A – Appointment of Individual as Claimant's Representative
VBA-21-0845 – Authorization to Disclose Personal Information to a Third Party

Forms Used for Ratings
VBA-21-2680 – Exam for Housebound Status or Permanent Need for Regular Aid and Attendance
VBA-21-0779 – Request for Nursing Home Information in Connection with Claim for Aid and Attendance

General-Purpose Communication Forms
VBA-21-4138 – Statement in Support of Claim (Blank)

Forms used for Fiduciary Appointments
VBA-21-4138 – Response to an Incompetency Proposal

VBA-21-0792 – Fiduciary Statement in Support of Appointment

Forms Used If Claimant Dies before the Claim Is Approved or Denied
VBA-21-0847 – Request for Substitution of Claimant upon Death of Claimant
VBA-21-534EZ – Application for DIC, Death Pension, and/or Accrued Benefits
VBA-21-601 – Application for Accrued Amounts due a Deceased Beneficiary

Forms Used to Verify Relationships Such As Marriage or Death
VBA-21-1775 – Statement of Disappearance
VBA-21-4170 – Statement of Marital Relationship
VBA-21-4171 – Supporting Statement Regarding Marriage
VBA-21-686c – Declaration of Status of Dependents
VBA-21-4103 – Information from Remarried Widower

Forms Used to Notify VA of Any Change in Income, Assets or Medical Expenses
VBA-21-8049 – Request for Details of Expenses
VBA-21P-8416 – Medical Expense Report
VBA-21-8416b – Report of Medical, Legal, and Other Expenses Incident to Recovery for Injury or Death
VBA-21-4709 – Certificate as to Assets
VBA-21-527 – Income, Net Worth and Employment Statement
VBA-21-4165 – Pension Claim Questionnaire for Farm Income
VBA-21-4185 – Report of Income from Property or Business

Under the folder titled "FV Forms" you will find several helpful forms. You will never use all of these forms for an initial application. Many are support or ancillary documents that will be called on depending on the situation. Here is a list of each form in this folder:

FV 11 – Cover Letter for Submission
FV 12 – Doctor's Report Addendum
FV 13 – Care Provider Certification of Services
FV 16 – Claimants Certification of Out of Pocket Expenses
FV 18 – Certification of Provided Information & Acknowledgment of Understanding
FV 22 – Independent Living Community Certification of Services
FV106 – Sample Care Invoice
Attendant Affidavit

Description of the Necessary Forms for a Fully Developed Claim

In this section we will discuss the forms that are the most important to produce a successful claim for Pension / Death Pension with the Aid and Attendance Allowance. As mentioned in a previous chapter, you want to give VA every possible document that the regional office or pension management center will require to make a decision. Any missing or incomplete documents may result in an inquiry (sometimes called a development letter) from VA and for each new inquiry; 30 - 60 days will typically lapse before the veterans service representative (VSR) will get back to your case. This is required by law in order to allow you enough time to respond. Unfortunately, too much of and too many of these response requirements can drag on application development for a year or more before a decision is made. You want to avoid any inquiries. The best way, obviously, is to send in a perfect claim the first time.

If a development letter is sent to a claimant you are assisting, or even a denial letter, it is generally not necessary to initiate an appeal. We warn you to you the word "appeal" cautiously and as a last resort. Generally, a response with new and/or clarifying information will satisfy an inquiry or give VA enough reason to re-open a denied claim without having to appeal. We have done this ourselves many times. In a response, remember to have the claimant write something like "with this new information I have enclosed, I am requesting that you continue (or re-open and reconsider) processing my application."

All of the forms that we use for the initial application are part of a process that VA calls a "Fully Developed Claim." VA describes the Fully Developed Claim program as such:

> "The Fully Developed Claim (FDC) Program is the fastest way to get your claim processed, and there is no risk to participate! Participation in the FDC Program is optional and will not affect the quality of care you receive or the benefits to which you are entitled. If you file a claim in the FDC Program and it is determined that other records exist and VA needs the records to decide your claim, then VA will simply remove the claim from the FDC Program (Optional Expedited Process) and process it in the Standard Claim Process. See [VBA Form 21-527ez of Form 21-534ez] for more information.

Using the fully developed claim concept and the forms that are designed around it, you can often cut your decision time from 12 months down to 3 months or less. You also have a greater probability of a favorable decision for benefits.

Unfortunately, we cannot promise any specific processing timeframe or guarantee a successful decision. Regional offices are known to make mistakes. Sometimes the very best prepared claim will not require any inquiry from the veteran service representatives (VSR) but still take 5-6 months to complete. We have no idea why this happens. We have sent almost identical claims to the same pension center and observed that one is processed in a matter of weeks and the other 5 months.

Below are descriptions of the most important forms that are used in the fully developed claim process.

SF 180 – Request Pertaining to Military Records
You must have the original or a certified copy of veteran's discharge. If you don't submit either of these with the initial application there is a high probability that you are going to slow things down considerably. The regional office will generally not proceed until they have a certified or original copy (some VSR's will let it slide). If you can't locate the original, you can submit Standard Form 180 to the Records Center in St. Louis to get a certified copy. This can take 4-8 weeks. Getting your hands on the discharge is the very first action that you must initiate before you do anything else. Even if you are viewing a copy that VA will not accept, still take time to verify the veteran's service (branch and dates). Take note of whether or not the veteran was a reservist (this can be a huge deal breaker).You can fill out the SF180 online, but the Records Center still needs a hard copy of the claimant's signature. You might as well go ahead and do a hard copy through slow mail. It takes about as long. There are also private services (e.g. aardvarkresearchgroup.com) that can get discharges for you in as little as 5 business days. You

can find them online and you will pay a fee around $90. Your state may also have a discharge archive for veterans. You can often get the county recorder to certify a copy for you.

VBA-21-527EZ – Application for Pension
This is the application that a veteran (married or single) will use to apply for VA Pension (with or without the aid and attendance or housebound allowance). The veteran is always the claimant if they are alive even if they are claiming expenses from the spouse's care. You must fill out every portion of the 527EZ. Don't leave any box blank. If a box isn't applicable write "0" or "none" or "n/a." If you leave questions unanswered, VA will send a development letter asking for explanations. It is especially important to remember that the marriage and income sections must be filled out completely. Complete marriage information includes full dates (month and year), locations (city/county and state), full names, and the type of marriage. Basically, no information can be missing and partial answers are not tolerated by VA. If you are not absolutely thorough with this form, the regional office or pension management center will return it to you to be completed accurately and you just lost another 30 - 60 days. Make sure everything is signed by the veteran, even if the veteran can only mark an "X". A Power of Attorney may not sign VA Forms on behalf of a claimant. Court appointed guardians or fiduciaries are the only individuals who may also sign for a claimant.

VBA-21-534EZ-ARE – Application for DIC, Death Pension, and/or Accrued Benefits
This is the application that a single surviving spouse will use for Death Pension. This form is also used for DIC and or for accrued benefits. If the claimant is filing for Death Pension only, you must fill out every portion of this form except for the portion pertaining to DIC and accrued benefits. You must fill out every portion of the 534EZ. Don't leave any box blank. If the question isn't applicable write "0" or "none" or "n/a." If you leave questions unanswered, VA will send a development letter asking for explanations. It is especially important to remember that the marriage and income sections must be filled out completely. Complete marriage information includes full dates (month and year), locations (city/county and state), full names, and the type of marriage (and an attached marriage certificate). Basically, no information can be missing and partial answers are not tolerated by VA. If you are not absolutely thorough with this form, the regional office or pension management center will return it to you to be completed accurately and you just lost another 30 - 60 days. Make sure everything is signed by the surviving spouse, even if he or she can only mark an "X". A Power of Attorney may not sign VA Forms on behalf of a claimant. Court appointed guardians or fiduciaries are the only individuals who may also sign for a claimant.

VBA-21-22a-ARE – Appointment of Individual as Claimant's Representative
This authorization allows an individual to act as a claimant's representative. Generally the best practice is to use VA accredited individuals or service organizations to act as the representative. Check the box titled "INDIVIDUAL PROVIDING REPRESENTATION UNDER SECTION 14.630" if the representative is not accredited. Avoid all of the restrictive options on the form.

VBA-21-0845-ARE – Authorization to Disclose Personal Information to a Third Party
This is the sister form to 21-22a above. Even though the 21-22a will allow you to act as the claimant's representative, the Regional Office will generally not share any information pertaining to the claim (by phone or mail) with your name is on this form. ONLY 1 NAME AND ADDRESS may be listed under #10a-b.

VBA-21-2680-ARE – Exam for Housebound Status or Permanent Need for Regular Aid and Attendance

This form is essential for earning a rating for aid and attendance or housebound. With a rating, a claimant can qualify for improved (or special monthly) pension rather than just basic pension. For example, basic pension will pay up to only $1,072/month for a single veteran. If that same veteran can earn a rating for aid and attendance, the veteran is eligible for up to $1,789/month improved pension.

Only an M.D. or D.O. may complete and sign this form. VA will not accept exams completed by a nurse or physician's assistant. Don't just give this form to the doctor and wait for the results. The doctor often doesn't understand that the rating service representative is looking for medical problems that produce disability which in turn justifies a medical reason for aid and attendance. Coach the doctor to make sure that the doctor understands the form is for a disability rating particularly directed towards activities of daily living. In short, VA is looking for language that justifies custodial care and highlights specific activities of daily living (ADLs) like bathing, walking, dressing, toileting, feeding, etc… Statements like "patient requires assistance with bathing and dressing" are far more convincing then vague statements like "poor motor skills and general weakness."

The basic criteria that VA follows to determine if a claimant requires the regular aid and attendance of another person or is permanently bedridden can be found in 38 CFR § 3.352.

Take special note that if the doctor indicates that the claimant has dementia or Alzheimer's and/or cannot manage their own financial affairs VA will 'propose to rate the beneficiary incompetent to handle their financial affairs.' This proposal will be given after an award is made. This action will hinder any back (retro) payments due and will likely lead the beneficiary down the path of fiduciary appointment. We will discuss this in more detail later on in this chapter.

VBA-21-0779-ARE – Request for Nursing Home Information in Connection with Claim for Aid and Attendance

If the applicant is a patient in a nursing home, a rating for aid and attendance is automatic. As long as #9 is marked "Skilled Nursing Care" there is no need for the doctor's form 21-2680 above nor for any caregiver to certify that that caregiver is providing custodial care. This form takes the place of that evidence. VA may ask for additional evidence if #9 is marked "Intermediate Nursing Care."

FV 12 – Doctor Report Addendum

We designed this form. It can be used for the veteran or spouse and acts as a wonderful supplement to VBA Form 21-2680. It is especially useful if the veteran is healthy and the spouse is disabled and generating long-term care medical costs for the deduction from income. VA rules require that the doctor for the unhealthy, non-veteran spouse must produce a letter that states that that spouse needs to be in a "protected environment" because of the health condition. Otherwise, deductions that rely on a rating will not be applied. Because the veteran is healthy, there is no rating and the benefit is much smaller for the couple (only $1,404/month as of December 2014).

FV13 – Care Provider Certification of Services
Even though the doctor is required to certify or produce medical evidence for the claimant to meet the criteria for aid and attendance or housebound outlined above, without evidence that the claimant is receiving and paying for these services there likely be no benefit. We designed this general-purpose form to cover all types of care services from facilities to family members providing care. Make sure that the form is completed accurately, that the proper sections are filled out and that it is signed by the provider. VA will likely reach out to the care provider to verify what is reported here. This is a very important document.

Consider backing up the care provider's statement with a recently paid invoice. Most of the time, you are seeking for VA to deduct unreimbursed medical expenses (UMEs) from the claimant's household income. This form will provide proof of these expenses, which by far are the claimant's biggest cost. After you submit the application, if the costs you report on this form change or if the claimant moves, notify VA immediately.

FV 16 – Claimants Certification of Out of Pocket Expenses
Sometimes the service representative will come back with a request that the claimant household certifies they are paying for the medical costs out-of-pocket. There may be some suspicion that these costs are reimbursed and are therefore not eligible for deduction. This form forces the claimant to show if they are being reimbursed from outside sources like long term care insurance and avoids any inquiries that might slow down the application process.

FV 22 – Independent Living Community Certification of Services
This form must be completed by an administrator of the facility. Remember that Independent living room and board expenses alone are not considered to be unreimbursed medical expenses (UMEs). VA simply does not consider housing, meals, emergency pull cords, 24-hour staffing, and locked exterior doors as a medical or nursing service (custodial care).

The following was taken from VA Fast Letter 12-23 (David R. McLenachen, Director | Pension and Fiduciary Service | October 26, 2012):

> To preserve the integrity of the pension program, VA considers a facility to provide custodial care if it assists an individual with two or more ADLs. Accordingly, for pension purposes, we interpret VA regulations as follows:
>
> - The cost of room and board at a residential facility is a UME if the facility provides custodial care to the individual, or the individual's physician states in writing that the claimant must reside in that facility to separately contract for custodial care with a third-party provider.
> - A facility provides custodial care if it assists the individual with two or more ADLs.
> - If the facility does not provide the claimant custodial care, or the claimant's physician does not prescribe care by a third-party provider in that facility, VA will not deduct room and board paid to the facility but will deduct the cost of any medical or nursing services obtained from a third-party provider.
>
> VA continues to receive claims for room and board as a UME when a facility provides assistance with IADLs, e.g., meal preparation. VA regulations define IADLs as "activities other than self-care that are needed for independent living, such as meal

preparation, doing housework and other chores, shopping, traveling, doing laundry, being responsible for one's own medications, and using a telephone." 38 C.F.R. § 4.124a note 3. As a general rule, charges for assistance with IADLs are not UMEs for pension purposes because such assistance is not a medical or nursing service.

FV 11 – Cover Letter for Submission
We have found that because all the forms that have to be submitted with an application for a rating, it is a good idea to organize the forms and identify the claim as fully developed for the veteran service representatives in the regional offices. We believe it helps move the claim along more quickly. The cover letter is provided in Word format so that you can edit it at your leisure.

Other Necessary Forms
Other possible necessary documentation might include supporting items like:

- a marriage certificate,
- a death certificate with a cause of death shown (VA is looking for instances of suspicious death, homicide, and whether or not it was service connected). VA will check to see if the veteran was married at the time of death.
- name change records,
- recently paid receipts/invoices from care providers
- bank statements, social security statement, insurance statements, asset statements, IRS records or supplemental insurances.

Filing an "Intent to File" - VBA Form 21-0966, formerly known as an "Informal Claim"

Before applying for benefits a veteran or the surviving spouse of a veteran (in either case, the claimant) may wish to establish an Effective Date by submitting an "Intent to File." An "Intent to File" can be submitted in three different ways (see 38 CFR 3.155). The most common and most convenient is faxing VBA Form 21-0966 to VA's Intake Center. Make sure to attention the appropriate pension management center. The "Intent to File," formerly known as an Informal Claim, can be sent to VA even though a claimant is not yet prepared to apply. This is done to 'lock-in a date' (for back-pay purposes) while the claimant is gathering supporting evidence to include in their application.

Using an "Intent to File" to establish an effective date before the claimant has sufficiently prepared his or her application will allow the claimant to receive a larger lump sum retroactive payment than he or she otherwise would have.

For pension claims with the aid and attendance allowance, if the applicant meets the medical requirement for a rating, is receiving aid and attendance services and can demonstrate having paid at least one month's worth of those services and in addition meets the war service test, and meets the asset test and the income test, you should file an "Intent to File" as soon as possible. This will establish an effective date with VA.

If you do not meet all of the criteria for an "Intent to File" above, ABSOLUTELY DO NOT FILE. It will mess up the process and create delays and confusion on the part of the service representatives or worse, cause ineligibility.

For pension, you should mail and fax the VBA Form 21-0966 to VA's Intake Center. Make sure to attention the appropriate pension management center. We recommend that you include a copy of the veteran's discharge in the mail or fax to help VA establish the veteran's identity and service. Save your fax transmission and mail certified so you can prove delivery. You will see on the Data Disk that we provide the addresses and fax numbers of the Pension Management Centers for your area of the country. You can also go to your local regional office and have it date-stamped before the end of the month and then send it on to the appropriate Pension Management Center.

Here is the "Intent to File" form that we provide you on the Data Disk. Look under the "Intent to File" folder for your type of claim and review the PDF titled *Important Information and Warnings regarding Effective Dates and Intent to File.*

VBA-21-0966 – INTENT TO FILE - Informal Claim

On the Data Disk, please refer to the PDF called "Where to Send Formal & Intent to File Claims for Pension" and the folder titled "Intent to File (Informal Claim)." Formal and VBA Form 21-0966 are sent VA's Intake Center in Jainesville, Wisconsin. Make sure to attention the appropriate pension management center. Fax and mail (to be safe) VBA Form 21-0966 to VA along with a copy of the veteran's honorable discharge (if possible). We recommend keeping a copy of your fax report in case an issue arises over when or if the 0966 was ever received.

Making Application for Pension or Death Pension Using Our Checklists

If you are filing a claim for those who are low income and are too healthy to earn a medical rating then simply follow the instructions we have given you above. You will not need a checklist. The checklists contained in the Claim Support Data Disk are meant for those:

- seeking a housebound or aid and attendance rating to qualify for maximum rates,
- wish to deduct burdensome long term care costs like home care or assisted living, and
- want to submit a fully developed claim and do it in an efficient manner.

As of October 2014 (according to the Veterans Benefits Administration Reports found on va.gov), only 8.3% of all claims sent to the three Pension Management Centers were pending longer than 125 days. On average, claims pended only 83 days. We are certain that if a claimant follows these checklists closely their claims will never fall behind these averages.

Even though you can bring these checklists up on your computer in PDF or print them, we will show them below so that you can get an appreciation of how the checklists work. The following pages are devoted to the 3 checklists. Because the borders on these checklists come very close to the inside edge of the book, you may not be able to examine them as closely as you want. Remember the PDF files are printable (most are fillable) and you can email them as attachments.

Checklist 1 - Pension – Unhealthy Veteran - Facility or Home Care

This two-page checklist covers the necessary documents to prepare a fully developed claim for a veteran (either single or married) receiving long term care under the following circumstances:

- Home Care from professional aides or Home Care from a private company or individual care giver
- Assisted Living or other Residential Care
- Independent Living plus 3rd party care
- Adult Day Services
- Nursing Home

Checklist 2 - Veteran - Unhealthy Spouse - Facility or Home Care

This two-page checklist covers the necessary documents to prepare a fully developed claim when the living and married veteran is reasonably healthy (and not generating any significant recurring medical costs), but the non-veteran spouse is. The medical and care costs of the spouse can be used to offset the household income for the claim. This type of application must go through the veteran and the veteran is the claimant. Since the veteran has no need for aid and attendance and is not housebound, there will be no rating allowance. This means that the couple's potential benefit will be cut down to the basic MAPR of $1,404/month which is about $700 less than the benefit would be if the veteran was rated for aid and attendance. This checklist covers the necessary documents to make application when the veteran's unhealthy spouse (who is not a veteran) is receiving long term care under the following circumstances:

- Home Care from professional aides or Home Care from a private company or individual care giver
- Assisted Living or other Residential Care
- Independent Living plus 3rd party care
- Adult Day Services
- Nursing Home

If the veteran has significant health problems but is not receiving care, it is advisable to submit VA Form 21-2680 on the veteran and request a rating for the veteran. VA has been known to issue a rating which then would result in VA paying the full couples benefit with the aid and attendance allowance. In some case it is worth a shot.

Checklist 3 - Surviving Spouse - Facility or Home Care

This two-page checklist covers the necessary documents to make application for a single surviving spouse receiving long term care under the following circumstances.

- Home Care from professional aides or Home Care from a private company or individual care giver
- Assisted Living or other Residential Care
- Independent Living plus 3rd party care
- Adult Day Services
- Nursing Home

Checklist 1 - Pension
Unhealthy Veteran - Facility or Home Care

Please complete or provide the forms and documents below as part of the application process.
This checklist will help you prepare a fully developed claim which should result in a faster processing time.
You, the veteran, are the claimant. Instructions on how to fill out each form are included with each form.

Agent's Name ________________________ Contact Information: ________________________________

Application for Pension with the Aid and Attendance Allowance

☐ **VBA Form 21-527EZ – APPLICATION FOR PENSION**
Use the attached instructions to complete this form in its entirety. The veteran must sign page 8.
If there are mistakes, a VA Accredited Claims Agent will correct them prior to submitting the application.

The Veteran Completes or Provides the Following Documentation

☐ **Original Discharge or Certified Copy of Original Discharge (DD 214 or equivalent)**

☐ **VBA 21-22a – APPOINTMENT OF IDIVIDUAL AS CLAIMANT'S REPRESENTATIVE**
The veteran should fill out this form as directed in the instructions and sign it.
An Accredited VA Claims Agent will sign the form to serve as the claimant's representative.

☐ **VBA 21-0845 - PERSONAL INFORMATION TO A THIRD PARTY**
The veteran should fill out this form as directed in the instructions and sign it.
An Accredited VA Claims Agent will list their information in #10a & #10b.

☐ **Marriage Certificate for current marriage (copy) – if applicable**

☐ **FV16 - CLAIMANT'S CERTIFICATION OF OUT-OF-POCKET EXPENSES**
Provide a recent receipt &/or paid invoice for each expense you list on this form to prove at least one month worth of payment. <u>If these expenses change in anyway, VA must be notified</u>.

☐ **FV17 - PENSION FULLY DEVELOPED CLAIM CERTIFICATION**
The veteran should fill out this form as directed in the instructions and sign it.

☐ **FV18 - CERTIFICATION OF PROVIDED INFORMATION & ACKNOWLEDGEMENT...**
The veteran <u>must</u> read this form in its entirety and sign it. An Accredited VA Claims Agent will sign the document as the claim representative.

Documents to Be Completed by the Veteran's Physician - M.D or D.O

☐ **VBA 21-2680 - DOCTOR'S EXAMINATION FOR A RATING**
This form is filled out and signed by the veteran's doctor (a nurse may not sign this form).

☐ **FV12 - DOCTOR'S REPORT ADDENDUM** (OPTIONAL)
This optional form is filled out and signed by the veteran's physician (a nurse may not sign this form).

Documents to Be Completed by the Veteran's Care Provider(s)

Complete the following if veteran is using assisted living, adult day services or home care

☐ **FV13 - CARE PROVIDER CERTIFICATION OF SERVICES**
A personal caregiver (private in-home attendant), care provider supervisor or facility administrator must complete and sign this document. VA will likely contact this provider to verify this information. You may also complete the **Attendant Affidavit** found in the FV Forms Folder.

☐ **A COPY OF THE PERSONAL CARE AGREEMENT / CONTRACT – if applicable**
This should be completed and signed by the veteran and care provider. All agreements and contracts should be reviewed by a qualified professional in order to meet all legal and Medicaid eligibility requirements specific to the claimant's state. The enclosed care agreements are only samples.

Complete the following if the vet is in independent living & contracting for 3rd party care

☐ **FV22 - INDEPENDENT LIVING COMMUNITY CERTIFICATION OF SERVICES**
A Community Administrator from the Independent Living Facility will fill out and sign this document. VA will likely contact this person to verify this information.

☐ **FV13 - CARE PROVIDER CERTIFICATION OF SERVICES**
The 3rd Party Care Provider must complete and sign this document. VA will likely contact this provider to verify this information.

☐ **DOCTOR'S STATEMENT – IMPORTANT!!!!**
In order for Independent Living Facility (ILF) room and board expenses to be deductable, the claimant's physician must certify in writing that the claimant must reside at the ILF to contract for the 3rd party care. The Physician must specifically name and prescribe the ILF and the 3rd party care's services for the claimant's well being. This statement must be written somewhere on VA Form 21-2680 (we recommend using #23, #25, or #32) or on the physician's letterhead:

"I, the signing medical practitioner, certify that ______________________ (claimant) must reside in ____________________________ (the Independent Living Community) to receive ________________________'s (the Contracted 3rd Party Care Provider) assistance with their Activities of Daily Living (ADLs) and custodial care. I prescribe the care outlined in the claimant's application that the 3rd Party Care Provider will offer the claimant in that facility."

Complete the following if the veteran is in a nursing home

☐ **VBA 21-0779 – VETERAN OR SPOUSE IN A NURSING HOME**
This form is filled out and signed by the Facility Administrator. If the veteran is in a skilled nursing home the VBA 21-2680 is not required.

Checklist 2 - Pension
Healthy Veteran - Unhealthy Non-Veteran Spouse in a Facility or Home Care

Please complete or provide the forms and documents below as part of the application process. This checklist will help you prepare a fully developed claim which should result in a faster processing time. Although your spouse is unhealthy and you will be making a claim for benefits based on your spouse's needs, you, the veteran, are the still claimant. Instructions on how to fill out each form are included with each form.

Agent's Name ______________________ Contact Information: ______________________________

Application for Pension with the Aid and Attendance Allowance

☐ **VBA Form 21-527EZ – APPLICATION FOR PENSION**
Use the attached instructions to complete this form in its entirety. The veteran must sign page 8.
If there are mistakes, a VA Accredited Claims Agent will correct them prior to submitting the application.

The Veteran Completes or Provides the Following Documentation

☐ **Original Discharge or Certified Copy of Original Discharge (DD 214 or equivalent)**

☐ **VBA 21-22a – APPOINTMENT OF IDIVIDUAL AS CLAIMANT'S REPRESENTATIVE**
The veteran should fill out this form as directed in the instructions and sign it.
An Accredited VA Claims Agent will sign the form to serve as the claimant's representative.

☐ **VBA 21-0845 - PERSONAL INFORMATION TO A THIRD PARTY**
The veteran should fill out this form as directed in the instructions and sign it.
An Accredited VA Claims Agent will list their information in #10a & #10b.

☐ **Marriage Certificate for current marriage (copy) – if applicable**

☐ **FV16 - CLAIMANT'S CERTIFICATION OF OUT-OF-POCKET EXPENSES**
Provide a recent receipt &/or paid invoice for each expense you list on this form to prove at least one month worth of payment. If these expenses change in anyway, VA must be notified.

☐ **FV17 - PENSION FULLY DEVELOPED CLAIM CERTIFICATION**
The veteran should fill out this form as directed in the instructions and sign it.

☐ **FV18 - CERTIFICATION OF PROVIDED INFORMATION & ACKNOWLEDGEMENT…**
The veteran must read this form in its entirety and sign it. An Accredited VA Claims Agent will sign the document as the claim representative.

Documents to Be Completed by the Spouse's Physician - M.D or D.O

☐ **VBA 21-2680 - DOCTOR'S EXAMINATION FOR A RATING**
This form is filled out and signed by the spouse's doctor (a nurse may not sign this form).
The spouse will appear as the claimant on this form.

☐ **FV12 - DOCTOR'S REPORT ADDENDUM**
This form is filled out and signed by the spouse's physician (a nurse may not sign this form).

Documents to Be Completed by the Spouse's Care Provider(s)

Complete the following ***if*** *the spouse is using* ***assisted living, adult day services*** *or* ***home care***

☐ **FV13 - CARE PROVIDER CERTIFICATION OF SERVICES**
A personal caregiver (private in-home attendant), care provider supervisor or facility administrator must complete and sign this document. VA will likely contact this provider to verify this information. You may also complete the **Attendant Affidavit** found in the FV Forms Folder.

☐ **A COPY OF THE PERSONAL CARE AGREEMENT / CONTRACT – if applicable**
This should be completed and signed by the spouse and care provider. All agreements and contracts should be reviewed by a qualified professional in order to meet all legal and Medicaid eligibility requirements specific to the claimant's state. The enclosed care agreements are only samples.

Complete the following ***if*** *the spouse is in* ***independent living & contracting for 3rd party care***

☐ **FV22 - INDEPENDENT LIVING COMMUNITY CERTIFICATION OF SERVICES**
A Community Administrator from the Independent Living Facility will fill out and sign this document. VA will likely contact this person to verify this information.

☐ **FV13 - CARE PROVIDER CERTIFICATION OF SERVICES**
The 3rd Party Care Provider must complete and sign this document. VA will likely contact this provider to verify this information.

☐ **DOCTOR'S STATEMENT – IMPORTANT!!!!**
In order for Independent Living Facility (ILF) room and board expenses to be deductable, the claimant's physician must certify in writing that the claimant must reside at the ILF to contract for the 3rd party care. The Physician must specifically name and prescribe the ILF and the 3rd party care's services for the claimant's well being. This statement must be written somewhere on VA Form 21-2680 (we recommend using #23, #25, or #32) or on the physician's letterhead:

"I, the signing medical practitioner, certify that ______________________ (claimant) must reside in ____________________________ (the Independent Living Community) to receive ________________________'s (the Contracted 3rd Party Care Provider) assistance with their Activities of Daily Living (ADLs) and custodial care. I prescribe the care outlined in the claimant's application that the 3rd Party Care Provider will offer the claimant in that facility."

Complete the following if the spouse is in a ***nursing home***

☐ **FV13 - CARE PROVIDER CERTIFICATION OF SERVICES (For nursing home)**
A Care Provider Supervisor or Facility Administrator will fill out and sign this document. VA will likely contact this person to verify this information about the unhealthy spouse.

Checklist 3 - Death Pension
Surviving Spouse - Facility or Home Care

Please complete the forms and documents below as part of the application process. This checklist will help you prepare a fully developed claim which should result in a faster processing time. You, the surviving spouse, are the claimant. Instructions on how to fill out each form are included with each form.

Agent's Name ________________________ Contact Information: ________________________________

Application for Death Pension with the Aid and Attendance Allowance

☐ **VBA Form 21-534EZ – APPLICATION FOR DEATH PENSION**
Use the attached instructions to complete this form in its entirety. The surviving spouse must sign pg 11. If there are mistakes, a VA Accredited Claims Agent will correct them prior to submitting the application.

The Spouse Completes or Provides the Following Documentation

☐ **Original Discharge or Certified Copy of Original Discharge (DD 214 or equivalent)**

☐ **VBA 21-22a – APPOINTMENT OF IDIVIDUAL AS CLAIMANT'S REPRESENTATIVE**
The surviving spouse should fill out this form as directed in the instructions and sign it.
An Accredited VA Claims Agent will sign the form to serve as the claimant's representative.

☐ **VBA 21-0845 - PERSONAL INFORMATION TO A THIRD PARTY**
The surviving spouse should fill out this form as directed in the instructions and sign it.
An Accredited VA Claims Agent will list their information in #10a & #10b.

☐ **Marriage Certificate for marriage to veteran (copy) – if applicable**

☐ **Death Certificate of the Veteran (Copy)**

☐ **FV16 - CLAIMANT'S CERTIFICATION OF OUT-OF-POCKET EXPENSES**
Provide a recent receipt &/or paid invoice for each expense you list on this form to prove at least one month worth of payment. <u>If these expenses change in anyway, VA must be notified</u>.

☐ **FV17 - PENSION FULLY DEVELOPED CLAIM CERTIFICATION**
The surviving spouse should fill out this form as directed in the instructions and sign it.

☐ **FV18 - CERTIFICATION OF PROVIDED INFORMATION & ACKNOWLEDGEMENT…**
The surviving spouse <u>must</u> read this form in its entirety and sign it. An Accredited VA Claims Agent will sign the document as the claim representative.

Documents to Be Completed by the Veteran's Physician - M.D or D.O

☐ **VBA 21-2680 - DOCTOR'S EXAMINATION FOR A RATING**
This form is filled out and signed by the surviving spouse's doctor (a nurse may not sign this form).

☐ **FV12 - DOCTOR'S REPORT ADDENDUM**
This form is filled out and signed by the surviving spouse's physician (a nurse may not sign this form).

Documents to Be Completed by the Surviving Spouse's Care Provider(s)

Complete the following if using assisted living, adult day services or home care

☐ **FV13 - CARE PROVIDER CERTIFICATION OF SERVICES**
A personal caregiver (private in-home attendant), care provider supervisor or facility administrator must complete and sign this document. VA will likely contact this provider to verify this information. You may also complete the **Attendant Affidavit** found in the FV Forms Folder.

☐ **A COPY OF THE PERSONAL CARE AGREEMENT / CONTRACT – if applicable**
This should be completed and signed by the surviving spouse and care provider. All agreements and contracts should be reviewed by a qualified professional in order to meet all legal and Medicaid eligibility requirements specific to the claimant's state. The enclosed care agreements are only samples.

Complete the following if living in independent living & contracting for 3rd party care

☐ **FV22 - INDEPENDENT LIVING COMMUNITY CERTIFICATION OF SERVICES**
A Community Administrator from the Independent Living Facility will fill out and sign this document. VA will likely contact this person to verify this information.

☐ **FV13 - CARE PROVIDER CERTIFICATION OF SERVICES**
The 3rd Party Care Provider must complete and sign this document. VA will likely contact this provider to verify this information.

☐ **DOCTOR'S STATEMENT – IMPORTANT!!!!**
In order for Independent Living Facility (ILF) room and board expenses to be deductable, the claimant's physician must certify in writing that the claimant must reside at the ILF to contract for the 3rd party care. The Physician must specifically name and prescribe the ILF and the 3rd party care's services for the claimant's well being. This statement must be written somewhere on VA Form 21-2680 (we recommend using #23, #25, or #32) or on the physician's letterhead:

"I, the signing medical practitioner, certify that ______________________ (claimant) must reside in ____________________________ (the Independent Living Community) to receive ______________________'s (the Contracted 3rd Party Care Provider) assistance with their Activities of Daily Living (ADLs) and custodial care. I prescribe the care outlined in the claimant's application that the 3rd Party Care Provider will offer the claimant in that facility."

Complete the following if the surviving spouse is in a nursing home

☐ **VBA 21-0779 – VETERAN OR SPOUSE IN A NURSING HOME**
This form is filled out and signed by the Facility Administrator. If the surviving spouse is in a skilled nursing home the VA Form 21-2680 is not required.

Paying Attention to Potentially Disastrous Pitfalls in the Application Process

Providing Information to VA

Over the years we have discovered there are some issues that claimants must treat very carefully or you and they will fall into a snare and possibly have the application denied from the beginning or more likely denied retroactively when the regional office gets notice concerning the claimant's taxes or income from the Internal Revenue Service (IRS) or the Social Security Administration. We see a number of letters, sometimes years after awards have been issued, demanding repayment of all of the benefits that were paid to that point. One in particular was a repayment demand of about $75,000.00.

IRS Crosschecks

The regional office that handles your claim continues to monitor the claimant/beneficiary from year-to-year to make sure they still qualify by meeting the income and asset tests. The agency receives 1099's and other information from the IRS as well as reports from the Social Security Administration concerning assets and income (including things like interest, dividends, and distributions from IRA accounts). These are entered into the computer and compared against what has been reported in an original application. If there appears to be a discrepancy an inquiry will be initiated. From this point on, veteran service officers will start demanding more and more detail until they make a decision.

Generally, anything that caused or will cause a tax event will eventually be seen by VA either now from last year's IRS records or on next year's IRS records. VA has been known to check as far as 3 years of records prior to an initial application for pension. Below and on the following page are instances where VA found items that were not unreported on the claimant's application.

Take special note that VA doesn't care that the tax event (or asset transfer if they discover one has been made) occurred before an effective date was established (before the application or VBA Form 21-0966 was submitted). Once VA discovers, for example, that an asset has been moved prior to application, one of the questions VA will then ask the claimant is if any portion of the moved asset is being used to pay for, no matter how small, the maintenance of the claimant. If the answer is YES to that question, VA will most likely count the entire amount as an asset belonging to the claimant even though it was moved. VA will also ask other questions like "why did you move the asset" and "do you have any type of control over this asset"? If the claimant cannot provide VA with good reasons and evidence, things will go south very quickly.

> We need additional evidence from you. **Please use the enclosed envelope (labeled FTI), put your VA file number on any correspondence or evidence you provide.**
>
> - On your application, you reported that you received in $ 1,664.28 in projected interest income for 2014 for $43,150.00 in Stock, bonds or mutual fund assets. VA received from the Internal Revenue Service information that in 2013 you received income of $11,460.00 in interest or pension distributions. The IRS also showed you reported $229,250.00 in real estate sales in 2013. The amount you reported on your application for this payment, $1,664.28, is $9,795.72 less than IRS reported to VA for the 2013 tax year. The $229,250.00 in real estate sales may be considered a conversion of assets if the proceeds are from the sale of your home.

File Number: [redacted]
[redacted]

On your application, you reported that you received in 2014 1323.90 for Social Security, Retirement of 368.28 a month and 808.38 a month from Genworth. VA received from the Internal Revenue Service information that in 2013 you received the following amounts and sources of income in 2013 that you did not report on your application:

$49,138.00 Distributions, from pensions, annuities, IRA's, Etc.... account #[redacted]

$1,617.00 Distributions, from pensions, annuities, IRA's, Etc.... account [redacted]

$171.00 Distributions, from pensions, annuities, IRA's, Etc.... account [redacted]

$1366.00 Distributions, from pensions, annuities, IRA's, Etc.... account [redacted]

To help us decide your claim, please provide information explaining the difference between the amount of income you reported on your application and the amount the IRS VA for 2013. If you believe the payment information reported by IRS or SSA is incorrect, please tell us in a written statement and provide any information you have to support the statement. Acceptable information to

What Do We Still Need from You?

We need additional evidence from you. ***Please use the enclosed envelope (labeled FTI), put your VA file number on any correspondence or evidence you provide.***

- On your application, you reported that you receive $430.69 in pension income and $1,242.90 in Social Security benfits. VA received from the Internal Revenue Service information that in 2013 you received gross distributions as follows; $108,195.00 from account [redacted], $1,219.00 from account [redacted], and $1,159.00 from account GA[redacted]. These amounts or income sources were not reported on your application.

To help us decide your claim, please provide information explaining why these incomes were not reported on your application. If you believe the payment information reported by the IRS is incorrect, please tell us in a written statement and provide any information you have to support the statement. Acceptable information to support a statement would include a statement from the person or entity that paid you showing the amount, type, frequency and date last paid. If you no longer receive the income reported by the IRS, please provide a statement from the person or entity that paid you showing the date this income stopped.

Financial Issues to Be Aware Of
Here's a brief description of most of the financial issues as well as other application issues you need to be aware of:

1. **The Home** – We discuss this in Chapter 5. If you are planning on selling your home after you apply or you are planning on not living in your home – either you or your spouse – after receiving a benefit, the Regional Office will find out about it from the IRS. Although unfavorable rulings based on the home are inconsistent, as a general rule, VA considers the home to be an asset if neither the veteran nor the spouse are living in it AND it is being rented or is earning income. The sale is usually discovered through a 1099s issued by the trust company when the property is sold. This document shows the owners' names on the property at the time of sale. VA considers this a conversion of an asset. You must do something prior to application if you are in this situation.

2. **Reporting Interest Income** – You are required to report interest and dividend income on the application. If there are not enough assets to support the amount of interest income you report, the service representative is required by the adjudication manual to find out where those assets are. If you can't provide a reasonable answer, the manual allows the VSR to deny your claim.

3. **Filling in Financial Data Entirely** – The application requires you to report income and assets on the application (VBA Form 21-527ez of 534ez). There are a whole bunch of blank boxes for you to report. If you don't use all the boxes, you must write $0.00 or "none" in the blank ones or the application will be sent back to you for completion and you'll have lost 30-60 days towards your decision on the application.

4. **Using the Word "Annuity"** – VA will likely follow up with a claimant if they report income streams from annuities. VA are not big fans of claimants using annuities to dilute assets by creating income streams just prior to application. In some cases, VA will seek to count a SPIA, for example, as an income and an asset. You may need to be prepared to argue your case with VA if this is a situation you put yourself in. VA has taken a hard line approach concerning the way they treat annuities even if the monies used to create the income stream no longer belong to the claimant in any shape of form (they think there is some underlying asset that you are not reporting). Please see Chapter 5 for more information on this subject.

   Service officers in the regional office (on occasion) do not seem to be very sophisticated (probably because of lack of guidance and rulings) when it comes to financial products. You may be receiving a pension income from your previous employment that is a commercial annuity. Or you may have yourself converted assets into a guaranteed income stream through a commercial immediate annuity. Consider not using the word "annuity" on an application even though it may be a legitimate income stream with no asset attached. Your application may be denied or held up. You might call the income "retirement income" because that is exactly what it is. The 1099r that VA receives for you concerning this income will reflect that it is retirement income and as a result, its existence as an income stream should never be questioned after the award is approved.

Again, be prepared to argue your case with VA if this is a situation you are in. You argument will carry more weight if the annuity is truly "non-transferable, non-assignable, non-commutable, non-surrenderable, totally and permanently irrevocable, and has no cash value." Statements that also indicate that the claimant's annuity truly cannot be converted to cash at any time during the life of the annuitants, that it is non-transferable and has no market value, and the monthly payments were already being counted towards income also will help make your case.

5. **Cashing out Tax Deferred Savings Accounts Prior to Application** – If done correctly, it is perfectly all right to do some sort of estate planning prior to applying, because assets or income prior to application don't count towards the income or asset test. Only those assets or income going forward 12 months and beyond, count. The problem is, any withdrawals or surrenders from retirement accounts such as IRAs, annuities, 401(k)s and so forth that occur in the year of your application will show up as income in that year. VA will also scrutinize these transfers heavily. The Regional Office will receive 1099's from the IRS concerning these surrenders, but service representatives have no idea whether this occurred before or after your benefit was approved. Just be aware that you may have to answer some sort of inquiry about any sort of a withdrawal or surrender in the year of application – possibly a year or two after your award is approved.

6. **Selling Property Prior to the Application** – This is the same issue as the one above. Even though it may have been a legitimate sale prior to application and the assets may have been reinvested for someone else or gifted, be prepared to provide an answer why this happened. Inquiry may come a year or two after the award has been approved.

7. **Incompetent to Handle Finances** - Take special note that if the doctor indicates on VBA Form 21-2680 (or on any other piece of medical evidence) that the claimant has dementia or Alzheimer's and/or cannot manage their own financial affairs VA will 'propose to rate the beneficiary incompetent to handle their financial affairs.' This proposal will be issued after an award is made. This action will hinder any back (retro) payments due and will likely lead the beneficiary down the path of fiduciary appointment. We will discuss this in more detail later on in this chapter. You may read more about this in the section below called "The Appointment of a Fiduciary."

8. **Long Term Care Insurance** (LTCi) – LTCi, when actively paying for something for a claimant, is a countable income. You must report LTCi on the application and take the monthly amount into account as you calculate a potential benefit. If the LTCi will not kick in until after a claim has filed an application, you must notify VA when the LTCi will begin payments and take into account the effects that new income will have.

9. **Life Insurance** – The cash value of the policy is the amount VA considers to be an asset.

10. **Reporting Costs Separately** – Never combine the costs for care or any other ongoing medical expense for a husband and wife into a single entry on an application for pension. Report each ongoing medical expense for the Veteran in separates rows distinguishable from the spouse's. If you are seeking to deduct care costs (e.g. home care or assisted

living) for both individuals, you must submit two VBA Form 21-2680s. One for the veteran, and one for the spouse.

Evidence for Medical Costs
There is only one exception to the rule that you do not have to provide supporting documents for any finances or income. That is the requirement to provide evidence that you have paid out-of-pocket for the approved medical costs that will result in a deduction from your income. You must provide evidence of recurring medical costs and show at least one month's worth of payments. Probably the best way to do this is to produce invoices with check numbers that are marked "paid." You cannot receive a deduction from your income without this evidence. The regional office will not accept an IOU or any form of deferred payment for the services as evidence. Money must exchange hands from you to the provider.

What Documents Not to Submit with the Claim

It is important to remember that your initial application or so-called "original" application for Pension/Death Pension is a best estimate of future income, future assets and future medical expenses. This is not like an application for a loan where you have to disclose every financial aspect of your life. Although VA requires full disclosure, they can verify most of the information submitted in the application through their own computer matching efforts. Remember they will look into historical data through IRS Crosschecks.

Certain Financial Statements and Paid Invoices
It is not requisite to submit evidence of financial status such as pay stubs, account statements, retirement plan statements, and insurance policies unless you feel that the evidence is required to highlight a certain income, asset, or ongoing medical cost that may come into question. Generally the most recent month's invoice or statement will suffice. The regional office does not need pages and pages of financial statements and invoices. There is no reason to confuse them with additional information. In fact, in some cases it may cause questions and result in an inquiry. As we have already discussed, inquiries can slow down your claim process.

Prescription Premiums
Generally VA will not allow prescription costs as deductable medical expenses. You shouldn't bother including any prescription information in a claim.

Black and White Non-Certified Copies of DD214s
Uncertified black and white photo copies of military records might not be considered as evidence by the regional office handling a claim. Always attempt to submit original DD214s or certified copies of an original.

Power of Attorney (POA) Forms
We are not talking about VBA Form 21-22a here. VA does not need statements of nor do they recognize a claimant's power of attorney. If a claimant's POA wants to represent the claimant, they may complete VBA Form 21-22a and mark the box called INDIVIDUAL PROVIDING REPRESENTATION UNDER SECTION 14.630. The POA may also complete VBA Form 21-

0845 so that they can receive copies or correspondence sent to the claimant. We recommend that family and POAs be listed on the 0845 and leave the 22a for accredited individuals to sign. POAs may not sign VA Forms on behalf of claimants under any circumstance.

VBA Form 21-0792
VA will completely disregard this form if you include it in an original application. This form is only considered after a claimant has agreed to an incompetency proposal. Send this form in when the claimant agrees with the incompetency proposal. Please see the section below titled "The Appointment of a Fiduciary" for more information.

If the Claimant Dies While the Application Is Pending or VA Owes the Claimant Money

Below we will show you how to apply for burial and accrued benefits. Here are the rules pertaining to what happens if a claim is pending and a decision has not been made when the claimant dies. The following is also applicable when un-paid monies are owed the deceased. This is found in Title 38 USC.

§5121. Payment of certain accrued benefits upon death of a beneficiary
(a) Except as provided in sections 3329 and 3330 of title 31, periodic monetary benefits (other than insurance and servicemen's indemnity) under laws administered by the Secretary to which an individual was entitled at death under existing ratings or decisions or those based on evidence in the file at date of death (hereinafter in this section and section 5122 of this title referred to as "accrued benefits") and due and unpaid, shall, upon the death of such individual be paid as follows:

(1) Upon the death of a person receiving an apportioned share of benefits payable to a veteran, all or any part of such benefits to the veteran or to any other dependent or dependents of the veteran, as may be determined by the Secretary.

(2) Upon the death of a veteran, to the living person first listed below:

(A) The veteran's spouse.
(B) The veteran's children (in equal shares).
(C) The veteran's dependent parents (in equal shares).

3) Upon the death of a surviving spouse or remarried surviving spouse, to the children of the deceased veteran.

(4) Upon the death of a child, to the surviving children of the veteran who are entitled to death Compensation, dependency and indemnity Compensation, or Death Pension.

(5) Upon the death of a child claiming benefits under chapter 18 of this title, to the surviving parents.

(6) In all other cases, only so much of the accrued benefits may be paid as may be necessary to reimburse the person who bore the expense of last sickness and burial.

Because of the requirement that at the death sufficient evidence had to be on file (in the regional office) in order to approve a claim, very few claims in the past were actually approved. No one really knew whether VA had the information are not because the claimant was dead and only a power of attorney could have demanded to know the true nature of the case. And even in this case, reasons for not awarding a benefit could easily be explained away. This injustice commonly resulted in the phrase "the claim dies with the claimant."

Congress recognized the inequity of this situation and passed legislation to correct it. Here is an explanation.

> This is an excerpt from an article by the following: Katrina J. Eagle is a veterans law attorney in San Diego. She can be reached at kjeagle@vetsjustice.com. Douglas J. Rosinski is of counsel in the law firm of Ogletree, Deakins, Nash, Smoak & Stewart in Columbia, South Carolina. He can be reached at doug.rosinski@ogletreedeakins.com.
>
> *In 2008, Congress passed a statute that explicitly created the right of certain family members to take the place of a claimant who dies awaiting a decision on a VA benefits claim. The law limits the pool of possible survivors eligible for substitution to spouses, children, and financially dependent parents of a veteran who died on or after October 10, 2008.*
>
> *The VA's proposed rules to comply with the act define a "pending claim" as one that has been filed at a regional office but has not yet been adjudicated, which means no rating decision has been issued.*
>
> *A "pending appeal" is created by the filing of a NOD in response to a denied claim. In either situation, if the claimant dies, an eligible survivor has one year from the date of the death to request substitution. Curiously, the VA's regulations do not require the agency to notify potentially eligible survivors--the onus is squarely on a survivor to request substitution.*
>
> *An eligible survivor must request substitution in writing from the same regional office where the original claim or appeal is pending and must include the term "substitute" or "substitution," the deceased claimant's name, his or her claim number, and evidence supporting eligibility. The survivor can also request substitution by completing and submitting VA Form 21-0847.*

Accrued Benefits and Final Expenses

Last sickness and burial expenses are part of a broader term VA uses called *Final Expenses*. These expenses are generally limited to hospice, hospital, funeral, and burial expenses. Paid invoices for nursing home, assisted living, or home care are not considered by VA to be final expenses.

If a claimant or beneficiary of VA Benefits has passed away, any person (e.g. a child or relative) may be eligible for accrued benefits if they personally paid for any of the claimant / beneficiary's final expenses AND there was money due (or likely due) the beneficiary or claimant. VA will reimburse the individual who paid for the final expenses up to the amount owed the deceased claimant / beneficiary.

Complete and mail the following in one envelope to the appropriate VA Pension Management Center in Jainesville, Wisconsin to apply for accrued benefits. Make sure to use the 4138 to explain the situation and make special comments to help the accrued claim.

VBA-21-4138-ARE – Statement in Support of Claim
VBA-21-601-ARE Application for Accrued Amounts due a Deceased Beneficiary
Copy of Claimant or Beneficiary's Death Certificate
Other applicable evidence (e.g. paid invoices of final expenses individual paid which can include hospice, hospital, funeral and/or burial).
***See the Claims Support Data Disc for submitting to VA's Claims Intake Center

If the Claimant Dies before the Claim Is Approved or Denied

Forms Used if Claimant Dies before the Claim Is Approved or Denied

VBA-21-4138-ARE – Statement in Support of Claim
VBA-21-0847-ARE Request for Substitution of Claimant upon Death of Claimant
VBA-21-534EZ-ARE – Application for DIC, Death Pension, and/or Accrued Benefits
***See the Claims Support Data Disc for submitting to VA's Claims Intake Center

When survivors are seeking all the back-pay possibly owed the deceased claimant, there must be someone in the line of succession to receive the full residual benefit (retro-payment) that would have been paid to the claimant. This is either a spouse or dependent children. It does not matter whether or not the spouse or dependent child paid for the veteran's final expenses.

For example, a veteran filed for Pension with Aid and Attendance in June and 4 months later passed away before an award was granted. Although deceased, there are 3 months of back-pay up for grabs (possibly over $6,300). The widow can file the above VBA Form 21-0847 (and the veteran's death certificate) to request substitution of claimant. VA will re-open the pension claim and release the back pay to the surviving spouse in full. For purposes of veterans benefits, a child is defined as a minor age 18 or less, a full-time student age 23 or less, any other child age 30 or less who is also a veteran or a child any age who became totally dependent prior to age 18. We will discuss below how children who do not fall under this description can become eligible.

Unfortunately, there is no option to pay to the estate of the claimant. If there are no individuals in the line of succession, there is no benefit. In this case, again, the benefit becomes an "accrued benefit for final costs" and the amount that would have been owed – if the application had been approved – could be used to pay for the out-of-pocket expenses of the person who bore the expense of paying off the final expenses of the deceased which are limited to hospital, hospice, funeral and burial expenses. A claim for accrued benefits must be filed within one year from the date of death of the deceased beneficiary using.

When there is a surviving spouse, application for Death Pension, DIC or an accrued benefit for final costs is made on the following form found on the Data Disk.

VBA-21-534EZ-ARE – Application for DIC, Death Pension, and or Accrued Benefits
***See the Claims Support Data Disc for submitting to VA's Claims Intake Center

Where there is no surviving spouse, application for this accrued benefit is made using the following form.

> VBA-21-601-ARE – Application for Accrued Amounts Due A Deceased Beneficiary
> ***See the Claims Support Data Disc for submitting to VA's Claims Intake Center

The Appointment of a Fiduciary

If the Veteran or Surviving Spouse's doctor indicates that the claimant has memory issues (dementia or Alzheimer's) and or cannot manage their own financial affairs on the VBA Form 21-2680 the VA will "propose to rate the beneficiary incompetent to handle their own financial affairs" at the time the Veteran or Surviving Spouse is awarded either Pension or Death Pension with the Aid and Attendance Allowance. This action will hinder any back payments due.

The beneficiary may (1) argue the incompetency proposal through a hearing, (2) remain silent and wait for VA to appoint a fiduciary to handle the beneficiary's finances, (3) respond and agree to the proposal of incompetency and simultaneously appoint their own fiduciary, or (4) disagree with the proposal and request that VA release the back pay.

About each option above:

1. If the Beneficiary wants a hearing, have them follow the instructions that the VA has provided them in the correspondence letter proposing incompetency. Our recommendation is to NEVER DO THIS. We recommend either #3 or #4

2. If the beneficiary remains silent, after 60 days the VA will begin to look for the most logical fiduciary (like a family member or VA fiduciary) through their own procedures.

3. If the Beneficiary wants to speed up things up and to appoint a fiduciary of their choosing (like a family member), use VBA Form 21-4138 Incompetency Statement and VBA Form 21-0792. We have pre-written a response for the beneficiary to use on the standard 21-4138 form (the beneficiary will have to complete, sign, and may edit the form). These forms are located in the Data Disk. Note that we have indicated that the beneficiary agrees with the proposal of incompetency (this statement is crucial). Have the person who the beneficiary wishes to be their fiduciary fill out the VBA Form 21-0792. Make sure to mail and fax the 2 VBA Forms to the address in the VA letter. Do not forget to list the claim # where applicable. In these situations, follow all the instructions in the VA correspondence sent to the beneficiary as the VA may want other forms or documents returned as well.

4. If the beneficiary believes that they can handle their own finances (and there was no major indication of memory issues on the VBA Form 21-2680 doctor's exam) but still needs a caregiver for their ADLs, they may "DISAGREE with the proposal of incompetency" and also state on a 21-4138 that "although I need help with several ADLs and personal care, I am still well enough to handle my finances". They must

also request that "VA no longer seek to appoint a fiduciary." If they do this, VA may stop the process and release the back pay. However, doing this runs the risk of VA believing that the claimant is too healthy to need the aid and attendance of another person because they can handle their own finances. So be careful.

Filling Out VBA Form 21-0792

The beneficiary's (veterans or surviving spouses) information goes under #6-12. All of the other boxes are completed by the person (e.g. family member) who wishes to be the fiduciary.

The Fiduciary Hubs

The hubs work on their own timeline (usually 3-5 months) as to the scheduling, interviewing, and eventual appointment of fiduciaries. Here is a direct link and contact information to VA's Fiduciary Program: http://www.benefits.va.gov/fiduciary/contact-us.asp

***See the Claims Support Data Disc for submitting to VA's Claims Intake Center

Notifying VA of Changes in Income, Assets and Medical Costs

The forms below have been used in the past for the Eligibility Verification Report which was due every calendar year between June and the end of February. These reports are no longer being used as VA will rely primarily on Social Security and the IRS to track the assets and income beneficiaries. Unfortunately, for many beneficiaries, VA will not know about changes in assets or income solely through the IRS or Social Security.

It is extremely important for you to report any changes in income or assets immediately to the one of the Pension management offices were your claim originated. We recommend you use the forms that were originally used for the EVR. These forms are on the Claim Support Data Disk.

VBA-21-4138-ARE – Statement in Support of Claim
VBA-21-0510-ARE – Eligibility Verification Report Instructions
VBA-21-8049-ARE – Request for Details of Expenses
VBA-21-0518-1-ARE – Improved Pension Eligibility Verification Report, Surviving Spouse
VBA-21-0516-1-ARE – Improved Pension Eligibility Verification Report, Veteran No Children
***See the Claims Support Data Disc for submitting to VA's Claims Intake Center

Pension Management Centers

We enjoy working with the Veterans Service Representatives (VSRs) employed by VA's three main pension management centers in the regional offices of St Paul, MN; Milwaukee, WI; and Philadelphia, PA. The VSRs that manage the application processing and call centers are skilled, friendly, and reasonable people.

Although we have not provided the call center phone numbers to you in this book, if you are accredited by VA and need the phone number of a certain call center, please get in touch with us. We will give you the number. The call center phone lines are generally not busy and the VSRs can give you updates on any claim and answer eligibility questions.

As of April, 2015, there were 19,230 pension claims pending at the three centers. Only 9% of these claims remain in development for over 125 days. This is a huge improvement from years past. All other regional centers combined in Aprul of 2015 were handling only 522 claims for pension. A staggering 55% of these claims were still being processed after 125 days.

Formal Claim Submission

Mail hardcopies (CERTIFIED with tracking, delivery guarantees, etc…) of your Fully Developed Claims to the pension management center PO Boxes listed on the following page. Make a copy of everything you send before you mail anything. VA is known to lose paperwork. Some people, to ensure receipt, choose to fax and mail claims to VA.

***Any material mailed directly to a Pension Management Centers (PMC) will automatically be re-directed by the U.S. Postal Service (USPS) to the intake center for scanning and processing. Jainsville, Wisconsin will scan and upload the digital images for processing. Please refer to the data disk for the appropriate PO Box in Jainesville for your claim.

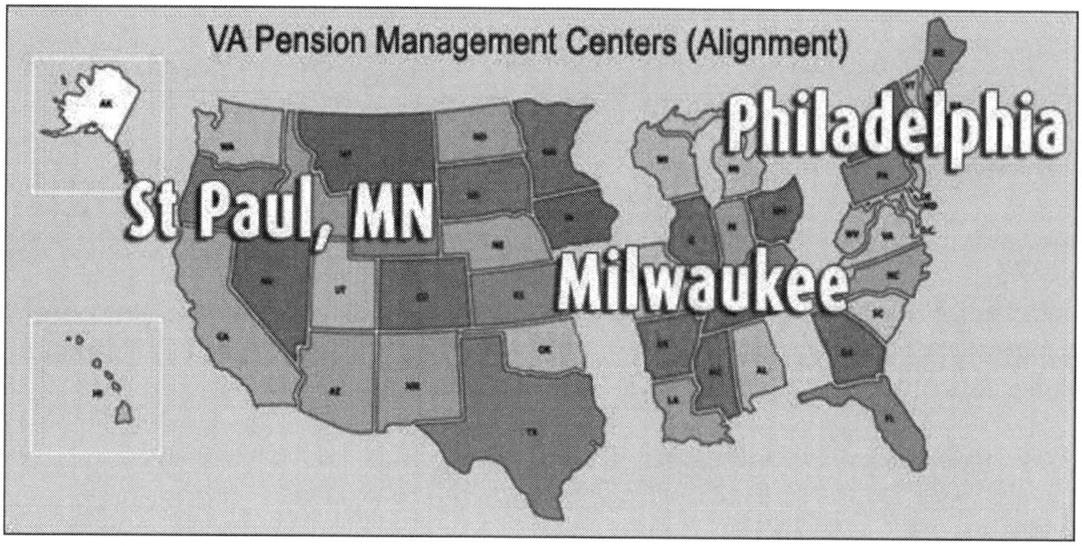

St. Paul Pension Management

Fax: (844) 822-5246
States: AK, HI, WA, OR, CA, NV, ID, MT, UT, AZ, WY, CO, NM, ND, SD, NE, KS, OK, TX, MN & IA
Mailing:

Claims Intake Center
*Attention: **St Paul** Pension Management*
*PO BOX **5365***
Janesville, WI 53547-5365

Milwaukee Pension Management

Fax: (844) 822-5246
States: WI, MI, IL, IN, OH, MO, KY, TN, AR, LA, MS, & AL
Mailing:

Claims Intake Center
*Attention: **Milwaukee** Pension Management*
*PO BOX **5192***
Janesville, WI 53547-5192

Philadelphia Pension Management

Fax: (844) 822-5246
States: ME, VT, RI, CT, NJ, NH, DE, DC, MD, MA, NY, PA, VA, NC, SC, GA, & FL
Mailing:

Claims Intake Center
*Attention: **Philadelphia** Pension Management*
*PO BOX **5206***
Janesville, WI 53547-5206

Claims Involving Independent Living Facilities (ILF)

Remember, ILF room, board, and the minimal care they can provide is not enough to satisfy VA's requirements to be an unreimbursed medical expense (UME). These facilities do not employ licensed individuals who are trained to provide hands on care services to their residents (i.e. independent living does not provide custodial care as assisted living or a nursing home does).

Until recently (see VA Fast Letter 12-23 (David R. McLenachen, Director | Pension and Fiduciary Service | October 26, 2012), "custodial care" was understood to be the same as room and board (see M21-1MR at 43.h.) "...because the individual needs to live in a protected environment, all unreimbursed fees paid to the institution for custodial care ('room and board') ... are deductible expenses".

However, as defined by Medicare (and now followed by VA), "custodial care assists persons with the activities of daily living (ADL). *See* e.g., Medicare Benefits Policy Manual, Chapter 16, section 110." As defined in VA regulations, ADLs are "basic self-care and includes bathing or showering, dressing, eating, getting in or out of bed or a chair, and using the toilet" (38 C.F.R. § 4.124a note 3). Therefore, to preserve the integrity of the pension program, VA now considers a facility to provide custodial care if it assists an individual with two or more ADLs. Accordingly, for pension purposes, VA regulations are as follows:

- The cost of room and board at a residential facility **is** a UME if the facility provides custodial care to the individual, or the individual's physician states in writing that the claimant must reside in that facility to separately contract for custodial care with a third-party provider.

- A facility provides custodial care if it assists the individual with two or more ADLs.

- If the facility does not provide the claimant custodial care, or the claimant's physician does not prescribe care by a third-party provider in that facility, VA will not deduct room and board paid to the facility but will deduct the cost of any medical or nursing services obtained from a third-party provider.

In addition, VA does not consider emergency pull cords, 24-hour staffing, and locked exterior doors as a medical or nursing service.

VA has revised M21-1MR, Part V, Subpart iii, Chapter 1, Section G, 43.d, h, and i to reflect the above clarifications.

In short, the following conditions must be met in order for ILF room and board expenses to be deductable. Use the Claims Support Data Disk to help you file this type of claim.

1. Claimant has needs for certain ADL care which is beyond what the ILF can provide (e.g. hands on help with bathing, dressing, hygiene, and walking),

2. Claimant hires additional 3rd party care (this can be contracted from the facility's in house 3rd party care or contracted outside the facility),

3. 3rd party care provides 2 or more ADL services,

4. VBA Form 21-2680 shows claimant has needs for 2 or more ADLs and earns the claimant an aid and attendance rating,

5. Physician certifies that claimant must reside at the ILF to contract for the 3rd party care. Physician must specifically name and prescribe the ILF and the 3rd party care entity for the claimant's well being. This statement must be written somewhere on the VBA Form 21-2680:

   "I, the signing medical practitioner, certify that ________________________ (claimant) must reside in ____________________________ (the Independent Living Community) to contract and receive ________________________'s (the Contracted 3rd Party Care Provider) assistance with their Activities of Daily Living (ADLs). I prescribe the care outlined in the application that the 3rd Party Care Provider will offer the claimant in that facility."

6. ILF completes Form FV22

7. 3rd Party Home Care completes Form FV13

If ALL of the above criteria are met, VA will deduct the ILF room and board and the 3rd party care costs. If not, VA will probably only deduct the 3rd party care costs.

CHAPTER 3
Understanding Compensation and DIC

SECTION A – HOW TO FILE A SUCCESSFUL CLAIM FOR BENEFITS

The Dilemma Presented to Your Regional Office

Most Claimants Don't Know It's Hard to Do It Right

The breadth of material in this chapter and the next chapter may seem to the reader to be overreaching and unnecessarily detailed. It is a mistake for you to assume this. You need to know this information before attempting to make a claim. Veterans Compensation benefits are not easily understood and claims for benefits are not as simple as VA would have you believe.

From reading information from the Department of Veterans Affairs, most of us receive the impression that the claimant simply has to provide a copy of the discharge and fill out a form of maybe three or four pages of information. We can now sit back and relax since the claim is well on its way to authorizing a benefit for the disability, that we are convinced, warrants payment from the Department. Hopefully a check will be in the mail in about 3 to 6 months. It's not that simple. We would like to share with you an online posting from a claims decision-maker – called a Rating Veterans Service Representative – who works for the Department in approving or disapproving claims. This was posted on an online web forum.

> Input from a Veterans Service Representative
>
> "Worth a read" - Tbird (webmaster HadIt.com)
>
> "First, allow me to introduce myself with some background info. I am a veteran, a nurse, a woman, and decide VA disability claims." Author Unknown
>
> I share many of the frustrations of veterans when I see claims that have not been properly or expeditiously decided. It is my mission to correct these where possible. I have called errors on prior decisions and awarded benefits back to the original claim date. I'm sure that I also have made errors and hope others have caught and corrected these.
>
> Please keep in mind that this is my personal perspective. I have no authority to speak for my Regional Office or any other.
>
> That said, I would like to
>
> 1) share some insight on how veterans can help themselves to get their claims through the system as quickly as possible.
>
> 2) share some of my frustrations with many system clogging claims that I get and must address.
>
> First, here's some general info on claims processing steps in my office:

Please be aware that many VA Regional Offices, including mine, receive thousands of pieces of mail every day. Each of these must be stamped with the date received. This takes time.

Next, for claims, the veteran's C-file is retrieved from the files and is sent to the development section. Development then sends a letter acknowledging receipt of the claim and lists the claims. This letter should also include release of information form(s) 4142 so that private medical records (not VAMC) that the veteran says are relevant to the claim can be obtained. When the veteran returns the signed forms, the VA contacts the care provider by mail requesting the records. Sometimes we receive no response and must request the records again. This also delays the decision process. *(Editing note: VA is not allowed to pay private physicians for copies of medical records. Private physicians are accustomed to being paid for their records and even though doctors must respond to government requests, doing it for free does not create a high priority for them.)*

When all records are received, or it is determined that records are unobtainable, the claim goes to the Rating Board.

1) Hints I hope are helpful:

- Be clear about what it is you are claiming. VA policy says that we must respond with a letter acknowledging and listing your claimed conditions or conditions for which you are claiming an increase. If we need to ask for clarification, it just slows the process. Example of unclear claim: "nerve condition" This could mean nerve damage or a mental condition. Please be specific.

- Put your claimed conditions where they can be found, at the beginning. The development people are buried in paper. A rambling explanation with claims hidden in lengthy text can get missed. I can't count the number of times that I've had to send a claim back to the development section for another letter to the veteran acknowledging the missed claim. Another delay.

- I understand that some veterans cannot afford to pay for copies of their private medical records. However, if at all possible, include copies of relevant medical records with your claim. It really does speed the process. We have to give the doctor or hospital 60 days to respond to our request before sending a second request. They have 30 days after that. If they don't respond, we do no more because it is ultimately the responsibility of the veteran to provide relevant private records. *(Editing note: VA is not allowed to pay private physicians for copies of medical records. Private physicians are accustomed to being paid for their records and even though doctors must respond to government requests, doing it for free does not create a high priority for them.)*

- Relevant is the key. I go through every piece of paper sent in support of the claim. If for instance, you are claiming knee problems, your psychiatry records, gynecologists records, billing/insurance statements, etc are not needed and just slow my ability to decide the claim. More is not better, relevant is.

-Help us to help you. Do get copies of your service medical records and service personnel records when you are discharged or from the National Personnel Records Center (NPRC). If VA has them request copies. It's free folks. It just takes a bit of effort on your part. Yes, VA and other agencies do lose/misfile records. It stinks, but this is the reality of any monstrously huge agency such as VA and NPRC. Without these records, my hands are tied. I may personally believe you, but I must have in-service medical evidence for most claims.

- Don't send in additional claims before you get a decision on the initial or increase claim. Depending on the issues, this can cause the processing of your claim to be sent back to the beginning.

2) Frustrations:

- Think before you claim. Is this really a disability? Is this a condition that occurred in service? I must address each claimed condition no matter what it is. We have daily production requirements. Therefore, a claim that has numerous issues, especially obviously merit less ones (more on that later), tends not to get handled as quickly.

- Most veterans are sincere and want only what they deserve. Some are in desperate financial shape and are hoping we can help. My heart and my best efforts go out to them. Others may not realize a claimed condition is not a disability. Others.... Here are just a few examples of some claims for disability that I have received which cause a slow down in an already overloaded system: Compensation for a venereal disease contracted and cured in 1971, abnormal PAP smears (weird cells but not malignant or showing other disease); tubal ligation, circumcision, vasectomy (the last 3 are voluntary: and unless there were medical complications are not disabling); exposure to local people; my wife's miscarriage; numbness of the legs due to spinal anesthesia administered in the 1960s (this from a veteran serving a life prison sentence. No spinal anything in service: but the prison treatment records show diabetes with leg neuropathy); claims for injuries, medical conditions, and diseases that occurred long after the veteran left service (that are not presumptive i.e.: Agent Orange, radiation related); claims for medical problems that occurred while a dependent spouse.

-Our office processes 600-700 claims per week. We come back to work on Monday, only to find that many or more new claims. Most of us are hard workers who care about the quality of our decisions. It is frustrating to be accused of delay tactics when the sheer volume of claims and the complexity of many claims makes it impossible to schedule a VA exam or render decisions as quickly as the veteran would like. I apologize to you, but I'm pedaling as fast as I can.

- Veterans working for the VA do NOT have their disability claims rated by the Regional Office in which they work. We employee veterans do not even have access to our VA files. They are stored at another VA office. And, I can personally attest that military veteran VA employees do not get preferential treatment for their claims. It is my experience and that of others in my office that we go through the exact same process as other veterans. The difference is that we know what is required to get a claim decided more quickly. I'm glad to share with you and hope it helps.

The Typical Claim Is Likely to Add to the Current Backlog

In a 2012 testimony to Congress, Under Secretary Adrian Hickey, Director of the Veterans Benefits Administration – the division of VA that manages Compensation benefits – talked about the backlog of claims and the composition of those claims. In her testimony she indicated roughly 77% of the veterans who currently have a claim pending for benefits are already receiving money for Compensation. In other words, 77% of all claims pending are for changes or increases in the benefit already being received. To turn this around, only 23% of all claims pending are new claims for benefit.

The advice from the veterans service representative above, allows us to reflect on what is happening. As a veteran gets older, his or her disability condition typically gets worse or the veteran develops a new disabling condition caused by the original one. VA will possibly provide a higher rating and more money if a veteran can show that the disability is indeed getting worse. We are pretty certain that these claims for an increase in benefit are never accompanied by medical evidence of current disability in a form that VA can use. Nor do they include other corroborative information needed to make a decision. It takes about 30 minutes to fill out VA Form 21-526EZ and about another 10 minutes to put it in an envelope and address it. That's all it takes to add one more claim to the backlog.

You – as the claimant or the claimant's representative – think you have done your job and you are satisfied that from this point VA has some magical way of knowing what to do to get information from you about the increased disability. On the contrary, you have just added another log to the huge pile of pending applications. Because of your lack of detail, you have added a burden that will require hours and hours of time and months and months of waiting with numerous veterans service representatives trying to get you and your doctors to submit more information, but at the same time having to go through the routine of setting up files, making computer entries, passing on information, writing letters and so forth. And just because you think that the you or the claimant deserves more money, there is still a long road to go down before you can even get a decision.

If you had read this book and this chapter and the next chapter before you had made the mistake above, you would have known the right way to submit a request for an increase in benefit. You would have made the job of the veteran service representatives in the regional office significantly easier and instead of a denial a year or two from now, you would have had a decision within a matter of months. And you would have helped reduce the backlog instead of adding to it.

AVOIDING YOUR CLAIM BECOMING ONE MORE JAM IN THE BACKLOG PILE IS WHY IT IS SO IMPORTANT FOR YOU TO UNDERSTAND THE CLAIM PROCESS AND HOW TO DO IT CORRECTLY.

An Incomplete Claim Will Languish for a Long Time and Likely Result in a Denial

The veteran service representative who made the blog at the beginning of this section alluded to the fact that an incomplete claim may not go anywhere for a long time. If you go back and reread it, she states that she has a requirement to process a certain number of claims each day with a decision. She also points out that a claim that will require more effort to gather information to make a decision will most likely be put aside for another day since she would not have the time to work on it and still meet her quota. In reality, this procrastination could mean months of delay. Information lacking on a claim is not just the responsibility of one veteran service representative. If the decision maker in this case has incomplete information, it will go back to another member of the team to gather information. Or an examination must be ordered. As many as five or more people from three different teams could be working on a claim. Incomplete claim files can languish for a month or more before they are reviewed again when responses to inquiries come in.

The Department does have a requirement to work on backlogged claims and not just let them sit. Computer diary entries keep track of the progress of a claim. It has been our experience that this often appears to be a token effort. For example, for a claim that is requiring a great deal of work to gather evidence – after about three months with no action – the service representative will pick it up, review for pending action and then send out a letter to you and or the claimant indicating that the regional office is working on your claim.

This delay tactic can only last so long as at some point a decision has to be made. Likely what will happen after a year or so; a letter will come out requesting specific evidence with the requirement for you to reply within 30 days. The letter will state that if you do not provide the evidence being requested, the rating authority will go ahead and make a decision based on the information they have in hand. This will mean a denial.

VA's Requirements under the Veterans Claims Assistance Act of 2000

The question you're going to ask next is if VA does need more information with the initial application, why don't they tell you that? The answer to this is the requirements imposed on the Agency by the Veterans Claims Assistance Act of 2000.

Prior to the Veteran's Claims Assistance Act of 2000 (VCAA), veterans had the burden of proof to show that they deserved a Compensation benefit. VA would not help them unless they provided their own evidence of service connection and disability. The pendulum had swung too far towards punishing the veteran for making application. Congress corrected this inequity with the Act but as a result caused the pendulum to swing too far towards putting the burden entirely on the Department of Veterans Affairs.

VCAA requires that as long as the veteran files a "substantially complete application," the VA has a duty to assist the veteran in finding all of the evidence necessary to support the claim – with, however, a number of limitations. Unfortunately, the bar is now set so low, that the duty to assist has become a tremendous burden on the department to assist in providing the evidence. This is what is causing the huge backlog in claims. A substantially complete claim is nothing more than this.

- claimant's name
- claimant's relationship to the Veteran, if applicable
- sufficient service information for the Department of Veterans Affairs (VA) to verify the claimed service, if applicable (a certified copy or original of the DD 214)
- benefit claimed
- disability(ies) for which the benefit is claimed (***Note***: These should be diagnosed conditions or identified symptoms. Exposure to certain agents, such as Agent Orange and anthrax, is not, in itself, a disability.)
- claimant's or guardian's signature, unless the application is submitted electronically via Veterans On Line Applications (VONAPP), and
- statement of income for nonservice-connected disability (NSC), Death Pension or Parents' Dependency and Indemnity Compensation (DIC).

That's it. The name, verification of service, indication that it's a request for Compensation, identifying a disability such as a backache, a headache, a nervous condition or some other nebulous assertion – which is often the case – and the correct signature. In the case of a Pension claim, the income must be provided.

From this point, as long as all of the substantially complete claim information is there, the VA must now help the claimant develop his or her case so that a decision can be made. It has to be obvious how challenging this is.

A substantially complete claim will generate hours and hours of back and forth requests, setting up of claims files, attempting to get private medical records over a period of months or years, computer entries, scheduling medically evaluations and on and on. And even when the medical records finally come in, they are typically not relevant to the disability.

Even more ridiculous is that a claim for an increased evaluation of a service-connected (SC) disability based on a statement from the claimant that the disability has worsened is considered substantially complete. That's the only information that is necessary, other than identifying who the claimant is. If the request has any merit at all, the VA must consider that to be a claim and help the claimant develop it for a decision.

Contrast all of this with a claim that contains all of the information that VA needs to make a decision, that can be processed fairly quickly and a decision made.

Here is a real-life example. The claimant is receiving benefits for service-connected hearing loss with tinnitus rated at 10% – about $130 a month. The claimant is convinced that the tinnitus is causing him to become mentally insane and is requesting that VA consider the claimant has developed a secondary disability due to the current disability. By VA granting secondary disability, this will result in a larger rating and more money. Perhaps the claimant doesn't really hold out any hope that VA will buy into this concept, but nevertheless the claimant has nothing to lose except to wait it out. The burden now lies in VA's lap and the claimant has plenty of time because it is unlikely he or she needs the extra money anyway.

An example of a request for an increase in rating that would have no merit might be one where the veteran has lost several of his teeth and is claiming it is related to his current agent orange disability award. Another true event. The loss of several teeth is not a disabling event – unless it is related to some major change in the ability to talk or eat – and VA will reject this claim out of hand unless more evidence can be provided that it is some sort of a disability. The problem is that because so many of these frivolous claims are filed, it simply burdens down the efficiency of the regional office.

On the other hand, VA does give the applicant the option to waive the duty to assist by the claimant providing all information necessary to make a decision. This is called a "fully developed claim." As mentioned above, prior to this duty to assist mandate, the department did put the entire burden on the veteran to show that the veteran deserved a benefit. With the current requirement for VA to assist, it would be unfair to ask veterans who have no money to produce all the necessary documents for a decision on a claim. Those with no money would not get a benefit and those with the money to do all of the research and produce the evidence would be more likely to get the benefit. Unfortunately, putting the burden on the claimant is still the best way to proceed if you are going to have success. By taking the burden of proof on yourself, you are going to have to spend a little bit of money and spend a great deal of your time, but in return you will gain a great deal more money by generating a benefit award with a timely decision.

Follow Our Instructions for Better Success through a Fully Developed Claim

You Must Take the Initiative to Get a Timely Decision through a Fully Developed Claim

In recent years, the department has come up with a solution to this dilemma of the claim getting pushed to the bottom of the pile. The regional office will continue to do its best for those individuals without the means for providing their own evidence, to assist in finding the proper evidence in order to avoid discrimination. But as we discussed – because of the current backload and pressure on service representatives – this could mean a long time before a decision is rendered. VA's solution to help you solve this problem is called a "fully developed claim." If you use the fully developed claim form and provide all of the documents necessary for VA to continue towards a decision on a claim, the Regional Office promises that it will take what you give it and move forward to make a decision.

Because of the subjective nature of disability decisions, we cannot promise a full proof approach to creating a fully developed claim. We can however, provide you strategies that will help you to be considerably more successful and receive a decision in a much shorter period of time. Also, we cannot promise a favorable decision. Decisions are not always consistent. For claims that are substantially the same, decisions by the various rating veteran service representatives in the same regional office tend to vary from one RVSR to the next. On the other hand, without the fully developed claim, you are at a higher risk for receiving a denial after waiting a long time.

How to Use the Information in This Book to File a Fully Developed Claim

Read Section C and gain a thorough understanding of the claim process before attempting to file a claim. Then identify the appropriate type of claim that you are going to file in Chapter 4 and follow the instructions for filing that type of claim.

Where to Submit Claims – Claims Intake Center

In order to improve timeliness and costliness of scanning claims into the Veterans Benefits Management System (VBMS), VA has implemented Centralized Mail Processing (CMP). Under these new procedures, claimants and beneficiaries should now send all mail directly to the scanning vendor (Jainesville, Wisconsin Intake Center), eliminating the need for Regional Office (RO) mail processing. The vendor will scan and upload the digital images for processing. Please refer to the data disk for the appropriate PO Box for your claim.

SECTION B – ABOUT DIC AND COMPENSATION

Description of DIC

Dependency and Indemnity Compensation (DIC) is a tax free monetary benefit generally payable to a surviving spouse, child, or parent of a service member who died while on active duty, active duty for training, or inactive duty training. It is also available to survivors of Veterans who died from their service-connected disabilities. DIC for parents is an income based benefit.

Dependency and Indemnity Compensation (D1C) is paid to surviving spouses and dependent children when the service member dies while on active duty; or, when death occurs after military service AND if a service-connected disability either directly caused or contributed substantially and materially to the death of the veteran. DIC can also be granted if the veteran dies from medical treatment received through the DVA medical system or from Vocational Rehabilitation training. DIC for spouses and dependent children is not means tested. The recipient of DIC can have any amount of income or assets. It is really a life insurance benefit.

DIC will be granted automatically when the veteran has been rated 100% service-connected for 10 or more years at the time of death and dies from non-service-connected causes other than willful misconduct. With this rule, there is no need to prove service connection death. For veterans passing away less than 10 years from the discharge date and succumbing from non-service-connected causes, DIC is payable when the veteran was rated 100% service-connected for at least 5 years prior to the date of death.

For veterans dying after January 1, 1993, a flat rate of D1C is payable. Prior to this date, DIC was paid based on the military rank of the veteran. Under the flat rate plan, an additional allowance is payable for those veterans rated totally disabled due to service connected condition(s) for 8 or more years at the time of their death with the surviving spouse having been married to the veteran for 8 or more years immediately preceding the death. Surviving spouses can also qualify for Housebound or Aid & Attendance allowances under 38 CFR§ 3.351.

If a surviving spouse remarries, DIC is terminated. However, if the subsequent marriage is dissolved by death, divorce, annulment, or voided, the now single spouse is eligible to reapply for DIC benefits.

On December 16, 2003, the President signed the Veterans Benefits Act of 2003. This Act amended Title 38 of the United States Code in several ways. Previously, 38 U.S.C. § 103(d) prohibited a surviving spouse who remarries from receiving DIC and related housing and education benefits during the length of the remarriage. The Act now allows a surviving spouse who remarries on or after his or her 57th birthday to remain eligible for DIC, home loan, and educational benefits.

The surviving spouse must have been married to the veteran for at least one year prior to the death of the veteran or for any length of time if a child was born of the marriage, or was born to them before the marriage. An exception is 38 CFR § 3.54 (c)(1), which covers marriages within fifteen years of leaving military service on or after January 1, 1957

A DIC claim is also a claim for Death Pension and accrued benefits. (The same form is used.) The applicant must designate which benefit is being applied for or VA will consider all of them if appropriate to the situation. If VA considers all three applications for an award, either VA or the beneficiary can determine which award would be the best. An individual can receive only one of these three benefits at any one time.

A surviving spouse receiving DIC is also eligible for The Civilian Health and Medical Program of the Department Of Veterans Affairs (CHAMPVA). This program provides reimbursement for most medical expenses for the surviving spouse through VA health care for the following.

- inpatient
- outpatient
- mental health
- prescription medication
- skilled nursing care, and
- durable medical equipment.

Dependency and Indemnity Compensation for 2015-16

Effective 12/1/14

Basic Monthly Rate = $1,254.19

Additional Allowances:

1. Add **$266.32** for veteran's death, if veteran was in receipt of or entitled to receive compensation for a service-connected disability rated totally disabling (including a rating based on individual unemployability) for a continuous period of at least 8 years immediately preceding death AND the surviving spouse was married to the veteran for those same 8 years. (38 U.S.C. 1311(a)(2))
2. Add the following allowance for each dependent child under age 18: Effective 12/1/14 **$310.71** per child (38 U.S.C. 1311(b))
3. If the surviving spouse is entitled to A&A, add **$310.71.** (38 U.S.C. 1311(c))
4. If the surviving spouse is entitled to Housebound, add **$145.55** (38 U.S.C. 1311(d))
5. If the surviving spouse has one or more children under the age 18 on the award, add the 2-year transitional benefit of **$270** effective, December 1, 2014 (38 U.S.C. 1311(f))

Description of Disability Compensation

Overview of Disability Compensation and Special Monthly Compensation (SMC)
Disability Compensation is a tax free monetary benefit paid to Veterans with disabilities that are the result of a disease or injury incurred or aggravated during active military service. Compensation may also be paid for post-service disabilities that are considered related or secondary to disabilities occurring in service and for disabilities presumed to be related to circumstances of military service, even though they may arise after service. Generally, the degrees of disability specified are also designed to compensate for considerable loss of working time from exacerbations or illnesses.

Special Monthly Compensation (SMC) is an additional tax-free benefit over Social Security disability or any other disability that can be paid to Veterans, their spouses, surviving spouses and parents. For veterans, Special Monthly Compensation is a higher rate of Compensation paid due to special circumstances such as the need of aid and attendance by another person or a specific disability, such as loss of use of one hand or leg.

Taken from "A 21st Century System for Evaluating Veterans for Disability Benefits, Committee on Medical Evaluation of Veterans for Disability Compensation 2006"

> "The VA Disability Compensation Program provides monthly benefit payments to veterans who become disabled as a result of or coincident with their military service. Payments generally are authorized based on an evaluation of the disabling effects of veterans' service-connected physical and/or mental health impairments. Monthly payments are authorized in percentage increments from 10 percent ($131 in 2014) to 100 percent ($2,858 in 2013). The process for determining ratings for Disability Compensation benefits uses the VA Schedule for Rating Disabilities (VASRD) to assign the level of severity of the disabilities.
>
> The VASRD contains over 700 diagnoses or disability conditions, each of which may have up to 11 levels of medical impairment. The lowest level of impairment starts at 0 percent then increases in 10 percent increments up to a maximum of 100 percent. Disability Compensation, as determined by the VASRD, is intended to replace average impairment in earnings capacity.
>
> Eligibility requires that a determination be made that the condition is a service-connected disability. Service-connected means that the condition occurred during or was aggravated by military service or, for chronic conditions, became evident within one year of discharge from the military. It does not require that the disability be work-related or be caused by conditions in the work environment. In this regard the VA Disability Compensation Program combines elements of both disability insurance voluntarily provided by employers and workers' Compensation programs mandated by government."
>
> **Individual Unemployability Benefits**
> "Claimants with a combined rating between 60 to 90 percent who are determined to be unemployable solely as a result of service-connected conditions qualify for IU (Individual Unemployability). Claimants determined to be entitled to IU qualify for the same benefit payment amount as those rated at the 100 percent disability level. Conditions or circumstances that result in the claimant not being employable override the medical impairment rating. IU is similar to the Social Security Disability Insurance (SSDI) program in that both provide payments because the beneficiary is deemed to be unemployable.

The number of IU cases has grown from about 101 thousand in September 2001 to 190 thousand cases in September 2007, an increase of almost 90 percent. PTSD cases constituted about one-third of the IU cases in 2007 and one-half of new IU cases between 2001 and 2007. Forty-four percent of the IU cases in 2007 were for veterans age 65 and older; 64 percent for veterans age 55 and older.

Although age is clearly related to employment, it is not considered in IU determinations. While IU is not intended for veterans who voluntarily withdraw from the labor market because of retirement, new awards are often made to veterans who are near or past normal retirement age for Social Security. In light of these circumstances it appears that IU determinations are made for veterans approaching or past retirement age based on providing retirement income or in recognition of loss of quality of life rather than for employment loss."

Special Monthly Compensation (SMC)
VA can pay additional Compensation to a veteran who, as a result of military service, incurred the loss or loss of use of specific organs or extremities.

Loss, or loss of use, is described as either an amputation or, having no effective remaining function of an extremity or organ. The disabilities VA can consider for SMC include:

- loss, or loss of use, of a hand or foot
- immobility of a joint or paralysis
- loss of sight of an eye (having only light perception)
- loss, or loss of use, of a reproductive organ
- complete loss, or loss of use, of both buttocks
- deafness of both ears (having absence of air and bone conduction)
- inability to communicate by speech (complete organic aphonia)
- loss of a percentage of tissue from a single breast, or both breasts, from mastectomy or radiation treatment

The Department will pay higher rates for combinations of these disabilities such as missing or loss of use of the feet, legs, hands, and arms, in specific monetary increments, based on the particular combination of the disabilities. There are also higher payments for various combinations of severe deafness with bilateral blindness. Additional SMC is available if a veteran is service connected for paraplegia, with complete loss of bowel and bladder control. In addition, if you have other service-connected disabilities that, in combination with the above special monthly Compensation, meet certain criteria, a higher amount of SMC can also be considered.

If a veteran is receiving Disability Compensation and is service connected at the 100% rate or is Individually Unemployable and is housebound, bedridden, or is so helpless to need the aid and attendance of another person, then an additional SMC rate is available. An aid and attendance allowance is also available to a veteran receiving SMC for whom a spouse needs aid and attendance or is housebound.

SMC for Assistance with Aid and Attendance or Housebound
Four different SMCs can be paid to veterans for assistance with aid and attendance or housebound: L, S, R1, and R2.

SMC L can be awarded either for loss of or loss of use of limbs or organs or to veterans rated 100 percent without such loss if they are in need of regular Aid and Attendance; in other words, if they need assistance with activities of daily living. The aid and attendance is in lieu of the other disabilities and is provided strictly based on this need for aid and attendance.

In 2007, 48 percent of 13,928 veterans receiving SMC L were receiving that award because they needed assistance, rather than for loss of or loss of use of organs or limbs.

SMC S can also be awarded to veterans rated 100 percent if they are housebound but do not meet the required level of assistance for SMC L. In other words they qualify strictly based on the fact that they are housebound and not on the fact that they have any other qualifying disabilities.

SMC R1 and R2 are awarded to catastrophically injured veterans, primarily to those with spinal cord injuries, who need the highest levels of assistance.

In 2007, 45,773 veterans received SMC L, S, R1, or R2 for assistance and they received $30,506,362 above the amount that would normally be paid for the 100 percent rating. This was an average of $660 per month above what would normally have been paid without the assistance allowance.

The information in this section was taken from a report to a congressional committee and we have not altered the notation in which SMC is referred to. Hereafter, we will refer to these more properly by the designations as SMC (l), (s), (r1) and (r2).

A rating of SMC (l) would include:

- The anatomical loss or loss of use of:
  - o Both feet,
  - o One hand and one foot OR
- Blindness in both eyes with visual acuity of 5/200 or less. OR
- Permanently bedridden. OR
- Regular need for aid and attendance to assist with activities of daily living such as dressing oneself, tending to personal hygiene, care and adjustment of assistive appliances or prosthetics, feeding oneself, and the like. (specific criteria is established in 38 CFR § 3.352(a)) (*if such services are not being provided at the expense of the U.S. Government due to hospitalization).

Ratings under SMC (s) are available if the veteran is permanently housebound. The VA defines "permanently housebound" as being substantially (as opposed to completely) confined to a dwelling as the result of service-connected disability and it is reasonably certain that that such disability will continue throughout the veteran's lifetime. These kinds of determinations should be made by a physician, whose written opinions or reports in this respect would serve as the best evidence to submit in support of a claim for "s" SMC benefits.

Ratings under SMC(r) are assigned for seriously disabled veterans in need of advanced levels of aid and attendance. SMC(r) ratings require a minimal combination of entitlement to both SMC(o) and SMC(l). Additionally, Veterans in receipt of SMC rates based on Aid and Attendance are strongly advised to contact their service representative and/or VA Regional Office should they become hospitalized at the expense of the U.S. Government (i.e. a VA medical facility) as failure to do so could create an overpayment of monetary benefits.

Ratings under SMC(t) are available to veterans who need regular aid A&A for residuals of Traumatic Brain Injury (TBI), but is not eligible for a higher level of A&A under (R)(2), and would require hospitalization, nursing home care, or other residential institutional care in absence of regular in-home aid and attendance.

Disability Compensation Rate Table for 2015-16

Basic Rates - 10%-100% Combined Degree Only

Rates for 2015-16 – In Dollars

Disability Percent	10%	20%	30%	40%	50%	60%	70%	80%	90%	100%
Veteran Alone	133.17	263.23	407.75	587.36	836.13	1,059.09	1,334.71	1,551.48	1,743.48	2,906.83
Veteran & Spouse			456.37	652.18	917.16	1,156.34	1,448.16	1,681.14	1,889.34	3,068.90
A/A for Spouse			44	59	74	88	104	118	133	148.64

If veteran has a spouse who requires A/A, add "A/A for spouse" to the amount of dependency and rate code above.

Special Monthly Compensation (SMC) Rate Table for 2015-16

Rates for 2015-16 – In Dollars

SMC Schedule	L	L½	M	M½	N	N½	O/P	R.1	R.2	S
Veteran Alone	3,617.02	3,803.58	3,991.74	4,266.32	4,540.89	4,807.36	5,075.60	7,252.63	8,318.95	3,253.67
Veteran & Spouse	3,779.09	3,965.65	4,153.80	4,428.38	4,702.96	4,969.43	5,237.67	7,414.70	8,481.02	3,415.74
A/A for Spouse	148.64	148.64	148.64	148.64	148.64	148.64	148.64	148.64	148.64	148.64

K	**$103.23**	Usually added to other rate or paid as the rate when percentage is zero.
Q	**$68.14**	Paid in place of a rate.

If veteran has a spouse who requires A/A, add "A/A for spouse" to the amount of dependency and rate code above.

Receiving Disability Benefit Payments

"The payment of military retirement pay, disability severance pay and separation incentive payments, known as SSB (Special Separation Benefits) and VSI (Voluntary Separation Incentives) affects the amount of VA Compensation paid to disabled veterans. Reductions or elimination for Compensation will be made if other benefits related to disability are being received.

Most veterans receive their disability benefit payments by direct deposit to a bank, savings and loan or credit union account. Other veterans may still be receiving benefits by paper check. Compensation and Pension beneficiaries can establish direct deposit through the Treasury's Go Direct helpline.

Veterans also have the option of receiving their benefits via a prepaid debit card, even if they do not have a bank account. There is no credit check, no minimum balance required, and basic services are free.

Veterans with disability ratings of at least 30 percent are eligible for additional allowances for dependents, including spouses, minor children, children between the ages of 18 and 23 who are attending school, children who are permanently incapable of self-support because of a disability arising before age 18, and dependent parents. The additional amount depends on the disability rating and the number of dependents." *Taken from "A 21st Century System for Evaluating Veterans for Disability Benefits, Committee on Medical Evaluation of Veterans for Disability Compensation 2006"*

All veterans who develop Amyotrophic Lateral Sclerosis (ALS), also known as Lou Gehrig's Disease, at any time after separation from service may be eligible for Compensation for that disability by only providing proof of the disorder. No other evidence is required.

Concurrent Retirement and Disability Payments (CRDP)

"Veterans receiving military retirement income cannot receive Disability Compensation at the same time except under certain special conditions. This rule does not apply to veterans receiving military retirement and who are also receiving Pension. There is no such prohibition. Typically, the veteran receiving Disability Compensation will choose not to receive the equivalent amount from his or her military retirement. This is called an offset election. The reason for preferring Disability Compensation to retirement is that Compensation is nontaxable in retirement is.

CRDP restores retired pay on a graduated 10-year schedule for retirees with a 50 to 90 percent VA-rated disability. Concurrent retirement payments increase 10 percent per year through 2013. Veterans rated 100 percent disabled or 100% due to individual unemployability by VA are entitled to full military retirement pay plus full Compensation benefits. This rule does not apply.

To qualify, under CRDP veterans must also meet the following criteria:

1. Have 20 or more years of active duty, or full-time National Guard duty, or satisfactory service as a reservist, or be in a retired status.

2. Be receiving retired pay (must be offset by VA payments).

Retirees do not need to apply for CRDP. Payment is coordinated between VA and the Department of Defense (DoD)." *Taken from "A 21st Century System for Evaluating Veterans for Disability Benefits, Committee on Medical Evaluation of Veterans for Disability Compensation 2006"*

Combat-Related Special Compensation (CRSC)
CRSC provides tax-free monthly payments to eligible retired veterans with combat-related injuries. With CRSC, veterans can receive both their full military retirement pay and their VA Disability Compensation if the injury is combat-related.

Retired veterans with combat-related injuries must meet all of the following criteria to apply for CRSC:

1. Active or Reserve component with 20 years of creditable service or medically retired.
2. Receiving military retired pay.
3. Have a 10 percent or greater VA-rated injury.
4. Military retired pay is being reduced by VA disability payments (VA Waiver).

In addition, veterans must be able to provide documentary evidence that their injuries were a result of one of the following:

- Training that simulates war (e.g., exercises, field training)
- Hazardous duty (e.g., flight, diving, parachute duty)
- An instrumentality of war (e.g. combat vehicles, weapons, Agent Orange)
- Armed conflict (e.g. gunshot wounds, Purple Heart)

Housing Adaptability Grants

Eligibility for up to $63,780: VA may approve a grant of not more than 50 percent of the cost of building, buying, or adapting existing homes or paying to reduce indebtedness on a currently owned home that is being adapted, up to a maximum of $63,780. In certain instances, the full grant amount may be applied toward remodeling costs. Veterans and servicemembers must be determined eligible to receive Compensation for permanent and total service-connected disability due to one of the following:

- Loss or loss of use of both lower extremities, such as to preclude locomotion without the aid of braces, crutches, canes or a wheelchair.
- Loss or loss of use of both upper extremities at or above the elbow.
- Blindness in both eyes, having only light perception, plus loss or loss of use of one lower extremity
- Loss or loss of use of one lower extremity together with (a) residuals of organic disease or injury, or (b) the loss or loss of use of one upper extremity which so affects the functions of balance or propulsion as to preclude locomotion without the use of braces, canes, crutches or a wheelchair.
- Severe burn injuries

Eligibility for up to $12,756: VA may approve a grant for the cost, up to a maximum of $12,756, for necessary adaptations to a veteran's or servicemember's residence or to help them acquire a residence already adapted with special features for their disability, to purchase and adapt a home, or for adaptations to a family member's home in which they will reside.

To be eligible for this grant, veterans and servicemembers must be entitled to Compensation for permanent and total service-connected disability due to one of the following:

- Blindness in both eyes with 5/200 visual acuity or less.
- Anatomical loss or loss of use of both hands.
- Severe burn injuries.

Temporary Residence Adaptation (TRA): Eligible veterans and servicemembers who are temporarily residing in a home owned by a family member may also receive a TRA grant to help the veteran or servicemember adapt the family member's home to meet his or her special needs. Those eligible for a $63,780 grant would be permitted to use up to $14,000 and those eligible for a $12,756 grant would be permitted to use up to $2,000. Grant amounts will also be adjusted annually based on a cost-of-construction index.

The first adjustment occurred on Oct. 1, 2009, with future adjustments each Oct. 1 thereafter. These adjustments will increase the grant amounts or leave them unchanged; they will not decrease the grant amounts. The maximum amount for a TRA grant is not indexed and remains unchanged.

The property may be located outside the United States, in a country or political subdivision which allows individuals to have or acquire a beneficial property interest, and in which the Secretary of Veterans Affairs, in his or her discretion, has determined that it is reasonably practicable for the Secretary to provide assistance in acquiring specially adapted housing. For more information on the use of such grants, contact Brian Bixler, Specially Adapted Housing via e-mail at brian.bixler@va.gov.

Supplemental Financing: Veterans and servicemembers with available loan guaranty entitlement may also obtain a guaranteed loan or a direct loan from VA to supplement the grant to acquire a specially adapted home. Amounts with a guaranteed loan from a private lender will vary, but the maximum direct loan from VA is $33,000. Additional information about the

Special Benefit Allowances
Other benefits may be available after an award for Compensation has been received. Here is a list of these special benefits.

Benefit	**Rate**	**Date Rate Changed**	**Public Law**
Automobile Allowance	$19,505 once	10-01-2012	PL 112-198
Clothing Allowance	$753 per year	12-01-2012*	PL 112-198
Medal of Honor Pension	$1,259 per month	12-01-2012	1.7% COLA

* The clothing allowance increase, while effective the date of the law, is not payable until the following August 1st. (Example: PL 97-306 effective October 1, 1982, increased the clothing allowance to $327.00. This rate was payable August 1, 1983.)

Automobile Allowance

This one-time allowance can be used toward the purchase of an automobile or other conveyance if the veteran has service-connected loss or permanent loss of use of

- one or both hands or feet or
- permanent impairment of vision of both eyes to a certain degree, or
- ankylosis (immobility) of one or both knees or one or both hips.

The veteran may also be eligible for adaptive equipment, and for repair, replacement, or reinstallation required because of disability or for the safe operation of a vehicle purchased with VA assistance.

Clothing Allowance

Any veteran who is service-connected for a disability for which he or she uses prosthetic or orthopedic appliances may receive an annual clothing allowance. This allowance also is available to any veteran whose service-connected skin condition requires prescribed medication that irreparably damages outer garments. To apply, contact the prosthetic representative at the nearest VA medical center.

Medal of Honor Pension

This income is available to any Medal of Honor recipient.

SECTION C – UNDERSTANDING THE ADJUDICATION PROCESS FOR CLAIMS

The Four Necessary Elements of a Claim for Disability Compensation or DIC

There are four elements that are essential to receiving a favorable claim decision from VA for Disability Compensation or DIC. All four must apply or there is no benefit.

1. The veteran – whether alive or dead – must meet service requirements for the benefit applied for.
2. A disabling condition or disease could be the result of an illness, injury or aggravation that happened while in service.
3. The veteran must be currently suffering from the disabling condition or disease that could be service-connected, and in most cases this condition must be ongoing and not temporary.
4. There must be convincing evidence of a link between the current disabling condition or disease and the illness, injury or aggravation that happened in service – establishing service connection.

1. Understanding Service Requirements for Veterans Benefits

Defining Who Is a Veteran

One must be a veteran in order to receive veterans benefits. Likewise, the benefit for a survivor must be linked to someone who was a veteran. "Veteran" is defined as a person who served in the active military, naval or air service and was discharged or released under conditions other than dishonorable. National Guard and Reserve members are not considered veterans unless they were called up to active duty by the President of the United States and served the appropriate length of time to receive an award for benefit or they honorably completed the length of obligation for which they were called.

Active duty service in order to qualify for veterans benefits includes the following:

- active duty
- any period of active duty for training during which a person is disabled or dies from
  - a disease or injury incurred or aggravated in the line of duty, or
  - an acute myocardial infarction, a cardiac arrest, or a cerebrovascular accident while proceeding directly to, or returning directly from, a period of active duty for training, and
- any period of inactive duty training during which a person is disabled or dies from an
  - injury incurred or aggravated in the line of duty, or
  - acute myocardial infarction, a cardiac arrest, or a cerebrovascular accident that occurred during such training or while proceeding directly to, or returning directly from, such training.

Generally National Guard or Reserve members are not eligible for Disability Compensation or Pension unless they were called up to active duty as mentioned above. There is, however, an exception to this pertaining to training and certain specialized service.

Reserve and Guard members without prior active service undergo a period of active duty for training (ACDUTRA), lasting from four to seven months. This training may be taken in a single period or as two separate periods. A Reservist or Guard Member may meet the criteria for establishing veteran status for Compensation and Pension purposes if he/she dies or becomes disabled from a disease or injury incurred or aggravated in the line of duty during a period of active duty for training, or an acute myocardial infarction, a cardiac arrest, or a cerebrovascular accident that occurred while the person was proceeding directly to, or returning directly from, a period of active duty for training.

Inactive duty training occurs for Reserve members typically on an annual basis where they spend full-time, for a period of weeks or months, training in their specialty. As with active duty training, a Reservist will be eligible for Disability Compensation or Pension if that person dies or becomes disabled from an injury incurred or aggravated in the line of duty during a period of inactive duty for training, or acute myocardial infarction, a cardiac arrest, or a cerebrovascular accident that occurred during such training or while the person was proceeding directly to, or returning directly from, a period of active duty for training.

Since the 1960's, the Reserve and Guard components have had several programs in which members serve full-time in operational or support positions but are never formally called to active duty. These positions are operated under military protocol and for all practical purposes would be considered full-time military service. This type of service, whether it lasts one day or three years, is classified by the service departments as active duty for training for the Reserve only. Even though these programs are not specifically tied to training, the VA has decided that because of the active service support provided by these full-time Reservists, they can also be eligible for Compensation or Pension. The DD 214 of these individuals indicates this service.

Even though the National Guard has a similar full-time program for members, VA will not consider these full-time support programs as active duty for Guard Members. For Guard Members there is no eligibility for Compensation or Pension from full-time support service.

Others Who Are Considered Veterans

There is a lengthy list of noncombatants who were exposed to combat conditions during World War II. This is found in 38 CFR 3.7. There are others found in this section who, for various reasons, are considered veterans. Here are those individuals.

- Aliens. Effective July 28, 1959, a veteran discharged for alienage during a period of hostilities (is considered a veteran) unless evidence affirmatively shows he or she was discharged at his or her own request. A veteran who was discharged for alienage after a period of hostilities and whose service was honest and faithful is not barred from benefits if he or she is otherwise entitled.

- Active service in the Coast Guard while under jurisdiction of the Treasury Department, Navy Department or the Department of Transportation (is considered a veteran)

- Contract surgeons performing their duty during a period of war if the disability or death was a result of line of duty (is considered a veteran)

In addition here are some other duty categories that are considered active service for certain veterans purposes.

- Cadets at US military academies when the individual commits to active service after schooling (for all benefits)
- Full-time duty of commissioned officers of the public health service for DIC only
- Commissioned officers of the Coast and Geodetic Survey, the Environmental Science Services Administration for DIC only

Minimum Period of Active Duty

Generally – for anyone enlisting after 1980 or entering active duty after October 16, 1981 – that person must meet a minimum of 24 months of continuous active duty or the full period for which that person was called or ordered to active duty in order to meet the requirements for veterans benefits. As an example of the call up period, many reserve and guard units that have been called up for the Gulf War, Afghanistan or Iraq are for periods of 12 months and not 24 months. This still meets the requirements. As already mentioned, an exception to the 24 month service requirement is eligibility for Compensation as a result of active duty training or inactive duty training. In addition, death benefits are available to any veteran who dies in service regardless of the amount of time spent in service. Anyone who becomes disabled and unable to perform his or her duty in the service, prior to completing 24 continuous months, is eligible for service-connected disability. Finally, any currently disabled veteran is eligible for Disability Compensation due to service-connected injury or illness regardless of the time on active duty.

Prior to 1980, there are no hard and fast rules for active duty service. Generally, there is a requirement for at least 90 days of continuous service. Travel time to return to the veteran's home after discharge is also used in computing length of service. In order to allow a reasonable time for travel, any veteran who is disabled or dies from an injury within 11 days from discharge may still be eligible for Compensation or DIC as if the veteran had been on active duty.

Character of Discharge

There are many different types of discharge categories. Not all of them are "honorable" or "dishonorable." The general requirement is that in order to be eligible for benefits, the veteran must have a discharge other than dishonorable. However, a discharge may not use the word "dishonorable" but may be considered such. For example conscientious objectors are barred from benefits as well as someone receiving sentence of general court-martial. Additional categories include resignation by an officer for the good of the service, a deserter and an alien serving in the Armed Forces who during a period of hostilities requested release from service. Other reasons for less than an honorable discharge would be committing a felony, committing a homosexual act that harmed another person or took advantage of that person because of rank or status or willful and persistent misconduct.

Discharges due to absent without leave (AWOL) may or may not bar an individual from receiving benefits. VA will weigh the conditions and circumstances and may or may not allow benefits based on the merits of the individual case.

Any veteran can challenge a discharge characterization and there are procedures to go through that process. Each service has discharge review processes where a challenge can be undertaken.

Some discharges are not characterized. In those cases, where a discharge is not characterized, the VA must determine whether that discharge is other than dishonorable or not.

38 CFR § 3.12 Character of discharge.

(k) Uncharacterized separations. Where enlisted personnel are administratively separated from service on the basis of proceedings initiated on or after October 1, 1982, the separation may be classified as one of the three categories of administrative separation that do not require characterization of service by the military department concerned. In such cases conditions of discharge will be determined by the VA as follows:
(1) Entry level separation. Uncharacterized administrative separations of this type shall be considered under conditions other than dishonorable.
(2) Void enlistment or induction. Uncharacterized administrative separations of this type shall be reviewed based on facts and circumstances surrounding separation, with reference to the provisions of §3.14 of this part, to determine whether separation was under conditions other than dishonorable.
(3) Dropped from the rolls. Uncharacterized administrative separations of this type shall be reviewed based on facts and circumstances surrounding separation to determine whether separation was under conditions other than dishonorable.

In the Line of Duty 38 CFR 3.1 (m) (n) and 38 CFR 3.301

In line of duty means an injury or disease incurred or aggravated during a period of active military, naval, or air service unless such injury or disease was the result of the veteran's own willful misconduct OR, for claims filed after October 31, 1990, was a result of his or her abuse of alcohol or drugs. Compensation, DIC and Pension are not paid if there is willful misconduct or abuse of alcohol or drugs. In line of duty also includes authorized leave.

(n) Willful misconduct means an act involving conscious wrongdoing or known prohibited action. A service department finding that injury, disease or death was not due to misconduct will be binding on the Department of Veterans Affairs unless it is patently inconsistent with the facts and the requirements of laws administered by the Department of Veterans Affairs.

> (1) It involves deliberate or intentional wrongdoing with knowledge of or wanton and reckless disregard of its probable consequences.
> (2) Mere technical violation of police regulations or ordinances will not per se constitute willful misconduct.
> (3) Willful misconduct will not be determinative unless it is the proximate cause of injury, disease or death.

Recreational use of alcohol is not considered abuse. Drug abuse is the use of illegal drugs including prescription drugs illegally obtained for a purpose other than medically intended use or for intoxicating purposes. Isolated use of drugs is not willful misconduct unless it results in a disabling condition or unless it can be shown is due to addiction. Contracting a venereal disease is not evidence of willful misconduct.

Example. A service member who was later honorably discharged, but during active duty, was on leave at a resort village in Italy with his buddy – also on leave. They rented a scooter, went to a bar, got drunk, went on a joyride on their scooter, crashed and the buddy was killed and the veteran ended up being a paraplegic. This was not willful misconduct because there was no deliberate or intentional wrongdoing with the knowledge of probable consequences. The accident was not intended as a probable consequence. It was considered an accident under the influence of alcohol.

Providing a Certified Copy of the Discharge Document

Even though the Department has access to discharge documents and can request them, a veteran must prove, through submitting a copy of his or her discharge document, that he or she is eligible for benefits. This is part of the requirement for a formal claim. Proving eligibility for benefits is the responsibility of the claimant. Without this, the VA will not proceed.

Prior to 1950, each service used a different identification method for designating an official discharge document. Since 1950, the document is called a DD 214. As a general rule, the VA will not accept a copy of the discharge unless it has been certified as a copy.

2. Establishing Evidence of the Illness, Injury or Aggravation That Occurred in Service

Presumptive Service-Connected Conditions

In Chapter 4, we have identified a number of different types of Disability Compensation claims. All of these types of claims are based on numerous regulations that are the result of Congress wanting to provide certain benefits to certain types of veterans. Over the years, Congress has felt that certain disabling conditions – presumably developed as a result of service – are automatically considered to be a result of service. These are called presumptive service-connected conditions or disabilities. With these particular types of claims, the veteran does not have to prove that an illness or injury or aggravation of an existing disability was incurred in the service. This burden of proof is removed, which makes it easier for these kinds of claims to be approved. All presumptive service-connected conditions require continuous service of 90 days or more and some require continuous service of six months or more.

Direct Service-Connected Conditions

These types of claims require that the veteran or the survivor must provide some sort of evidence that a particular injury or disease resulting in disability was incurred coincident with service in the Armed Forces OR if that condition was pre-existing to entry in the service it was aggravated through service. These claims do not require any specific amount of service as do the presumptive service connected claims.

Service Induction Examination – Presumption of Soundness

The veteran is presumed to be in sound condition after the induction examination except when defects, infirmities or disorders were noted in the records at entrance into service. Nevertheless, even though pre-existing conditions are not noted at entrance, the VA still must provide clear and unmistakable evidence that the disease or injury did not exist prior to service and was not aggravated by service.

For those conditions that were known at entry, the service representative will establish a baseline for determining whether the pre-existing condition was aggravated by service based on the veteran's entire history of service medical records for that condition.

Accident, Injury or Illness as a Matter of Record – Personnel or Service Treatment Records STR
The Regional Office must review the evidence of record to include personnel and service treatment records (STR's), to ensure the injury occurred during service and in the line of duty. If the record does not exist, corroborative evidence can be used if it is consistent with the conditions that would have caused the accident injury or illness. Perhaps the veteran was treated for the injury or illness at a civilian location. If these records can be found, this can also provide the proper evidence. A sworn statement by the veteran is not acceptable unless accompanied by other evidence.

Unreported Accident, Injury or Illness
A discharge medical evaluation may uncover unreported accidents injuries or illnesses. It is not unreasonable to assume that the rigors of military service for certain assignments would result in back injuries, muscle injuries or other joint injuries. For various reasons, these injuries might go unreported. Perhaps illnesses are also unreported that could have a chronic effect many years after discharge. Where any evidence from service records is lacking, it is up to the claimant to try and come up with enough evidence to provide a reasonable assumption that the existing disability was due to an unreported accident, injury or illness. This is a large burden of proof and it may not always be possible to win these kinds of claims. A sworn statement by the veteran is not acceptable unless accompanied by other evidence.

Exposure to Hazards or Stressors Resulting in Post Service Disability
Some exposures are already covered under presumptive service connection. This would include ionizing radiation, tropical diseases, prisoner of war, Agent Orange and other herbicide exposures, and to some degree posttraumatic stress syndrome which is not presumptive but in some respects is often acknowledged as occurring in service because of combat stress or the fear of imminent danger. Other exposures such as asbestos, loud noises, fumes, fuels and solvents, vibration, extreme heat, extreme cold and so forth are not considered presumptive. On the other hand, when it can be shown that a current disabling condition is likely the result of one of these kinds of exposures and that the claimant was indeed exposed because of duty assignment, these kinds of disability conditions are much easier to get acknowledged as incurred in service. A sworn statement by the veteran is not acceptable unless accompanied by other evidence.

Combat
Illnesses or injuries claimed incurred in combat are generally treated in a more liberal manner as far as acceptance of happening in service. Scars may be used as evidence of wounds, but they may not always be due to combat and thus corroborating evidence is necessary. If there is a medical discharge evaluation, combat injuries or illnesses will show up in this evaluation. In the absence of any service records, lay statements from the veteran or other individuals corroborating the statements will be accepted that an injury or disease was incurred OR aggravated in combat, if the evidence is consistent with circumstances, conditions, or hardships of such service even though there is no official record of such incurrence or aggravation. Such evidence should be sufficient by itself – meaning it is consistent and plausible and not refuted by clear and convincing evidence to the contrary.

Aggravation of an Existing Condition during Service
Aggravation is covered under 38 CFR 3.306 and 38 CFR 3.307. Service treatment records must indicate an aggravation during the period of service. Temporary or intermittent flare ups of pre-

existing injury or disease are not sufficient to be considered aggravation in service unless the underlying condition has worsened. Rehabilitation from surgery shall not be considered as an aggravation. For a veteran entering the service with a hereditary disease, aggravation and thus service connection can be established if the disease manifests itself after entry on duty. A genetic disease that is predisposed for development is not service-connected.

3. Establishing Evidence for a Current Disabling Illness or Condition

Medical evidence is required for a current disabling illness or condition. VA will always want to see the current private medical file of the claimant pertaining to the disabling illness or condition that is being claimed. You should be aware that the regional office does not want to see medical records that are not pertinent. They are useless and end up bogging down the decision process. It is important that the condition be chronic (persistent or long-lasting) and not temporary in nature. VA will want to see evidence of the so-called "chronicity" of the disability or condition.

In addition, your current medical records pertaining to the disability may not actually identify a disability associated with your illness or other condition. In other words, your doctors may devote a great deal of information pertaining to diagnosis, treatment and prognosis but not even mention disability. This is also not always useful information as it requires VA to infer from the records that there may be a disability or there may not be. On the other hand, such conditions as stage IV cancer or congestive heart failure or other debilitating conditions, carry with them an inherent disability and it is not necessary to know disability.

It is important that if your records do not reflect disability and it is necessary to establish, you should always consult with your doctor or doctors and have them do a disability assessment related to your condition. We will provide you instructions on what documents to use for this disability assessment in Chapter 4. As part of establishing a link between your current condition and service, your doctors will also need to offer an opinion that the illness, injury or exposure that you experienced in the service is likely or most probably a cause of your current condition.

A layperson may be competent "to establish a diagnosis of a condition when (1) a layperson is competent to identify the medical condition, (2) the layperson is reporting a contemporaneous medical diagnosis, or (3) lay testimony describing symptoms at the time supports a later diagnosis by a medical professional." Jandreau, 492 F.3d at 1377 (footnote omitted).

A final word is in order. You are not eligible for benefits if you are not suffering from disability. There are some conditions such as presumptive conditions or hearing loss that will result in a rating, but without disabling conditions that will trigger the proper rating decision in 38 CFR Part 4, the rating will be 0%. Do not bother to make application if your condition is acute (temporary) or is not principally chronic – meaning that it persists over a long period of time. In fact, your medical records or the assessment that you have done must reflect the chronicity of your condition.

It is important to note that if you have a chronic disabling condition that can be rated at 0%, you should definitely make application, as you have established service connection even though you will receive no money. This service connection could be very valuable later if your condition gets worse or causes a secondary disability that could be ratable and result in an award. It saves you going back and establishing service connection.

4. Establishing a Link between the Current Disability and the Illness, Injury or Condition That Occurred in Service.

Presumptive Service Connection

Ninety days of service is required for certain defined presumptive conditions manifesting within one year after service and for tropical diseases. If a current disease or condition is considered presumptive service-connected, there is no need to establish a link between that disease or condition and active duty service. It is automatically considered to be caused by service. On the other hand, the existence of a disease or condition that is presumptive SC does not necessarily mean an award for Compensation or DIC. The disease or condition must also be chronic and be disabling and be ratable in 10% increments on a scale from 0% to 100%.

It is important to note that some VA-listed presumptive conditions may not actually be the result of service, but many years after discharge may be the result of other non-service health developments. Some of the presumptive conditions must have manifest within a certain period of time after leaving the service – usually to a degree of 10% disability within the first year. Where the condition has been recently diagnosed and the time between discharge and the claim is significant, the VA will question whether the condition is service connected. In this case, a continuity of symptoms must be produced to show that the condition would have been or was manifest – meeting the proper time frame – even though it was not necessarily diagnosed. Diagnosis is not required, only that evidence of its manifesting is.

For other presumptive conditions – such as Agent Orange or ionizing radiation or exposure to certain chemicals – there does not have to be a continuity of symptoms, nor do they have to show up within any period of time. Symptoms from these conditions could show up many years after discharge. 38 CFR 3.303

Direct Service Connection

Because direct service connection is not presumptive, a direct link between the current disability and any injury or illness or exposure in service that is claimed as the cause of the current disability must be established. There is no required time in service for receiving an award through direct service connection.

The disabling condition that the veteran is currently experiencing could have been caused by an illness, injury or aggravation in the service. It could also be caused by exposure to hazardous material or environment. A veteran seeking service connection for an existing condition, has several ways to prove –based on the place, the timing, or the circumstances of his service – something occurred that can be tied to a current disability. Medical treatment records and personnel records are available from the National Records Center in St. Louis for providing this evidence.

Evidence that is not a matter of service treatment records or it is not self-evident that the veteran was exposed to threats or stressors such as combat, or hazardous materials or hazardous environment, can sometimes be hard to come by. We will provide you sources for finding extraneous evidence under the fully developed claims discussion in Chapter 4.

Many times, these occurrences in the service may not have direct evidence to support them. Nevertheless, through presumption of being in the right place at the wrong time, testimonies from others who were there, squadron or battalion historical records, your own testimony or the use of common sense might dictate that they did occur.

With some claims, a principal used by the rating activity in the regional office could come to your aid. It is called "reasonable doubt" and is found in 38 CFR 3.102.

> "It is the defined and consistently applied policy of the Department of Veterans Affairs to administer the law under a broad interpretation, consistent, however, with the facts shown in every case. When, after careful consideration of all procurable and assembled data, a reasonable doubt arises regarding service origin, the degree of disability, or any other point, such doubt will be resolved in favor of the claimant. By reasonable doubt is meant one which exists because of an approximate balance of positive and negative evidence which does not satisfactorily prove or disprove the claim. It is a substantial doubt and one within the range of probability as distinguished from pure speculation or remote possibility. It is not a means of reconciling actual conflict or a contradiction in the evidence. Mere suspicion or doubt as to the truth of any statements submitted, as distinguished from impeachment or contradiction by evidence or known facts, is not justifiable basis for denying the application of the reasonable doubt doctrine if the entire, complete record otherwise warrants invoking this doctrine. The reasonable doubt doctrine is also applicable even in the absence of official records, particularly if the basic incident allegedly arose under combat, or similarly strenuous conditions, and is consistent with the probable results of such known hardships."

Once a service link can reasonably be established for the current disability, medical evidence must show that the current disability is likely a result of the injury, illness or exposure in the service.

After an evaluation with your doctor or through a medical evaluation from VA, information from this evaluation is carefully reviewed by the rating authority in the regional office to see if the doctor or doctors are of the opinion that the disability is linked to the injury, illness or exposure in service. Medical records may use words that indicate a casual linkage or they may use words that indicate a strong linkage. The stronger the language asserting the link, the more likely service connection will be granted. We list the language below which is used in conjunction with examinations ordered by the regional office when an opinion is requested. Your private physician or physicians should use this same language if they are going to express an opinion.

- "is due to" (physician is 100% sure it is service-connected);
- "more likely than not" (physician feels probability is greater than 50% it is service-connected);
- "at least as likely as not" (physician feels probability is equal to or greater than 50% it is service-connected); and
- "not at least as likely as not" (physician feels probability is less than 50% it is service-connected)

VA will often order its own medical exam at a local regional medical center or through contract with a private examining company. In addition to medical information, such as the results of tests or examinations, the examiner may be asked to provide an expert opinion on such questions as whether a condition is related to a specific event during service in the military, or a preexisting condition was aggravated in service, or a condition may be a secondary manifestation or consequence of a condition that previously was service connected. In these cases, the examiner is asked to use the same opinion terminology above.

If you can amass enough relevant evidence and medical evidence that indicates or might lead to the conclusion that the current condition is a result of the illness, injury or exposure incurred during service and the Rating Veterans Service Representative in the regional office cannot counter with any better medical evidence against you, then they will usually rule in your favor. These decisions come into play more often than most people think and usually involve the principle of reasonable doubt discussed above.

You should always try and get your personal or treating physician to write an opinion letter for you whether that the current condition is likely or likely not a result of what you relate to that physician has what happened to you in the service.

Oftentimes, a private physician is unwilling to provide an opinion that the current medical condition is a result of the service connection the veteran is claiming. You may be able to find a physician who will write an opinion letter that there is a a little better than a 50-50 chance the current disability is service-connected. This poses less risk to the examining medical practitioner. The physician will use the words that the current disability is "at least as likely as not" to have been incurred in the service based on information provided by the veteran and an examination by the physician. The physician has opined that there is a little better than a 50-50 chance it was incurred in service and if VA has no evidence to the contrary – under the doctrine of reasonable doubt (38 CFR 3.102) – the veteran will receive an award.

The 50% threshold is extremely important because it might make the difference between an approval or a denial. Assuming all other evidence is equal (courts use the term equipose), at 50%, the rating activity must follow the principle of reasonable doubt and give the award to the claimant.

In Chapter 4, we will go into more detail on the forms that you should use for disability evaluations as well as how you should approach your own personal physician or specialist on doing an evaluation for you. The stronger your own private evidence, the less likely that VA will rely on its own medical evaluation to make a decision. On the other hand, even though they are not allowed to do so, the rating authority in the regional office often feel that private physicians, especially ones who have been treating the claimant for number of years, might be biased towards recommending a service-connected link. The rater may feel a contract doctor might not demonstrate as much bias. Because of its own bias in this situation, the rating service authority may tend to favor the results of the VA examination over possibly more convincing results from private physicians. Technically, they are not allowed by regulation to show this bias, but we are sure it occurs. Thus, the more credible your private source and the less the personal bond, the more likely your own evidence will hold sway over the VA's evidence.

The Consequences of Incomplete Evidence or Failure to Submit What VA Wants

On receipt of a "substantially complete application" (which includes the claimant's name, his or her relationship to the veteran, sufficient service information for VA to verify the veteran's service and claimed medical condition or conditions), VA will begin to process the claim.

After VA receives your Application for Compensation, it sends you a letter. The letter explains what VA needs in order to help grant your claim. It states how VA assists in getting records to support your claim. The letter may enclose forms for you to complete, such as medical releases. These additional documents help the Department obtain pertinent medical records from your doctor or hospital. You should try to complete and return all forms the regional office sends within a month. Your claim will be processed more quickly if you send a copy of your own medical records. You should never rely on VA to order your medical records for you.

In accordance with the Veterans Claims Assistance Act (VCAA) of 2000, VA has a "duty to assist" the claimant. VA must give the claimant written notification of the evidence necessary to substantiate the claim. It must also tell the claimant whether VA or the claimant is responsible for obtaining that evidence. The regional office must make reasonable efforts to obtain relevant records not in the custody of the federal government, and it must make as many requests as necessary to obtain relevant records within the custody of federal departments or agencies, including the veteran's service medical records and VA records of examination or treatment. However, the Department encourages applicants to submit copies of their own medical records to expedite the claim. You should always do this when the records are available.

The evidence development phase of disability claims processing is often the most time-consuming part of the entire process. Multiple requests may be necessary to obtain needed information. This phase of the claims process is managed by the predetermination team in the VSC (Veterans Service Center). The team sets diaries (deadline dates) for receipt of requested information, then determines the need for a VA medical examination to assess the current level of disability or to provide a medical opinion about whether the current disability is related to the veteran's military service (referred to as "medical nexus").

Every time a request for information goes out, the claimant has 30 days to submit evidence. If enough evidence is on file after the end of the 30 day period, the claim may be forwarded to the rating authority for a decision. The file cannot be sent to the rating authority without at least some medical information. With incomplete information, a denial is likely the result. Or the rating authority could have enough information to make a partial rating and then send a claim back to predetermination in order to ask for more evidence. If the claimant only furnishes part of the information requested before the end of 30 days, and that evidence does not permit a grant of benefits, the predetermination team will continue to follow-up to try and get more information.

If no more evidence is forthcoming after the end of another 30 day period, the claim will be denied and the claimant will be notified that there is a one-year time limit for the submission of additional evidence to reopen the case or the claimant may wish to appeal.

The claimant or his or her representative may also request an extension in order to gather more evidence. The extension will be granted if there is a valid reason for it.

The best advice we can give you to avoid a situation where you are being pressured for additional evidence and you simply cannot obtain it or it is being delayed, is not to submit a formal claim in the first place. Submit an informal claim to establish an effective date and then take all the time you want – up to a year if necessary – to collect the evidence.

Understanding the Claims Process in the Regional Office

Claimants and beneficiaries for Compensation, Pension, Survivor Benefits and other benefits should now send all mail directly to VA's Intake Center in Jainesville, Wisconsin. Any material mailed directly to Regional Offices (RO) or Pension Management Centers (PMC) will automatically be re-directed by the U.S. Postal Service (USPS) to the intake center for scanning and processing. Jainsville, Wisconsin will scan and upload the digital images for processing. Please refer to the data disk for the appropriate PO Box in Jainesville for your claim

Overview of the Veterans Benefits Administration

Taken from "A 21st Century System for Evaluating Veterans for Disability Benefits, Committee on Medical Evaluation of Veterans for Disability Compensation 2006"

> "The Veterans Benefits Administration is the division of the Department of Veterans Affairs that administers disability benefits such as Pension and Compensation. The VA has approximately 14,000 employees. Approximately half of the staff is directly devoted to the administration of the Disability Compensation program and the cost of this program represents about half of VA's annual $130 billion budget. The other half of the budget goes to health care. VBA has 57 regional offices, including at least one in every state in the nation (except Wyoming, which is served by the Denver, Colorado, regional office), as well as offices in Puerto Rico and the Philippines, and additional locations in Korea and Germany. Some states have multiple offices. Texas, Pennsylvania and New York each have 2 regional offices and California has 3 regional offices. A list of these regional offices is contained in the appendix in this book.
>
> Within VBA, the Compensation and Pension (C&P) Service administers the Disability Compensation program. C&P Service also administers the dependency and indemnity Compensation (DIC), death Compensation, disability Pension, Death Pension, burial benefits, automobile allowance/adaptive equipment, clothing allowance, and specially adapted housing programs. Claims that you submit for any of these benefits, you will be sent to the regional office in your state or to the office that services the region in your state if there is more than one office.
>
> The other program components of VBA are the Vocational Rehabilitation, Education, Loan Guaranty, and Insurance Services. These benefits are administered out of designated regional offices throughout the country, depending on the benefit. For example, the Philadelphia Regional Office is responsible for insurance services.
>
> Each regional office includes a veterans service center (VSC), which is the component that processes Disability Compensation claims. These centers function under a standardized structure called the claims process improvement (CPI) model, which was recommended in 2001 by the Claims Processing Task Force appointed by the VA secretary to address the growing backlog of claims. The model was designed to increase efficiency in processing Compensation and Pension claims and to reduce the number of errors. The model was fully implemented in 2002, and it established a consistent organizational structure and standard work processes across all regional offices.
>
> The model provides the following:

- requires triage of incoming mail and analysis of incoming claims;
- emphasizes the importance of complete and accurate development of claims by veterans service representatives (VSRs) specially trained to do the work; and
- promotes specialization that improves quality and the expeditious handling of claims, while at the same time allowing management the flexibility to adjust resources to meet the demands of changing workload requirements.

Specialized Team Structure
Each VSC uses six separate teams specialized to handle specific steps in the Compensation claim process.

Public Contact Team
The public contact team handles personal interviews and telephone inquiries. Team members assist walk-ins, answer telephones, answer routine correspondence (including e-mails), respond to veterans assistance inquiries, and address outreach and fiduciary issues.

VSRs on the public contact team interview veterans and collect as much information as possible to complete a veteran's claim. If the veteran provides a birth certificate and the master record indicates an award can be prepared immediately, a VSR on the public contact team can prepare the veteran's award. If additional records are needed, such as from a VA medical center, or if the veteran was recently released from the military and his or her service medical records and separation examination are on record, the public contact team will forward the claim to the triage team.

The public contact team's regular outreach activities include contacts with veterans service organizations (VSOs), nursing homes, state fairs, stand-downs, and benefit clinics. Personnel on the public contact team could have a large number of people but would include this category of supervisor or specialist:

- coach (GS-13);
- assistant coach (GS-12);
- VSR (rotational) (GS-11);
- public contact and outreach specialist (GS-10);
- public contact specialist (GS-9);
- field examiner (GS-10);
- legal instrument examiner (GS-9); and
- intake specialist (GS-7).

One of the primary objectives of the public contact team is to promote a bilateral exchange of information with the triage team.

Triage Team
The triage team helps coordinate the work of the other specialized teams. Team members review, control, and process all incoming mail. They also process actions that can be completed with little or no review of the claim folder. Personnel in the triage team include the following categories:

- coach (GS-13);
- assistant coach (GS-12);
- rating VSR (GS-12);
- senior VSR (GS-12);
- VSR (GS-11);
- claims assistant (GS-6);
- file bank coach (GS-6); and
- file clerk/program clerk (GS-4).

Predetermination Team
The predetermination team's primary role is to develop evidence necessary for a rating to be made. This team is responsible for most of the medical development activity in the following cases:

- original and reopened Compensation;
- Compensation claimed due to injury or death caused by VA medical care or evaluation;
- original and reopened disability Pension;
- original and reopened dependency and indemnity Compensation
- (DIC); and
- basic eligibility issues requiring a rating decision.
- character of discharge;
- line of duty;
- willful misconduct;
- deemed valid marriage (death claims); and
- common law marriage (live claims).

Staff on the team also prepare administrative decisions, including decisions on claims not requiring a rating. Personnel in the predetermination team are the same as in the triage team.

Rating Team
The rating team makes decisions on claims that require consideration of medical evidence. Rating VSRs (RVSRs – Rating Veteran Service Representatives) on the rating team rate claims that have been certified by the predetermination team as "ready to rate." They may prepare a rating for partial grant if there is insufficient evidence to rate all of a veteran's medical conditions (referred to as issues), if there is sufficient evidence to make an award on one or more issues. In such a case, the rating specialist rates the issue(s) ready to be rated, prepares a separate deferred rating for the unresolved issues, and returns the claims file to the predetermination team for further development. Personnel on the rating team include the following people:

- coach – over more than one team (GS-13);
- assistant coach – over selected teams (GS-12);
- RVSR – one or more rating people (GS-12); and
- claims assistant – one or more assistants (GS-6).

The RVSR determines

- service connection;
- percentage of disability;
- permanent and total disability;
- entitlement to Compensation, Pension, and vocational training;
- medical and dental treatment;
- automobiles or other conveyances;
- insurance;
- specially adapted housing;
- dependent education allowances; and
- other ancillary benefits.

There are also RVSRs on the triage and predetermination teams because those teams perform a limited number of the ratings in certain circumstances and also assess whether the medical evidence is sufficient to support a rating decision. He or she is fully accountable for proper analysis, appropriate development, proper application of the Rating Schedule, and final rating determinations.

Postdetermination Team
The postdetermination team develops evidence for non-rating issues, processes awards, and notifies claimants of decisions. This team also completes entitlement determinations for issues that do not require a rating, such as

- accrued benefits;
- apportionment decisions;
- competency issues;
- income changes; • original Pension;
- dependency issues;
- burials;
- Death Pension;
- hospital adjustments;
- specially adapted housing; and
- the Civilian Health and Medical Program.

Personnel on the post determination team include a

- coach (GS-13);
- assistant coach (GS-12);
- senior VSR (GS-12);
- VSR (GS-11); and
- claims assistant (GS-6).

The rating process, which involves the interpretation and application of VA's Schedule for Rating Disabilities, is described in more detail in the next section.

.

Appeals Team
The appeals team handles decisions with which claimants have formally disagreed (i.e., appealed). The appeals team processes both appeals submitted by veterans and cases returned by the Board of Veterans' Appeals (BVA) for further development, called remands. The appeals team is also responsible for development of remands, which may involve returning the case to VHA for a medical examination or opinion and for making a decision on the basis of the additional information. If the adjudicator reaffirms the original denial of the case, the case is sent back to BVA for review and decision. The team is intended to increase the level of accountability and maintain control over the appeal workload. Personnel on the appeals team include the following:

- coach (GS-13);
- decision review officer (GS-13);
- senior VSR (GS-12);
- RVSR (GS-12);
- VSR (GS-11);
- claims assistant (GS-6); and
- file clerk/program clerk (GS-4). "*Entire section on how VA operates is taken from "A 21st Century System for Evaluating Veterans for Disability Benefits, Committee on Medical Evaluation of Veterans for Disability Compensation 2006"*

How the Rating Activity in the Regional Office Makes a Decision

The Job of the Rating Activity

After all development actions are complete, the VSC predetermination team refers the claim to the rating team for a rating. The rating team reviews all the evidence associated with the claim, makes decisions on issues raised by the claimant, and identifies any inferred issues that should be addressed. The team documents the rating decision in a standard format, using an automated rating preparation system called Rating Board Automation (RBA) 2000. After completing the rating decision, the team routes the claim to the post determination team. The post determination team implements the rating decision by preparing either a monetary award or a denial. It also prepares notification letters for the claimant and representative.

When performing a rating evaluation, RVSRs consider all evidence associated with the claim. This includes service medical records, VA medical examination records, clinical summaries from VA medical centers where treatment has been provided to the veteran, and evidence provided from private sources, such as the veteran's treating physician.

The job of the rating service representative consists primarily of interpreting medical records in deciding if the medical evidence is sufficient enough to result in a favorable or unfavorable decision. First of all, medical evidence must show the disabling condition that is ratable and that is ongoing and not acute. Second, medical evidence from service records or evidence of duty assignment or statements from others or corroborative history must show that an illness or injury that could have resulted in the current condition was incurred in service. Finally, the medical evidence must tie together such that there is a link established between the current chronic disability of the claimant and the illness or injury or exposure that occurred in the service.

Rating Decisions Are Not Made by Individuals with a Medical Background

It is interesting to note that RVSR's are not required to have a medical background, although some of them might be nurses or have served as medics in the service. At one time, rating decisions were made by a so-called "rating board" that consisted of two non-medical rating experts along with a physician. In fact, an analog to veterans disability is Social Security disability where decisions regarding disability are made involving a doctor.

Rating boards were replaced in the early 1990s by several non-medical individuals making the decision or more recently by a single non-medical rater making a decision. This removal of medical personnel is due to a ruling by the Court of Appeals for Veterans Claims which has become famous, not only for its impact on not using in-house medical personnel, but also for its impact on the concept of new and material evidence in rating and appeal decisions.

> Colvin v. Derwinski, 1 Vet. App. 171 (1991) CAVC
> Taken from The Veterans Advocate, January-June 2008
>
> Colvin stands for a now deeply embedded and fundamental principle of veterans law – that VA may use only independent medical evidence to support its benefits decisions. The VA may not use the medical opinion or judgment of the VA rater or BVA Veterans Law Judge to support a decision.

For many years prior to Colvin, VA decisions were based on the findings of VA physicians who were part of the decision-making process. A doctor employed by VA would not only provide the medical opinion that would be used to decide the claim, he or she would participate in deciding whether to grant or deny benefits.

This practice of having VA doctors play a decision making role was ended by Colvin. The Court held that:

"If the medical evidence of record is insufficient, or, in the opinion of the BVA, of doubtful weight or credibility, the BVA is always free to supplement the record by seeking an advisory opinion, ordering a medical examination or citing recognized medical treatises in its decisions that clearly support its ultimate conclusions . . . . This procedure ensures that all medical evidence contrary to the veteran's claim will be made known to him and be part of the record before this Court. Colvin, 1 Vet.App. at 175."

But advocates must watch out . . . even though the formal procedure of having a VA doctor play a decision making role stopped after Colvin, VA raters and BVA Veterans Law Judges persist in relying on their own medical judgments to decide claims. For example, the VA and BVA may often make a determination that an in-service injury was "acute, without chronic residual disability." However, the degree of injury and whether any disabilities resulted from the injury are medical assessments that the VA and the Board are not competent to make unless there is independent medical evidence to support that conclusion. This means that in many cases the VA's determination that an in-service injury was acute and did not result in chronic disability may violate Colvin.

Another common problem is that the VA may dismiss favorable medical evidence of record without citing to medical evidence in the record or medical literature to support its rejection.

A good rule of thumb based on Colvin is that if there is a VA-made medical conclusion – not directly based on a medical examination report, advisory opinion, or medical literature – the conclusion may be erroneous because the VA has no independent medical support for its findings. Decisions containing unsupported medical conclusions should be appealed.

Instructions for Raters from the Adjudication Manual (M21-1MR, Part III, Subpart iv, Chapter 5)

1. GUIDELINES FOR EVALUATING EVIDENCE

a. When to Evaluate Evidence

If VA's duty to assist has been fulfilled, analyze the evidence for and against the claim.

Note: Evaluate all the evidence, including oral testimony given under oath and certified statements submitted by claimants.

b. Points to Consider When Evaluating Evidence

When evaluating evidence and making decisions

- maintain objectivity
- never allow personal feelings to enter into the process, and
- show fairness and courtesy **at** all times to claimants.

Example: An antagonistic, critical, or even abusive attitude on the part of the claimant should not in any way influence the handling of the case.

Reference: For more information on the attitude of the rating officers, see 38 CFR 4.23.

c. Provisions Applied by the RVSR (Rating Veterans Service Representative)

When making decisions or taking action on claims that require a rating decision, the Rating Veterans Service Representative (RVSR) must apply the provisions of all pertinent

- laws
- regulations
- schedules for rating disabilities
- policy statements
- procedures
- administrators' decisions
- VA Secretaries' decisions
- Court of Appeals for Veterans Claims (CAVC) precedents, and
- other legal precedents governing Department of Veterans Affairs (VA).

d. Determining the Value of Testimony

The RVSR determines the probative value of medical or lay testimony.

e. Determining the Issues

The issues in some claims will be clear and unambiguous, while others may involve interpreting difficult to understand claims.

Reference: For more information on determining the issues, see M21-1MR, Part III, Subpart iv, 6.B.

2. EVIDENCE TO CONSIDER

a. Types of Evidence to Consider

Consider the following evidence when making decisions:

- medical records, such as

    - service medical records
    - VA examination reports
    - private and VA hospital reports, and
    - outpatient treatment reports
- lay evidence, such as letters from
    - veterans and claimants, including reports of specific traumatic experience related as stressors for post-traumatic stress disorder (PTSD) claims, and
    - other people who have knowledge of the claimed disability or relevant events
- medical opinions by examining or treating physicians, and
- medical treatises regarding
    - etiology of a disability
    - complications of a disease process, and
    - employment records.

3. RESPONSIBILITY FOR REVIEWING EVIDENCE

a. Who Is Responsible

The RSVR is responsible for reviewing the evidence, including

- recognizing the need for evidence in relation to a claim, and
- determining the
    - admissibility of the evidence
    - weight to be afforded evidence that is presented
    - need for additional evidence, and
    - need for a physical examination.

4. CREDIBLE AND PROBATIVE EVIDENCE

a. Evaluating Evidence

Evaluating evidence

- is the heart of the Reasons for Decision section of a rating decision, and
- may entail assessing the credibility and probative value of evidence before weighing the evidence in order to arrive at a decision on the claim.

Notes:

- Accept evidence at face value unless called into question by other evidence of record or sound medical or legal principles.
- In the presence of questionable or conflicting evidence, further development may be needed to reconcile the disparity.

b. Definition:

Credible Evidence

Credible evidence refers to evidence that is inherently believable or has been received from a competent source.

c. Definition:
Probative Evidence
Probative evidence must be

- relevant to the issue in question, and
- have sufficient weight, either by itself or in combination with other evidence, to persuade the decision-maker about a fact.

Note: For medical evidence to be probative, it generally must be recent enough to adequately evaluate the current state of the claimant's disability.

d. Assessing the Credibility of Evidence

Weigh the evidence by assessing its credibility and probative value in regard to the pending issue or issues. Weigh only credible evidence in reaching the ultimate decision. Evidence that is incredible carries no weight or probative value.

Example: Joseph Smith, a World War II veteran, submitted a statement from his primary care physician that noted the veteran's seizure disorder was secondary to his service-connected (SC) head injury.

Upon recent neurological examination, conducted at the VA Medical Center (VAMC) in West Palm Beach, the examiner opined there was no evidence linking the veteran's current seizure disorder to the veteran's head injury in service. Specifically, the neurologist stated that the veteran's nonservice-connected (NSC) vascular condition was causing the seizures. He went on to say that this is one of the most common causes of seizures that have their onset after age 60.

e. Example of Credible Evidence

VA receives a statement from a physician who expresses an opinion regarding the nexus, or link, between the veteran's current disability and an injury or disease in military service.

Note: As a result of the physician's medical expertise, the physician's statement is considered credible.

f. Example of Non-Credible Evidence

VA receives a statement from a claimant's spouse regarding the link between the veteran's current disability and an injury in service. The spouse is not known to be a medical professional.

Note: Since the spouse is not a medical professional, and a lay person is not considered capable of answering questions of medical causation or diagnosis, the evidence is not considered credible.

Exception: If the spouse is a medical professional, then the evidence is considered credible and weighed during the decision-making process.

g. Determining the Probative Value of Evidence

Determine the probative value of the evidence once the evidence has been determined credible.

Note: It is not necessary to accord equal weight to each item of evidence contained in the record.

h. Explaining the Persuasiveness of Evidence

Clearly explain in the rating decision why the evidence is found to be persuasive or not.

Example: Service connection for a seizure disorder secondary to the veteran's SC head injury is denied. Although the veteran's private physician provided an opinion linking the veteran's seizure disorder to his SC head injury, more weight was assigned to the VA examiner due to his specialization in neurological disorders.

5. MEDICAL EVIDENCE

a. Non-Adversarial Adjudication

VA's system of claims adjudication is non-adversarial.

Do not minimize the weight of a treating physician's opinion based upon the idea that he/she has become an advocate for the patient, since doing so may appear adversarial and biased.

b. Weighing Physicians' Opinions

Greater weight may be placed on one physician's opinion than another's, depending on several factors, such as

- the specialty of the physician
- the reasoning employed by the physician, and
- the extent to which the physician reviewed prior clinical records and other evidence.

An opinion may be discounted if it materially relies on a layperson's unsupported history as the premise for the opinion.

Note: Treating physician records are not necessarily dispositive of an issue and must be analyzed and discussed like all other evidence.

Reference: For more information on discounting opinions based on unsupported history, see Wood v. Derwinski, 1 Vet. App. 190 (1991).

c. Evaluating Medical Evidence

Consider the key elements listed below when evaluating medical evidence.

- Basis for the physician's opinion, such as
  - theory
  - observation
  - practice
  - clinical testing
  - subjective report, and
  - conjecture.
- Physician's knowledge of the veteran's accurate medical and relevant personal history.
- Length of time the physician has treated the veteran.
- Reason for the physician's contact with the veteran, such as for
  - treatment, or
  - substantiation of a medical disability claim.
- Physician's expertise and experience.
- Degree of specificity of the physician's opinion.
- Degree of certainty of the physician's opinion.

Reference: For more information on determining a physician's expertise and experience, see Black v. Brown, 10 Vet. App. 279, (1997).

d. Rejecting Medical Evidence

Unless the historical facts upon which a medical conclusion is based are dubious or untenable, reject medical evidence only on the basis of other medical evidence.

The RSVR may not rely upon his/her own unsubstantiated medical conclusions to reject expert medical evidence provided by the claimant.

Reference: For more information on the basis for rejecting medical evidence, see

- Shipwash v. Brown, 8 Vet. App. 218, (1995), and
- Colvin v. Derwinski, Vet. App. 175 (1991).

e. Supporting Medical Conclusions

Support medical conclusions with evidence in the claims folder.

Cite medical information and reasoning to

- link or separate two disabilities, or
- establish or refute prior inception or aggravation.

Cite recognized medical treatises or an independent medical opinion to support a conclusion.

Note: If evidence such as medical treatises or independent medical opinions were relied upon when the rating decision was made, explain this in the rating decision.

f. Considering the POW Protocol Examination Report

Carefully consider the prisoner of war (POW) protocol examination reports, because they may provide sufficient background information to relate the veteran's current symptomatology to the POW experience.

g. Evaluating STRs

Service treatment records (STRs) are generally highly probative, but not necessarily determinative, in the resolution of service connection.

h. Statements From Physicians as Acceptable Evidence

A statement from any physician can be accepted for rating purposes without further examination if it

- is otherwise adequate for rating purposes, and
- includes clinical manifestations and substantiation of diagnosis by findings of diagnostic techniques generally accepted by medical authorities.

Examples: Diagnostic techniques generally accepted by medical authorities are

- pathological studies
- x-rays, and
- appropriate laboratory tests.

i. Considering Information in the Claims Folder

The information in the claims folder must support the medical conclusions.

Consider the following information in the claims folder:

- applicable dates of events such as
  - treatment reports, and
  - hospitalizations
- dates covered by the service medical record, identifying at least the month and year
  - VA and private medical facilities
  - private physicians, and
  - other information sources, and
- items of evidence that were requested but not received.

6. INSUFFICIENT EXAMINATIONS

a. Improper Denials

Do not deny a claim or reduce an evaluation based upon an insufficient examination.

b. Explaining Necessary But Unscheduled Examinations

If the rating activity decides to rate a case where a specialist exam has been recommended by the medical examiner but not scheduled by the Veterans Health Administration (VHA), explain the reason in the rating decision.

7. REVIEWING HOSPITAL REPORTS FOR ADEQUACY

a. Handling Inadequate VA Hospital Reports

Request the original clinical records, including the nurses' and doctors' orders, if a VA report of hospitalization is inadequate for rating purposes in cases involving either

- injury, aggravation of injury, or death as the result of
    - hospitalization
    - medical treatment
    - surgical treatment, or
    - examination, or
- the death of a veteran from NSC causes if
    - the veteran had an SC neuropsychiatric disability that reasonably may have impeded, obstructed, or otherwise interfered with the treatment of the condition that caused death , and
    - the hospital report does not clarify this issue.

b. Handling Inadequate Non-VA Hospital Reports

Request clarification of any hospital report that is inadequate for rating purposes and is received from a

- State hospital
- county hospital
- municipal hospital
- contract hospital, or
- private hospital.

Important: Authorize a VA examination if a satisfactory corrected report cannot be obtained within a reasonable period of time.

8. REVIEWING TESTIMONY

a. Using Testimony

To be admitted as proper evidence, certain types of testimony must be sworn under oath or properly certified.

Examples: Evidence from court proceedings, depositions, and so on.

b. Handling Unsworn or Uncertified Testimony

Make an exact copy of unsworn or uncertified testimony and return the original copy for notarization or certification to the

- claimant
- representative, or
- person testifying.

Note: Return unsworn or uncertified testimony only if the RVSR or Decision Review Officer (DRO) considers the evidence material to a favorable determination of a claim.

Reference: For more information on certifying testimony, see M21-1MR, Part III, Subpart iii, 1.B.8.

9. LAY EVIDENCE

a. Acceptable Lay Evidence

Lay evidence is acceptable for the purpose of establishing service incurrence or aggravation, in the absence of STRs, for a combat veteran or former POW, if the evidence

- is satisfactory
- is consistent with the circumstances, conditions, or hardships of combat or POW internment, and
- can prevail in spite of the absence of official records showing incurrence or aggravation of the disease or injury during service.

Important: Medical evidence of a link to a current condition is still needed to establish service-related incurrence or aggravation.

b. When to Use Lay Evidence

A medically untrained individual is not competent to offer medical opinion regarding the etiology of disorders, and such an opinion is generally assigned to little probative weight.

The value accorded to other types of lay evidence depends on such factors as

- the accuracy or clarity of the individual's memory
- direct personal knowledge or experience, and
- the competence of the reporting person.

Note: An opinion may be discounted if it materially relies on a layperson's unsupported history as the premise for the opinion.

References: For more information on

- discounting opinions that rely upon a layperson's history, see Wood v. Derwinski, 1 Vet. App. 190 (1991), and
- using lay evidence to support a claim, see Espiritu v. Derwinski, 2 Vet. App. 492 (1992).

10. REQUIRING FURTHER DEVELOPMENT

a. Evidence Requiring Further Development

Further development may be needed to corroborate testimony if the evidence is questionable or conflicting.

This development may include field examinations and/or social surveys to obtain transcripts of original or other appropriate records.

11. EVIDENCE FROM NON-DEPARTMENT OF VETERANS AFFAIRS (VA) SOURCES

a. Evaluating Evidence From Non-VA Sources

When evaluating medical and lay evidence from non-VA sources

- accept it at face value unless there is reason to question it, and
- question it if it is conflicting.

b. Considering Conflicting Evidence

Use good judgment when evaluating conflicting evidence.

Consider the following issues:

- whether witnesses have a personal interest in the issue
- if there is a basis for bias
- if one party had a better opportunity to know the facts, and
- which version is more reasonable and probable.

12. WEIGHING THE EVIDENCE

a. Assigning Weight to the Evidence

After assigning weight to the evidence

- review the evidence in its totality, and
- determine the balancing of scales.

Note: Do not assign weight unjustly or arbitrarily.

b. Questions to Ask When Weighing Evidence

Ask the questions listed below when weighing evidence.

- Did the evidence originate in service or in close proximity to service?
- Is the medical opinion supported by clinical data?
- How detailed is the opinion?
- Is the opinion based on personal knowledge or on history provided by another person?

c. Handling Imbalanced Evidence

If the evidence shows an overwhelming imbalance, then the evidence requires a decision in that direction, either for or against.

Note: The claim must be granted if all of the evidence is favorable.

d. Handling Evidence in Equipoise

Resolve reasonable doubt in favor of the claimant if all procurable evidence, after being weighed, is found in approximate balance or equipoise. 38 CFR 3.102 dictates that the veteran prevails when the evidence neither satisfactorily proves nor disproves an issue.

Reference: For more information on applying reasonable doubt, see Alemany v. Brown, 9 Vet. App. 518 (1996).

e. Considering Reasonable Doubt

Consider reasonable doubt only when the evidence is in equipoise, not when the evidence weighs either in favor or against the claimant.

f. Example of Evidence in Equipoise

In the following example there is no compelling justification to side with either expert:

"Evidence supportive of the claim includes the July 1991 opinion of Dr. T., who treated the veteran for several years prior to his death, that PTSD had been the major factor in the veteran's suicide. Evidence against the claim includes the January 1992 opinion of the VA physician that the evidence did not point to PTSD as the actual cause of suicide and that the veteran's suicide had occurred in the setting of alcohol dependence, family breakdown, and depression."

g. Reaching a Conclusion

When weighing the evidence to reach a conclusion

- discuss the evidence in favor of the claim
- discuss the evidence against the claim, and
- explain that

- one set of evidence outweighs the other set, or
- the evidence is in equal balance for and against the claim.

13. HANDLING OTHER CONSIDERATIONS IN THE ANALYSIS

a. Explaining Grants

Grants may not require as extensive an explanation as denials and may be simply explained with a statement, such as "The service medical records demonstrate that the veteran fractured his left leg in service."

b. Explaining Denials

Provide a more in-depth recitation of the facts and a citation or paraphrase of pertinent law and regulations to explain the basis for a denial. Carefully craft the explanation to provide basic information as succinctly as possible.

c. Supporting Denials

Support the denial of NSC Pension or individual unemployability due to failure to meet the schedular requirements by explaining

- how the disability percentages were assigned for each disability by applying the pertinent diagnostic codes to the evidence, and
- why the veteran is considered to be able to perform work duties, given his/her employment background, and the degree or nature of the SC or NSC disabilities.

d. Danger of Paraphrasing

Paraphrasing in easy-to-understand language requires care because the paraphrase might

- misstate the law, or
- misstate or mistake medical facts.

Example: Use paraphrased language to help explain why the claim has been disallowed, but do not expressly state, "The law says that…." Simply insert the paraphrase.

e. Addressing Complex Issues

Discuss complex issues, such as secondary service connection and aggravation of NSC disabilities by SC disabilities, more thoroughly than simple issues of service connection.

Example: In claims for secondary service connection, address the relationship of the disability claimed by the veteran to the condition for which service connection has already been established.

f. Handling Inferred Issues

When an inferred issue is considered in a rating decision, explicitly address the inferred issue in the Reasons for Decision. If the inferred issue and the primary issue

- share the same fact pattern, then the inferred issue may be incorporated in the same Issue, Decision, and Reasons for Decision numbered item as the primary issue, or
- are each itemized in a separate Decision and Reasons for Decision paragraph, then the discussion of the common fact pattern may be confined to the Reasons for Decision of the primary issue.

Example: The issue statement on the rating decision could be worded as follows: "1. Evaluation of psychotic disorder currently evaluated as 30 percent disabling; Competency to handle disbursement of funds."

Reference: For more information on inferred issues, see M21-1MR, Part III, Subpart iv, 6.B.3.

Assigning a Rating Level

> "RVSRs assign evaluation levels based on the tables, diagnostic codes, and the percentages provided in the Rating Schedule, correlating the medical evidence in the individual case to the criteria and percentages provided in the Rating Schedule. Most recent innovations in the regional office include computer-based rating calculators that save a great deal of time and are more accurate and avoid common mistakes when ratings were calculated by hand.
>
> When multiple conditions have been evaluated, a combined rating evaluation is performed according to a "combined rating table" found in 38 CFR 4.25. To the extent that the Rating Schedule reflects current medical diagnostic knowledge, assessment of disability, and treatment, the resultant rating evaluation should accurately reflect disability. To the extent that the Rating Schedule is outdated, the resultant rating evaluation will be subject to distortions and imprecision. We include a copy of 38 CFR Section 4 on the data disk if you are interested in looking at various ratings for various conditions. Just a word of advice on using the rating table. If you can't find the symptoms coincident with a particular condition you are looking for, the rating table allows you to substitute the same symptoms from another condition to determine a rating for the situation you cannot find.
>
> The standard rating evaluation decision format contains the following sections: Introduction, Decision, Statement of Evidence, and Reasons and Bases for the Decision. It also includes a section called Coded Conclusion, containing statistical information about the veteran, the specific evaluations, and the combined evaluation. The RVSR signs the completed rating decision.
>
> The discussion above shows that the rating process is complicated and multifaceted. The technicians who execute the ratings are expected to have substantial expertise in VA law and the medical aspects of the Rating Schedule. Rating team personnel are generally grouped together in a section or sections of the VSC. The RVSRs do their evaluations individually, however. They do not have routine access to medical practitioners or legal experts as they conduct their assessments. They have only their training guides and regulations to interpret." *"Information on writing is taken from "A 21st Century System for Evaluating Veterans for Disability Benefits, Committee on Medical Evaluation of Veterans for Disability Compensation 2006"*

CHAPTER 4
The Claims Process for Compensation, DIC and SMC

SECTION A – ELEMENTS OF THE FULLY DEVELOPED CLAIM PROCESS

Where to Submit Claims – Claims Intake Center

In order to improve timeliness and costliness of scanning claims into the Veterans Benefits Management System (VBMS), VA has implemented Centralized Mail Processing (CMP). Under these new procedures, claimants and beneficiaries should now send all mail directly to the scanning vendor (Jainesville, Wisconsin Intake Center), eliminating the need for Regional Office (RO) or Pension Management Center (PMC) mail processing. The vendor will scan and upload the digital images for processing. Please refer to the data disk for the appropriate PO Box for your claim.

The Fully Developed Claim Is a Wonderfully Useful Procedure for Getting Results
Please do not attempt to file a claim until you have read this section. Also, in order to understand the information in this section, you really need to understand the information in Chapter 3, Section C. A thorough understanding of the adjudication process in Chapter 3 allows you to follow the rationale and understand the verbiage outlined in this section for submitting a fully developed claim.

The concept behind a fully developed claim is that you will give the Regional Office every scrap of relevant and probative evidence you can get your hands on to make your case. You will provide this information up front when you make your formal application by filling out the appropriate benefit forms and including all of your evidence with it. The goal is for all of the evidence that you assemble to be sufficient enough for the Regional Office development team to pass on to the rating activity for a final decision. This fully developed claim concept could get you a decision within a matter of a few months instead of the typical 8 to 18 months that it takes by simply applying and waiting for VA to assist you in developing your evidence.

Laid out below in this section are the steps you will take to implement a fully developed claim. This is important information. Read it carefully.

1. Decide Whether the Condition Warrants Making a Claim
Many veterans seem to think that because of their service, they have an entitlement to disability benefits even if they aren't currently disabled. Or, if they are currently disabled they seem to think that all of their ailments are a result of being a veteran. This attitude causes a number of veterans or their survivors to make application thinking that VA owes them something whether they qualify are not. Unfortunately, this attitude leads to a great number of claims that are filed where there is no benefit. It is also unfortunate that many people with this attitude come away from their experience with a denial with a bad taste in their mouth.

The filing of an unjustified claim with a denial that has taken many years, often leads to resentment towards the Department of Veterans Affairs and to the VA employees and to an attitude of recrimination. This recrimination often takes the form of angry letters or accusations in in a public forum against the Department for not providing something that the veteran or the survivor felt was his or her just due. Many people who feel they have been wronged, go on a crusade on the Internet or with their congressional representatives to try and correct the perceived wrong treatment from DVA. Or, they will often initiate the appeals process, more out of an attitude of retribution, than out of a need for extra income.

Please don't misunderstand. Always file a claim if you believe that your disability is a result of service connection. Don't file a claim if you are pretty sure that your disability condition is a result of non-service connection. If you are convinced the disability is non-service-connected, don't file a claim anyway just to see what you can get. This is not fair to you nor to the other veterans who are waiting for their claims to be adjudicated. An unjustified claim – or so-called claim without merit – is only going to add to the current backlog in the system making it harder for everyone else.

Here's an example. A Vietnam era veteran has learned through an Internet source that even though he was not in Vietnam, the stateside base where he was stationed for two weeks of training was storing herbicides in transit for use in Vietnam. The veteran has no agent orange presumptive conditions but he has developed cirrhosis of the liver. He doesn't know if he was exposed to Agent Orange are not. He does have a medical condition, however, and by filing a claim he might get something even though it may not even be on the presumptive list. Who knows? A friend of his convinces him that regardless of whether he thinks he is eligible or not, he should make a claim because he needs to get what he can out of VA for his cirrhosis. After all, what can it hurt to turn in the claim? The worst that can happen is he will be turned down.

2. Always File an "Intent to File", VBA Form 21-0966

Once you feel that you can justify a claim for benefits and not waste your time or VA's time, you should proceed to submit an "intent to file." An "intent to file," before March of 2015, was known as an "informal claim" for benefits. The "intent to file" allows you to notify your Regional Office that you will be submitting a substantially complete claim with the appropriate claims form in order to start the process at some future date. Actually, you have one year from filing an "intent to file" to providing the formal application for a substantially complete claim. Most importantly, the "intent to file" with establish an effective date for back-pay purposes. The effective date with be the first day of the month following receipt of the "intent to file."

An "intent to file" is typically used for application for new benefits. If you are applying for an revaluation of existing benefits or a change in existing benefits, you should use a formal request either on the appropriate VA form or using VBA Form 21-4138, to establish an effective date. Here is the information that you should send to establish an effective date.

- VBA Form 21-0966 INTENT TO FILE
- A copy Veteran's Discharge (DD214 or equivalent)

We have provided the VBA 21-0966 INTENT TO FILE for you on the "Claim Support Data Disk" under the folder name "2 Application for Compensation and DIC." On the 0966, ignore #15 entirely (it is a huge hassle to have the claimant's rep sign). The claimant should be the only one signing. Also, do not use the electronic signature under #14a.

Always include a copy of the veteran's honorable discharge when you fax or mail the form to the Jainesville Intake Center or hand deliver the "intent to file" to a regional office. Sometimes, with only a 0966 in hand, the regional office will struggle to locate the veteran's records and establish his or her identity and service. Including the discharge will help VA immensely.

Again, the primary purpose of an "intent to file" is to establish an effective date for back-pay purposes. When the "intent to file" is received, it will be date stamped and that date will become your effective date under most conditions. The effective date could be a later date if you don't meet the qualifications for the benefit at the time of filing. Remember, do not file an "intent to file" unless you are sure that you do have a valid claim for benefits.

The effective date governs the date of payment for benefits. For example, if your effective date is July 15, 2016 and the application gets approved on November 10, 2016, you will receive two payments by deposit. The first is a lump sum back-payment dating back to and starting on August 1, 2016 for the months of August, September, and October. The second payment will be the first of the monthly payments. The monthly payment, in this example, will be deposited on or around November 1, 2016. VA pays in arrears so this payment will represent October's benefit.

If you don't think that you can hand carry your "intent to file" into your Regional Office before the end of the current month, you are going to have to fax or mail it to VA's Intake Center in Jainesville, Wisconsin if you do not want to miss a month of payment. VA will not use a postal date or a delivery receipt or a mailroom diary for an effective date. The "intent to file" must officially be handled by a VSR and stamped by hand with the date stamp machine. We highly recommend faxing before the month's end. Save the original (or certified copy of the) discharge as well as the original 0966 and fax report to include in the fully developed claim you will submit later on. The fax report will act as your insurance in case the department loses it. See the data disc for fax information.

3. Get a Copy of Your Discharge and Locate Your Own Service Treatment Records (STR)
You will need a certified copy of your discharge for filing the formal fully developed claim. If you do not have the original, you can order a certified copy using Form SF 180. This form is found on the "Claim Support Data Disk" under the folder name "2 Application for Compensation and DIC." If you have an original of the discharge, and you do not want to send it in with your formal application, generally the County Recorder's Office should provide a certified copy for the veteran. Although not all counties are that cooperative. If your state has an archive of discharge records, which many states do, call your state Department of Veterans Affairs and they will send you a certified copy.

If your claim is going to be tied to service treatment records – which not all claims are – then you should use Form SF 180 to get those records from the Service Center in St. Louis. This does not mean that the Regional Office would not order these for you, it just may take them two or three months to get around to it. Go ahead and get them up front as part of the evidence collection you will be doing for your fully developed claim.

The Official Military Personnel Files (OMPF), held at the National Personnel Records Center (NPRC), are administrative records containing information about the subject's military service history. Many OMPFs contain both personnel and former active duty health records, but the service branches discontinued retiring the health record portion to the NPRC in the 1990s. In the past, all of the military services retired the individual health record, along with the personnel record, to the NPRC upon a service member's separation from service. The Army and the Air Force retired its health records with the Official Military Personnel File, while the Department of the Navy (including the Navy, Marine Corps and Coast Guard) retired these files separately to the NPRC until the 1980s.

Health records cover the outpatient, dental and mental health treatment that former members received while in military service. Health records include induction and separation physical examinations, as well as routine medical care (doctor/dental visits, lab tests, etc.) when the patient was not admitted to a hospital.

In comparison, clinical (hospital inpatient) records were generated when active duty members were actually hospitalized while in the service. Typically, these records are NOT filed with the health records but are generally retired to the NPRC by the facility which created them (see clinical records for more information). Medical records from the Department of Veterans Affairs (VA) are also not included.

In the 1990s, the military services discontinued the practice of filing health records with the personnel record portion at the NPRC. In 1992, the Army began retiring most of its former members' health records to the Department of Veterans Affairs (VA). Over the next six years, the other services followed suit:

Branch	Status	Health Record to VA
Army	Discharged, retired, or separated from any component	October 16, 1992
Navy	Discharged, retired, or separated from any component	January 31, 1994
Air Force	Discharged, retired, or separated from Active Duty Discharged or retired from Reserves or National Guard	May 1, 1994 June 1, 1994
Marine Corps	Discharged, retired, or separated from any component	May 1, 1994
Coast Guard	Discharged, retired, or separated from Active Duty - Reservists with 90 days active duty for training	April 1, 1998

After the dates listed above, the Department of Veterans Affairs (VA), Records Management Center, in St. Louis, MO, became responsible for maintaining active duty health records and managing their whereabouts when on loan within the VA. Call the VA toll free number at 1-800-827-1000 to identify the current location of specific health records and to find out how to obtain releasable documents or information.

4. Obtain Your Own Private Medical Records

As part of the fully developed claim process, you should never have VA order your personal medical records. Your doctors and specialists are used to being paid a fee to provide copies of your records to third-party organizations. Sometimes these copy fees can be as much as $100 or more. As a general rule, you will not be charged for copies of your own private medical records. When VA puts in a request for your medical records, it will not pay a fee because it is prohibited by the regulation cited below. This does not mean that your doctors can refuse to supply copies, because they are required to respond to government agencies.

Unfortunately, it has been our experience over the years, in obtaining medical records for others, that without the fee, the request often gets delayed by months. The reality of this is that most doctor's offices or clinics have outside companies who come in and make the copies for third-party requests. These copy service people have to be paid. Government requests do not include fees and as such the office staff has to take time out from their regular duties to make the copies. Oftentimes, they have so much to do they just don't get around to making copies. Never rely on VA to order your medical records. Besides, by so doing, you have destroyed the continuity of the fully developed claims program and reverted back to the slow way of doing things.

> **38 CFR §3.159 Department of Veterans Affairs assistance in developing claims.**
> (c) VA's duty to assist claimants in obtaining evidence. Upon receipt of a substantially complete application for benefits, VA will make reasonable efforts to help a claimant obtain evidence necessary to substantiate the claim. In addition, VA will give the assistance described in paragraphs (c)(1), (c)(2), and (c)(3) to an individual attempting to reopen a finally decided claim. VA will not pay any fees charged by a custodian to provide records requested.

If you use the VA health care system, you can obtain copies of your medical records. Use either of the forms below (found on the Data Disk under the folder "Compensation and DIC Forms.") To request your records be sent to someone else such as your private physician, use 10-5345 or that the records be sent to you, use 10-5345a. Request both the hospital summary and the treatment notes. Look up the address of your VA medical center where your records will be kept. Don't use the outpatient clinic where you see your doctors but use the main center. Include in the address title the following, "Medical Records Request."

VHA-10-5345 – Request for and Authorization to Release Medical Records
VHA-10-5345a – Individual's Request for a Copy of Their Own Health Information

5. Have Your Private Doctors or Specialists Do Disability Evaluations

For many of the presumptive service connected conditions such as cancer, heart disease, diabetes and other chronic diseases or disorders, description of the disease process, symptoms and past and current treatment protocols are enough to guide the rating activity to assign a level of disability. Debilitating diseases or disorders are already inherently disabling. Your private medical records might be enough for the rater to make a decision. On the other hand, some conditions or diseases need a level of disability to be determined in order to make a rating decision. This is especially true for conditions involving range of motion limitations, requirements for assistance from others and cognitive impairment.

VA has designed disability rating forms for private consultation for most of the disorders or diseases for which applications are made. There are currently 70 of these and the Department does not feel that it needs any more at this time. These are called Disability Benefits Questionnaires. Copies of these are found on your "Claim Support Data Disk" under the folder "2 Application for Compensation and DIC," and under the subfolder "Disability Benefits Questionnaires." There are no DBQ's for hearing loss or mental disorders (other than PTSD) as these require specialists from VA to do the evaluations. Even though these conditions do not have DBQ's, you should still obtain a private evaluation for any condition that is not covered by the DBQ's to include hearing loss and mental disorders. We will give you instructions for the hearing loss evaluation for that particular claim under Section B below.

This is extremely important for you to establish your own line of evidence and not rely on VA to provide all the evidence for your disability or your service connection. Whether the application you are making is presumptive service-connected or not, always do your own private disability evaluation. VA will often not consider your application to be a fully developed claim unless you complete one of these forms – prerequisite filing of a DBQ depends on the condition. So go ahead and do it anyway.

6. Have Your Doctors/Specialists Provide Opinion Letters If Service Connection Is Needed
Where your claim is for a condition for which you have no service records and for which you must rely on the logical nexus of your current disabling condition tied to an exposure, unreported injury, unreported disease or other incident incurred in the service, you have to establish – through medical evidence – that a service connection exists. This will almost always require an expert opinion from a doctor or psychiatrist or psychologist that the current condition is probably or definitely a result of that incident incurred in the service. If you do not provide this evidence, the VA will either try to infer from your other nonmedical evidence that it is service-connected or VA may likely order a Compensation and Pension Examination with the request that the examiner offer an expert opinion on the service connection.

If you rely entirely on VA to help you establish the service connection, you have a higher probability of losing the contest. You must provide your own offsetting evidence of the service connection in case the rating authority in the Regional Office – based on other evidence, including a VA-ordered expert opinion from a medical examiner – decides that your current condition is not service-connected.

If you need to prove service connection, do the following. When you have your disability examination with your private doctor or specialist or both, ask them for this expert opinion on the service connection. Of course, you will have to provide them with the details and these details must be in the opinion letter they produce for you. You must give them these written details when you show up for your examination. You must write out these details exactly as you will give them to VA in your own sworn statement as to what was incurred in service. The background information your doctor is using must concur with what you are telling VA. The more detailed the explanation in the opinion letter, the better the evidence. Explain to private medical examiners the importance of this opinion.

Your medical examiners should use the following terminology in determining whether, in their expert opinion, the current condition is tied to the incident incurred in the service based on your written description that will be inserted in the letter.

"is due to"
(examiner is 100% sure that the current disability condition was incurred as a result of illness, injury or exposure in service);

"more likely than not"
(examiner feels there is a greater than 50% probability that the current disability condition was incurred as a result of illness, injury or exposure in service);

"at least as likely as not"
(examiner feels there is an equal to or greater than 50% probability that the current disability condition was incurred as a result of illness, injury or exposure in service);

"not at least as likely as not"
(examiner feels there is less than a 50% probability that the current disability condition was incurred as a result of illness, injury or exposure in service)

Oftentimes, a private physician is unwilling to provide an opinion that the current medical condition is a result of the service connection the veteran is claiming. You may be able to find a physician who will write an opinion letter that there is a 50-50 chance or greater the current disability is service-connected. This seems more reasonable to the examining medical practitioner. The physician will use the words that the current disability is "at least as likely as not" to have been incurred in the service based on information provided by the veteran and an examination by the physician. The physician has opined that there is a 50-50 chance or greater it was incurred in service and if VA has no evidence to the contrary – under the doctrine of reasonable doubt (38 CFR 3.102) – the veteran will receive an award.

7. Obtain or Produce Lay Evidence
In order to provide corroborating evidence for service connection, where service records are missing or nonexistent, or to prove that you meet the duty requirements for conditions that are presumed to be service-connected, you will have to provide evidence of that service or the duty to which you were assigned. Or in other cases where service records are missing, you may need to provide evidence that you sustained an unreported injury, exposure or illness while in service that has resulted in a current disability. Statements from you and from others laying out the facts in great detail pertaining to where you were in the service, what happened and what the physical results were, can be accepted as evidence of possible incurrence in service under the right conditions.

You should also look for any physical evidence that will back up your assertions that the injury, illness or exposure was incurred in service especially if you are trying to tie the condition you have now to a specific base, country or command posting. This might include photos, newsletters, newspaper articles, unit histories or yearbooks, locally postmarked letters mentioning specific assignments and so on. For example, a quicker way than ordering service records to prove that you were in Vietnam and exposed to herbicides is to produce postcards of known sites in the country signed by you and dated. Or perhaps your Squadron or Battalion had a newsletter and your picture or name was mentioned in it. Or maybe you retained a letter from your assigned unit that identified where you were located physically in the body of the letter.

Lay statements cannot include opinions about medical conditions or diagnoses of medical conditions unless the person making the statement has a medical degree. However, a lay statement can include an assertion that the claimant was diagnosed in the past with a certain condition as long as details of that knowledge are spelled out in the statement. This may not, however, carry much weight, since medical evidence should be the way to establish diagnoses. Statements that are short on fact of observations of disability or incidents, and are long on medical opinions will be discounted and perhaps even thrown out by the rater. A layperson cannot provide an opinion on whether a condition is service connected or not. That is also going to be thrown out. Observations on the current disabling conditions with detailed descriptions of the disabilities – refraining from any medical opinions – is good evidence.

Lay Statements for Direct Service Connection: The claimant's and possible witness' statements of the unreported injury, illness, exposure or other unreported in-service-incurred incident can be used as corroborating evidence for service connection by providing facts and details that the current condition could have occurred as a result of service. If the claimant's and witnesses' lay statements cannot be supported by other evidence such as personnel records, unit histories and so forth, the evidence in these statements is not acceptable.

Lay Statements for Presumed Service Connection: In the absence of any corroborating evidence for a claim for service connection that is presumed service-connected, lay statements can be used to establish that the claimant was in the service for the period claimed and did meet the duty requirements for the "presumed service-connected" claim.

Lay Statements for Direct Service Connection Related to Combat or POW Internment: Lay statements that pertain to combat or POW internment do not need corroborating history to prove that the participants were there and could have sustained an unreported illness or injury. This evidence is acceptable by itself as long as it is satisfactory to the rater, is consistent with the circumstances, conditions, or hardships of combat or POW internment, and can prevail in spite of the absence of official records showing incurrence or aggravation of the disease or injury during service.

For direct service-connected claims, establishing a link between the current condition and the supporting lay statements along with other corroborating evidence, that the condition may be due to an unreported incident in service requires a medical opinion. All lay statements should be signed by the person making the statement and should we notarized. In addition VA requires certification of evidence submitted. If the evidence is copies of physical evidence, the following statement is to be attached to those records.

"*I hereby certify that the following (or attached) is a true transcript of my records pertaining to this case.*"

If the evidence is a direct statement by a friend or member of the family or by a witness, the following certification should be part of that statement.

"I hereby certify that the information given above is true and correct to the best of my knowledge and belief."

Using VA Form 21-4138 for providing statements, does not require certification because use of the form is inherent with the certification above.

8. Locate Records to Establish Assignment Location or Type of Duty Where Applicable
Standard Form 180 (SF 180), which is found on the Data Disk, is used to request copies of records from the Records Management Center, in St. Louis, Missouri. The following records are kept there unless they were destroyed by the fire.

- DD 214
- service treatment records
- personnel records

The form SF 180 is also rich in information on where to find records kept by the various services. For claims for conditions that are presumed service-connected or that are direct service-connected through evidence on file, you will need your STR's and possibly your personnel records from the records center. For other direct service-connected claims where evidence of incurrence in service is missing, your service treatment records will not be helpful but your personnel records may be valuable.

Perhaps you need additional evidence to demonstrate that you were in a particular assignment or a particular place that is not reflected in your personnel records or your personnel records were destroyed in the fire. Here are some additional sources for you to locate records.

- Army History Website – http://history.army.mil/websites.html
- Naval Operation Records from 1965 through 1974 – http://www.history.navy.mil/branches/org10-8.htm
- Air Force Records in Addition to Those Found at the National Records Center http://www.af.mil/questions/topic.asp?id=4

9. Make Sure the Evidence Conforms with the Rating Decision Criteria in Section C
After you have gathered all of your evidence, make sure that it is compliant with the rating decision criteria in Chapter 3, Section C found under the following portion of that section. **"Instructions for Raters from Adjudication Manual M21-1MR."** Understanding exactly what the rater is looking for, will give you a tremendous advantage towards getting a favorable decision.

10. Understand the Claim Forms and the Forms for Obtaining Records
Here are the fully developed claim forms that you will find under the subfolder on the Data Disk entitled "2 Application for Compensation and DIC." Here is a list of the forms in this folder on the Data Disk.

"Intent to File" for New Benefits, Obtaining Records and Communication with VA

VA Form 21-0966 – INTENT TO FILE
VBA-21-4138-ARE – Statement in Support of Claim
FV1 SF 180 Request Pertaining to Military Records

Initial Application for Disability Compensation or SMC Benefits

VHA-10-5345 – Request for and Authorization to Release Medical Records
VHA-10-5345a – Individual's Request for a Copy of Their Own Health Information
VBA-21-526EZ-ARE – Application for Disability Compensation and Related Compensation Benefits
VBA-21-0781a-ARE – Statement in Support of Claim for Service Connection for PTSD Secondary to Personal Assault
VBA-21-0781-ARE – Statement in Support of Claim for Service Connection for PTSD
VBA-21-686c-ARE – Declaration of Status of Dependents
VBA-21-4192-ARE – Request for Employment Information in Connection With Claim for Disability Benefits
VBA-21-4176-ARE – Report of Accidental Injury in Support of Claim for Compensation or Pension Statement of Witness to Accident
VBA-21-4142-ARE – Authorization and Consent to Release Information to the Department of Veterans Affairs

Forms for Representation for Assistance
VBA-21-22A-ARE – Appointment of Individual a Claimant's Representative
VBA-21-0845-ARE – Authorization to Disclose Personal Information to a Third Party

Initial Application for Other Benefits Associated with Compensation

VHA-10-0103 – Assistance in Acquiring Home Improvement and Structural Alterations (HISA Grant)
VBA-21-4502-ARE – Application for Automobile or Other Conveyance and Adaptive Equipment
VBA-26-4555-ARE – Application in Acquiring Special Housing Adaptations
VBA-21-4142-ARE – Authorization and Consent to Release Information to the Department of Veterans Affairs

Forms for Representation for Assistance
VBA-21-22A-ARE – Appointment of Individual a Claimant's Representative
VBA-21-0845-ARE – Authorization to Disclose Personal Information to a Third Party

Application for Reevaluation or Change in Benefits for Existing Compensation Award

VBA-21-526EZ-ARE – Application for Disability Compensation and Related Compensation Benefits
VBA-21-8940-ARE – Veteran's Application for Increased Compensation Based on Unemployability

VBA-21-4192-ARE – Request for Employment Information in Connection With Claim for Disability Benefits
VBA-21-4142-ARE – Authorization and Consent to Release Information to the Department of Veterans Affairs

Forms for Representation for Assistance
VBA-21-22A-ARE – Appointment of Individual a Claimant's Representative
VBA-21-0845-ARE – Authorization to Disclose Personal Information to a Third Party

Initial Application for Dependency and Indemnity Compensation (DIC)

VBA-21-534EZ-ARE – Application for DIC, Death Pension, and or Accrued Benefits
FV30 – Determining Cause of Death for Awarding Income Benefit
VBA-21-4170-ARE – Statement of Marital Relationship
VBA-21-4171-ARE – Supporting Statement Regarding Marriage
VBA-21-4103-ARE – Information from Remarried Widow
VBA-21-1775-ARE – Statement of Disappearance
VBA-21-601-ARE – Application for Accrued Amounts Due a Deceased Beneficiary
VBA-21-8416b-ARE – Report of Medical, Legal, and Other Expenses Incident to Recovery for Injury or Death
VBA-21-4142-ARE – Authorization and Consent to Release Information to the Department of Veterans Affairs

Forms for Representation for Assistance
VBA-21-22A-ARE – Appointment of Individual a Claimant's Representative
VBA-21-0845-ARE – Authorization to Disclose Personal Information to a Third Party

Application for Aid and Attendance or Housebound Benefits w/ Compensation or DIC

VBA-21-2680-ARE – Exam for Housebound Status or Permanent Need for Regular A&A
VA-21-4138-ARE – Statement in Support of Claim
FV13 – Care Provider Certification of Services
VBA-21-0779-ARE – Request for Nursing Home Info in Connection with Claim for Aid and Attendance
VBA-21-4142-ARE – Authorization and Consent to Release Information to the Department of Veterans Affairs

Forms for Representation for Assistance
VBA-21-22A-ARE – Appointment of Individual a Claimant's Representative
VBA-21-0845-ARE – Authorization to Disclose Personal Information to a Third Party

Post Application Issues

VBA-21-0790-ARE – Your Rights to Representation and a Hearing (Possible Overpayment)
VBA-21-0847-ARE – Request for Substitution of Claimant upon Death of Claimant
VBA-21-651-ARE – Election of Compensation In Lieu Of Retired Pay

VBA-21-8951-2-ARE-1 – Notice of Waiver of VA Compensation to Receive Military Pay and

Allowances
We will explain the use of the forms in Section B below. When you choose the particular type of claim in Section B, that you will be submitting, we will describe the principle forms that you will be using.

Primary Forms for Application
Most of the forms that we have listed above are secondary to the application and in many cases won't be used or the forms will be used in specific instances where they are needed by VA. Here are the primary forms that are used for applications.

Release of Medical Information
VBA-21-4142-ARE – Authorization and Consent to Release Information to the Department of Veterans Affairs
VHA-10-5345 – Request for and Authorization to Release Medical Records
VHA-10-5345a – Individual's Request for a Copy of Their Own Health Information

Primary Form for Application for Disability Compensation
VBA-21-526EZ-ARE – Application for Disability Compensation and Related Compensation Benefits
VBA-21-0781-ARE – Statement in Support of Claim for Service Connection for PTSD
VBA-21-8940-ARE – Veteran's Application for Increased Compensation Based on Unemployability

Primary Form for Application for DIC
VBA-21-534EZ-ARE – Application for DIC, Death Pension, and or Accrued Benefits

Form to Support Applications If There Are Dependents Such As a Spouse or a Dependent Child
VBA-21-686c-ARE – Declaration of Status of Dependents

Forms for Representation for Assistance
VBA-21-22A-ARE – Appointment of Individual a Claimant's Representative
VBA-21-0845-ARE – Authorization to Disclose Personal Information to a Third Party

11. Fill out the "Fully Developed Claim" Forms for the Claimed Benefit
For Disability Compensation and for DIC, the VA has designed forms that recognize the fully developed claims concept. When you submit these forms for new benefits, you are essentially waiving your rights under the duty to assist. Even though the application does not state it directly, the Regional Office will ignore the duty to assist and take the information you give it and pass this information on to the rating activity for a decision.

<u>You must be very careful that you submit all the evidence that is needed to make a decision with the initial application. If you go back and submit additional evidence – whether VA requests it or not – you will lose the special tracking of the fully developed claim and your claim will revert</u>

back to the duty to assist rules. As a result of losing special handling, the process could end up taking forever as many of these "standard" claims do.

To avoid losing special treatment is why it is so important to file an "Intent to File" first. An "Intent to File" is not considered a substantially complete claim, and VA will not start any process on it until the Regional Office actually gets your formal claim application with all of the information for a fully developed claim. The "Intent to File" will establish a payment date while at the same time allowing you to gather all of the evidence you need. The clock starts ticking with the actual adjudication process when you submit the full application package.

Don't assume that there will be a final decision. With some claims, the rating authority must order a medical evaluation from veterans health care or from a contracting organization that does these types of exams. On the other hand, special treatment as a fully developed claim will often result in that special examination being ordered perhaps within a matter of weeks of receiving the initial application.

12. Check and Double Check Everything and Include All Necessary Forms

Make sure all pertinent boxes on your application forms are filled out or if they are not applicable put "N/A" in them. Answer all questions pertaining to marriage, dependents and relationships and put in the appropriate places and dates. If you cannot provide places and dates you can sometimes estimate them or if you cannot you must provide copies of marriage certificates or the equivalent. For an application for DIC you must provide a marriage certificate or the equivalent. You must also provide a death certificate where that is appropriate for the application being filed. More information on marriages and death are found in the Appendix of this book.

All required signature blanks must be signed by the veteran or the claimant if the claimant is not the veteran. If the veteran or claimant is considered incompetent by the state to sign documents, as long as they can move their hands, the VA has no competency requirement. Make sure they sign. Marks or thumbprints must have two witnesses or a veteran service officer can witness independently.

The Triage team in the Regional Office will return the application if signatures are missing. Other missing information generally does not require returning the application but it will slow down the process. Make sure that all of your lay statements are notarized and that the certifications for all evidence are provided. The exception will be medical records where the doctor provides identification as a licensed physician. As a general rule, opinions by physicians assistants or nurse practitioners may be admissible, but always go with an M.D. or D.O.

Make sure you submit the form below with any application that you send in. This form is a release to obtain medical records from the private physicians or from VA health care. If you submit a fully developed claim, it is unlikely that VA will need to use this release. Always obtain your own private medical records and send them in with the application. On the other hand, if the Veterans Service Center decides it wants this form for one reason or another, and you have not furnished it, you have probably added another 60 days to the claim process.

VBA-21-4142-ARE – Authorization and Consent to Release Information to the Department of Veterans Affairs
Finally, check and make sure that you have not left out any of the required forms, statements, evidence and other records that are necessary for a fully developed claim.

13. Arrange for Representation and Third-Party Help If Needed
If the reader of this book is not the claimant but someone assisting the claimant, you will want to complete the two documents below and submit them with the application so that you can be included in the flow of information from the Regional Office. The veteran or claimant who is not the veteran (this means the veteran is deceased) must sign both of these. If you are not an accredited agent or accredited attorney check off the box titled "INDIVIDUAL PROVIDING REPRESENTATION UNDER SECTION 14.630 (*See required statement below. Signatures are required in Items 7C and 7D)" on VBA-21-22a. Don't limit the information flow with all of the special requirements and boxes to check on either of these documents. Just set them up so that there's no special requirement.

Forms for Representation for Assistance
VBA-21-22A-ARE – Appointment of Individual a Claimant's Representative
VBA-21-0845-ARE – Authorization to Disclose Personal Information to a Third Party

14. Provide a Cover Letter to Help the Service Representative Understand the Claim
If you are including a number of documents, organize them in logical order and put appropriately titled cover sheets on the private records you are providing. Staple them together so that they don't get lost. Finally, provide a cover letter explaining to the veteran service representative that you are submitting a claim for "whatever benefit it is you are submitting" and that you are providing the information as a fully developed claim. Make the following statement is on your cover letter.

"I am providing all of the information to you necessary to make a rating decision on this application. I have no other information to furnish you. Please take my information and make a rating decision as quickly as possible."

Make a list on the cover letter of all of the documents that you are providing. This includes all of your private evidence as well as all of the VA forms that you are submitting. If you are acting as a power of attorney under VA Form 21-22a include that on the cover letter is well.

15. Submit Claim to the Claims Intake Center
In order to improve timeliness and reduce the cost of scanning claims into the Veterans Benefits Management System (VBMS), VA has implemented Centralized Mail Processing (CMP). Under these new procedures, claimants and beneficiaries should now send all mail directly to the scanning vendor (Jainesville, Wisconsin Intake Center), eliminating the need for Regional Office (RO) or Pension Management Center (PMC) mail processing. The vendor will scan and upload the digital images for processing. Please refer to the data disk for the appropriate PO Box for your claim.

16. Understand the Acknowledgment Letter from Your Veterans Service Center

A number of weeks after you submit your application, you may receive a letter of acknowledgment. This letter will also list all of the documents that you sent. Oftentimes, the list of documents does not include some of the documents that you are sure that you provided. Generally, this is not a problem as the triage team that created this letter may not have seen all the documents that were submitted. If you are nervous that VA has lost something, resend those documents. One baffling aspect of these acknowledgment letters is the fact that the letter will give you a list of what you sent and then proceed to tell you that you must send the same things in order to start your claim. For whatever reason, the powers that be from VA have not bothered to check the logic of these computer-generated forms. Disregard this odd conflict in the letter.

17. Use VA Form 21-4138 for Purposes of Correspondence on the Claim

If the Regional Office comes back and requests any additional information, always use "VBA-21-4138-ARE – Statement in Support of Claim" for this purpose. This form was designed for communication purposes and VA recognizes it readily. Not that letters could suffice as well, just go ahead and use the form VA is used to. ***See the Claims Support Data Disk for submitting to VA's Claims Intake Center.

18. Expect Scheduling of a Compensation and Pension Examination

A Compensation and Pension examination (C&P) may be ordered for your claim. The fully developed claim system incorporates "Disability Benefits Questionnaires" that VA encourages you to use with your private physician to turn in with your application. In many cases, the VA will accept DBQ's and not order a C&P exam. You should always do a DBQ, whether an exam is needed or not, as this provides an additional source of evidence that is available to the rater and can be compared to the results of the C&P exam if one is ordered.

Obtaining a C&P medical examination is part of VA's duty to assist the applicant. Examinations are allowed by regulation and could be required under the following circumstances.

- when a veteran files a claim for service connection and submits evidence of disability;
- when a service-connected veteran asserts a worsened condition;
- to provide medical nexus;
- to reconcile diagnoses;
- as directed by BVA; and
- as required by regulation

VA may accept a medical report from a private physician if it is "adequate for rating purposes." Prior to the fully developed claims process, C&P examinations were ordered in most Disability Compensation claims for several reasons:

- to obtain current medical information;
- to obtain information relevant to disability (such as functional impacts of an impairment) rather than the diagnostic and treatment information sought in a standard medical examination; and
- to have information from someone more independent than the applicant's treating physician might be.

If you submit the appropriate "Disability Benefits Questionnaire" with your application, chances are a C&P examination will not be needed.

In some cases, such as PTSD, neurological conditions, mental conditions and hearing loss, you can still submit your own DBQ (except for hearing loss) and it will provide counterbalancing evidence to the C&P exam that VA is required to order. Even for hearing loss, you should go to a doctor who has a hearing lab and have a state certified audiologist conduct a hearing test just in case VA's state certified audiologists make a mistake. Besides, for hearing loss, you almost always have to have tinnitus to get a ratable award. It is helpful to have a consultation with an ear nose and throat doctor (Otolaryngologist) to establish additional evidence that you have tinnitus.

The Disability Benefits Questionnaires are found on the Claim Support Data Disk. Find the appropriate one for your condition and have your doctor fill it out for you.

"In FY 2005 VA obtained more than a half million C&P examinations. VHA performed 84 percent of these examinations in its own medical facilities, and the remaining 16 percent were obtained from a contract examination provider (QTC, 2006). Examinations from VHA generally take about 35 days to complete, and those from the contract provider take about 38 days. Using contractors was part of a test program started in 2003, and VA has had good success with it and most Regional Offices currently continue to use contractors for some or all of the examinations.

Generally, the predetermination team in the Regional Office's VSC (Veterans Service Center) determines the kind of examination needed based on the available medical records and uses one or more of 54 examination worksheets (referred to as AMIE worksheets, after the Automated Medical Information Exchange system for which they were originally developed in 1997) to describe for the examiner the specific requirements of the examination. There are separate worksheets for specific diagnoses (e.g., diabetes mellitus, hypertension, cold injury, posttraumatic stress disorder [PTSD]) and for certain body systems (e.g., eye, genitourinary, dental and oral, mental, hemic disorders). There is also one sheet for a general medical examination. Although there are 54 different examination worksheets, the 10 most frequently requested examinations account for 67 percent of C&P exams." *"Information in these two paragraphs is taken from "A 21st Century System for Evaluating Veterans for Disability Benefits, Committee on Medical Evaluation of Veterans for Disability Compensation 2006"*

We have included 54 of these C&P examination worksheets from 2005 on the Data Disk for you. If you are scheduled to take a C&P exam, review the worksheet for the exam that you will be taking to make sure that you can be well prepared for it. It is very useful to know in advance what to expect so that you can think about your responses – if they are required – before you take the examination.

The Regional Office requesting an examination is responsible for specifying the type of examination required and any special reports or studies needed. The VHA health-care facility decides who will perform the examination and where and how the examination will be conducted. There is no requirement for the examiner to be a licensed physician or to be board-certified for most of the exams. For the hearing exam a state certified audiologist must be used. For mental disorders, including PTSD, a psychiatrist or PhD psychologist must be used or the examiner must be under the supervision of such a person. For neurological examinations, a neurologist is required. For other exams, the examiner could be a physician's assistant or a resident or possibly even a third-year medical student in a VA hospital. VA hospitals are teaching hospitals and always have a number of medical students and residents on staff.

In addition to medical information, such as the results of tests or examinations, the examiner may be asked to provide an expert opinion on such questions as whether a condition is related to a specific event during service in the military, or a preexisting condition was aggravated in service, or a condition may be a secondary manifestation or consequence of a condition that previously was service connected. In these cases, the examiner is asked to use the following terminology in the report from the examination:

is due to (100% sure);
more likely than not (greater than 50%);
at least as likely as not (equal to or greater than 50%); and
not at least as likely as not (less than 50%)

In 2006, VA's under secretary for health and under secretary for benefits initiated a mandatory certification procedure for clinicians who perform C&P examinations, directing CPEP to provide every clinician who performs C&P exams for VHA, whether employee or contractor, the necessary training to have a full understanding of the requirements of the process. . . . Individuals who meet the training requirements for certification will be tracked, and this data will be made available to the credentialing and privileging authority for their respective health care facility.

19. Decide How to Proceed if the Claimant Dies before the Claim Is Adjudicated
Here are the current rules governing what happens if a claim decision is not made and the claimant dies.

38 USC §5121. Payment of certain accrued benefits upon death of a beneficiary
(a) Except as provided in sections 3329 and 3330 of title 31, periodic monetary benefits (other than insurance and servicemen's indemnity) under laws administered by the Secretary to which an individual was entitled at death under existing ratings or decisions or those based on evidence in the file at date of death (hereinafter in this section and section 5122 of this title referred to as "accrued benefits") and due and unpaid, shall, upon the death of such individual be paid as follows:
(1) Upon the death of a person receiving an apportioned share of benefits payable to a veteran, all or any part of such benefits to the veteran or to any other dependent or dependents of the veteran, as may be determined by the Secretary.
(2) Upon the death of a veteran, to the living person first listed below:
(A) The veteran's spouse.
(B) The veteran's children (in equal shares).
(C) The veteran's dependent parents (in equal shares).
(3) Upon the death of a surviving spouse or remarried surviving spouse, to the children of the deceased veteran.
(4) Upon the death of a child, to the surviving children of the veteran who are entitled to death Compensation, dependency and indemnity Compensation, or Death Pension.
(5) Upon the death of a child claiming benefits under chapter 18 of this title, to the surviving parents.

(6) In all other cases, only so much of the accrued benefits may be paid as may be necessary to reimburse the person who bore the expense of last sickness and burial.
(b) No part of any accrued benefits shall be used to reimburse any political subdivision of the United States for expenses incurred in the last sickness or burial of any beneficiary.
(c) Applications for accrued benefits must be filed within one year after the date of death. If a claimant's application is incomplete at the time it is originally submitted, the Secretary shall notify the claimant of the evidence necessary to complete the application. If such evidence is not received within one year from the date of such notification, no accrued benefits may be paid.

If you read this law carefully, it says that evidence had to be on file at the time of death to determine a decision on the application. We are not sure, but we think that VA has found it convenient to say that regardless of what was in the claims file at the time of death, there is no benefit at the death of the claimant. Whether this is just convenient to avoid processing the claim or whether it is fairly common, we do not know. Prior to the substitution law, it was commonly accepted that "the claim – and thus the benefit – died with the claimant."

There must also be someone in the line of succession to receive the residual benefit that would have been paid to the death of the claimant. This is either a spouse or children. For purposes of veterans benefits, a child is defined as a minor age 18 or less, a full-time student age 23 or less, any other child age 30 or less who is also a veteran or a child any age who became totally dependent prior to age 18.

There is no option to pay to the estate of the claimant. Therefore if there are no individuals in the line of succession, there is no benefit. In this case, the benefit becomes an "accrued benefit for final costs" and the amount that would have been owing, if the application had been approved, could be used to pay for the out-of-pocket expenses of the person or persons who bore the expense of last sickness and burial. When there is a surviving spouse, application for an accrued benefit for final costs is made on the following form found on the Data Disk.

VBA-21-534EZ-ARE – Application for DIC, Death Pension, and or Accrued Benefits

Where there is no surviving spouse, application for this accrued benefit is made using the following form.

VBA-21-601-ARE – Application for Accrued Amounts Due A Deceased Beneficiary

The claim dying with the claimant was the situation prior to 2008 when Congress passed legislation allowing for someone to step in and take over the claim. This substitution can only take effect if there is someone in the line of succession to inherit the benefit from the first day of the month following the effective date to the month of death. For most senior veterans, there will be no children in the line of succession unless an adult child became totally dependent prior to age 18. This means for most senior veterans or their surviving spouses if the claim is for the surviving spouse and he or she dies before a decision is made, there is no benefit and there is no reason to file a substitution in case of death because it will be turned back. Here is the new law.

38 USC §5121A. Substitution in case of death of claimant

(a) Substitution.—(1) If a claimant dies while a claim for any benefit under a law administered by the Secretary, or an appeal of a decision with respect to such a claim, is pending, a living person who would be eligible to receive accrued benefits due to the claimant under section 5121(a) of this title may, not later than one year after the date of the death of such claimant, file a request to be substituted as the claimant for the purposes of processing the claim to completion.
(2) Any person seeking to be substituted for the claimant shall present evidence of the right to claim such status within such time as prescribed by the Secretary in regulations.
(3) Substitution under this subsection shall be in accordance with such regulations as the Secretary may prescribe.
(b) Limitation.—Those who are eligible to make a claim under this section shall be determined in accordance with section 5121 of this title.

Katrina J. Eagle is a veterans law attorney in San Diego. She can be reached at kjeagle@vetsjustice.com. Douglas J. Rosinski is of counsel in the law firm of Ogletree, Deakins, Nash, Smoak & Stewart in Columbia, South Carolina. He can be reached at doug.rosinski@ogletreedeakins.com.

In 2008, Congress passed a statute that explicitly created the right of certain family members to take the place of a claimant who dies awaiting a decision on a VA benefits claim. The law limits the pool of possible survivors eligible for substitution to spouses, children, and financially dependent parents of a veteran who died on or after October 10, 2008.

The VA's proposed rules to comply with the act define a "pending claim" as one that has been filed at a Regional Office but has not yet been adjudicated, which means no rating decision has been issued.

A "pending appeal" is created by the filing of a NOD in response to a denied claim. In either situation, if the claimant dies, an eligible survivor has one year from the date of the death to request substitution. Curiously, the VA's regulations do not require the agency to notify potentially eligible survivors--the onus is squarely on a survivor to request substitution.

An eligible survivor must request substitution in writing from the same Regional Office where the original claim or appeal is pending and must include the term "substitute" or "substitution," the deceased claimant's name, his or her claim number, and evidence supporting eligibility. The survivor can also request substitution by completing and submitting VA Form 21-0847.

If sufficient evidence is not provided or located in the existing file, the applicant may be asked to provide additional evidence. The VA will mail its response to the substitution request, but it has no deadline, so survivors cannot know how long a Regional Office will take to process and respond to a substitution request.

If a claimant dies after a NOD has been filed, a substitution request will put the claim or appeal on hold until the request has been processed. If no substitution request is forthcoming within a year from the claimant's death, the Regional Office will close the case.
When an appeal is already before the BVA when the veteran dies, the VA's proposed rules require the BVA to dismiss a pending appeal "without prejudice" when it receives notice of the death and return the entire claim to the Regional Office to await a substitution request. Again, if no substitution request is forthcoming within a year after the claimant's death, the case is closed.

If a request is received and approved, the case is returned to the BVA for resolution of the underlying claim.

Despite Congress's desire to ensure that a veteran's closest family members can step in and obtain the benefits that the veteran had earned but lost because of VA delay, the substitution process as currently proposed still contains pitfalls for the unwary. Therefore, it is important for attorneys and other advocates counseling veterans and their family members to know of the right of substitution and to persevere in exercising that right. The ultimate reward--the veteran's hard-earned benefits--is certainly worth it.

Use this form on the Data Disk to make a substitution claim.

VBA-21-0847-ARE – Request for Substitution of Claimant upon Death of Claimant

SECTION B – SUBMITTING APPLICATIONS FOR SPECIFIC TYPES OF CLAIMS

Claimants and beneficiaries for Compensation, Pension, Survivor Benefits and other benefits should now send all mail directly to VA's Intake Center in Jainesville, Wisconsin. Any material mailed directly to Regional Offices (RO) or Pension Management Centers (PMC) will automatically be re-directed by the U.S. Postal Service (USPS) to the intake center for scanning and processing. Jainsville, Wisconsin will scan and upload the digital images for processing. Please refer to the data disk for the appropriate PO Box in Jainesville for your claim

Below are the various types of claims found in this Section:

1. Submitting an "Intent to File" VBA Form 21-0966
2. Application for Aid & Attendance or Housebound with Compensation and DIC
3. Application for an Original Claim for DIC
4. Reconsidering or Reopening a Claim for A & A, Compensation or DIC
5. Specific Chronic Conditions Presumed Service-Connected with a Time Limit
6. Prisoner of War – Chronic Conditions, Service-Connected with No Time Limit
7. Ionizing Radiation – Chronic Conditions Presumed Service-Connected
8. Agent Orange – Chronic Conditions, Service-Connected with No Time Limit
9. Disability Caused by Illness, Combat or Other Injury Incurred in the Service
10. Secondary Service Connection or Aggravation of an Existing Condition
11. Exposure to Hazards, Chemicals and Harmful Environmental Conditions
12. PTSD – Posttraumatic Stress Disorder
13. Hearing Loss with or without Tinnitus
14. PTIU – Permanent and Total Disability Due to Individual Unemployability
15. Gulf War Disorders – Service Connection Is Presumed with a Time Limit
16. Request for Reevaluation or Change for an Existing Benefit
17. Section 1151 Claim
18. Tropical Diseases – Service Connection Is Presumed with a Time Limit
19. Special Monthly Compensation (SMC)
20. Specific Special Allowances
21. HISA (Housing Improvement and Structural Alterations) Grants

Understanding the Disability Rating System

Disability Ratings
If a claim is approved, VA will assign a disability rating from 0% to 100%. A 0% disability rating does not pay any benefit. Why then would one want such a rating? The answer is that by receiving a 0% rating, your Service Center has recognized that the disability is service-connected. You have already overcome a large hurdle towards getting a benefit. If, in the future, the disability worsens or causes a secondary disability, then service connection is already established and you now only have to provide evidence that the condition has worsened or that it has caused a secondary condition. We post the rates for 2015 below. You will notice that the difference between 90% and 100% is significant. This represents the loss of earnings capacity

between someone who might possibly still be employed and someone who at 100% is considered unemployable.

Disability Compensation Rate Table for 2015-16

Basic Rates - 10%-100% Combined Degree Only

Rates for 2016– In Dollars

Disability Percent	10%	20%	30%	40%	50%	60%	70%	80%	90%	100%
Veteran Alone	133.17	263.23	407.75	587.36	836.13	1,059.09	1,334.71	1,551.48	1,743.48	2,906.83
Veteran & Spouse			456.37	652.18	917.16	1,156.34	1,448.16	1,681.14	1,889.34	3,068.90
A/A for Spouse			44	59	74	88	104	118	133	148.64

If veteran has a spouse who requires A/A, add "A/A for spouse" to the amount of dependency and rate code above.

Combined Ratings

A single rating percentage can also be a combination of a number of disabilities rated at different percentages. For example, suppose a veteran has a rating for 50% for PTSD, a rating for 10% for hearing loss and a rating for 20% for back injury. These are all plausible ratings for a veteran exposed to the rigors of combat. The combined rating is not the sum of the individual ratings – 80%. It is a little bit more complicated. Here's how it works. To calculate the combined rating, you sort the percentages descending from the largest to the smallest. In this case the order is 50%, 20%, 10%. Next subtract the largest from 100% which yields 50%. This is the first number that is used to determine the combined rating. VA assumes that if the veteran is 50% disabled he or she only has the efficiency to perform work at a 50% level. Therefore if a veteran is 20% disabled from back injury on top of being 50% then the veteran can only perform 20% times 50% of the remaining efficiency. This is 10%. This is the next number that is added to the total. Now subtract the 10 % new efficiency-based rating from the 50% remaining efficiency for the first disability and you have a 40% remaining efficiency to perform work. Multiply this remaining efficiency of 40% times 10% for hearing loss and you get 4%. Now we add up the following numbers to get the combined rating – 50% +10% + 4% = 64 all %. This final number is rounded up or rounded down to the nearest 10% multiple and in this case the combined disability is 60% instead of the 80% that you would expect.

"A claimant who has three disabilities with each disability rated at 10 percent, receives a combined rating of 30 percent. A veteran with two service-connected disabilities, one rated 60 percent and one rated 10 percent, receives Compensation only at the 60 percent rate. The effect of combining additional ratings gives greater weight to multiple 10 percent ratings at the low end of the scale. The effect of additional 10 percent ratings is diminished if the primary diagnosis has a high rating. Having multiple low ratings increases the payment dramatically for a veteran whose primary diagnosis has a low rating; but it has a negligible or much smaller effect for veterans who have a single condition with a high rating such as 80 percent or more. A veteran at 90% single disability rating with multiple 10% to 30% secondary ratings will likely never get to 100%." *Information on rating is taken from "A 21st Century System for Evaluating Veterans for Disability Benefits, Committee on Medical Evaluation of Veterans for Disability Compensation 2006"*

If this is all confusing, we have included on the claim support Data Disk, "38 CFR Part 4 – Schedule for Rating Disabilities." This portion of 38 CFR is often referred to as the VASRD – standing for VA Schedule for Rating Disabilities. This 243 pages of material covers over 700 different conditions and how they are rated. It also contains information on using the rating schedule and how to calculate a combined rating. For those who don't want to calculate a combined rating, it includes rating tables for you that determine what the final combined rating is from a combination of different ratings. Rating service officers in the Regional Office, in the past, had to manually determine what the rating was for each condition and then derive them from the table if they were combined ratings. Now they have a computer program that does it for them. It has reduced a lot of error.

We believe that the schedule for rating disabilities can be useful to you if you want to see what sort of rating you will get for any given condition and how much you expect to be paid.

Disability Compensation Replaces the Earnings Capacity Lost Because of the Disability

> "Disability Compensation, as determined by the VASRD, is intended to replace average impairment in earnings capacity.
>
> Eligibility requires that a determination be made that the condition is a service-connected disability. Service-connected means that the condition occurred during or was aggravated by military service or, for chronic conditions, became evident within one year of discharge from the military. It does not require that the disability be work-related or be caused by conditions in the work environment. In this regard the VA Disability Compensation Program combines elements of both disability insurance voluntarily provided by employers and workers' Compensation programs mandated by government.
>
> Claimants with a combined rating between 60 to 90 percent who are determined to be unemployable solely as a result of service-connected conditions, qualify for IU (individual unemployability). Claimants determined to be entitled to IU qualify for the same benefit payment amount as those rated at the 100 percent disability level. Conditions or circumstances that result in the claimant not being employable override the medical impairment rating. IU is similar to the Social Security Disability Insurance (SSDI) program in that both provide payments because the beneficiary is deemed to be unemployable.
>
> Overall, veterans with service-connected disabilities have earnings plus Disability Compensation 7 percent above their average expected earnings. The average was higher at each rating level except at the 100 percent rating level where the combined earnings and Compensation was 9 percent less than expected. On average, veterans with a 30 percent or less combined disability rating do not experience serious wage loss. Approximately, 55 percent of 2.6 million veterans receiving Disability Compensation in 2007 were rated at 30 percent or less. Earnings losses for veterans with 40 percent to 90 percent combined rating did have wage losses, but their VA Disability Compensation more than made up the loss. In contrast, actual earnings losses plus Disability Compensation for veterans with 100 percent combined rating fall short of average expected earnings by about 9 percent. In 2007, 9.1 percent of veterans receiving Disability Compensation had a combined rating of 100 percent, up from 7.5 percent in 2001.
>
> On the other hand, there are considerable differences in earnings loss across different diagnoses for a given rating level, resulting in serious inequity in the payment system. For example, for veterans with a 50 percent combined rating, the range was from no earnings losses for genitourinary or endocrine medical conditions to over 40 percent earnings losses for non-PTSD mental conditions. Veterans with PTSD, Other Mental Disorders, and infectious diseases experience greater earnings losses than veterans diagnosed with other medical conditions rated at the same level." *Information on rating is taken from "A 21st Century System for Evaluating Veterans for Disability Benefits, Committee on Medical Evaluation of Veterans for Disability Compensation 2006"*

Identify below the Type of Claim or Claims That Fit Your Situation

Below are descriptions of various types of claims found in this chapter for the following:

1. Submitting an "Intent to File" VBA Form 21-0966
2. Application for Aid & Attendance or Housebound with Compensation and DIC
3. Application for an Original Claim for DIC
4. Reconsidering or Reopening a Claim for A & A, Compensation or DIC
5. Certain Chronic Conditions Presumed Service-Connected with a Time Limit
6. Prisoner of War – Chronic Conditions, Service-Connected with No Time Limit
7. Ionizing Radiation – Chronic Conditions Presumed Service-Connected
8. Agent Orange – Chronic Conditions, Service-Connected with No Time Limit
9. Disability Caused by Illness, Combat or Other Injury Incurred in the Service
10. Secondary Service Connection or Aggravation of an Existing Condition
11. Exposure to Hazards, Chemicals and Harmful Environmental Conditions
12. PTSD – Posttraumatic Stress Disorder
13. Hearing Loss with or without Tinnitus
14. PTIU – Permanent and Total Disability Due to Individual Unemployability
15. Gulf War Disorders – Service Connection Is Presumed with a Time Limit
16. Request for Reevaluation or Change for an Existing Benefit
17. Section 1151 Claim
18. Tropical Diseases – Service Connection Is Presumed with a Time Limit
19. Special Monthly Compensation (SMC)
20. Specific Special Allowances
21. HISA (Housing Improvement and Structural Alterations) Grants

Please read through the descriptions to identify the type of claim that best fits yours or the claimant's particular situation and then locate that particular type of claim further down in this chapter. Then follow the instructions for filing that particular claim.

Before you proceed with an application, it is extremely important that you read through all of the information pertaining to how to submit claims and how to provide evidence found in Chapter 3 in Section C and to understand the fully developed claim process in Section A above.

1. Submitting Application for an Intent to File, VA Form 21-0966

An "Intent to File" can be submitted in one of the following three ways (38 CFR 3.155):

(i) Saved electronic application. When an application otherwise meeting the requirements of this paragraph (b) is electronically initiated and saved in a claims-submission tool within a VA web-based electronic claims application system prior to filing of a complete claim, VA will consider that application to be an intent to file a claim.

(ii) Written intent on prescribed intent to file a claim form. The submission to an agency of original jurisdiction of a signed and dated intent to file a claim, on the form prescribed by the Secretary for that purpose, will be accepted as an intent to file a claim.

(iii) Oral intent communicated to designated VA personnel and recorded in writing. An oral statement of intent to file a claim will be accepted if it is directed to a VA employee designated to receive such a communication, the VA employee receiving this information follows the provisions set forth in § 3.217(b), and the VA employee documents the date VA received the claimant's intent to file a claim in the claimant's records.

Once you feel that you can justify a claim for benefits and not waste your time or VA's time, you should proceed to submit an "intent to file." An "intent to file," before March of 2015, was known as an "informal claim" for benefits. The "intent to file" allows you to notify your Regional Office that you will be submitting a substantially complete claim with the appropriate claims form in order to start the process at some future date. Actually, you have one year from filing an "intent to file" to providing the formal application for a substantially complete claim. Most importantly, the "intent to file" with establish an effective date for back-pay purposes. The effective date with be the first day of the month following receipt of the "intent to file."

***See the Claims Support Data DisK for submitting to VA's Claims Intake Center.

An "intent to file" is typically used for application for new benefits. If you are applying for an revaluation of existing benefits or a change in existing benefits, you should use a formal request either on the appropriate VA form or using VBA Form 21-4138, to establish an effective date. Here is the information that you should send to establish an effective date.

- VBA Form 21-0966 INTENT TO FILE
- A copy Veteran's Discharge (DD214 or equivalent)

We have provided the VBA 21-0966 INTENT TO FILE for you on the "Claim Support Data Disk" under the folder name "2 Application for Compensation and DIC." On the 0966, ignore #15 entirely (it is a huge hassle to have the claimant's rep sign). The claimant should be the only one signing. Also, do not use the electronic signature under #14a.

<u>Always include a copy of the veteran's honorable discharge (DD214 or equivalent) when you fax or deliver the "intent to file" to a regional office. Sometimes, with only a 0966 in hand, the regional office struggles to locate the veteran's records and establish his or her identity and service. Including the discharge will help VA immensely.</u>

Again, the primary purpose of an informal claim is to establish an effective date. When the "intent to file" is received, it will be date stamped and that date will become your effective date under most conditions. The effective date could be a later date if you don't meet the qualifications for the benefit at the time of filing. Remember, do not file an "intent to file" unless you are sure that you do have a valid claim for benefits.

The effective date governs the date of payment for benefits. For example, if your effective date is July 15, 2016 and the application gets approved on November 10, 2016, you will receive two payments by deposit. The first is a lump sum back-payment dating back to and starting on August 1, 2016 for the months of August, September, and October. The second payment will be the first of the monthly payments. The monthly payment, in this example, will be deposited on or around November 1, 2016. VA pays in arrears so this payment will represent October's benefit.

If you don't think that you can hand carry your "intent to file" into your Regional Office before the end of the current month, you are going to have to fax or mail it to VA's Intake Center in Jainesville, Wisconsin if you do not want to miss a month of payment. VA will not use a postal date or a delivery receipt or a mailroom diary for an effective date. The "intent to file" must officially be handled by a VSR and stamped by hand with the date stamp machine. We highly recommend faxing before the month's end. Save the original (or certified copy of the) discharge as well as the original 0966 and fax report to include in the fully developed claim you will submit later on. The fax report will act as your insurance in case the department loses it. See the data disc for fax information.

***See the Claims Support Data Disc for submitting to VA's Claims Intake Center

2. Application for Aid & Attendance or Housebound with Compensation and DIC

Understanding Claims for Aid and Attendance or Housebound Allowances
If the claimant is receiving the aid and attendance of another person because the claimant is so helpless as to be unable to perform certain activities of daily living independently, or the claimant is considered housebound, meaning he or she is basically confined to living quarters for life, there are additional benefits available as monetary allowances.

Please do not confuse the meaning of "aid and attendance" or "housebound." These phrases pertain to about 16 different monetary allowances that are available with Pension, Death Pension, Compensation and certain forms of Special Monthly Compensation. The phrase "aid and attendance" is especially confusing because most individuals have been led to believe that this is the name for Pension or Death Pension. Unfortunately, the media has chosen to call Pension and Death Pension "aid and attendance." There is no such VA disability benefit as an aid and attendance benefit. When we talk about aid and attendance or housebound benefits with Compensation or DIC or SMC, most people think we are talking about Pension. This is not the case.

VA rules do not allow a veteran or surviving spouse to receive Compensation or DIC at the same time they are receiving Pension or Death Pension. You must choose one or the other benefits but you cannot have any degree of both benefits together.

Aid and attendance and housebound allowances are additional amounts of money available with all VA disability income benefits to help individuals receiving these benefits cope with the added burden of helplessness or being housebound.

Criteria for the Need for Aid and Attendance
The criteria for a need for aid and attendance is found in the following:

§ 3.352 Criteria for determining need for aid and attendance and "permanently bedridden."
(a) Basic criteria for regular aid and attendance and permanently bedridden. The following will be accorded consideration in determining the need for regular aid and attendance (§3.351(c)(3):

- inability of claimant to dress or undress himself (herself),
- or to keep himself (herself) ordinarily clean and presentable;
- frequent need of adjustment of any special prosthetic or orthopedic appliances which by reason of the particular disability cannot be done without aid (this will not include the adjustment of appliances which normal persons would be unable to adjust without aid, such as supports, belts, lacing at the back, etc.);
- inability of claimant to feed himself (herself) through loss of coordination of upper extremities or through extreme weakness;
- inability to attend to the wants of nature;
- or incapacity, physical or mental, which requires care or assistance on a regular basis to protect the claimant from hazards or dangers incident to his or her daily environment.
- "Bedridden" will be a proper basis for the determination (meaning determination for aid and attendance). For the purpose of this paragraph "bedridden" will be that condition which, through its essential character, actually requires that the claimant remain in bed. The fact that claimant has voluntarily taken to bed or that a physician has prescribed rest in bed for the greater or lesser part of the day to promote convalescence or cure will not suffice.

It is not required that all of the disabling conditions enumerated in this paragraph be found to exist before a favorable rating may be made. The particular personal functions which the veteran is unable to perform should be considered in connection with his or her condition as a whole. It is only necessary that the evidence establish that the veteran is so helpless as to need regular aid and attendance, not that there be a constant need. Determinations that the veteran is so helpless, as to be in need of regular aid and attendance will not be based solely upon an opinion that the claimant's condition is such as would require him or her to be in bed. They must be based on the actual requirement of personal assistance from others.

Regular Aid and Attendance Provided by Relative (not the higher level)
(c) Attendance by relative. The performance of the necessary aid and attendance service by a relative of the beneficiary or other member of his or her household will not prevent the granting of the additional allowance.

Discussion of the Criteria

The Regular Need for Aid and Attendance

Because, certain of the criteria listed under the need for aid and attendance are a little unclear, here is the list of our experience with what VA considers aid and attendance activities.

1. Assistance with bathing/showering
2. Assistance with toileting
3. Assistance with feeding
4. Assistance with dressing/undressing
5. Assistance with transferring in/out of bed/chair
6. Assistance with incontinence
7. Assistance with ambulating
8. Assistance with keeping oneself ordinarily clean and presentable
9. Assistance with frequent need of adjustment of special prosthetic or orthopedic devices which cannot be done without aid
10. Having an incapacity (physical or mental) requiring care/assistance on a regular basis to protect patient from hazards or dangers incident to his/her daily environment
11. Is blind or so nearly blind as to have corrected visual acuity of 5/200 or less, in both eyes, or concentric contraction of the visual field to 5 degrees or less
12. Is a patient in a nursing home because of mental or physical incapacity
13. Meets the criteria of being totally bedridden as defined above

As is mentioned in the regulation, there does not need to be a certain number of these incapacities in order to determine a rating for aid and attendance. The rating service representative simply must determine from the evidence whether the claimant is so helpless as to require the regular aid and attendance of another person based on one or more of these conditions.

From our experience with the rating authority, the person who is applying or the spouse of the veteran who is applying should exhibit the need for and be receiving at least two of the services from #1 through #8 above and from #9 through #13, only one of these need apply.

It is also important to note that a relative or a member of the household providing aid and attendance services is acceptable for granting the additional regular – not the higher amount – allowance for aid and attendance. (The so-called higher amount is only available with SMC Schedule (r).) We suggest a note of caution when it comes to relatives or members of the household. To avoid any appearance of fraud, it is advisable that a care contract be written up between the member of the household or the relative providing the care, spelling out exactly what is provided and on what schedule. We recommend this person or persons keep a daily or weekly care log.

Since Compensation, DIC and SMC are not means tested programs – like Pension or Death Pension – it is unlikely that VA would require a relative or member of the household to be paid for services. This would only be the case if VA suspected that the service was not being provided as claimed. Payment for those services might be required on the same basis as any other professional or licensed entity providing these services to make the services appear legitimate.

Definition of Housebound

The definition of housebound from 38 CFR § 3.350(i) (1)(2) is the following:

(1) Has additional service-connected disability or disabilities independently ratable at 60 percent, separate and distinct from the 100 percent service-connected disability and involving different anatomical segments or bodily systems,

OR

(2) Is permanently housebound by reason of service-connected disability or disabilities. This requirement is met when the veteran is substantially confined as a direct result of service-connected disabilities to his or her dwelling and the immediate premises or, if institutionalized, to the ward or clinical areas, and it is reasonably certain that the disability or disabilities and resultant confinement will continue throughout his or her lifetime.

Most veterans are going to qualify for being "housebound" under the second option above. Not very many veterans are going to qualify by being 100% rated disabled and then having VA say that they have an equivalent combined rating of 60% from other disabilities. Please note that any veteran in this situation would not have a final rating of 160%. The most available is 100%. What this is saying is that VA has determined there are additional disabilities that could be rated at 60% independently without actually paying the veteran.

A number of appeals in the past have addressed what "substantially confined" means. Previous board decisions had determined that substantially confines means that the claimant is restricted to his house except for medical treatment purposes. The Court of Appeals for Veterans Claims overturned those previous BVA decisions.

> *Howell versus Nicholson, March 23, 2006 number 04-0624 CAVC*
> *"The term "substantially confined" is not defined by statute or regulation. See id. Because the meaning of the term "substantially confined" is ambiguous and there is no regulatory interpretation, "the Court must determine the meaning" of the term "and the Board's obligation" thereunder. Thompson v. Brown, 8 Vet. App. 169, 175 (1995); see also Jackson and Cropper, both supra. The Secretary submits that the clear implication of this term is that the requirement that one be "substantially confined" is met when the claimant is restricted to his house except for medical treatment purposes. The Secretary, citing to Senate Report No. 1745 (June 27, 1960), notes that in passing section 1114(s) Congress intended to provide additional Compensation for veterans who were unable to overcome their particular disabilities and leave the house in order to earn an income as opposed to an inability to leave the house at all. Mr. Howell does not contest this interpretation.*
>
> *To the extent substantial confinement does not include departures for medical purposes, we agree that the interpretation that the Secretary presents in his supplemental briefing is reasonable and consistent with statute and regulations. See Jackson, Thompson, and Cropper, all supra.*
>
> *Accordingly, we hold that leaving one's house for medical purposes cannot, by itself, serve as the basis for finding that one is not substantially confined for purposes of SMC-*

HB benefits, and the Board's interpretation of section 1114(s) to preclude the grant of SMC benefits on the basis of Mr. Howell's leaving his house in order to attend VA medical appointments was erroneous as a matter of law.

It should be noted that there are no housebound allowances for regular Compensation. The only allowances are for aid and attendance. There are only two situations concerning Compensation or DIC where there is a housebound allowance.

1. The first is a housebound allowance for a surviving spouse receiving DIC.

2. The second is an alternative higher level of payment under SMC(s) where a veteran who is totally disabled can get an additional monthly income if that veteran is considered housebound but is not in need of aid and attendance.

Identifying the Various Allowances Available for Application
Here are the aid and attendance allowances or housebound allowances available with Disability Compensation, DIC and SMC

Aid and Attendance or Housebound Allowances for Spouses or Surviving Spouses of Veterans

1. Gradually increasing allowances for the spouse of a veteran who needs aid and attendance and the veteran is at least 30% disabled. A different benefit corresponds to each 10% rating increase from 30% up to 100%
2. An aid and attendance or housebound allowance for a surviving spouse receiving DIC
3. An allowance for the spouse of a veteran who needs aid and attendance and the veteran is receiving SMC

Aid and Attendance or Housebound Incomes for Veterans who are Totally Disabled

1. An income under SMC Schedule (l) for a veteran who needs aid and attendance or is housebound and is receiving Disability Compensation at 100% disability
2. An income under SMC Schedule (s) for veterans 100% disabled or TDIU (with one single rating of 60%), who do not meet criteria for aid and attendance but do meet criteria for being housebound
3. Two special increased aid and attendance allowances for severely disabled veterans receiving SMC under Schedule (r) under very specific conditions

We will discuss each of these allowances and their application process below in the order in which they are listed above. Here are the forms that you will use with these applications.

VBA-21-4138-ARE – Statement in Support of Claim
VBA-21-2680-ARE – Exam for Housebound Status or Permanent Need for Regular A&A
FV13 – Care Provider Certification of Services
VBA-21-0779-ARE – Request for Nursing Home Information in Connection with Claim for Aid and Attendance
VBA-21-4142-ARE – Authorization and Consent to Release Information to the Department of Veterans Affairs
VBA-21-686c-ARE – Declaration of Status of Dependents

Applications for Aid and Attendance or Housebound for Spouses or Surviving Spouses

Basic Overview

These applications cover the following allowances.

1. Gradually increasing allowances for the spouse of a veteran who needs aid and attendance and the veteran is at least 30% disabled. A different benefit corresponds to each 10% rating increase from 30% up to 100%
2. An aid and attendance or housebound allowance for a surviving spouse receiving DIC
3. An allowance for the spouse of a veteran who needs aid and attendance and the veteran is receiving SMC

Disability Compensation Rate Table for 2015-16

Basic Rates - 10%-100% Combined Degree Only

Rates for 2016– In Dollars

Disability Percent	10%	20%	30%	40%	50%	60%	70%	80%	90%	100%
Veteran Alone	133.17	263.23	407.75	587.36	836.13	1,059.09	1,334.71	1,551.48	1,743.48	2,906.83
Veteran & Spouse			456.37	652.18	917.16	1,156.34	1,448.16	1,681.14	1,889.34	3,068.90
A/A for Spouse			44	59	74	88	104	118	133	148.64

If veteran has a spouse who requires A/A, add "A/A for spouse" to the amount of dependency and rate code above.

Dependency and Indemnity Compensation for 2015-16

Effective 12/1/14

Basic Monthly Rate = $1,254.19

Additional Allowances:

1. Add **$266.32** for veteran's death, if veteran was in receipt of or entitled to receive compensation for a service-connected disability rated totally disabling (including a rating based on individual unemployability) for a continuous period of at least 8 years immediately preceding death AND the surviving spouse was married to the veteran for those same 8 years. (38 U.S.C. 1311(a)(2))
2. Add the following allowance for each dependent child under age 18: Effective 12/1/14 **$310.71** per child (38 U.S.C. 1311(b))
3. If the surviving spouse is entitled to A&A, add **$310.71.** (38 U.S.C. 1311(c))
4. If the surviving spouse is entitled to Housebound, add **$145.55** (38 U.S.C. 1311(d))
5. If the surviving spouse has one or more children under the age 18 on the award, add the 2-year transitional benefit of **$270** effective, December 1, 2014 (38 U.S.C. 1311(f))

Instructions for Application

These are additional allowances that are tacked onto an existing benefit that the spouse or the veteran is receiving. There is no need here for an original application. You must simply notify VA that you qualify for the benefit and that you are requesting the additional amount. All of the forms are found under the folder "2 Application for Compensation and DIC" on the Data Disk.

If it is going to take you awhile to assemble the evidence for aid and attendance or housebound, do an "intent to file" using the following form:

VA Form 21-0966 INTENT TO FILE

1. First of all, you must provide medical evidence that you are in need of the aid and attendance of another person or you are housebound. Use the following form for this and have the physician or specialist treating the person who needs aid and attendance or is housebound fill out the form.

VBA-21-2680-ARE – Exam for Housebound Status or Permanent Need for Regular A&A

2. In the case of an application for aid and attendance, you must show that someone is providing those services. Use the following form.

FV13 – Care Provider Certification of Services

If the applicant is confined to a nursing home use this form instead.

VBA-21-0779-ARE – Request for Nursing Home Info in Connection with Claim for Aid and Attendance

3. In the case of an application for housebound for DIC, you must provide evidence that the claimant is housebound. This is a letter that you ask the claimant's physician to write. The letter should state that_because of the condition or conditions outlined in the letter "the patient is confined to his or her dwelling and the immediate premises or, if institutionalized, to the ward or clinical areas, and it is reasonably certain that the disability or disabilities and resultant confinement will continue throughout his or her lifetime." The physician should identify the condition or conditions that are causing his patient to be housebound. If the physician is uncertain whether the patient will be housebound for the remainder of his or her life the physician might use the more acceptable probability statement of "more likely than not that (*"name of the patient"*) will be housebound for the remainder of her life." For a lengthier discussion of housebound, reread the section above pertaining to that.

4. Use the following form to request the additional allowance.

VBA-21-4138-ARE – Statement in Support of Claim

Enter the name of the veteran whether the veteran is living or deceased. Enter the VA case number for the Disability Compensation or SMC or DIC.

A. If the request is for aid and attendance or housebound with DIC use the following.

"I am the surviving spouse of the above name deceased veteran and I am receiving DIC. I am requesting that you provide the additional allowance under 38 CFR for *(use either "aid and attendance" or "housebound" here whichever applies)* as I now qualify for this additional benefit. I am enclosing medical evidence of the need for this additional allowance as well as evidence that my physical environment requires this additional support. I also include authorization for you to request my medical records if you so choose."

The signature is that of the person receiving DIC.

B. If the request is for the aid and attendance allowance with regular Compensation or SMC, use the following.

   The above name veteran is currently receiving *(use either "Disability Compensation" or "SMC" here whichever applies)* from the Department of Veterans Affairs. I am the legal spouse of this veteran and we have been living together continuously since he first received his award. I now qualify for the aid and attendance allowance under *("Disability Compensation" or "SMC").* I am enclosing medical evidence of the need for the aid and attendance of another person as well as certification of service by the care provider who is providing aid and attendance. In addition, I am attaching the appropriate form to verify our current marital status. I also include authorization for you to request my medical records if you so choose."

   Include the following form with a request for aid and attendance.

   VBA-21-686c-ARE – Declaration of Status of Dependents

5. Sign the release below for VA to obtain your medical records if they so choose.

   VBA-21-4142-ARE – Authorization and Consent to Release Information to the Department of Veterans Affairs

***See the Claims Support Data Disc for submitting to VA's Claims Intake Center

Application for Aid and Attendance or Housebound for Veterans Totally Disabled

Description of Aid and Attendance or Housebound under SMC
For veterans totally disabled, and who need aid and attendance or are housebound, there are Special Monthly Compensation benefits available to assist them with their needs.

Four different SMC's can be paid to veterans for assistance with aid and attendance or housebound: (l), (s), (r1) and (r2).

In 2007, 45,773 veterans received SMC (l), (s), (r1), (r2) for assistance and they received $30,506,362 above the amount that would normally be paid for the 100 percent rating. This was an average of $660 per month above what would normally have been paid without the assistance allowance.

We will discuss the application process below for two of these benefits – SMC (l) and SMC (s). For these benefits the general qualification is that the claimant is rated 100% disabled – SMC (l) – or is 100% or TDIU with at least one single disability rated at 60% or more – SMC (s).

It may be possible for an older claimant to make a new application or request an increase in rating and possibly get 100% or get 60% and then go for unemployability. (No other combinations will get you these special benefits.) In this case, you would have to go to the particular type of claim further on in this document and make new application or request for reevaluation, which new claim, would include evidence of needing aid and attendance or housebound, which in turn would lead to one of the two SMC's – (l) or (s) – all based on a single application for benefit.

***See the Claims Support Data Disc for submitting to VA's Claims Intake Center

Special Monthly Compensation (SMC) Rate Table for 2015-16

Rates for 2016– In Dollars

SMC Schedule	L	L½	M	M½	N	N½	O/P	R.1	R.2	S
Veteran Alone	3,617.02	3,803.58	3,991.74	4,266.32	4,540.89	4,807.36	5,075.60	7,252.63	8,318.95	3,253.67
Veteran & Spouse	3,779.09	3,965.65	4,153.80	4,428.38	4,702.96	4,969.43	5,237.67	7,414.70	8,481.02	3,415.74
A/A for Spouse	148.64	148.64	148.64	148.64	148.64	148.64	148.64	148.64	148.64	148.64

K	**$103.23**	Usually added to other rate or paid as the rate when percentage is zero.
Q	**$68.14**	Paid in place of a rate.

If veteran has a spouse who requires A/A, add "A/A for spouse" to the amount of dependency and rate code above.

Application for SMC (l) for Aid and Attendance
SMC (l) can be awarded either for loss of or loss of use of limbs or organs or to veterans rated 100 percent without such loss if they are in need of regular Aid and Attendance; in other words, if they need assistance with activities of daily living.

In 2007, 48 percent of 13,928 veterans receiving SMC (l) were receiving that award because they needed assistance, rather than for loss of or loss of use of organs or limbs. We are primarily interested in the award for aid and attendance and not for loss of use.

A rating of SMC(l) would include:

- The anatomical loss or loss of use of:
  - o Both feet,
  - o One hand and one foot
- Blindness in both eyes with visual acuity of 5/200 or less.
- Permanently bedridden.
- Regular need for aid and attendance to assist with activities of daily living such as dressing oneself, tending to personal hygiene, care and adjustment of assistive appliances or prosthetics, feeding oneself, and the like. (specific criteria is established in 38 CFR § 3.352(a)) (*if such services are not being provided at the expense of the U.S. Government due to hospitalization).

If it is going to take you some time to assemble the evidence for aid and attendance or housebound, do an "Intent to File" using the following form:

VA Form 21-0966 – INTENT TO FILE

Here are the documents to use if you are moving from Compensation with a rating of 100% to SMC (l)

VBA-21-4138-ARE – Statement in Support of Claim
VBA-21-2680-ARE – Exam for Housebound Status or Permanent Need for Regular A&A
FV13 – Care Provider Certification of Services
VBA-21-0779-ARE – Request for Nursing Home Info in Connection with Claim for Aid and Attendance (use this only if you are in nursing home and don't use FV 13 above, this form is sufficient)

1. First of all, you must provide medical evidence that you are in need of the aid and attendance of another person. Use the following form for this and have the physician or specialist treating the person who needs the aid and attendance or who is housebound fill out the form.

A. Proof for regular need for aid and attendance

VBA-21-2680-ARE – Exam for Housebound Status or Permanent Need for Regular A&A

2. In the case of an application for aid and attendance, you must show that someone is providing those services. Use the following form.

FV13 – Care Provider Certification of Services

If the applicant is confined to a nursing home use this form instead.

VBA-21-0779-ARE – Request for Nursing Home Info in Connection with Claim for Aid and Attendance

Where the request is for the aid and attendance allowance with SMC, use the following narrative and insert it into a VA Form 21-4138. Make sure you identify the veteran receiving SMC on this form.

> "I am the above name veteran and I am currently receiving a monetary award from the Department of Veterans Affairs for disability. I now believe I qualify for the aid and attendance allowance under SMC Schedule (l). I am enclosing medical evidence of the need for the aid and attendance of another person as well as certification of service by the care provider who is providing aid and attendance. In addition, I am attaching the appropriate form to verify my current marital status. I also include authorization for you to request my medical records if you so choose."

5. Sign the release below for VA to obtain your medical records if they so choose.

VBA-21-4142-ARE – Authorization and Consent to Release Information to the Department of Veterans Affairs

PLEASE NOTE THAT THE CONDITION THAT CAUSES THE APPLICANT TO NEED AID AND ATTENDANCE MUST BE RELATED TO OR BE A DIRECT RESULT OF THE SERVICE-CONNECTED CONDITION FOR WHICH THE VETERAN IS RECEIVING COMPENSATION. Make absolutely sure that the medical report that the doctor provides indicates that the need for aid and attendance is a result of one or more of the service-connected conditions for which the veteran is receiving compensation. Without this important information, the claim will be denied.

Application for SMC (s) for Housebound

In essence, one way to qualify for this benefit is that you must either have a combined or single total rating of 100% OR you must have received a rating from VA as TDIU based on a single rating – not based on multiple ratings. TDIU is available in two ways. Either having a single rating of 60% or more or having multiple independent ratings that combine to 70% or more with at least one of the independent ratings at 40%. You cannot get SMC (s) based on the second option – only on the single 60% or more rating. Note that the 60% rating can be due to a number of disabilities that share a common cause or condition.

You qualify as housebound in two ways. You can be totally confined to your home or apartment and expect to be such for the remainder of your life – Or, the alternative way to qualify is to be rated 100% disabled and have a second independently rated disability at 60% or more. The first condition for housebound requires medical evidence from a doctor but the second condition automatically qualifies for housebound and the evidence for further application below under is not needed. If the veteran is entitled to Housebound benefits by statute (without demonstrating need, under 38 U.S.C. 1114(s)), the additional disability(ies), rated 60 percent or more disabling, must

- be separate and distinct from the single disability, rated totally disabling, and
- involve separate anatomical segments or body systems.

If it is going to take you some time to assemble the evidence for aid and attendance or housebound, do an "Intent to File" using the following form:

VA Form 21-0966 – INTENT TO FILE

If application is to be made based on a rating of 100% only or TDIU with a single rating of 60%, here's how you would approach it.

1. First of all, if you qualify for being housebound by being totally confined, you must provide medical evidence that you are housebound. Use the following form for this and have the physician or specialist treating the person who is housebound fill out the form.

VBA-21-2680-ARE – Exam for Housebound Status or Permanent Need for Regular A&A

In addition to the exam above you need to ask the doctor to write a letter for you expressing an opinion that you are housebound. This is a letter that the claimant's physician writes. The letter should state that_because of the condition or conditions outlined in the letter "the patient is confined to his or her dwelling and the immediate premises or, if institutionalized, to the ward or clinical areas, and it is reasonably certain that the disability or disabilities and resultant confinement will continue throughout his or her lifetime." The physician should identify the condition or conditions that are causing his patient to be housebound. If the physician is uncertain whether the patient will be housebound for the remainder of his or her life the physician might use the more acceptable probability statement of "more likely than not that (*"name of the patient"*) will be housebound for the remainder of her life." For a lengthier discussion of housebound, reread the section above pertaining to that.

2. Use the following form to request the additional allowance.

    VBA-21-4138-ARE – Statement in Support of Claim

Enter the name of the veteran. Enter the VA case number for the Disability Compensation benefit the veteran is receiving.

A. Use the following written request.

    "I am requesting that you provide the housebound allowance under 38 USC for SMC Schedule (s). I now believe I qualify for this additional benefit. I am enclosing medical evidence of the need for this additional allowance as well as evidence that my physical environment requires this additional support. I also include authorization for you to request my medical records if you so choose."

    The signature is that of the veteran receiving Compensation.

PLEASE NOTE THAT THE CONDITION THAT CAUSES THE APPLICANT TO BE HOUSEBOUND MUST BE RELATED TO OR BE A DIRECT RESULT OF THE SERVICE-CONNECTED CONDITION FOR WHICH THE VETERAN IS RECEIVING COMPENSATION. Make absolutely sure that the medical report that the doctor provides indicates that the need for aid and attendance is a result of one or more of the service-connected conditions for which the veteran is receiving compensation. Without this important information, the claim will be denied.

Application for SMC (r1) or (r2) Special Aid and Attendance Allowance and Higher Level
Ratings under SMC(r) are assigned for seriously disabled veterans in need of advanced levels of aid and attendance. SMC(r) ratings require a minimal combination of entitlement to both SMC(o) and SMC(l). Additionally, Veterans in receipt of SMC rates based on Aid and Attendance are strongly advised to contact their service representative and/or VA Regional Office should they become hospitalized at the expense of the U.S. Government (i.e. a VA medical facility) as failure to do so could create an overpayment of monetary benefits.

SMC (r1) is a level of aid and attendance allowance that is available for this particular rating. SMC (r2) is the so-called higher-level of aid and attendance above that level in the sentence above. This level is for daily specialized care in the home by licensed health care providers.

This is not an application that you would do yourself. If a veteran is currently 100% disabled and needing aid and attendance in a home on a daily basis or in a facility due to loss of use of various bodily physical systems, this particular benefit may be available.

You must contact a service organization to find out how to apply for this benefit.

3. Application for an Original Claim for DIC

Understanding DIC
Dependency and Indemnity Compensation or DIC for short is a death benefit available to a surviving spouse and or dependent children after the death of a veteran. In order to receive a benefit, the veteran must have died during service or have died after service from a service-connected condition or from negligent treatment in a veterans health facility.

There are a number of ways to create eligibility for an award. Any one of these could trigger a benefit.

1. The veteran died while on active service
2. The veteran had a service-connected disability or disabilities that were either the principal or contributory cause of the veteran's death
3. The veteran died from non service-connected injury or disease AND was receiving, or entitled to receive VA Compensation for a service-connected disability rated totally disabling (rated 100% or TDIU) for at least 10 years immediately before death;
4. The veteran died from non service-connected injury or disease AND was receiving, or entitled to receive VA Compensation for a service-connected disability rated totally disabling (rated 100% or TDIU) for at least 5 years after the veteran's release from active duty preceding death;
5. The veteran died from non service-connected injury or disease AND was receiving, or entitled to receive VA Compensation for a service-connected disability rated totally disabling (rated 100% or TDIU) for at least 1 year before death, if the veteran was a former prisoner of war who died after September 30, 1999

It is important to note that total disability for purposes of DIC means either a rating of 100% or being totally disabled due to individual unemployability (TDIU). This alternative allows a veteran rated 60% or more for a single disability or 70% or more for combined disabilities (with at least one at 40%) to qualify due to unemployability for the 100% rating. For a further discussion on unemployability please go to the appendix.

Here are the current rates for DIC. You will notice that there is a bonus of $258 a month for a surviving spouse if the veteran died as a result of service-connected disability and was on claim for a continuous period of at least eight years before death and the two of them lived together continuously for that period of time. You also note that there is an additional allowance of $301 a month if the surviving spouse needs aid and attendance and an additional $141 a month if the surviving spouse is housebound. Also a dependent child under the age of 18 could receive an additional $301 a month if living with the surviving spouse or the child could receive it if there was no surviving spouse.

Dependency and Indemnity Compensation for 2015-16

Effective 12/1/14

Basic Monthly Rate = $1,254.19

Additional Allowances:

1. Add **$266.32** for veteran's death, if veteran was in receipt of or entitled to receive compensation for a service-connected disability rated totally disabling (including a rating based on individual unemployability) for a continuous period of at least 8 years immediately preceding death AND the surviving spouse was married to the veteran for those same 8 years. (38 U.S.C. 1311(a)(2))
2. Add the following allowance for each dependent child under age 18: Effective 12/1/14 **$310.71** per child (38 U.S.C. 1311(b))
3. If the surviving spouse is entitled to A&A, add **$310.71.** (38 U.S.C. 1311(c))
4. If the surviving spouse is entitled to Housebound, add **$145.55** (38 U.S.C. 1311(d))
5. If the surviving spouse has one or more children under the age 18 on the award, add the 2-year transitional benefit of **$270** effective, December 1, 2014 (38 U.S.C. 1311(f))

Different Types of Claims

The different benefit triggers for receiving DIC result in a number of different options for filing claims for the benefit. Although all claims for DIC have certain elements that are common, each of these options has a somewhat different approach to making application that is beyond these common elements. Here are the most common types of claims.

1. ***Automatic Benefit***
   The veteran was on claim for Disability Compensation and was married to a surviving spouse when the veteran died. The veteran did meet one of the three non-service-connected death requirements at 100% disability or TDIU and as such the benefit should be automatically awarded based on a formal claim for DIC.

2. ***The Veteran Was on Claim for Compensation but Fails Test for Automatic Benefit***
   The veteran was on claim for Disability Compensation and was married to a surviving spouse when the veteran died. The veteran did not meet any of the requirements for non-service-connected death for the automatic benefit at total disability, but it appears that the service-connected disability was the cause of or contributory to the death.

3. ***The Veteran Never Made a Claim for Compensation but Could Be Presumed Service-Connected***
   The veteran was not on claim for Disability Compensation and was married to a surviving spouse when the veteran died. A claim for Disability Compensation was never made while the veteran was alive, but the surviving spouse believes that the death was caused by an injury, exposure or illness incurred during service that is presumed to be service-connected. This type of claim could be very feasible if the veteran was in

Vietnam and exposed to Agent Orange and died as a result of one of the presumptive conditions for Agent Orange such as type II diabetes or arteriosclerotic heart disease. However, the veteran never made claim while the veteran was alive.

4. ***The Veteran Never Made a Claim and the Survivor Must Prove Service Connection***
The veteran was not on claim for Disability Compensation and was married to a surviving spouse when the veteran died. A claim for Disability Compensation was never made while the veteran was alive, but the surviving spouse believes that the death was caused by an injury, exposure or illness incurred during service that requires evidence to be service-connected.

5. ***The Veteran's Death Could Be the Result of a Section 1151 Claim That Has Not yet Been Filed***
In order to support a claim for DIC under 38 USC 1151, the evidence must show the deceased veteran died as a result of undergoing VA hospitalization, medical or surgical treatment, examination, or training; and the death was:

    - the direct result of VA fault such as carelessness, negligence, lack of proper skill, or error in judgment; OR
    - the direct result of an event that was not a reasonably expected result or complication of the VA care or treatment; OR
    - the direct result of participation in a VA Vocational Rehabilitation and Employment or compensated work therapy

6. ***The Surviving Spouse Needs Aid and Attendance or Is Housebound***
The surviving spouse, making application for DIC under one of the options above, also has a need for aid and attendance or is housebound.

Further on we will provide you the steps to take for filing an application for each one of these claim options. In the meantime, let us examine the elements common to DIC claims.

Elements Common to Every Type of Claim for DIC

- You must submit a death certificate for the deceased veteran for a claim for DIC. If the veteran died under circumstances where there is no death certificate or has been missing and presumed dead, there are equivalent ways to establish death. There is a form on the Data Disk if the veteran has been missing and presumed dead for seven years or longer. VA will accept that as evidence of death if the absence is of this length or longer. For alternative evidence of death, there is a section on evidence for death and marriage in the Appendix of the book.

- A copy of the marriage license is required for application for DIC. It may not be required for other applications for other benefits, but it is in this case. If a marriage license is not available there are alternative ways to establish a marriage relationship. Please read the section on evidence for death and marriage in the Appendix of the book.

- Entitlement to DIC will be from the first of the month in which the veteran died if a claim is made within one year of the date of the veteran's death.

- If a claim is made beyond one year of the date of the veteran's death, entitlement will from the date in which the claim was received.

- Claims for a surviving spouse or a child are treated the same. A child is defined as a minor younger than age 18, or an individual younger than age 23, attending school full-time or an adult child who became helpless and totally dependent due to a mental or physical disability prior to his or her 18th birthday.

Elements Common to All Claims for DIC except the Automatic Benefit Claim

- Where they are available, always obtain private medical records of the deceased veteran. Don't rely on VA to do this for you.

- Each claim should be accompanied by opinion letters from the deceased veteran's primary care physician or from physicians who treated the deceased veteran prior to death, that the death was caused by a service-connected condition. We have provided such a form for you on the Data Disk and a copy of it is included below. Print out copies of this form and persuade the attending physicians to produce the appropriate opinion letters for you. This could often make the difference between receiving the award and receiving a denial.

***See the Claims Support Data Disk for submitting to VA's Claims Intake Center.

FV30 – Determining Cause of Death for Awarding an Income Benefit for Survivors of a Veteran (DIC)

Name of the Deceased Veteran ______________________________ SSN __________

Address of the Deceased Veteran ______________________________

______________________________ Date ______________

Dear Physician,

The above named veteran was a patient of yours prior to this person's death, or you treated this person proximate to this person's death.

The surviving spouse and/or dependent children of the above patient are applying for a monthly death benefit income from the Department of Veterans Affairs that could be payable as a result of this death. In order to apply for this benefit, we need your opinion as to which illnesses, disorders or disabling conditions of the patient were the principal cause of death and in addition which illnesses, disorders or disabling conditions were contributory causes of death. The definitions of "principal cause" and "contributory cause" are included below as excerpts from government regulations.

The purpose of this opinion letter is to determine whether the patient's chronic conditions, prior to death, that were attributed to an injury, illness or exposure incurred during active duty service in the military, are the cause of death. If death was a result of one or more pre-death, military service-connected conditions, then there is a payable benefit for the spouse or children. We are not asking you to determine if these conditions are connected to service.

Please use the following phraseology when expressing your opinion as to the likelihood of causes of death. Please identify when expressing your opinion whether it is for a principal cause or a contributory cause of death

"is due to"
(Physician is 100% sure that the identified illness, disease, disorder or chronic disabling condition is either a principal cause of death or a contributing cause of death);

"more likely than not"
(Physician feels there is a greater than 50% probability that the identified illness, disease, disorder or chronic disabling condition is either a principal cause of death or a contributing cause of death);

"at least as likely as not"
(Physician feels there is an equal to or greater than 50% probability that the identified illness, disease, disorder or chronic disabling condition is either a principal cause of death or a contributing cause of death);

"not at least as likely as not"
(Physician feels there is less than a 50% probability that the identified illness, disease, disorder or chronic disabling condition is either a principal cause of death or a contributing cause of death);

Guidelines for Determining the Principal and Contributory Causes of Death

Principal Cause of Death

The chronic disability or chronic condition will be considered as the principal (primary) cause of death when such disability, singly or jointly with some other condition, was the immediate or underlying cause of death or was etiologically related thereto.

Contributory Causes of Death

1. **Contributory cause shared substantially or materially in producing death.** Contributory cause of death is inherently one not related to the principal cause. In determining whether the chronic disability or chronic condition contributed to death, it must be shown that it contributed substantially or materially; that it combined to cause death; that it aided or lent assistance to the production of death. It is not sufficient to show that it casually shared in producing death, but rather it must be shown that there was a causal connection.

2. **A condition quiescent or static in nature did not materially affect vital body functions and was likely not contributory.** Generally, minor chronic disabilities or chronic conditions, particularly those of a static nature or not materially affecting a vital organ, would not be held to have contributed to death primarily due to unrelated disability. In the same category there would be included disease or injuries of any evaluation (even though evaluated as 100 percent disabling) but of a quiescent or static nature involving muscular or skeletal functions and not materially affecting other vital body functions.

3. **Conditions involving active processes weakened the patient's ability to resist the effects of the primary cause and are likely contributory.** Diseases or injuries involving active processes, affecting vital organs, should receive careful consideration as a contributory cause of death, the primary cause being unrelated from the viewpoint of whether there were resulting debilitating effects and general impairment of health to an extent that would render the person materially less capable of resisting the effects of other disease or injury primarily causing death. Where the chronic condition affects vital organs as distinguished from muscular or skeletal functions and is evaluated as 100 percent disabling, debilitation may be assumed.

4. **A primary cause that eventually leads to death but in this instance was secondary unless it affected a vital organ.** There are primary causes of death which by their very nature are so overwhelming that eventual death can be anticipated irrespective of coexisting conditions, but, even in such cases, there is for consideration whether there may be a reasonable basis for holding that a chronic condition was of such severity as to have a material influence in accelerating death. In this situation, however, it would not generally be reasonable to hold that a chronic condition accelerated death unless such condition affected a vital organ and was of itself of a progressive or debilitating nature.

List chronic illnesses, chronic diseases, chronic disorders and chronic disabilities of the patient.

Condition #1 ____

____

Your Opinion – principal cause, contributory cause or not related to death ______________

____

Condition #2 ____

____

Your Opinion – principal cause, contributory cause or not related to death ______________

____

Condition #3 ____

____

Your Opinion – principal cause, contributory cause or not related to death ______________

____

Condition #4 ____

____

Your Opinion – principal cause, contributory cause or not related to death ______________

____

Condition #5 ____

____

Your Opinion – principal cause, contributory cause or not related to death ______________

____

Condition #6 ____

____

Your Opinion – principal cause, contributory cause or not related to death ______________

____

Name of Physician ______________________________

Address of Physician ____

Signature of Physician (must be licensed Doctor) ______________________

I, the above signing medical practitioner, hereby certify that the information given above is true and correct to the best of my knowledge and belief.

SVSA form FV30, March 2013

Elements of the Fully Developed Claim Process for DIC

1. Decide Whether the Condition Warrants Making a Claim
2. Always File an "INTENT TO FILE"
3. Get a Copy of Your Discharge and Locate Your Own Service Treatment Records (STR)
4. Obtain Your Own Private Medical Records
5. Have Your Private Doctors or Specialists Do Disability Evaluations
6. Have Your Doctors/Specialists Provide Opinion Letters If Service Connection Is Needed
7. Obtain or Produce Lay Evidence
8. Locate Records to Establish Assignment Location or Type of Duty Where Applicable
9. Make Sure the Evidence Conforms with the Rating Decision Criteria in Section C
10. Understand the Claim Forms and the Forms for Obtaining Records
11. Fill out the "Fully Developed Claim" Forms for the Claimed Benefit
12. Check and Double Check Everything and Include All Necessary Forms
13. Arrange for Representation and Third-Party Help If Needed
14. Provide a Cover Letter to Help the Service Representative Understand the Claim
15. Submit the Claim to Your Regional Office of Jurisdiction
16. Understand the Acknowledgment Letter from Your Veterans Service Center
17. Use VA Form 21-4138 for Purposes of Correspondence on the Claim
18. Expect Scheduling of a Compensation and Pension Examination
19. Decide How to Proceed if the Claimant Dies before the Claim Is Adjudicated

List of All Forms Needed for DIC Claims
These forms are found on the Data Disk under the folder entitled "2 Application for Compensation and DIC." These are the forms that would pertain to all of the application types listed below. Not every application type will require all of these forms.

VA Form 21-0966 – INTENT TO FILE
VBA-21-534EZ-ARE – Application for DIC, Death Pension, and or Accrued Benefits
FV30 – Determining Cause of Death for Awarding Income Benefit
VBA-21-4170-ARE – Statement of Marital Relationship
VBA-21-4171-ARE – Supporting Statement Regarding Marriage
VBA-21-4103-ARE – Information from Remarried Widow
VBA-21-1775-ARE – Statement of Disappearance
VBA-21-8416b-ARE – Report of Medical, Legal, and Other Expenses Incident to Recovery for Injury or Death
VBA-21-4142-ARE – Authorization and Consent to Release Information to the Department of Veterans Affairs

Forms for Representation for Assistance if Desired
VBA-21-22A-ARE – Appointment of Individual as a Claimant's Representative
VBA-21-0845-ARE – Authorization to Disclose Personal Information to a Third Party

Procedures for the Application Types below
Following this section, are 6 different types of applications for DIC. We will approach every application using these same procedures.

- First, you need to print out the document found on the Data Disk entitled "Elements of the Fully Developed Claim Process." This allows you to follow the steps in the claim process without having to go back and forth to the fully developed claim section in this book. A printout provides you a separate document that you can refer to as you read the instructions for each type of claim. You can also make notes on the document that you print out.

- Second, we will mention pertinent details pertaining to each particular kind of claim .

- Third, we will list the forms that should be used with each particular kind of claim application.

- Fourth, we will provide you the steps from the elements of the fully developed claim process that you will use for each particular type of claim.

1. Application for the Automatic Benefit

Details:
The veteran was on claim for Disability Compensation and was married to a surviving spouse when the veteran died. The veteran did meet one of the three non-service-connected death requirements at 100% disability and as such the benefit should be automatically awarded based on a formal claim for DIC. Here are the triggers for this automatic benefit award.

1. The veteran died from a non service-connected injury or disease AND was receiving, or entitled to receive VA Compensation for a service-connected disability rated totally disabling (rated 100% or TDIU) for at least 10 years immediately before death; OR

2. The veteran died from a non service-connected injury or disease AND was receiving, or entitled to receive VA Compensation for a service-connected disability rated totally disabling (rated 100% or TDIU) for at least 5 years after the veteran's release from active duty preceding death; OR

3. The veteran died from a non service-connected injury or disease AND was receiving, or entitled to receive VA Compensation for a service-connected disability rated totally disabling (rated 100% or TDIU) for at least 1 year before death, AND the veteran was a former prisoner of war who died after September 30, 1999

Forms to Use:
A copy of the death certificate or equivalent evidence
A copy of the marriage certificate or equivalent evidence

VBA-21-534EZ-ARE – Application for DIC, Death Pension, and or Accrued Benefits

Forms for Representation for Assistance if Desired
VBA-21-22A-ARE – Appointment of Individual as a Claimant's Representative
VBA-21-0845-ARE – Authorization to Disclose Personal Information to a Third Party

Steps in the Fully Developed Claim Process to Follow:
Because the veteran was already on claim prior to death, you simply need to notify VA of the death and the Department will send you the appropriate form to apply. This should be your only requirement.

2. Application for a Veteran Who Was on Claim for Compensation but Fails the Test for the Automatic Benefit

Details:
The veteran was on claim for Disability Compensation and was married to a surviving spouse when the veteran died. The veteran did not meet any of the requirements for non-service-connected death for the automatic benefit at total disability, but it appears that the service-connected disability was the cause of or contributory to the death.

This is similar to the automatic benefit above, in that you do not have to prove service connection for the disabilities for which the veteran was receiving benefits. There is one caveat to this however. If the veteran had developed secondary disabilities but had never made a claim and the secondary disabilities were the result of death, you will have to go through the process of establishing service connection for these disabilities. For this, you must go to application #3 below and follow that process.

When establishing service connection for a previously unclaimed service-connected disability, do not use VA form 526EZ. Use VA Form 21-534EZ that you normally use for DIC but submit all the evidence that you would normally submit for a new claim for Compensation. Follow all the steps in "The Elements of the Fully Developed Claim Process" as if you are filing a claim for Compensation.

If you are reasonably certain that the death was primarily due or secondarily due to the disabilities for which the veteran was receiving a benefit, then proceed with the process for this type of claim.

You will report the death to the Department and you will receive the appropriate instructions and forms to file a claim for DIC. Please follow our instructions below.

If it is going to take you some time to assemble the evidence for DIC, do an "Intent to File" using the following form:

VA Form 21-0966 – INTENT TO FILE

Forms to Use:
A copy of the death certificate or equivalent evidence
A copy of the marriage certificate or equivalent evidence
VBA-21-534EZ-ARE – Application for DIC, Death Pension, and or Accrued Benefits
FV30 – Determining Cause of Death for Awarding Income Benefit
VBA-21-4142-ARE – Authorization and Consent to Release Information to the Department of Veterans Affairs
VBA-21-4170-ARE – Statement of Marital Relationship (if needed)
VBA-21-4171-ARE – Supporting Statement Regarding Marriage (if needed)
VBA-21-4103-ARE – Information from Remarried Widow (if needed)
VBA-21-1775-ARE – Statement of Disappearance (if needed)

Forms for Representation for Assistance if Desired
VBA-21-22A-ARE – Appointment of Individual as a Claimant's Representative
VBA-21-0845-ARE – Authorization to Disclose Personal Information to a Third Party

Steps in the Fully Developed Claim Process to Follow:
1. Decide Whether the Condition Warrants Making a Claim
2. Always File an "Intent to File"
4. Obtain Your Own Private Medical Records
8. Locate Records to Establish Assignment Location or Type of Duty Where Applicable
10. Understand the Claim Forms and the Forms for Obtaining Records
11. Fill out the "Fully Developed Claim" Forms for the Claimed Benefit
12. Check and Double Check Everything and Include All Necessary Forms
13. Arrange for Representation and Third-Party Help If Needed
14. Provide a Cover Letter to Help the Service Representative Understand the Claim
15. Submit the Claim to Your Regional Office of Jurisdiction
16. Understand the Acknowledgment Letter from Your Veterans Service Center
17. Use VA Form 21-4138 for Purposes of Correspondence on the Claim
19. Decide How to Proceed if the Claimant Dies before the Claim Is Adjudicated

3. Application for a Veteran Who Never Made a Claim for Compensation but Whose Death Could Be Presumed Service-Connected

Details:
The veteran was not on claim for Disability Compensation and was married to a surviving spouse when the veteran died. A claim for Disability Compensation was never made while the veteran was alive, but the surviving spouse believes that the death was caused by an injury, exposure or illness incurred during service that is presumed to be service-connected.

You should read the information about making application for Compensation for presumed service-connected disabilities further on. Your claim is going to be a combination of a claim for presumed service-connected disability and DIC. For older veterans, the presumed service-connected is likely due to Agent Orange exposure in Vietnam. Read the section on Agent Orange claims below. Such Agent Orange conditions such as type II diabetes, Parkinson's disease, a number of common types cancers and ischemic heart disease which could have contributed to any number of heart conditions resulting in death, could very likely be the cause of death even though the veteran never made claim. Look at the other presumed service-connected disabilities to see if the deceased veteran may have qualified under one of these as well.

You can make claim years later and likely establish the service connection and then establish the connection between the disease or condition and the death of the veteran. When establishing presumed service connection for a previously unclaimed service-connected disability, do not use VA form 526 EZ. Use VA Form 21-534ezEZ that you normally use for DIC but submit all the evidence that you would normally submit for a new claim for Compensation. Follow all the steps in "The Elements of the Fully Developed Claim Process" as if you are filing a claim for Compensation combined with the claim for DIC.

If it is going to take you some time to assemble the evidence for DIC, do an "Intent to File" using the following form:

VA Form 21-0966 – INTENT TO FILE

Forms to Use:
The necessary forms to be used for an original claim for Compensation, which can be combined with the following forms:

A copy of the death certificate or equivalent evidence
A copy of the marriage certificate or equivalent evidence
VBA-21-534EZ-ARE – Application for DIC, Death Pension, and or Accrued Benefits
FV30 – Determining Cause of Death for Awarding Income Benefit
VBA-21-4142-ARE – Authorization and Consent to Release Information to the Department of Veterans Affairs
VBA-21-4170-ARE – Statement of Marital Relationship (if needed)
VBA-21-4171-ARE – Supporting Statement Regarding Marriage (if needed)
VBA-21-4103-ARE – Information from Remarried Widow (if needed)
VBA-21-1775-ARE – Statement of Disappearance (if needed)

Forms for Representation for Assistance if Desired
VBA-21-22A-ARE – Appointment of Individual as a Claimant's Representative
VBA-21-0845-ARE – Authorization to Disclose Personal Information to a Third Party

Steps in the Fully Developed Claim Process to Follow:
1. Decide Whether the Condition Warrants Making a Claim
2. Always File an "Intent to File"
3. Get a Copy of Your Discharge and Locate Service Treatment Records (STR)
4. Obtain Your Own Private Medical Records
5. Have Your Private Doctors or Specialists Do Disability Evaluations
7. Obtain or Produce Lay Evidence
8. Locate Records to Establish Assignment Location or Type of Duty Where Applicable
9. Make Sure the Evidence Conforms with the Rating Decision Criteria in Section C

10. Understand the Claim Forms and the Forms for Obtaining Records
11. Fill out the "Fully Developed Claim" Forms for the Claimed Benefit
12. Check and Double Check Everything and Include All Necessary Forms
13. Arrange for Representation and Third-Party Help If Needed
14. Provide a Cover Letter to Help the Service Representative Understand the Claim
15. Submit the Claim to Your Regional Office of Jurisdiction
16. Understand the Acknowledgment Letter from Your Veterans Service Center
17. Use VA Form 21-4138 for Purposes of Correspondence on the Claim
19. Decide How to Proceed if the Claimant Dies before the Claim Is Adjudicated

4. Application for a Veteran who Never Made a Claim and Whose Survivor Must Prove Service Connection

Details:
The veteran was not on claim for Disability Compensation and was married to the surviving spouse when the veteran died. A claim for Disability Compensation was never made while the veteran was alive, but the surviving spouse believes that the death was caused by an injury, exposure or illness incurred during service that requires evidence to be service-connected.

You must be reasonably certain that the deceased veteran did die as a result of a disability or condition incurred in the service. This is going to be a very difficult claim to make and could take a great deal of effort and time. No sense in wasting your time unless you are reasonably certain.

When establishing service connection for a previously unclaimed service-connected disability, do not use VA form 526 EZ. Use VA Form 21-534ezEZ that you normally use for DIC but submit all the evidence that you would normally submit for a new claim for Compensation. Follow all the steps in "The Elements of the Fully Developed Claim Process" as if you are filing a claim for Compensation.

Not only must you establish the service connection as if you were making an application for Compensation and prove that the condition or conditions the deceased veteran had were service-connected, but you must also follow through and provide evidence that the veteran actually died as a result of this possible service-connected condition. Read the section or sections below that pertain to this type of Compensation claim. The claim can involve two types of service connection: one which can be proven through service records and the other which cannot be proven, but private evidence is available to establish the service connection.

If it is going to take you some time to assemble the evidence for DIC, do an "Intent to File" using the following form: VA Form 21-0966 – INTENT TO FILE

Forms to Use:
The necessary forms to be used are for an original claim for Compensation, which can be combined with the following forms:

A copy of the death certificate or equivalent evidence
A copy of the marriage certificate or equivalent evidence
VBA-21-534EZ-ARE – Application for DIC, Death Pension, and or Accrued Benefits
FV30 – Determining Cause of Death for Awarding Income Benefit
VBA-21-4142-ARE – Authorization and Consent to Release Information to the Department of Veterans Affairs
VBA-21-4170-ARE – Statement of Marital Relationship (if needed)
VBA-21-4171-ARE – Supporting Statement Regarding Marriage (if needed)
VBA-21-4103-ARE – Information from Remarried Widow (if needed)
VBA-21-1775-ARE – Statement of Disappearance (if needed)

Forms for Representation for Assistance if Desired
VBA-21-22A-ARE – Appointment of Individual as a Claimant's Representative
VBA-21-0845-ARE – Authorization to Disclose Personal Information to a Third Party

Steps in the Fully Developed Claim Process to Follow:

1. Decide Whether the Condition Warrants Making a Claim
2. Always File an "Intent to File"
3. Get a Copy of Your Discharge and Locate Service Treatment Records (STR)
4. Obtain Your Own Private Medical Records
5. Have Your Private Doctors or Specialists Do Disability Evaluations
6. Have Your Doctors/Specialists Provide Opinion Letters for Service-Connected
7. Obtain or Produce Lay Evidence
8. Locate Records to Establish Assignment Location or Type of Duty Where Applicable
9. Make Sure the Evidence Conforms with the Rating Decision Criteria in Section C
10. Understand the Claim Forms and the Forms for Obtaining Records
11. Fill out the "Fully Developed Claim" Forms for the Claimed Benefit
12. Check and Double Check Everything and Include All Necessary Forms
13. Arrange for Representation and Third-Party Help If Needed
14. Provide a Cover Letter to Help the Service Representative Understand the Claim
15. Submit the Claim to Your Regional Office of Jurisdiction
16. Understand the Acknowledgment Letter from Your Veterans Service Center
17. Use VA Form 21-4138 for Purposes of Correspondence on the Claim
19. Decide How to Proceed if the Claimant Dies before the Claim Is Adjudicated

Some of these applications may involve establishing direct service connection for a veteran who never applied for benefits. There may not be a lot of evidence, but under some conditions it can be inferred that the veteran would have qualified for Compensation if VA cannot produce any evidence to the contrary. This situation will likely involve the doctrine of reasonable doubt.

A very good way to tip the scales in a decision that involves reasonable doubt is to find a physician who will write an opinion letter that the disability causing death was "at least as likely as not" to have been incurred in the service based on information provided by the veteran or spouse and an examination by the physician. This type of opinion does not put the pressure on the doctor to provide an opinion one way or another. You are very likely to get a doctor to give you this kind of opinion. The physician has opined that there is a 50-50 chance or greater it was incurred in service and if VA has no evidence to the contrary – under the doctrine of reasonable doubt (38 CFR 3.102) – the veteran will receive an award.

5. Application for a Veteran's Death that Could Be the Result of a Section 1151 Claim That Has Not yet Been Filed

Details:
In order to support a claim for DIC under 38 USC 1151, the evidence must show the deceased veteran died as a result of undergoing VA hospitalization, medical or surgical treatment, examination, or training; and the death was:

- the direct result of VA fault such as carelessness, negligence, lack of proper skill, or error in judgment; OR
- the direct result of an event that was not a reasonably expected result or complication of the VA care or treatment; OR
- the direct result of participation in a VA Vocational Rehabilitation and Employment or compensated work therapy

These types of claims are extremely difficult to prove unless there is good evidence that the treating personnel were negligent or incompetent. There is no question that negligence or incompetence associated with health care or other social services does occur. You will have to have access to the records of the treating facilities or organizations. Hearsay evidence or evidence of witnesses is not sufficient enough. You need some hard evidence of some kind.

If it is going to take you some time to assemble the evidence for DIC, do an "Intent to File" using the following form:

VA Form 21-0966 – INTENT TO FILE

Forms to Use:
A copy of the death certificate or equivalent evidence
A copy of the marriage certificate or equivalent evidence
VBA-21-534EZ-ARE – Application for DIC, Death Pension, and or Accrued Benefits
FV30 – Determining Cause of Death for Awarding Income Benefit
VBA-21-4142-ARE – Authorization and Consent to Release Information to the Department of Veterans Affairs
VBA-21-4170-ARE – Statement of Marital Relationship (if needed)
VBA-21-4171-ARE – Supporting Statement Regarding Marriage (if needed)
VBA-21-4103-ARE – Information from Remarried Widow (if needed)
VBA-21-1775-ARE – Statement of Disappearance (if needed)

Forms for Representation for Assistance if Desired
VBA-21-22A-ARE – Appointment of Individual as a Claimant's Representative
VBA-21-0845-ARE – Authorization to Disclose Personal Information to a Third Party

Steps in the Fully Developed Claim Process to Follow:

1. Decide Whether the Condition Warrants Making a Claim
2. Always File an "Intent to File"
3. Get a Copy of Your Discharge and Locate Service Treatment Records (STR)
4. Obtain Your Own Private Medical Records
5. Have Your Private Doctors or Specialists Do Disability Evaluations
6. Have Your Doctors/Specialists Provide Opinion Letters for Service-Connected
7. Obtain or Produce Lay Evidence
8. Locate Records to Establish Assignment Location or Type of Duty Where Applicable
9. Make Sure the Evidence Conforms with the Rating Decision Criteria in Section C
10. Understand the Claim Forms and the Forms for Obtaining Records
11. Fill out the "Fully Developed Claim" Forms for the Claimed Benefit
12. Check and Double Check Everything and Include All Necessary Forms
13. Arrange for Representation and Third-Party Help If Needed
14. Provide a Cover Letter to Help the Service Representative Understand the Claim
15. Submit the Claim to Your Regional Office of Jurisdiction
16. Understand the Acknowledgment Letter from Your Veterans Service Center
17. Use VA Form 21-4138 for Purposes of Correspondence on the Claim
19. Decide How to Proceed if the Claimant Dies before the Claim Is Adjudicated

6. Application to include a Surviving Spouse Who Needs Aid and Attendance or Is Housebound

Details:

The surviving spouse, making application for DIC under one of the options above, also has a need for aid and attendance or is housebound. This application is to be combined with one of the types already discussed above. Use the information in the section previously that provided for making application for aid and attendance with DIC and combine it with your original application for DIC based on any of the 5 types of possible claims above.

The Rating Decision for DIC

A reasonable probability of service-connected (SC) death exists if based on a rating decision made during the veteran's lifetime, one or more of the following exists:

- service connection was granted for any chronic disease under 38 CFR 3.309
- service connection was granted for a condition affecting any vital organ, or
- the veteran
  - had at least one SC disease or disability evaluated at 50 percent or more disabling
  - was rated 100 percent for an SC disease or disability, or
  - was entitled to individual unemployability (IU).

The rating activity must determine if, based on all evidence of record, it is at least as likely as not that the veteran's death was related to service. <u>If the answer to either of the questions listed below is "yes," grant service connection for the cause of death, otherwise deny it.</u>

1. Was service connection previously established for the disability that either caused the veteran's death or substantially or materially contributed to it?

2. If not, is service connection in order (able to be proved) for the disability that either substantially or materially contributed to or caused the veteran's death?

Note that the words "at least as likely as not" is VA verbiage for a 50-50 chance or greater that the conditions for an award are met. This is an important issue, because if this happens, this becomes the principle of reasonable doubt and VA must award the benefit if a 50-50 chance is present.

Offsets to DIC
DIC will not be paid if the survivors receive an award for damages due to the veteran's death of any of the following:

- judicial or administrative proceeding
- settlement
- administrative award,
- tort award,
- compromise, or
- Radiation Exposure Compensation Act (RECA) settlement payment.

Any such awards will be deducted from DIC or demanded back for overpayment. Attorney's fees, court costs, and other expenses incident to the civil claim are not deductible from the total amount awarded or accepted.

Benefits for DIC and the Survivor Benefit Plan (SBP) cannot be received concurrently. SBP is paid to the survivor of a deceased retired military service person who was receiving military retirement pay. If there are concurrent benefits, the military finance center will deduct the amount of DIC from SBP and pay the difference to the surviving spouse. If the amount is less than zero, there is no SBP and DIC is the only benefit. This offset does not apply if the SBP is being paid to a child or parent. One note. If DIC is being paid as a result of a deceased veteran spouse who was not retired military and SBP is being paid as a result of another deceased veteran spouse who was retired military, both benefits can be received concurrently.

4. Reconsidering or Reopening a Claim for A & A, Compensation or DIC

Reconsidering Evidence before a Final Decision Is Made
There is some confusion as to when a decision is final from VA and how that affects the effective date and the payment date for benefits. Until VA has made a final decision, the effective date remains the same unless the applicant was not eligible at the time of the effective date, in which case the date at which the claimant was eligible will become the new effective date.

A case can go on for many years until a denial is made. Once the denial is made, the claimant has one year to challenge that denial and still keep the effective date. After one year – with no new evidence for reversing the decision – the denial is referred to as a finally denied claim. After one year without a valid challenge, the effective date is lost. A lost effective date can be recaptured if new and material evidence is submitted that shows that clear and unmistakable error (CUE) resulted in the denial. In other words, if VA really screwed up and did not follow the proper regulation or adjudication procedure, a claim that was denied 20 years ago could go back to the original effective date and pay a retroactive benefit.

For various reasons, it is advantageous, in some cases, to keep VA from making a decision as more evidence is uncovered. This keeps open the effective date. On the other hand, at some point, the Regional Office will recognize that a claim is going on too long and that a considerable liability for back payment could be the result. This will often cause a rush to make a decision even if there is not enough evidence in the file to make that decision. Of course, this will result in a denial.

As we have mentioned previously, it is much better to file an informal claim and keep the final decision process open for at least a year until a formal claim needs to be filed. That is how long you have to act on the informal claim.

It is also important to understand that under 38 CFR 3.160, making requests on an existing award such as increasing a rating, filing for unemployability, applying for aid and attendance or housebound or reapplying for Pension (which is not an existing award) do not keep the original effective date. These are all considered new claims and you cannot go back to the original effective date to get back payment for an increase in benefit.

Reopening a Claim after a Denial Decision Is Made

Definition of a Reopened Claim and New and Material Evidence
A reopened claim is any claim for service connection, received after a finally denied claim, which VA must reconsider because the evidence it presents is new and material. A finally denied claim means that at least one year has elapsed since the letter was sent notifying the claimant of the decision to deny the benefit sought. Correspondence from a claimant asking for reconsideration for service connection is a claim to reopen.

New and material evidence is required before the Department of Veterans Affairs (VA) will reconsider a finally denied claim for service connection for a particular disability. A determination by VA that information constitutes new and material evidence means that the information, by itself, or when considered with previous evidence of record, relates to an un-established fact necessary to substantiate the claim and raises a reasonable possibility of substantiating the claim.

New information does not necessarily mean that the evidence warrants revision of a prior determination. A decision by the Regional Office not to reopen a claim because the evidence submitted is not new and material is an appealable decision. The date of receipt of statements from the claimant that are held to be new and material evidence may constitute an effective date for increased benefits under 38 CFR 3.400(q).

Description of New Evidence
New evidence is evidence not previously of record. Evidence is any means by which an alleged matter of fact is established or disproved. Examples of evidence include the following:

- testimony, to include
    - statements
    - contentions, and
    - arguments
- documentary proof
- medical examinations or reports, and
- other material not previously considered.

To qualify as "new evidence" under 38 CFR 3.156, evidence must be submitted to VA for the first time, whether documentary, testimonial, or in some other form. A claimant's own statement, covering in sufficient detail a condition that is within his/her ability to describe, such as his/her own symptoms, may to that extent constitute new evidence. While such statements have self-serving aspects, the claimant is often the most qualified source to describe the circumstances of the disabling effects of the disease or injury. If such statements are new and material and of sufficient probative value, they may serve as a basis for ordering a VA examination.

As an example of new evidence, a veteran injured while on duty may not have realized immediately that the condition required medical attention and may have sought treatment later that evening from a private physician. A Compensation claim might be denied if the service treatment records (STRs) contain no mention of treatment for the condition. Should the claimant subsequently submit proof of treatment by the civilian physician, that information would constitute new evidence on which the claim could be reopened.

The following does not constitute new evidence:

- a photocopy or other duplication of information already contained in a VA claims folder (since it was previously considered), or
- information confirming a point already established, such as a statement from a physician verifying the existence of a condition that has already been diagnosed and reported by another physician.

<u>Even though a medical evaluation is from a different doctor, it offers no new basis on which the claim might be reopened, unless it contains new information, such as evidence that the condition first manifested itself earlier and much closer to service than previously established.</u>

Description of Material Evidence
Material evidence is information that is relevant and relates to an un-established fact necessary to substantiate the claim, and has a legitimate influence or bearing on the decision in the case. In order to be considered "material evidence" under 38 CFR 3.156, the additional information must

bear directly and substantially on the specific matter under consideration. A medical opinion is not material if it relies on historical facts that are wholly inaccurate.

Here's an example of material evidence. VA has previously determined that a currently diagnosed back condition claimed by a World War II veteran is not service-connected (SC) because it is not related to an event, injury, or disease in-service. If VA receives evidence that the claimant received treatment shortly after release from active duty, this evidence might be considered new and material if VA had previously been unaware of that treatment, or addressing only the current severity of the condition submitted now, over 50 years after service, this evidence may not have a bearing on the issue of whether the condition was incurred or aggravated during military service and may not warrant reopening the prior claim.

Statements and affidavits attesting to the claimant's good character since his/her release from active duty are irrelevant, if the issue is the character of the claimant's military service. However, any new information offering mitigating circumstances for an action that resulted in an "other than honorable" discharge does address the specific issue under consideration, and therefore warrants reopening the claim.

Below Are Various Categories of Applications for Disability Compensation

Definition of service connection: Service connected disabilities are current chronic disabilities diagnosed by a medical professional and determined by the United States Department of Veterans Affairs (USDVA) to have been caused or aggravated by military service or secondary to an existing service connected disability.

5. Specific Chronic Conditions Presumed Service-Connected with a Time Limit
6. Prisoner of War – Chronic Conditions, Service-Connected with No Time Limit
7. Ionizing Radiation – Chronic Conditions Presumed Service-Connected
8. Agent Orange – Chronic Conditions, Service-Connected with No Time Limit
9. Disability Caused by Illness, Combat or Other Injury Incurred in the Service
10. Secondary Service Connection or Aggravation of an Existing Condition
11. Exposure to Hazards, Chemicals and Harmful Environmental Conditions
12. PTSD – Posttraumatic Stress Disorder
13. Hearing Loss with or without Tinnitus
14. PTIU – Permanent and Total Disability Due to Individual Unemployability
15. Gulf War Disorders – Service Connection Is Presumed with a Time Limit
16. Request for Reevaluation or Change for an Existing Benefit
17. Section 1151 Claim
18. Tropical Diseases – Service Connection Is Presumed with a Time Limit
19. Special Monthly Compensation (SMC)
20. Specific Special Allowances
21. HISA (Housing Improvement and Structural Alterations) Grants

5. Specific Chronic Conditions Presumed Service-Connected with a Time Limit

We approach this application using these procedures.

- First, you need to print out the document found on the Data Disk entitled "Elements of the Fully Developed Claim Process." This allows you to follow the steps in the claim process without having to go back and forth to the fully developed claim section in this book. A printout provides you a separate document that you can refer to as you read the instructions for each type of claim. You can also make notes on the document that you print out.

- Second, we will mention pertinent details pertaining to this particular kind of claim .

- Third, we will list the forms that should be used with this particular kind of claim application. These forms are found on the Data Disk under the folder entitled "2 Application for Compensation and DIC."

- Fourth, we will provide you the steps from the elements of the fully developed claim process that you will use for this particular type of claim.

Details:
The veteran must have 90 continuous days or more of service. Having one or more of these 41 chronic diseases or disorders below is considered to have been caused by service if they manifest themselves to a degree of disability of 10% or more within one year after discharge. Manifesting does not necessarily mean medical diagnosis, only that evidence shows the existence. There are some exceptions to the one year rule which are: Hansen's Disease (leprosy) must have appeared within three years after separation. Tuberculosis must have appeared within three years after separation. Multiple sclerosis must have appeared within seven years after separation.

Amyotrophic Lateral Sclerosis (ALS), also known as Lou Gehrig's Disease can appear any time after separation from service. Because service connection is presumed, it is not required to produce evidence for service connection – only evidence of the manifestation of the disorder or disease. Here's the list.

- Anemia, primary.
- Arteriosclerosis.
- Arthritis.
- Atrophy, Progressive muscular.
- Brain hemorrhage.
- Brain thrombosis.
- Bronchiectasis.
- Calculi of the kidney, bladder, or gallbladder.
- Cardiovascular-renal disease, including hypertension. (This term applies to combination involvement of the type of arteriosclerosis, nephritis, and organic heart disease, and since hypertension is an early symptom long preceding the development of those diseases in

their more obvious forms, a disabling hypertension within the 1-year period will be given the same benefit of service connection as any of the chronic diseases listed.)

- Cirrhosis of the liver.
- Coccidioidomycosis.
- Diabetes mellitus.
- Encephalitis lethargica residuals.
- Endocarditis. (This term covers all forms of valvular heart disease.)
- Endocrinopathies.
- Epilepsies.
- Hansen's disease.
- Hodgkin's disease.
- Leukemia.
- Lupus erythematosus, systemic.
- Myasthenia gravis.
- Myelitis.
- Myocarditis.
- Nephritis.
- Other organic diseases of the nervous system.
- Osteitis deformans (Paget's disease).
- Osteomalacia.
- Palsy, bulbar.
- Paralysis agitans.
- Psychoses.
- Purpura idiopathic, hemorrhagic.
- Raynaud's disease.
- Sarcoidosis.
- Scleroderma.
- Sclerosis, amyotrophic lateral.
- Sclerosis, multiple.
- Syringomyelia.
- Thromboangiitis obliterans (Buerger's disease).
- Tuberculosis, active.
- Tumors, malignant, or of the brain or spinal cord or peripheral nerves.
- Ulcers, peptic (gastric or duodenal) (A proper diagnosis of gastric or duodenal ulcer (peptic ulcer) is to be considered established if it represents a medically sound interpretation of sufficient clinical findings warranting such diagnosis and provides an adequate basis for a differential diagnosis from other conditions with like symptomatology; in short, where the preponderance of evidence indicates gastric or duodenal ulcer (peptic ulcer). Whenever possible, of course, laboratory findings should be used in corroboration of the clinical data.

You do not have to prove service connection with any condition listed above as it is presumed service-connected. Your challenge is, if you have never filed a claim for any of the conditions above, and it has been a number of years since leaving the service, you have to demonstrate some sort of evidence that the conditions manifested themselves within the proper time frame. Otherwise, you can have the condition, but VA will assume that you did not incur it in service.

If it is going to take you some time to assemble the evidence for the application, do an "Intent to File" using the following form:

VA Form 21-0966 INTENT TO FILE

Forms to Use:
VHA-10-5345 – Request for and Authorization to Release Medical Records
VHA-10-5345a – Individual's Request for a Copy of Their Own Health Information
VBA-21-526EZ-ARE – Application for Disability Compensation and Related Compensation Benefits
VBA-21-4142-ARE – Authorization and Consent to Release Information to the Department of Veterans Affairs
VBA-21-4142-ARE – Authorization and Consent to Release Information to the Department of Veterans Affairs
VBA-21-0847-ARE – Request for Substitution of Claimant upon Death of Claimant

Forms for Representation for Assistance if Desired
VBA-21-22A-ARE – Appointment of Individual a Claimant's Representative
VBA-21-0845-ARE – Authorization to Disclose Personal Information to a Third Party

Steps in the Fully Developed Claim Process to Follow:
1. Decide Whether the Condition Warrants Making a Claim
2. Always File an "Intent to File"
3. Get a Copy of Your Discharge and Locate Service Treatment Records (STR)
4. Obtain Your Own Private Medical Records
5. Have Your Private Doctors or Specialists Do Disability Evaluations
7. Obtain or Produce Lay Evidence
8. Locate Records to Establish Assignment Location or Type of Duty Where Applicable
9. Make Sure the Evidence Conforms with the Rating Decision Criteria in Section C
10. Understand the Claim Forms and the Forms for Obtaining Records
11. Fill out the "Fully Developed Claim" Forms for the Claimed Benefit
12. Check and Double Check Everything and Include All Necessary Forms
13. Arrange for Representation and Third-Party Help If Needed
14. Provide a Cover Letter to Help the Service Representative Understand the Claim
15. Submit the Claim to Your Regional Office of Jurisdiction
16. Understand the Acknowledgment Letter from Your Veterans Service Center
17. Use VA Form 21-4138 for Purposes of Correspondence on the Claim
18. Expect Scheduling of a Compensation and Pension Examination
19. Decide How to Proceed if the Claimant Dies before the Claim Is Adjudicated

6. Prisoner of War – Chronic Conditions, Service-Connected with No Time Limit

We approach this application using these procedures.

- First, you need to print out the document found on the Data Disk entitled "Elements of the Fully Developed Claim Process." This allows you to follow the steps in the claim process without having to go back and forth to the fully developed claim section in this book. A printout provides you a separate document that you can refer to as you read the instructions for each type of claim. You can also make notes on the document that you print out.

- Second, we will mention pertinent details pertaining to this particular kind of claim .

- Third, we will list the forms that should be used with this particular kind of claim application. These forms are found on the Data Disk under the folder entitled "2 Application for Compensation and DIC."

- Fourth, we will provide you the steps from the elements of the fully developed claim process that you will use for this particular type of claim.

Details:
The veteran must have 90 continuous days or more of service. There are 20 diseases or disorders considered service-connected for a prisoner of war depending on the length of imprisonment and manifested any time after separation to a disabling degree of 10% or more. Manifesting does not necessarily mean medical diagnosis, only that evidence shows the existence. Because service connection is presumed, it is not required to produce evidence for service connection – only evidence of the manifestation of the disorder or disease. That said, evidence must be provided that shows the claimant was a prisoner of war for the prescribed amount of imprisonment. Here is the list.

- psychosis,
- any of the anxiety states,
- dysthymic disorder,
- organic residuals of frostbite,
- post-traumatic osteoarthritis,
- atherosclerotic heart disease or hypertensive vascular disease and their complications,
- stroke and its complications,
- residuals of stroke and
- effective October 10, 2008, osteoporosis if the veteran has post-traumatic stress disorder (PTSD).

For former POWs who were imprisoned for at least 30 days, the following conditions are also presumed to be service-connected:

- avitaminosis,
- beriberi,

- chronic dysentery,
- helminthiasis,
- malnutrition (including optic atrophy associated with malnutrition),
- pellagra and/or other nutritional deficiencies,
- irritable bowel syndrome,
- peptic ulcer disease,
- peripheral neuropathy except where related to infectious causes,
- cirrhosis of the liver,
- and effective September 28, 2009, osteoporosis.

Prisoners of war. Where Disability Compensation is claimed by a former prisoner of war, omission of history or findings from clinical records made upon repatriation is not determinative of service connection, particularly if evidence of comrades in support of the incurrence of the disability during confinement is available. Special attention will be given to any disability first reported after discharge, especially if poorly defined and not obviously of intercurrent origin. The circumstances attendant upon the individual veteran's confinement and the duration thereof will be associated with pertinent medical principles in determining whether disability manifested subsequent to service is etiologically related to the prisoner of war experience.

If it is going to take you some time to assemble the evidence for the application, do an "Intent to File" using the following form:

VA Form 21-0966 INTENT TO FILE

Forms to Use:
VHA-10-5345 – Request for and Authorization to Release Medical Records
VHA-10-5345a – Individual's Request for a Copy of Their Own Health Information
VBA-21-526EZ-ARE – Application for Disability Compensation and Related Compensation Benefits
VBA-21-4142-ARE – Authorization and Consent to Release Information to the Department of Veterans Affairs

Forms for Representation for Assistance if Desired
VBA-21-22A-ARE – Appointment of Individual a Claimant's Representative
VBA-21-0845-ARE – Authorization to Disclose Personal Information to a Third Party

Steps in the Fully Developed Claim Process to Follow:
1. Decide Whether the Condition Warrants Making a Claim
2. Always File an "Intent to File"
3. Get a Copy of Your Discharge and Locate Service Treatment Records (STR)
4. Obtain Your Own Private Medical Records
5. Have Your Private Doctors or Specialists Do Disability Evaluations
7. Obtain or Produce Lay Evidence
8. Locate Records to Establish Assignment Location or Type of Duty Where Applicable
9. Make Sure the Evidence Conforms with the Rating Decision Criteria in Section C
10. Understand the Claim Forms and the Forms for Obtaining Records
11. Fill out the "Fully Developed Claim" Forms for the Claimed Benefit

12. Check and Double Check Everything and Include All Necessary Forms
13. Arrange for Representation and Third-Party Help If Needed
14. Provide a Cover Letter to Help the Service Representative Understand the Claim
15. Submit the Claim to Your Regional Office of Jurisdiction
16. Understand the Acknowledgment Letter from Your Veterans Service Center
17. Use VA Form 21-4138 for Purposes of Correspondence on the Claim
18. Expect Scheduling of a Compensation and Pension Examination
19. Decide How to Proceed if the Claimant Dies before the Claim Is Adjudicated

7. Ionizing Radiation – Chronic Conditions Presumed Service-Connected

We approach this application using these procedures.

- First, you need to print out the document found on the Data Disk entitled "Elements of the Fully Developed Claim Process." This allows you to follow the steps in the claim process without having to go back and forth to the fully developed claim section in this book. A printout provides you a separate document that you can refer to as you read the instructions for each type of claim. You can also make notes on the document that you print out.

- Second, we will mention pertinent details pertaining to this particular kind of claim .

- Third, we will list the forms that should be used with this particular kind of claim application. These forms are found on the Data Disk under the folder entitled "2 Application for Compensation and DIC."

- Fourth, we will provide you the steps from the elements of the fully developed claim process that you will use for this particular type of claim.

Details:
Careful attention is paid to whether the veteran was actually exposed to radiation to a degree to cause a number of conditions which are mostly cancers. Exposure is generally assumed to be related to nuclear detonations or experiments of which there is a specific list and the veteran must prove he was involved at the time. Manifestation of these diseases or disorders can occur generally any time after a certain prescribed period of time, depending on the condition. Manifesting does not necessarily mean medical diagnosis, only that evidence shows the existence.

Because service connection is presumed, it is not required to produce evidence for service connection – only evidence of the manifestation of the disorder or disease. That said, the claimant must provide evidence of being in the defined locations where the claimant was presumably exposed to ionizing radiation and in sufficient doses to result in one of the chronic conditions on the list. This might prove a difficult task. Here is the list.

- all forms of leukemia (except for chronic lymphocytic leukemia);

- cancer of the thyroid, breast, pharynx, esophagus, stomach, small intestine, pancreas, bile ducts, gall bladder, salivary gland, urinary tract (renal pelvis, ureter, urinary bladder and urethra), brain, bone, lung, colon, and ovary;
- bronchiolo-alveolar carcinoma;
- multiple myeloma;
- lymphomas (other than Hodgkin's disease), and
- primary liver cancer (except if cirrhosis or hepatitis B is indicated).

If it is going to take you some time to assemble the evidence for the application, do an "Intent to File" using the following form:

VA Form 21-0966 INTENT TO FILE

Forms to Use:
VHA-10-5345 – Request for and Authorization to Release Medical Records
VHA-10-5345a – Individual's Request for a Copy of Their Own Health Information
VBA-21-526EZ-ARE – Application for Disability Compensation and Related Compensation Benefits
VBA-21-4142-ARE – Authorization and Consent to Release Information to the Department of Veterans Affairs

Forms for Representation for Assistance if Desired
VBA-21-22A-ARE – Appointment of Individual a Claimant's Representative
VBA-21-0845-ARE – Authorization to Disclose Personal Information to a Third Party

Steps in the Fully Developed Claim Process to Follow:

1. Decide Whether the Condition Warrants Making a Claim
2. Always File an "Intent to File"
3. Get a Copy of Your Discharge and Locate Service Treatment Records (STR)
4. Obtain Your Own Private Medical Records
5. Have Your Private Doctors or Specialists Do Disability Evaluations
7. Obtain or Produce Lay Evidence
8. Locate Records to Establish Assignment Location or Type of Duty Where Applicable
9. Make Sure the Evidence Conforms with the Rating Decision Criteria in Section C
10. Understand the Claim Forms and the Forms for Obtaining Records
11. Fill out the "Fully Developed Claim" Forms for the Claimed Benefit
12. Check and Double Check Everything and Include All Necessary Forms
13. Arrange for Representation and Third-Party Help If Needed
14. Provide a Cover Letter to Help the Service Representative Understand the Claim
15. Submit the Claim to Your Regional Office of Jurisdiction
16. Understand the Acknowledgment Letter from Your Veterans Service Center
17. Use VA Form 21-4138 for Purposes of Correspondence on the Claim
18. Expect Scheduling of a Compensation and Pension Examination
19. Decide How to Proceed if the Claimant Dies before the Claim Is Adjudicated

8. Agent Orange – Chronic Conditions, Service-Connected with No Time Limit

We approach this application using these procedures.

- First, you need to print out the document found on the Data Disk entitled "Elements of the Fully Developed Claim Process." This allows you to follow the steps in the claim process without having to go back and forth to the fully developed claim section in this book. A printout provides you a separate document that you can refer to as you read the instructions for each type of claim. You can also make notes on the document that you print out.

- Second, we will mention pertinent details pertaining to this particular kind of claim .

- Third, we will list the forms that should be used with this particular kind of claim application. These forms are found on the Data Disk under the folder entitled "2 Application for Compensation and DIC."

- Fourth, we will provide you the steps from the elements of the fully developed claim process that you will use for this particular type of claim.

Details:
The veteran must have 90 continuous days or more of service. Herbicides were used in Vietnam to defoliate trees in order to remove cover for the enemy. During the manufacturing process, significance amounts of harmful contaminants called dioxins were produced. Different blends of herbicides were used but the most common was one called "Agent Orange." Being on the ground in Vietnam, during the war or on the inland waterways is sufficient for presumption for service connection. Harmful exposure other than the automatic "boots on the ground" for Vietnam is generally considered to be inhalation and not topical.

Exposure also occurred in Thailand, the demilitarized zone in Korea and presumably on certain ships offshore from Vietnam (those proven to be in harbor). In addition, numerous storage, spraying operations, testing and loading sites – outside the country and inside the US – could have resulted in exposure. The claimant must prove that he or she was exposed to Agent Orange. Proving that the claimant was in Vietnam is relatively easy, based on service records. Being exposed to Agent Orange under other circumstances might be a difficult task. These following illnesses are presumed by VA to be service-connected for Agent Orange veterans:

- AL amyloidosis,
- chloracne or other acneform disease similar to chloracne,
- porphyria cutanea tarda,
- soft-tissue sarcoma (other than osteosarcoma, chondrosarcoma,
- Kaposi's sarcoma or mesothelioma),
- Hodgkin's disease,
- multiple myeloma,
- respiratory cancers (lung, bronchus, larynx, trachea),
- non-Hodgkin's lymphoma,
- prostate cancer,

- acute and subacute peripheral neuropathy,
- diabetes mellitus (Type 2),
- all chronic B-cell leukemias (including, but not limited to, hairy-cell leukemia and chronic lymphocytic leukemia),
- Parkinson's disease, and
- ischemic heart disease.

You will note that some of these disorders such as type II diabetes, ischemic heart disease (insufficient blood supply to the heart likely due to cardiovascular disease) and Parkinson's disease are fairly common among the elderly. We expect the number of claims for Agent Orange to go up considerably because of the aging population of Vietnam Era veterans.

Here is how VA defines ischemic heart disease.

"***Arteriosclerotic heart disease***, also diagnosed as ischemic heart disease and coronary heart disease, is a disease of the heart caused by the diminution of blood supply to the heart muscle due to narrowing of the cavity of one or both coronary arteries due to the accumulation of fatty material on the inner lining of the arterial wall."

Here is the rating table for ischemic heart disease.

7005 Arteriosclerotic heart disease (Coronary artery disease):	
With documented coronary artery disease resulting in:	
Chronic congestive heart failure, or; workload of 3 METs or less results in dyspnea, fatigue, angina, dizziness, or syncope, or; left ventricular dysfunction with an ejection fraction of less than 30 percent	100
More than one episode of acute congestive heart failure in the past year, or; workload of greater than 3 METs but not greater than 5 METs results in dyspnea, fatigue, angina, dizziness, or syncope, or; left ventricular dysfunction with an ejection fraction of 30 to 50 percent	60
Workload of greater than 5 METs but not greater than 7 METs results in dyspnea, fatigue, angina, dizziness, or syncope, or; evidence of cardiac hypertrophy or dilatation on electrocardiogram, echocardiogram, or X-ray	30
Workload of greater than 7 METs but not greater than 10 METs results in dyspnea, fatigue, angina, dizziness, or syncope, or; continuous medication required	10
Note: If nonservice-connected arteriosclerotic heart disease is superimposed on service-connected valvular or other non-arteriosclerotic heart disease, request a medical opinion as to which condition is causing the current signs and symptoms.	

Here is the rating table for diabetes.

7913 Diabetes mellitus	
Requiring more than one daily injection of insulin, restricted diet, and regulation of activities (avoidance of strenuous occupational and recreational activities) with episodes of ketoacidosis or hypoglycemic reactions requiring at least three hospitalizations per year or weekly visits to a diabetic care provider, plus either progressive loss of weight and strength or complications that would be compensable if separately evaluated	100
Requiring insulin, restricted diet, and regulation of activities with episodes of ketoacidosis or hypoglycemic reactions requiring one or two hospitalizations per year or twice a month visits to a diabetic care provider, plus complications that would not be compensable if separately evaluated	60
Requiring insulin, restricted diet, and regulation of activities	40
Requiring insulin and restricted diet, or; oral hypoglycemic agent and restricted diet	20
Manageable by restricted diet only	10
Note (1): Evaluate compensable complications of diabetes separately unless they are part of the criteria used to support a 100 percent evaluation. Noncompensable complications are considered part of the diabetic process under diagnostic code 7913.	
Note (2): When diabetes mellitus has been conclusively diagnosed, do not request a glucose tolerance test solely for rating purposes.	

Remember, the key issue here is you must prove you were in Vietnam during the war. Your service and personnel records from the National Records Center, should prove this, but if your records were lost in the fire, you will need to look for an alternative source. Generally, your discharge does not reflect that you were in Vietnam – but it could. If you are trying to prove exposure in some location other than Vietnam, your job is definitely cut out for you, but we understand some people have won awards based on exposure outside of Vietnam.

In the appendix of this book, we have a list of all of the storage and testing sites known for Agent Orange in the United States and internationally. If you want to pursue a claim for exposure beyond Vietnam, this will give you a head start. In addition this topic in the appendix includes several newsletters from the VA and some additional information on the subject.

If it is going to take you some time to assemble the evidence for the application, do an "Intent to File" using the following form:

VA Form 21-0966 INTENT TO FILE

Forms to Use:
VHA-10-5345 – Request for and Authorization to Release Medical Records
VHA-10-5345a – Individual's Request for a Copy of Their Own Health Information
VBA-21-526EZ-ARE – Application for Disability Compensation and Related Compensation Benefits

VBA-21-4142-ARE – Authorization and Consent to Release Information to the Department of Veterans Affairs

Forms for Representation for Assistance if Desired
VBA-21-22A-ARE – Appointment of Individual a Claimant's Representative
VBA-21-0845-ARE – Authorization to Disclose Personal Information to a Third Party

Steps in the Fully Developed Claim Process to Follow:
1. Decide Whether the Condition Warrants Making a Claim
2. Always File an "Intent to File"
3. Get a Copy of Your Discharge and Locate Service Treatment Records (STR)
4. Obtain Your Own Private Medical Records
5. Have Your Private Doctors or Specialists Do Disability Evaluations
7. Obtain or Produce Lay Evidence
8. Locate Records to Establish Assignment Location or Type of Duty Where Applicable
9. Make Sure the Evidence Conforms with the Rating Decision Criteria in Section C
10. Understand the Claim Forms and the Forms for Obtaining Records
11. Fill out the "Fully Developed Claim" Forms for the Claimed Benefit
12. Check and Double Check Everything and Include All Necessary Forms
13. Arrange for Representation and Third-Party Help If Needed
14. Provide a Cover Letter to Help the Service Representative Understand the Claim
15. Submit the Claim to Your Regional Office of Jurisdiction
16. Understand the Acknowledgment Letter from Your Veterans Service Center
17. Use VA Form 21-4138 for Purposes of Correspondence on the Claim
18. Expect Scheduling of a Compensation and Pension Examination
19. Decide How to Proceed if the Claimant Dies before the Claim Is Adjudicated

9. Disability Caused by Illness, Combat or Other Injury Incurred in the Service

We approach this application using these procedures.

- First, you need to print out the document found on the Data Disk entitled "Elements of the Fully Developed Claim Process." This allows you to follow the steps in the claim process without having to go back and forth to the fully developed claim section in this book. A printout provides you a separate document that you can refer to as you read the instructions for each type of claim. You can also make notes on the document that you print out.

- Second, we will mention pertinent details pertaining to this particular kind of claim .

- Third, we will list the forms that should be used with this particular kind of claim application. These forms are found on the Data Disk under the folder entitled "2 Application for Compensation and DIC."

- Fourth, we will provide you the steps from the elements of the fully developed claim process that you will use for this particular type of claim.

Details:

This type of disability is not presumed to be service-connected. Evidence must be produced to show that it was service-connected. Proving service connection adds an additional degree of difficulty over those conditions that are presumed. Generally, evidence of the illness or injury should be contained in service medical records of the claimant. If no medical evidence is available, service connection can still be established through other means such as lay testimony or historical reports from individuals who observed the injury or illness of the claimant. There is no time frame for making a claim.

Sometimes, the injury or illness does not manifest as chronically disabling for many years after separation. Medical evidence soon after separation of the existence of the illness or injury and prior to manifestation of disability is often necessary in establishing service connection and what VA calls "chronicity" or duration of the chronic condition. These types of claims are very common for any age of veteran, be it a young veteran or a veteran who is aged. For some other types of claims involving direct service connection, chronicity must be established but not necessarily manifestation early on. Some disabling conditions may not show up for years.

Here's an interesting ruling from the Board of the Veterans Appeals concerning these kinds of claims. We think it is an interesting study in detail as to how decisions for these types of claims are made.

> Service connection may be granted for disability resulting from a disease or injury incurred in or aggravated by military service. 38 U.S.C.A. § 1110; 38 C.F.R. § 3.303. In addition, service connection may be presumed for certain chronic diseases, including arthritis, that are manifested to a compensable degree within one year after service. 38 U.S.C.A. §§ 1101, 1112; 38 C.F.R. §§ 3.307, 3.309(a). For the showing of chronic disease in service, there must be a combination of manifestations sufficient to identify the disease entity and sufficient observation to establish chronicity at the time. If chronicity in service is not established, evidence of continuity of symptoms after discharge is required to support the claim. 38 C.F.R. § 3.303(b). Service connection may also be granted for a disease diagnosed after discharge when all the evidence, including that pertinent to service, establishes that the disease was incurred in service. 38 C.F.R. § 3.303(d).
>
> To establish service connection, there must be (1) medical evidence of current disability; (2) medical, or in certain circumstances, lay evidence of in-service incurrence or aggravation of a disease or injury; and (3) medical evidence of a nexus between the claimed in-service disease or injury and the current disability. Hickson v. West, 12 Vet. App. 247 (1999); see also Degmetich v. Brown, 104 F.3d 1328 (Fed. Cir. 1997); Brammer v. Derwinski, 3 Vet. App. 223 (1992). This determination is based on an analysis of all the evidence of record and evaluation of its credibility and probative value. Baldwin v. West, 13 Vet. App. 1 (1999).
>
> There is no reference to back problems, symptoms, or diagnoses in any of the veteran's service medical records. Nor is there any mention of the veteran's use of any back support, as he testified.
>
> Moreover, there is no record of any complaint of or treatment for any back disorder for many years after service. Indeed, on a September 1951 reserve service examination, the veteran's spine was clinically normal. On an accompanying medical history report, the veteran denied any back injury or back problems.

The first mention of any back symptoms was in non-VA treatment in December 2001, that is, over 50 years after service. The diagnosis at that time was backache.

None of the available competent VA or non-VA records attributes any current back problems to the veteran's service.

The Board is mindful of an August 2004 VA examination that concluded that degenerative joint disease of the lumbar spine was "at least as likely as not related to an inservice back injury." The examiner noted having reviewed the claims folder. The examiner specifically described a history of an in-service fall (in 1944); the use of a back brace throughout the remainder of the veteran's active service; treatment for back problems at a VA facility in Memphis, Tennessee, in 1962; and constant back pain ever since the in-service incident. However, that history cannot be based on a review of the claims folder and relevant medical history, since there is no documentation of the specified treatment at those particular times. Indeed, the VA facility in Memphis has replied that it does not have records of any treatment for the veteran. Moreover, the service medical records do not document any treatment for a 1944 or other in-service back injury or the use of a back brace in service. Thus, it appears that the August 2004 VA examination is premised on the veteran's recitations.

A bare conclusion (even from a medical professional) is not probative without a factual predicate in the record. Miller v. West, 11 Vet. App. 345 (1998). A medical opinion premised on an unsubstantiated account is of no probative value and does not verify the occurrences described. Swann v. Brown, 5 Vet. App. 229 (1993); cf. Howell v. Nicholson, No. 04-0624, __ Vet. App. __, 2006 WL 760181 (Vet. App. Mar. 23, 2006). The Board is not bound to accept a doctor's opinion based exclusively on a claimant's recitations. Reonal v. Brown, 5 Vet. App. 458, 461 (1993). As a result, the August 2004 VA examination is not probative as to any relationship between the veteran's service and any current back disorder.

Thus, the Board finds that the weight of the credible, competent evidence demonstrates that the veteran did not develop a back disorder during his service or because of any incident therein. As the preponderance of the evidence is against this claim, the "benefit-of-the-doubt" rule does not apply, and the Board must deny the claim. 38 U.S.C.A. § 5107(b) (West 2002).

In this particular case, the doctor's opinion was not very strong or convincing. If enough evidence is produced to show that there is a reasonable assumption or inference that the current disability is service-connected, then a strong opinion letter from a physician might sway VA to make a favorable decision.

Oftentimes, a private physician is unwilling to provide an opinion that the current medical condition is a result of the service connection the veteran is claiming. You may be able to find a physician who will write an opinion letter that there is a 50-50 chance or greater the current disability is service-connected. This seems more reasonable to the examining medical practitioner. The physician will use the words that the current disability is "at least as likely as not" to have been incurred in the service based on information provided by the veteran and an examination by the physician. The physician has opined that there is a 50-50 chance or greater it was incurred in service and if VA has no evidence to the contrary – under the doctrine of reasonable doubt (38 CFR 3.102) – the veteran will receive an award.

Also remember that for these types of claims, especially where there is scanty evidence of the incurrence of an illness or injury in the service, current disabling conditions that could be attributed to combat or being a prisoner of war are usually accepted based on the testimony of the claimant alone with no other corroborating evidence. For peacetime service or noncombatant service, testimony of the claimant or other witnesses is not enough without other supporting physical evidence.

If it is going to take you some time to assemble the evidence for the application, do an "Intent to File" using the following form:
VA Form 21-0966 INTENT TO FILE

Forms to Use:
VHA-10-5345 – Request for and Authorization to Release Medical Records
VHA-10-5345a – Individual's Request for a Copy of Their Own Health Information
VBA-21-526EZ-ARE – Application for Disability Compensation and Related Compensation Benefits
VBA-21-4176-ARE – Report of Accidental Injury in Support of Claim for Compensation or Pension Statement of Witness to Accident
VBA-21-4142-ARE – Authorization and Consent to Release Information to the Department of Veterans Affairs

Forms for Representation for Assistance if Desired
VBA-21-22A-ARE – Appointment of Individual a Claimant's Representative
VBA-21-0845-ARE – Authorization to Disclose Personal Information to a Third Party

Steps in the Fully Developed Claim Process to Follow:
1. Decide Whether the Condition Warrants Making a Claim
2. Always File an "Intent to File"
3. Get a Copy of Your Discharge and Locate Service Treatment Records (STR)
4. Obtain Your Own Private Medical Records
5. Have Your Private Doctors or Specialists Do Disability Evaluations
6. Have Your Doctors/Specialists Provide Opinion Letters for Service-Connected
7. Obtain or Produce Lay Evidence
8. Locate Records to Establish Assignment Location or Type of Duty Where Applicable
9. Make Sure the Evidence Conforms with the Rating Decision Criteria in Section C
10. Understand the Claim Forms and the Forms for Obtaining Records
11. Fill out the "Fully Developed Claim" Forms for the Claimed Benefit
12. Check and Double Check Everything and Include All Necessary Forms
13. Arrange for Representation and Third-Party Help If Needed
14. Provide a Cover Letter to Help the Service Representative Understand the Claim
15. Submit the Claim to Your Regional Office of Jurisdiction
16. Understand the Acknowledgment Letter from Your Veterans Service Center
17. Use VA Form 21-4138 for Purposes of Correspondence on the Claim
18. Expect Scheduling of a Compensation and Pension Examination
19. Decide How to Proceed if the Claimant Dies before the Claim Is Adjudicated

10. Secondary Service Connection or Aggravation of an Existing Condition

Details:

Here are the rules for this type of claim from 38 CFR § 3.310 and § 3.322

(Section 3.310)
(a) General. Except as provided in §3.300(c), disability which is proximately due to or the result of a service-connected disease or injury shall be service connected. When service connection is thus established for a secondary condition, the secondary condition shall be considered a part of the original condition.

(b) Aggravation of nonservice-connected disabilities. Any increase in severity of a nonservice-connected disease or injury that is proximately due to or the result of a service-connected disease or injury, and not due to the natural progress of the nonservice-connected disease, will be service connected. However, VA will not concede that a nonservice-connected disease or injury was aggravated by a service-connected disease or injury unless the baseline level of severity of the nonservice-connected disease or injury is established by medical evidence created before the onset of aggravation or by the earliest medical evidence created at any time between the onset of aggravation and the receipt of medical evidence establishing the current level of severity of the nonservice-connected disease or injury. The rating activity will determine the baseline and current levels of severity under the Schedule for Rating Disabilities (38 CFR part 4) and determine the extent of aggravation by deducting the baseline level of severity, as well as any increase in severity due to the natural progress of the disease, from the current level.

(c) Cardiovascular disease. Ischemic heart disease or other cardiovascular disease developing in a veteran who has a service-connected amputation of one lower extremity at or above the knee or service-connected amputations of both lower extremities at or above the ankles, shall be held to be the proximate result of the service-connected amputation or amputations.

(Section 3.322)
(a) Aggravation of preservice disability. In cases involving aggravation by active service, the rating will reflect only the degree of disability over and above the degree of disability existing at the time of entrance into active service, whether the particular condition was noted at the time of entrance into active service, or whether it is determined upon the evidence of record to have existed at that time. It is necessary to deduct from the present evaluation the degree, if ascertainable, of the disability existing at the time of entrance into active service, in terms of the rating schedule except that if the disability is total (100 percent) no deduction will be made. If the degree of disability at the time of entrance into service is not ascertainable in terms of the schedule, no deduction will be made.

(b) Aggravation of service-connected disability. Where a disease or injury incurred in peacetime service is aggravated during service in a period of war, or conversely, where a disease or injury incurred in service during a period of war is aggravated during peacetime service, the entire disability flowing from the disease or injury will be service connected based on the war service.

Here is a summary of these rules.

Service connection can be granted under 38 CFR 3.310 above when disabilities are proximately due to or the result of a service-connected condition or the increase in severity of a non-service-connected disability. This increase in severity of a non-service-connected disability has to be attributable to aggravation by a service-connected disability and not due to the natural progress of that non-service-connected disability.

The baseline of the non-service connected disability which was aggravated by a service-connected disability must be established by medical evidence created before the onset of aggravation. Or if this is not possible, the earliest medical evidence that can be created between the onset of aggravation and receipt of medical evidence establishing the current level of severity of the non-service connected disability. If it is impossible to establish a baseline to determine the severity of aggravation, it is unlikely that there will be an award. Medical records are critical to this type of claim. The veteran must furnish medical evidence of the current level of severity of the non-service connected disability and medical evidence of its level of severity prior to the point at which it was being aggravated by the service-connected disability.

Once the rating authority has this information, a C&P medical examination will be requested directing an opinion by the examiner to establish whether the examiner feels that the severity of the non-service connected disability is proximately due to the service-connected disability. The examiner must have all of the private records of the veteran establishing the baseline for review when providing an opinion on the issue of aggravation. The examiner's report must separately address all of the following medical issues in order to be considered adequate for rating a claim for secondary service connection based on aggravation:

- the current level of severity of the non-service connected disease or injury
- an opinion as to whether a service-connected disability proximately caused the non-service connected disability to increase in severity, and
- the medical considerations supporting this opinion.

The rating activity will use this information as the primary source of evidence for making a decision whether there was aggravation or not and whether it is ratable or not.

If enough evidence is produced to show that there is a reasonable assumption or inference that the non-service connected secondary disability is due to the service-connected disability, then a strong opinion letter from a physician might sway VA to make a favorable decision.

Oftentimes, a private physician is unwilling to provide an opinion that the current medical condition is a result of the service connection the veteran is claiming. You may be able to find a physician who will write an opinion letter that there is a 50-50 chance or greater the current disability is service-connected. This seems more reasonable to the examining medical practitioner. The physician will use the words that the current disability is "at least as likely as not" to have been incurred in the service based on information provided by the veteran and an examination by the physician. The physician has opined that there is a 50-50 chance or greater it was incurred in service and if VA has no evidence to the contrary – under the doctrine of reasonable doubt (38 CFR 3.102) – the veteran will receive an award.

If it is going to take you some time to assemble the evidence for the application, do an "Intent to File" using the following form:

VA Form 21-0966 INTENT TO FILE

Forms to Use:
VHA-10-5345 – Request for and Authorization to Release Medical Records
VHA-10-5345a – Individual's Request for a Copy of Their Own Health Information
VBA-21-4142-ARE – Authorization and Consent to Release Information to the Department of Veterans Affairs
VBA-21-526EZ-ARE – Application for Disability Compensation and Related Compensation Benefits

Forms for Representation for Assistance if Desired
VBA-21-22A-ARE – Appointment of Individual a Claimant's Representative
VBA-21-0845-ARE – Authorization to Disclose Personal Information to a Third Party

Steps in the Claim Process to Follow:
This is not a new application. You will use form 21-526EZ for this application. VA already has you on an award for service connection and you are simply trying to increase your rating by establishing additional ratable, non-service-connected disabilities that are presumably caused by your service connected disabilities. The key to this application is support from your private medical records by establishing a level of disability from the non-service connected condition prior to aggravation. Later records must show a worsening of the non-service-connected disability and the presumption that it is connected to the service-connected disability. The better these records can show a contrast from the so-called "baseline," the better your chance of getting a favorable opinion, if indeed the service-connected disability is the cause.

Also, have your physicians or specialists prepare a "Disability Benefit Questionnaire" pertaining to the particular condition or illness for which you are requesting an evaluation. These DBQ's are found on the claim support Data Disk.

Make sure that you submit all of your private medical records as well as the DBQ pertaining to the new condition along with the change request form. This will allow your application to be treated as fully developed and should result in a C&P examination fairly quickly. Otherwise, without all of the additional information, the development team may take a long time to get around to getting more evidence in order to have the rating activity order a C&P exam.

11. Exposure to Hazards, Chemicals and Harmful Environmental Conditions

We approach this application using these procedures.

- First, you need to print out the document found on the Data Disk entitled "Elements of the Fully Developed Claim Process." This allows you to follow the steps in the claim process without having to go back and forth to the fully developed claim section in this book. A printout provides you a separate document that you can refer to as you read the instructions for each type of claim. You can also make notes on the document that you print out.

- Second, we will mention pertinent details pertaining to this particular kind of claim .

- Third, we will list the forms that should be used with this particular kind of claim application. These forms are found on the Data Disk under the folder entitled "2 Application for Compensation and DIC."

- Fourth, we will provide you the steps from the elements of the fully developed claim process that you will use for this particular type of claim.

Details:
The veteran may have been exposed to any one or more of the following during active duty:

- Harmful sounds from guns, equipment and machinery used during military service
- Vietnam Era veterans who are at risk for hepatitis C
- Depleted uranium used in military tank armor and some bullets
- Sulfur fire at Al Mishraq, Iraq – Sulfur plant burned almost a month in June 2003; large amounts of sulfur dioxide released into the air
- (Qarmat Ali) Hexavalent chromium in contaminated sodium dichromate dust; water treatment plant in 2003
- Camp Lejeune Water Supplies
- Tap water contaminated by industrial chemicals at Marine Corps Base Camp in the 1950s to 1980s
- Burn Pits – Open-air pit waste disposal at military sites
- (Gulf War) Substances used to repel or destroy pests such as insects and pathogens
- Depleted Uranium – Uranium used in military tank armor and some bullets
- PCBs – Polychlorinated biphenyls used as coolant and insulating fluid
- Industrial Solvents – Usually a liquid used to dissolve, degrease, clean, strip paint, etc.
- Exposure during military service to the airborne hazards listed below could potentially cause certain health problems in Veterans, depending on a number of other factors.
    - Burn Pits
    - Atsugi Waste Incinerator Atsugi, Japan: Combustion waste disposal that burned industrial and medical waste
    - Oil Well Fire, Smoke (Gulf War)
    - Oil or gas wells that caught on fire and burned during the 1990-1991 Gulf War
    - Sand, Dust and Particulates Tiny airborne matter that can cause respiratory and other health problems
    - Sulfur Fire (Al Mishraq, Iraq)
    - Responding to concerns of many returning Veterans, VA will continue to study the health risks of pollution in Iraq and Afghanistan, including burn pit smoke, and establish a burn pit registry for eligible
- Asbestos Mineral – fiber used in older buildings and an older ships; if inhaled deeply into the lungs can cause health problems
- Vibration – Periodic back and forth movement that if severe, can cause health conditions
- Lead Metal that can be toxic for certain uses
- Noise – Harmful sounds from guns, equipment, airplanes, combat vehicles and machinery that is often experienced during military service
- Exposure to extreme heat or extreme cold
- Heavy equipment including armored vests that may cause deterioration of bodily joints

- Herbicide Tests and Storage
- Radiation – Dental technicians, nuclear weapons technicians, and others with routine and usually safe exposure
- CARC Paint – Chemical Agent Resistant Coating (CARC) used on military vehicles to resist corrosion and chemical agents
- Fuels (Petroleum, Oils, Lubricants) – Fuels such as diesel and JP-8 used to operate vehicles in the military
- Use of biological toxins or infectious agents with intent to kill or incapacitate
- Nerve Agents – Toxic chemicals that attack the body's nervous system
- Mustard Gas – Odorless, poisonous gas used during World War I, II, and military tests in the 1940s
- Project 112/Project SHAD – Military tests of chemical/biological warfare materials conducted in the 1960s to early 1970s
- Edgewood/Aberdeen Experiments – Classified medical studies of low-dose chemical agents conducted from 1955-1975
- Agent Orange and other herbicides used in Vietnam. Agent Orange and other herbicides used in Vietnam were tested or stored elsewhere, including some military bases in the United States.
    - Exposure to Agent Orange in Vietnam Exposure on land in Vietnam or on a ship operating on the inland waterways of Vietnam between January 9, 1962 and May 7, 1975
    - Blue Water Veterans Possible exposure on open sea ships off the shore of Vietnam during the Vietnam War
    - U.S. Navy and Coast Guard Ships in Vietnam List of ships and boats with operations in Vietnam between January 9, 1962 and May 7, 1975
    - Korean Demilitarized Zone Exposure along the demilitarized zone in Korea between April 1, 1968 and August 31, 1971
    - Thailand Military Bases Possible exposure on or near the perimeters of military bases between February 28, 1961 and May 7, 1975
    - Herbicide Tests and Storage Outside Vietnam Possible exposure due to herbicide tests and storage at military bases in the United States and locations in other countries
    - Agent Orange Residue on Airplanes Used in the Vietnam War Possible exposure of crew members to herbicide residue in C-123 planes flown after Vietnam War

<u>In the appendix of this book, we have a list of all of the storage and testing sites known for Agent Orange in the United States and internationally. If you want to pursue a claim for exposure beyond Vietnam, this will give you a head start.</u>

The key to this type of application is demonstrating that "you were in the wrong place at the right time" so to speak. The more likely the nexus between your current condition and the exposure, the more likely the inference that it occurred in service. Conditions caused by these types of exposure may not manifest until many years after getting out of the service. Trying to show evidence of the continuity of chronicity, as in other claims, is more difficult with one of these claims. The crucial issue in establishing service connection is that the chronic condition that you currently have is known to be caused by the particular exposure that you incurred in service.

You most definitely must have an opinion letter from your treating physicians as to the probability of this link to service connection.

This is likely going to be one of those claims based on reasonable doubt. VA will not be able to prove beyond a 50-50 probability that you did not incur the current disability because of an exposure in service, and as such must use the principle of reasonable doubt to award you the benefit.

Proving you were at an assignment where you were exposed to the hazard, the chemicals or the environment is crucial. There also has to be some sort of evidence that the level of exposure was sufficient enough to cause injury, disease or disorder. Or this must be self-evident because of the assignment.

If enough evidence is produced to show that there is a reasonable assumption or inference that the current disability is service-connected, then a strong opinion letter from a physician might sway VA to make a favorable decision.

Oftentimes, a private physician is unwilling to provide an opinion that the current medical condition is a result of the service connection the veteran is claiming. You may be able to find a physician who will write an opinion letter that there is a 50-50 chance or greater the current disability is service-connected. This seems more reasonable to the examining medical practitioner. The physician will use the words that the current disability is "at least as likely as not" to have been incurred in the service based on information provided by the veteran and an examination by the physician. The physician has opined that there is a 50-50 chance or greater it was incurred in service and if VA has no evidence to the contrary – under the doctrine of reasonable doubt (38 CFR 3.102) – the veteran will receive an award.

If it is going to take you some time to assemble the evidence for the application, do an "Intent to File" using the following form:

VA Form 21-0966 INTENT TO FILE

Forms to Use:
VHA-10-5345 – Request for and Authorization to Release Medical Records
VHA-10-5345a – Individual's Request for a Copy of Their Own Health Information
VBA-21-526EZ-ARE – Application for Disability Compensation and Related Compensation Benefits
VBA-21-4192-ARE – Request for Employment Information in Connection With Claim for Disability Benefits
VBA-21-4192-ARE – Request for Employment Information in Connection With Claim for Disability Benefits
VBA-21-8951-2-ARE-1 – Notice of Waiver of VA Compensation to Receive Military Pay and Allowances

Forms for Representation for Assistance if Desired
VBA-21-22A-ARE – Appointment of Individual a Claimant's Representative
VBA-21-0845-ARE – Authorization to Disclose Personal Information to a Third Party

Steps in the Fully Developed Claim Process to Follow:

1. Decide Whether the Condition Warrants Making a Claim
2. Always File an "Intent to File"
3. Get a Copy of Your Discharge and Locate Service Treatment Records (STR)
4. Obtain Your Own Private Medical Records
5. Have Your Private Doctors or Specialists Do Disability Evaluations
6. Have Your Doctors/Specialists Provide Opinion Letters for Service-Connected
7. Obtain or Produce Lay Evidence
8. Locate Records to Establish Assignment Location or Type of Duty Where Applicable
9. Make Sure the Evidence Conforms with the Rating Decision Criteria in Section C
10. Understand the Claim Forms and the Forms for Obtaining Records
11. Fill out the "Fully Developed Claim" Forms for the Claimed Benefit
12. Check and Double Check Everything and Include All Necessary Forms
13. Arrange for Representation and Third-Party Help If Needed
14. Provide a Cover Letter to Help the Service Representative Understand the Claim
15. Submit the Claim to Your Regional Office of Jurisdiction
16. Understand the Acknowledgment Letter from Your Veterans Service Center
17. Use VA Form 21-4138 for Purposes of Correspondence on the Claim
18. Expect Scheduling of a Compensation and Pension Examination
19. Decide How to Proceed if the Claimant Dies before the Claim Is Adjudicated

12. PTSD – Posttraumatic Stress Disorder

We approach this application using these procedures.

- First, you need to print out the document found on the Data Disk entitled "Elements of the Fully Developed Claim Process." This allows you to follow the steps in the claim process without having to go back and forth to the fully developed claim section in this book. A printout provides you a separate document that you can refer to as you read the instructions for each type of claim. You can also make notes on the document that you print out.

- Second, we will mention pertinent details pertaining to this particular kind of claim .

- Third, we will list the forms that should be used with this particular kind of claim application. These forms are found on the Data Disk under the folder entitled "2 Application for Compensation and DIC."

- Fourth, we will provide you the steps from the elements of the fully developed claim process that you will use for this particular type of claim.

Details:
Posttraumatic Stress Disorder is a mental disorder classified as an "anxiety" by VA. It is a mental health problem that can occur after someone goes through a traumatic event like war, assault, or disaster. Most people have some stress reactions after a trauma. If the reactions don't

go away over time or disrupt your life, you may have PTSD. Because PTSD can affect a person's ability to make an income, it is considered a disabling condition subject to Compensation if it is severe enough to be rated. Oftentimes, these are difficult claims to approve, because PTSD cannot be quantifiably measured like other conditions. It requires special evaluations from psychiatrists and employment assessment specialists. In addition, the service connection is sometimes difficult to establish when PTSD is not caused by engaging in combat. For many sufferers this is the case. If you or the claimant believes you are suffering from PTSD as a result of service and it is causing chronic disability, go to this claim category in Section E for more instructions.

PTSD is becoming a very common claim for disability with applications soaring in the last 10 or so years. This condition also leads to the inability to work and as such many PTSD claims are combined with individual unemployability claims.

(f) Posttraumatic stress disorder. Service connection for posttraumatic stress disorder requires medical evidence diagnosing the condition in accordance with §4.125(a) of this chapter; a link, established by medical evidence, between current symptoms and an in-service stressor; and credible supporting evidence that the claimed in-service stressor occurred. The following provisions apply to claims for service connection of posttraumatic stress disorder diagnosed during service or based on specified in-service stressors:

(1) If the evidence establishes a diagnosis of posttraumatic stress disorder during service and the claimed stressor is related to that service, in the absence of clear and convincing evidence to the contrary, and provided that the claimed stressor is consistent with the circumstances, conditions, or hardships of the veteran's service, the veteran's lay testimony alone may establish the occurrence of the claimed in-service stressor.

(2) If the evidence establishes that the veteran engaged in combat with the enemy and the claimed stressor is related to that combat, in the absence of clear and convincing evidence to the contrary, and provided that the claimed stressor is consistent with the circumstances, conditions, or hardships of the veteran's service, the veteran's lay testimony alone may establish the occurrence of the claimed in-service stressor.

(3) If the evidence establishes that the veteran was a prisoner-of-war under the provisions of §3.1(y) of this part and the claimed stressor is related to that prisoner-of-war experience, in the absence of clear and convincing evidence to the contrary, and provided that the claimed stressor is consistent with the circumstances, conditions, or hardships of the veteran's service, the veteran's lay testimony alone may establish the occurrence of the claimed in-service stressor.

(4) If a posttraumatic stress disorder claim is based on in-service personal assault, evidence from sources other than the veteran's service records may corroborate the veteran's account of the stressor incident. Examples of such evidence include, but are not limited to: records from law enforcement authorities, rape crisis centers, mental health counseling centers, hospitals, or physicians; pregnancy tests or tests for sexually transmitted diseases; and statements from family members, roommates, fellow service members, or clergy. Evidence of behavior changes following the claimed assault is one

type of relevant evidence that may be found in these sources. Examples of behavior changes that may constitute credible evidence of the stressor include, but are not limited to: a request for a transfer to another military duty assignment; deterioration in work performance; substance abuse; episodes of depression, panic attacks, or anxiety without an identifiable cause; or unexplained economic or social behavior changes. VA will not deny a posttraumatic stress disorder claim that is based on in-service personal assault without first advising the claimant that evidence from sources other than the veteran's service records or evidence of behavior changes may constitute credible supporting evidence of the stressor and allowing him or her the opportunity to furnish this type of evidence or advise VA of potential sources of such evidence. VA may submit any evidence that it receives to an appropriate medical or mental health professional for an opinion as to whether it indicates that a personal assault occurred.

We have more information on PTSD in the appendix of this book. You may want to read this information to learn more about it before you make a claim.

In order to provide your own private evaluations, you should always seek treatment with a psychiatrist or a PhD psychologist for the evaluation, treatment and an opinion letter. Any other expert would not be considered comparable to the examiners that VA uses. Here are the examiners that VA will use when ordering a C&P examination, which is required for this type of claim.

- Board-certified psychiatrists.
- Psychiatrists who have successfully completed an accredited psychiatry residency and who are appropriately credentialed and privileged.
- Licensed doctoral-level psychologist.
- Non-licensed doctoral-level psychologists working toward licensure under close supervision by a board-certified, or board-eligible, psychiatrist or a licensed doctoral-level psychologist.
- Psychiatry residents under close supervision by a board-certified, or board-eligible,

If enough evidence is produced to show that there is a reasonable assumption or inference that the PTSD is service-connected, then a strong opinion letter from a psychiatrist or PhD psychologist might sway VA to make a favorable decision.

Oftentimes, a private physician is unwilling to provide an opinion that the current medical condition is a result of the service connection the veteran is claiming. You may be able to find a physician who will write an opinion letter that there is a 50-50 chance or greater the current disability is service-connected. This seems more reasonable to the examining medical practitioner. The physician will use the words that the current disability is "at least as likely as not" to have been incurred in the service based on information provided by the veteran and an examination by the physician. The physician has opined that there is a 50-50 chance or greater it was incurred in service and if VA has no evidence to the contrary – under the doctrine of reasonable doubt (38 CFR 3.102) – the veteran will receive an award.

If it is going to take you some time to assemble the evidence for the application, do an "Intent to File" using the following form:

VA Form 21-0966 INTENT TO FILE

Forms to Use:
VHA-10-5345 – Request for and Authorization to Release Medical Records
VHA-10-5345a – Individual's Request for a Copy of Their Own Health Information
VBA-21-526EZ-ARE – Application for Disability Compensation and Related Compensation Benefits
VBA-21-0781a-ARE – Statement in Support of Claim for Service Connection for PTSD Secondary to Personal Assault
VBA-21-0781-ARE – Statement in Support of Claim for Service Connection for PTSD
VBA-21-4142-ARE – Authorization and Consent to Release Information to the Department of Veterans Affairs

Forms for Representation for Assistance if Desired
VBA-21-22A-ARE – Appointment of Individual a Claimant's Representative
VBA-21-0845-ARE – Authorization to Disclose Personal Information to a Third Party

Steps in the Fully Developed Claim Process to Follow:
1. Decide Whether the Condition Warrants Making a Claim
2. Always File an "Intent to File"
3. Get a Copy of Your Discharge and Locate Service Treatment Records (STR)
4. Obtain Your Own Private Medical Records
5. Have Your Private Doctors or Specialists Do Disability Evaluations
6. Have Your Doctors/Specialists Provide Opinion Letters for Service-Connected
7. Obtain or Produce Lay Evidence
8. Locate Records to Establish Assignment Location or Type of Duty Where Applicable
9. Make Sure the Evidence Conforms with the Rating Decision Criteria in Section C
10. Understand the Claim Forms and the Forms for Obtaining Records
11. Fill out the "Fully Developed Claim" Forms for the Claimed Benefit
12. Check and Double Check Everything and Include All Necessary Forms
13. Arrange for Representation and Third-Party Help If Needed
14. Provide a Cover Letter to Help the Service Representative Understand the Claim
15. Submit the Claim to Your Regional Office of Jurisdiction
16. Understand the Acknowledgment Letter from Your Veterans Service Center
17. Use VA Form 21-4138 for Purposes of Correspondence on the Claim
18. Expect Scheduling of a Compensation and Pension Examination
19. Decide How to Proceed if the Claimant Dies before the Claim Is Adjudicated

13. Hearing Loss with or without Tinnitus

We approach this application using these procedures.

- First, you need to print out the document found on the Data Disk entitled "Elements of the Fully Developed Claim Process." This allows you to follow the steps in the claim process without having to go back and forth to the fully developed claim section in this book. A printout provides you a separate document that you can refer to as you read the instructions for each type of claim. You can also make notes on the document that you print out.

- Second, we will mention pertinent details pertaining to this particular kind of claim .

- Third, we will list the forms that should be used with this particular kind of claim application. These forms are found on the Data Disk under the folder entitled "2 Application for Compensation and DIC."

- Fourth, we will provide you the steps from the elements of the fully developed claim process that you will use for this particular type of claim.

Details:
Tinnitus and hearing loss are the #1 and #2 most common awarded conditions for Compensation. Tinnitus connected to service is ratable at 10% disability. Tinnitus is a ringing or rushing or other sound only perceived by the individual and not by anyone else. Most people describe it as extremely high-pitched. Depending on the degree, it can be very disconcerting and interfere with normal functioning. Generally, service-connected tinnitus should be persistent – meaning it is present most of the time. This establishes it as chronic. Establishing service connection for tinnitus by itself is generally not that difficult. This is because there is no definitive test for this condition and VA must accept the word of the person afflicted that it exists.

Tinnitus at 10% – as a combined rating – is often awarded in combination with noise induced hearing loss which is typically rated at 0%. This is because tinnitus is a common symptom of noise induced hearing loss. The hearing loss is much easier to establish as a service connection because the condition can be recognized through testing and because it is well-known that certain noise exposure conditions will cause it. For most cases of hearing loss, you must have the tinnitus or you will only get a 0% rating. With the tinnitus you will get 10% as a combined rating.

As long as duty can be established where the claimant was exposed sufficiently to loud noise or sudden air pressure changes resulting in hearing loss, these types of claims are not that difficult to generate an award. If the hearing loss by itself is severe enough, it could result in a combined or single rating of 20%, 30% or even 100%.

Establishing an assignment in the service that is consistent with producing noise induced hearing loss and enough exposure over time is often important to winning one of these claims. Your personnel records or other evidence should show that you had such assignments in the service. For example, you may have been assigned to a gunnery unit or you may have worked in the belly of a ship in the engine room or on the flight deck exposed to engine noise or catapult noise or on the flight line on a land base or you were in combat firing weapons or the list goes on.

When initiating one of these claims, you should always go to a private ear nose and throat doctor (otolaryngologist) who has a hearing lab and a state certified audiologist on staff. This will tell you whether you have noise induced hearing loss or not. Without your own lab test, you cannot do a fully developed claim and it could take a long time before VA will order its own hearing test. In your consultation with the doctor, you must establish – as a matter of record and based on your own testimony – that the hearing loss or the tinnitus or both manifest within a reasonable time of leaving the service. If it has been 50 years, and you just developed tinnitus, the VA is going to question whether it was service-connected even though it may take that many years to catch up to you.

Perhaps you are convinced the hearing loss or tinnitus or both are due to service, but you cannot prove that you were exposed to any conditions that may have caused the hearing loss and/or tinnitus. If enough evidence is produced to show that there is a reasonable assumption or inference that the current disability is service-connected, then a strong opinion letter from a physician might sway VA to make a favorable decision even in the absence of any evidence of exposure.

If your examining physician feels very strongly about writing an opinion letter for you, you should always do this. Even if the physician doesn't feel comfortable doing an opinion letter, try and find out if he or she has any feelings about whether the condition is service connected or not. If he or she indicates a willingness to write even a weak opinion, by all means do whatever you can to facilitate this opinion letter.

This soft approach may seem more reasonable to the examining medical practitioner. The physician will use the words that the current disability is "at least as likely as not" to have been incurred in the service based on information provided by the veteran and an examination by the physician. The physician has opined that there is a 50-50 chance or greater it was incurred in service and if VA has no evidence to the contrary – under the doctrine of reasonable doubt (38 CFR 3.102) – the veteran will receive an award.

Make sure you include your hearing test along with the doctor consultation – establishing that you have had persistent tinnitus for a long time – with your initial claim. VA will usually order a C&P examination for this kind of claim unless the opinion letter from your doctor is very strong. Because you have paved the way with fully developed information, the exam – if it is ordered – will likely be scheduled within a matter of months of filing. Otherwise, who knows how long you would have to wait if you did not pave the way with fully developed information. When you show up for the VA hearing exam, you must also establish as a matter of record, with your own testimony, that the tinnitus is persistent and that it first manifested sometime close to getting out of service.

This is another one of those claims that rely on inference and probability. VA typically cannot provide evidence that your hearing loss and accompanying tinnitus was not incurred in service. Again it's a 50-50 probability that it was service-connected or was not. Just as it is with the exposure claims above – which noise is – VA will have to use the principle of reasonable doubt and award you the claim. This is why there are so many veterans on hearing loss claims or hearing loss with tinnitus or tinnitus alone.

If it is going to take you some time to assemble the evidence for the application, do an "Intent to File" using the following form:

VA Form 21-0966 INTENT TO FILE

Forms to Use:
VHA-10-5345 – Request for and Authorization to Release Medical Records
VHA-10-5345a – Individual's Request for a Copy of Their Own Health Information
VBA-21-526EZ-ARE – Application for Disability Compensation and Related Compensation Benefits
VBA-21-4142-ARE – Authorization and Consent to Release Information to the Department of Veterans Affairs
VBA-21-526EZ-ARE – Application for Disability Compensation and Related Compensation Benefits

Forms for Representation for Assistance if Desired
VBA-21-22A-ARE – Appointment of Individual a Claimant's Representative
VBA-21-0845-ARE – Authorization to Disclose Personal Information to a Third Party

Steps in the Fully Developed Claim Process to Follow:

1. Decide Whether the Condition Warrants Making a Claim
2. Always File an "Intent to File"
3. Get a Copy of Your Discharge and Locate Service Treatment Records (STR)
4. Obtain Your Own Private Medical Records
5. Have Your Private Doctors or Specialists Do Disability Evaluations
6. Have Your Doctors/Specialists Provide Opinion Letters for Service-Connected
7. Obtain or Produce Lay Evidence
8. Locate Records to Establish Assignment Location or Type of Duty Where Applicable
9. Make Sure the Evidence Conforms with the Rating Decision Criteria in Section C
10. Understand the Claim Forms and the Forms for Obtaining Records
11. Fill out the "Fully Developed Claim" Forms for the Claimed Benefit
12. Check and Double Check Everything and Include All Necessary Forms
13. Arrange for Representation and Third-Party Help If Needed
14. Provide a Cover Letter to Help the Service Representative Understand the Claim
15. Submit the Claim to Your Regional Office of Jurisdiction
16. Understand the Acknowledgment Letter from Your Veterans Service Center
17. Use VA Form 21-4138 for Purposes of Correspondence on the Claim
18. Expect Scheduling of a Compensation and Pension Examination
19. Decide How to Proceed if the Claimant Dies before the Claim Is Adjudicated

14. PTIU – Permanent and Total Disability Due to Individual Unemployability

Details:
We have provided detailed information on unemployability in the appendix of this book. You may want to read this information in order to understand the claim before submitting any information.

This is a rating increase for someone already on claim to produce the equivalent of 100% disabled, even though the existing underlying rating remains the same. However, Individual Unemployability pays out at the 100% rate. The veteran must currently be service connected for a single disability evaluated at least 60 percent disabling or service connected for multiple disabilities evaluated at least 70 percent disabling, with one of the multiple disabilities rated at least 40 percent disabling. There are circumstances where the requirement for a single 60 or 40 percent disability may be met by a combination of disabilities that can be considered a single disability. There is no age test for this rating. This means a retired 85-year-old who meets the criteria could just as well be considered unemployable as a younger person.

Unemployability means the inability of a veteran to secure or follow a substantially gainful occupation. A finding of unemployability cannot be made if the evidence shows that the veteran is engaged in, or is capable of being engaged in, a substantially gainful occupation. However, a finding could be made if the evidence shows marginal employment. Marginal employment is defined in terms of a veteran's earned annual income.

For a voluntarily-retired individual, not producing earned income, this alternative test for marginal employment would not be appropriate and the test of "capable of being engaged in a substantially gainful occupation" would have to be the test. This marginal employment income should generally not exceed the government's established poverty threshold for one person. Exceeding this threshold may indicate a substantially gainful occupation, as noted by the Court of Appeals for Veteran's Claims (CAVC) in Faust v. West, 13 Vet.App. 342 (2000), where a substantially gainful occupation was defined as "one that provides annual income that exceeds the poverty threshold for one person."

In addition to the income criterion, evidence showing that employment is marginal rather than substantially gainful may also exist on a "facts found" basis. Examples of this marginal status include employment in the protected environment of a family business or sheltered workshop. Such fact-based marginal employment is consistent with a finding of unemployability.

Just filling out the appropriate form and submitting it to the Regional Office is an extremely ineffective way to get an award. This approach will most likely result in a denial after a year or two of sitting on the shelf. These claims are very difficult and require a great deal of effort and evidence in order to pull them off. On the other hand, the difference in income between 60% or 70% and 100% is significant and often warrants the effort. In addition, anyone needing the aid and attendance of another person or being housebound and wanting these allowances as additional income under Compensation, must be 100% disabled or individually unemployable (IU) in order to receive the additional monetary allowances for aid and attendance or housebound.

We highly suggest that you receive expert opinion letters on unemployability due to your service connected disability, not only from your private physician, but also engage the services of a qualified employment counseling specialist who makes determinations of this sort for Social Security disability. You can generally find these people by calling a law office that deals in Social Security and explaining to them what you are doing. Generally, they will cooperate with you because they are not interested in this type of representation but they do want to help veterans.

If it is going to take you some time to assemble the evidence for the application, do an "Intent to File" using the following form:

VA Form 21-0966 INTENT TO FILE

Forms to Use:
VHA-10-5345 – Request for and Authorization to Release Medical Records
VHA-10-5345a – Individual's Request for a Copy of Their Own Health Information
VBA-21-4142-ARE – Authorization and Consent to Release Information to the Department of Veterans Affairs
VBA-21-8940-ARE – Veteran's Application for Increased Compensation Based on Unemployability

Forms for Representation for Assistance if Desired
VBA-21-22A-ARE – Appointment of Individual a Claimant's Representative
VBA-21-0845-ARE – Authorization to Disclose Personal Information to a Third Party

Steps in the Claim Process to Follow:
This is not an original claim but a request for a change in your current disability rating. You will fill out the appropriate form above and provide the following information below with your claim.

4. Obtain Your Own Private Medical Records
5. Have Your Private Doctors or Specialists Do Disability Evaluations
6. Have Your Doctors/Specialists Provide Opinion Letters for Service-Connected
7. Obtain or Produce Lay Evidence
9. Make Sure the Evidence Conforms with the Rating Decision Criteria in Section C
18. Expect Scheduling of a Compensation and Pension Examination
19. Decide How to Proceed if the Claimant Dies before the Claim Is Adjudicated

15. Gulf War Disorders – Service Connection Is Presumed with a Time Limit

We approach this application using these procedures.

- First, you need to print out the document found on the Data Disk entitled "Elements of the Fully Developed Claim Process." This allows you to follow the steps in the claim process without having to go back and forth to the fully developed claim section in this book. A printout provides you a separate document that you can refer to as you read the instructions for each type of claim. You can also make notes on the print out.

- Second, we will mention pertinent details pertaining to this particular kind of claim .

- Third, we will list the forms that should be used with this particular kind of claim application. These forms are found on the Data Disk under the folder entitled "2 Application for Compensation and DIC."

- Fourth, we will provide you the steps from the elements of the fully developed claim process that you will use for this particular type of claim.

Details:
Veterans may receive Disability Compensation for chronic disabilities resulting from undiagnosed illnesses and/or medically unexplained chronic multi-symptom illnesses defined by a cluster of signs or symptoms. A disability is chronic if it has existed at least 6 months.

The undiagnosed illnesses must have appeared either during active service in the Southwest Asia Theater of Operations during the Gulf War period of Aug. 2, 1990, to July 31, 1991, or to a degree of at least 10 percent at any time since then through Dec. 31, 2011. This theater of operations includes Iraq, Kuwait, Saudi Arabia, the neutral zone between Iraq and Saudi Arabia, Bahrain, Qatar, the United Arab Emirates, Oman, the Gulf of Aden, the Gulf of Oman, the Persian Gulf, the Arabian Sea, the Red Sea, and the airspace above these locations.

Because service connection is presumed, it is not required to produce evidence for service connection – only evidence of the manifestation of the disorder or disease. That said, the claimant must provide evidence of being in the service in the particular theater of operation. Disability has to become manifest to 10% or more from the time of active duty and no later than December 31, 2011. Examples of symptoms of an undiagnosed illness and medically unexplained chronic multi-symptom illness defined by a cluster of signs and symptoms include:

- chronic fatigue syndrome,
- fibromyalgia,
- irritable bowel syndrome,
- fatigue,
- signs or symptoms involving the skin,
- skin disorders,
- headache,
- muscle pain,
- joint pain,

- neurological signs or symptoms,
- neuropsychological signs or symptoms,
- signs or symptoms involving the respiratory system (upper or lower),
- sleep disturbances,
- gastrointestinal signs or symptoms,
- cardiovascular signs or symptoms,
- abnormal weight loss, and
- menstrual disorders.

If no previous claim has been made or if a previous claim was made but there was no chronic disability for an award, it may be possible to submit a new claim or reopen the previous claim as long as this is done within one year of any correspondence with VA. It is important to note that the condition had to have manifest itself at 10% or more prior to December 31, 2011. You would have to provide concrete medical evidence of the manifestation of symptoms prior to December 31, 2011 to even proceed. Otherwise, don't bother to make a claim.

If it is going to take you some time to assemble the evidence for the application, do an "Intent to File" using the following form:

VA Form 21-0966 INTENT TO FILE

Forms to Use:
VHA-10-5345 – Request for and Authorization to Release Medical Records
VHA-10-5345a – Individual's Request for a Copy of Their Own Health Information
VBA-21-526EZ-ARE – Application for Disability Compensation and Related Compensation Benefits
VBA-21-4142-ARE – Authorization and Consent to Release Information to the Department of Veterans Affairs

Forms for Representation for Assistance if Desired
VBA-21-22A-ARE – Appointment of Individual a Claimant's Representative
VBA-21-0845-ARE – Authorization to Disclose Personal Information to a Third Party

Steps in the Fully Developed Claim Process to Follow:
1. Decide Whether the Condition Warrants Making a Claim
2. Always File an "Intent to File"
3. Get a Copy of Your Discharge and Locate Service Treatment Records (STR)
4. Obtain Your Own Private Medical Records
5. Have Your Private Doctors or Specialists Do Disability Evaluations
7. Obtain or Produce Lay Evidence
8. Locate Records to Establish Assignment Location or Type of Duty Where Applicable
9. Make Sure the Evidence Conforms with the Rating Decision Criteria in Section C
10. Understand the Claim Forms and the Forms for Obtaining Records
11. Fill out the "Fully Developed Claim" Forms for the Claimed Benefit
12. Check and Double Check Everything and Include All Necessary Forms
13. Arrange for Representation and Third-Party Help If Needed
14. Provide a Cover Letter to Help the Service Representative Understand the Claim

15. Submit the Claim to Your Regional Office of Jurisdiction
16. Understand the Acknowledgment Letter from Your Veterans Service Center
17. Use VA Form 21-4138 for Purposes of Correspondence on the Claim
18. Expect Scheduling of a Compensation and Pension Examination
19. Decide How to Proceed if the Claimant Dies before the Claim Is Adjudicated

16. Request for Reevaluation or Change for an Existing Benefit

Details:
As we mentioned previously, changes to an existing benefit represent about three quarters of all 900,000 claims pending for approval. Veterans already on claim are getting older and in many cases their disabilities are increasing in severity. If they have legitimate medical or work-related evidence of an increase in disability, there is a possibility for an increased rating and more monthly income.

It can also work in the opposite direction. Sometimes, a request for reevaluation of a rating can result in downgrading that rating or even reevaluating whether a service connection exists. We have heard of veterans not only losing the rating but losing the service connection and the entire award. You should always be careful in requesting a change that you have a legitimate increase in disability and that a reevaluation won't reduce your existing award. If you have been service-connected for at least 10 years, that service connection is protected and VA cannot take it away from you. If you have had the same rating for at least 20 years, that rating is protected and VA can only increase it but not decrease it.

Some veterans have developed secondary conditions, meaning that their primary disability has resulted in conditions that are caused by the primary disability. For example, service-connected diabetes can result in cardiovascular disease which would be a new condition but would be considered secondary to the diabetes and therefore service-connected. If the cardiovascular disease results in disability with a rating, the VA will combine those ratings to produce a new larger rating. Combined ratings are not additive. For example a 40% rating for diabetes and a 20% rating for cardiovascular disease results in a 50% combined rating not a 60% additive rating.

If you have developed a disability that has been aggravated or caused by a service-connected disability, do not continue in this section. Instead, go to the section above that is devoted to this type of claim " #10. Secondary Service Connection or Aggravation of an Existing Condition."

Also please note that if your disability has worsened or you have developed new disabilities to the point that you are severely disabled and could qualify under "Special Monthly Compensation," (SMC) go ahead and go to that section below – claim type #19 – for this type of application instead of going to claim type #10.

If enough evidence is produced to show that there is a reasonable assumption or inference that the current disability is worsened, then a strong opinion letter from a physician might sway VA to make a favorable decision.

Oftentimes, a private physician is unwilling to provide an opinion that the current condition has worsened. You may be able to find a physician who will write an opinion letter that there is a 50-50 chance the current condition causes greater disability. This seems more reasonable to the examining medical practitioner. The physician will use the words that the current disability is "at least as likely as not" to have caused greater disability based on information provided by the veteran and an examination by the physician. The physician has opined that there is a 50-50 chance things are worse and if VA has no evidence to the contrary – under the doctrine of reasonable doubt (38 CFR 3.102) – the veteran will receive an award.

You should not submit a request for a change or increase in rating unless you are sure that your disability has worsened or you have developed a new service-connected disability. We suspect many veterans submit a request not really understanding what they are doing and simply hope that they will somehow get a larger check. For example, a veteran with diabetes has developed numbness in his feet – a possible new service-connected disability associated with diabetes for Agent Orange exposure – but it has not affected his ability to ambulate, to dress, to bathe or in any other way to function over what he had experienced in the past. An increase or change may not justified. The claimant has to justify any increase or change with medical evidence that the service-connected disability has worsened, a new ratable service-connected disability has appeared or a new secondary disability has developed. Without this, you are wasting the time of the veteran service representatives and adding to the backlog – preventing other veterans from getting benefits.

If it is going to take you some time to assemble the evidence for the application, do an "Intent to File" using the following form:

VA Form 21-0966 INTENT TO FILE

Forms to Use:
VHA-10-5345 – Request for and Authorization to Release Medical Records
VHA-10-5345a – Individual's Request for a Copy of Their Own Health Information
VBA-21-4192-ARE – Request for Employment Information in Connection With Claim for Disability Benefits
VBA-21-526EZ-ARE – Application for Disability Compensation and Related Compensation Benefits

Forms for Representation for Assistance if Desired
VBA-21-22A-ARE – Appointment of Individual a Claimant's Representative
VBA-21-0845-ARE – Authorization to Disclose Personal Information to a Third Party

Steps to Follow:
Fill out VA form 21-526EZ and check the appropriate box and provide a narrative on why you are requesting a change or reevaluation. Make sure that you submit all pertinent private medical records with this application. This is important, because otherwise the development team could take forever to obtain enough information to send to the rating team to then order a C&P exam for you. You need to justify up front what you are requesting so that it can be treated as if it were fully developed. You should also have your physicians prepare opinion letters whether they think the condition has worsened or whether you have developed a new service-connected disability because of an underlying condition. Read the section on fully developed claims above on how to do these opinion letters.

Finally, have your physician or physicians prepare a "Disability Benefits Questionnaire" pertaining to the particular kind of condition you are having VA examine. These DBQ's are found on the claim support Data Disk. Turn all of this information in at once when you submit your change form. This is important. Based on all of this evidence, the VA should order a C&P examination fairly quickly to evaluate the issue.

17. Section 1151 Claim

We approach this application using these procedures.

- First, you need to print out the document found on the Data Disk entitled "Elements of the Fully Developed Claim Process." This allows you to follow the steps in the claim process without having to go back and forth to the fully developed claim section in this book. A printout provides you a separate document that you can refer to as you read the instructions for each type of claim. You can also make notes on the document that you print out.

- Second, we will mention pertinent details pertaining to this particular kind of claim .

- Third, we will list the forms that should be used with this particular kind of claim application. These forms are found on the Data Disk under the folder entitled "2 Application for Compensation and DIC."

- Fourth, we will provide you the steps from the elements of the fully developed claim process that you will use for this particular type of claim.

Details:
This non-service-connected disability benefit is named after the section in Title 38 United States Code where it is found. If a non-service-connected disabling condition is caused by or aggravated by VA examination, hospital care, medical or surgical treatment, Vocational Rehabilitation, or (beginning November 1, 2000) a program of Compensated Work Therapy under 38 USC 1718, then Compensation is payable for that condition as though the condition was service-connected.

Remember, however, that even though Compensation is being paid, the condition is in fact NOT service-connected, and should not be called such. Ancillary benefits beyond Compensation are limited in Section 1151 cases: in general, they are restricted to the applicable priority medical care; a clothing allowance (where applicable); and, where the qualifying level of compensable disability is present, an automobile and appropriate special adaptive equipment under 38 USC, Chapter 39 and special adapted housing under 38 USC, Chapter 21.

Compensation for disabilities under Section 1151 may be combined with Compensation for any service-connected conditions the veteran may also have. If the veteran is awarded any amount from a judicial award, settlement, or compromise for the same condition(s) for which compensation under Section 1151 has been (or will be) authorized, the Compensation otherwise payable for such condition(s) must be withheld until the full amount of the award, settlement, or compromise has been recovered. [38 USC 1151; 38 CFR §§ 3.358, 3.361–3.363, 3.800] Such recovery does not affect entitlement to any Compensation payable for service-connected disabilities, however.

These types of claims are not common because the burden of proof is so high. In order to meet the qualifications of 38 U.S.C. 1151, the proximate cause of additional disability or death must be

- carelessness, negligence, lack of proper skill, error in judgment, or similar instance of fault on the part of VA in furnishing the hospital care, medical or surgical treatment, or examination
- an event not reasonably foreseeable, or
- the provision of
  - training and rehabilitation by VA or one of its service providers as part of an approved rehabilitation program under 38 U.S.C. Chapter 31, or
  - a CWT program.

Even if you succeed in getting one division of VA to blame the other division of VA for doing wrong, you still have to demonstrate the exact nature of your disability before and after the treatment. Evidence for this claim must be some sort of hardcopy evidence from hospital or clinical or organizational records. You would have a difficult time establishing an award based on personal testimony or testimony of witnesses. This is not to say it can't be done.

For example, if you had a knee operation for joint replacement and they did it on your good knee instead of your bad knee, this is pretty easy to establish. Or if you have a mastectomy and they removed the wrong breast, that's pretty simple to prove. Or if they operated on you and left a surgical instrument inside – pretty straightforward. It's the errors or negligence involving treatment protocols or surgical procedures and what was right and what was wrong for the particular condition that might be difficult to prove.

VA will consider as an informal claim for benefits under 38 U.S.C. 1151, any statement showing an intent to file a claim for benefits resulting from

- hospital, medical or surgical treatment by VA
- examination by VA, or
- pursuit of a course of vocational rehabilitation.

VA Form 21-0966 INTENT TO FILE

A claim for Section 1151 may also be filed as a formal claim on

- *VA Form 21-526ez, Veteran's Application for Compensation or Pension.*
- *VA Form 21-534ez, Application for Dependency and Indemnity Compensation or Death Pension and Accrued Benefits by a Surviving Spouse or Child, or all talk during this is to*
- *VA Form 21-535, Application for Dependency and Indemnity Compensation by Parent(s).*

Note: If an individual or his/her representative files an informal claim, send him/her the appropriate application form.

You should seek help with representation for such a claim. Likely it will require an attorney who specializes in these types of medical malpractice claims for veterans. Perhaps a service organization has experience with these claims as well.

18. Tropical Diseases – Service Connection Is Presumed with a Time Limit

We approach this application using these procedures.

- First, you need to print out the document found on the Data Disk entitled "Elements of the Fully Developed Claim Process." This allows you to follow the steps in the claim process without having to go back and forth to the fully developed claim section in this book. A printout provides you a separate document that you can refer to as you read the instructions for each type of claim. You can also make notes on the document that you print out.

- Second, we will mention pertinent details pertaining to this particular kind of claim .

- Third, we will list the forms that should be used with this particular kind of claim application. These forms are found on the Data Disk under the folder entitled "2 Application for Compensation and DIC."

- Fourth, we will provide you the steps from the elements of the fully developed claim process that you will use for this particular type of claim.

Details:
The veteran must have 90 continuous days or more of service. The disorder or disease must manifest disability to a degree of 10% or more within one year from date of separation or at the end of the standard incubation period. Disorders or diseases caused by treatment may also be considered service-connected. Because service connection is presumed, it is not required to produce evidence for service connection – only evidence of the manifestation of the disorder or disease. Manifesting does not necessarily mean medical diagnosis, only that evidence shows the existence.

- Amebiasis.
- Blackwater fever.
- Cholera.
- Dracontiasis.
- Dysentery.
- Filariasis.
- Leishmaniasis, including kala-azar.
- Loiasis.
- Malaria.
- Onchocerciasis.
- Oroya fever.
- Pinta.

- Plague.
- Schistosomiasis.
- Yaws.
- Yellow fever.

Qualifying periods of service for these infectious diseases include active military, naval, or air service in the above stated Southwest Asia theater of operations during the Gulf War period of August 2, 1990, to July 30, 1991, or active military, naval, or air service on or after September 19, 2001, in Afghanistan.

- Brucellosis,
- Campylobacter jejuni,
- Coxiella burnetti (Q fever),
- Malaria,
- Mycobacterium tuberculosis,
- Nontyphoid Salmonella,
- Shigella,
- Visceral leishmaniasis, and
- West Nile virus.

If it is going to take you some time to assemble the evidence for the application, do an "Intent to File" using the following form:

VA Form 21-0966 INTENT TO FILE

Forms to Use:
VHA-10-5345 – Request for and Authorization to Release Medical Records
VHA-10-5345a – Individual's Request for a Copy of Their Own Health Information
VBA-21-526EZ-ARE – Application for Disability Compensation and Related Compensation Benefits
VBA-21-4142-ARE – Authorization and Consent to Release Information to the Department of Veterans Affairs

Forms for Representation for Assistance if Desired
VBA-21-22A-ARE – Appointment of Individual a Claimant's Representative
VBA-21-0845-ARE – Authorization to Disclose Personal Information to a Third Party

Steps in the Fully Developed Claim Process to Follow:

1. Decide Whether the Condition Warrants Making a Claim
2. Always File an "Intent to File"
3. Get a Copy of Your Discharge and Locate Service Treatment Records (STR)
4. Obtain Your Own Private Medical Records
5. Have Your Private Doctors or Specialists Do Disability Evaluations
7. Obtain or Produce Lay Evidence
8. Locate Records to Establish Assignment Location or Type of Duty Where Applicable
9. Make Sure the Evidence Conforms with the Rating Decision Criteria in Section C
10. Understand the Claim Forms and the Forms for Obtaining Records

11. Fill out the "Fully Developed Claim" Forms for the Claimed Benefit
12. Check and Double Check Everything and Include All Necessary Forms
13. Arrange for Representation and Third-Party Help If Needed
14. Provide a Cover Letter to Help the Service Representative Understand the Claim
15. Submit the Claim to Your Regional Office of Jurisdiction
16. Understand the Acknowledgment Letter from Your Veterans Service Center
17. Use VA Form 21-4138 for Purposes of Correspondence on the Claim
18. Expect Scheduling of a Compensation and Pension Examination
19. Decide How to Proceed if the Claimant Dies before the Claim Is Adjudicated

19. Special Monthly Compensation (SMC)

You may approach this application using these procedures below. Or, if the veteran is currently on award and seeking a higher level of disability, you should treat an application for SMC as a request for reevaluation under claim type "16. Request for Reevaluation or Change for an Existing Benefit" above. If this is the case, go directly to #16 and don't use the procedures in this section.

- First, you need to print out the document found on the Data Disk entitled "Elements of the Fully Developed Claim Process." This allows you to follow the steps in the claim process without having to go back and forth to the fully developed claim section in this book. A printout provides you a separate document that you can refer to as you read the instructions for each type of claim. You can also make notes on the document that you print out.

- Second, we will mention pertinent details pertaining to this particular kind of claim .

- Third, we will list the forms that should be used with this particular kind of claim application. These forms are found on the Data Disk under the folder entitled "2 Application for Compensation and DIC."

- Fourth, we will provide you the steps from the elements of the fully developed claim process that you will use for this particular type of claim.

Details:
The majority of service-connected disabilities are defined by a percentage ranging from 0 to 100 percent to reflect the severity of the condition(s) and the disabling effects they have on the veteran. These percentages are explicitly defined by Federal Regulations under the Schedule for Rating Disabilities (there is a copy of this on the Data Disk) and are assigned a monetary Compensation award based on the vocational limitations that these injuries or disorders cause and subsequently the effect they may have on monetary earnings.

Some injuries and disorders are more severe in nature and result in several additional debilitating residual conditions that can have additional adverse affects on an individual's socioeconomic state. To better assist with meeting the specialized needs of these individuals, additional benefits are available under Special Monthly Compensation (SMC) ratings provided under Title 38 of U.S.C. 1114. These ratings are in addition to the numerical ratings established under the standard rating schedule and are identified by letters such as SMC (k), SMC (l), SMC (m), SMC (n), SMC (o), SMC(p), SMC (r), SMC (s) and the recently added SMC (t). These rates are simply named after the subsections of the Code of Federal Regulations that outline the required eligibility requirements for each level of SMC. SMC provides additional monetary Compensation awards and where applicable can establish entitlement to additional ancillary benefits such as the VA's Specially Adapted Housing Grant and the Automobile and Adaptive Equipment Grants.

The basic elements of Special Monthly Compensation Ratings include anatomical (or physical) loss or the loss of use of limbs, hands, feet and/or reproductive organs; aphonia; deafness; blindness; loss of bowel and bladder control; being permanently housebound; and a need for regular aid and attendance with activities of daily living or a higher level of care–all of which must be a result of the veteran's service-connected disabilities.

Most veterans suffering these disabilities are fully aware of the possibility of receiving SMC where it is appropriate and have long since applied. One never knows, however, if someone fell through the cracks and never bothered to apply.

If it is going to take you some time to assemble the evidence for the application, do an "Intent to File" using the following form:

VA Form 21-0966 INTENT TO FILE

Forms to Use:
VHA-10-5345 – Request for and Authorization to Release Medical Records
VHA-10-5345a – Individual's Request for a Copy of Their Own Health Information
VBA-21-526EZ-ARE – Application for Disability Compensation and Related Compensation Benefits
VBA-21-4142-ARE – Authorization and Consent to Release Information to the Department of Veterans Affairs

Steps in the Fully Developed Claim Process to Follow:
1. Decide Whether the Condition Warrants Making a Claim
2. Always File an "Intent to File"
3. Get a Copy of Your Discharge and Locate Service Treatment Records (STR)
4. Obtain Your Own Private Medical Records
5. Have Your Private Doctors or Specialists Do Disability Evaluations
6. Have Your Doctors/Specialists Provide Opinion Letters for Service-Connected
7. Obtain or Produce Lay Evidence
8. Locate Records to Establish Assignment Location or Type of Duty Where Applicable
9. Make Sure the Evidence Conforms with the Rating Decision Criteria in Section C
10. Understand the Claim Forms and the Forms for Obtaining Records
11. Fill out the "Fully Developed Claim" Forms for the Claimed Benefit
12. Check and Double Check Everything and Include All Necessary Forms
13. Arrange for Representation and Third-Party Help If Needed
14. Provide a Cover Letter to Help the Service Representative Understand the Claim
15. Submit the Claim to Your Regional Office of Jurisdiction
16. Understand the Acknowledgment Letter from Your Veterans Service Center
17. Use VA Form 21-4138 for Purposes of Correspondence on the Claim
18. Expect Scheduling of a Compensation and Pension Examination

19. Decide How to Proceed if the Claimant Dies before the Claim Is Adjudicated

20. Specific Special Allowances

Details:
Even though most disabled veterans are aware of these special allowances, it doesn't hurt to reiterate what is available. Perhaps the veteran is in need at this point and never bothered to apply previously. This is a reminder of these benefits. We provide no further instructions other than for the veteran to get in touch with an appropriate service officer for application where applicable. Here is a list of these special allowances.

Specially Adapted Housing Grants
Automobile Allowance
Clothing Allowance
Medal of Honor Pension
Temporary Residence Adaptation (TRA)
Supplemental Financing

The clothing allowance is available through the Veterans Health Administration. You need to be enrolled in health care to get this. The other benefits requires special application due to certain severe disabilities. Contact a service organization if you need help getting these special allowances. Here are the forms that are appropriate to these benefits.

VHA-10-0103 – Assistance in Acquiring Home Improvement and Structural Alterations (HISA Grant)
VBA-21-4502-ARE – Application for Automobile or Other Conveyance and Adaptive Equipment
VBA-26-4555-ARE – Application in Acquiring Special Housing Adaptations

21. HISA Grants (Home Improvement and Structural Alterations)

Details:
These are one-time grants of either $2,000 or $6,800 to any veteran who qualifies for modifying the home for disability. They are awarded through the local regional medical center. The veteran must be enrolled in VA health care and receive a prescription from the health care provider for this grant. The grant comes from the veterans local regional medical center.

Applying for a HISA Grant
The veteran must be registered with VA health care. In order to receive a HISA grant, the Veteran must first have a prescription from a VA or fee-basis physician. This must include:

- The diagnosis with medical justification
- The Veteran's name, address, SSN, and phone number(s)

To apply, the Veteran must first provide:

- A completed VA Form 10-0103, <u>VETERANS APPLICATION FOR ASSISTANCE In Acquiring Home Improvement and Structural Alterations</u>

- If a leased or rented property, written permission from the owner
- Quotes from at least 3 licensed contractors (if required by state law), to include:
- The contractors name, address, telephone, and Federal tax ID number or social security number
- The Veteran's name, address, and telephone number
- Plans and drawings
- An itemized list of estimated materials, cost, and labor cost
- All permits required (it is the contractors responsibility to obtain these)
- A picture of the work site prior to construction

Following are the types of projects that HISA grants will pay for. This is not all inclusive and other appropriate projects may be approved.

(1) Roll-in showers

(2) Construction of wooden or concrete, permanent ramping to provide access to the home

(3) Widening doorways to bedroom, bathroom, etc., to achieve wheelchair access

(4) Lowering of kitchen or bathroom counters and sinks

(5) Improving entrance paths and driveways in immediate area of home to facilitate access to the home

(6) Construction of concrete pads and installation of exterior types of wheelchair lift mechanisms if the installation cost exceeds $500.00

(7) Interior and exterior railing deemed necessary for patients with ambulatory capability or for veterans rated legally blind if the installation cost is over $500.00

(8) Improvements to plumbing or electrical systems made necessary due to the installation of dialysis equipment in the home

(9) Any cost associated with permits, inspection fees, etc., that are required by local ordinances.

HISA will not pay for:

- Walkways to exterior buildings
- Widening of driveways (in excess of a 7ft x 6ft area)
- Spa, hot tub, or Jacuzzi
- Exterior decking (in excess of 8ft x 8ft)

***See the Claims Support Data Disk for submitting to VA's Claims Intake Center

CHAPTER 5
State Veterans Benefits

State Tax Discounts, Special Services and Other Savings for Veterans

Generally Available in All States
All states offer veterans special services, tax breaks and fee waivers . Many available benefits are unique to each state. But in general, all states offer at least the following programs.

- state veterans homes
- burial in state veterans cemeteries
- specialty license plates
- free license plates for disabled veterans
- hiring preference
- credit for state retirement plans

We will discuss briefly benefits common to all states

State Veterans Homes
Every state now has at least one veterans home. The most homes are maintained in Texas which has eight. There are still a number of states that only have one home. There is great demand for this type of housing and it appears from news releases and Internet articles that a number of states are in the process of considering for construction or actually building more veterans homes.

Veterans Homes are generally available to active duty veterans but some states have beds for people who served with the reserves or National Guard and the spouses of veterans. The majority of these homes offer nursing care but some may offer assisted living or domiciliary care. Generally there is no income or asset test. Most veterans in most states would qualify. Many states have waiting lists of weeks to months for available beds. Each facility has different eligibility rules and there is an application process. You cannot simply walk in the door and arrange for nursing care on the spot. You must contact the veterans home you are interested in to find out the availability of beds and the application process.

We discuss state veterans homes in more detail below.

Burial in State Veterans Cemeteries
At least 43 states have established state veterans cemeteries. Some states only have one cemetery while other states such as Hawaii offer as many as 8 different cemeteries. Eligibility is similar to Department of Veterans Affairs (VA) national cemeteries, but may include residency requirements. Even though state cemeteries may have been established or improved with Government funds through VA's State Cemetery Grants Program, state veterans cemeteries are run solely by the states.

Motor vehicles and License Plates
Motor vehicle registration, sales tax on a vehicle and license plates are generally free in those states where veterans are receiving disability grants from VA towards purchase or modification of a motor vehicle. In most states special design license plates identifying status, discharge or other service status of a veteran are available at no charge or additional charge. In most states, veterans who are disabled can receive license plates and registration for free.

Other Available Benefits

- free hunting or fishing licenses for disabled veterans
- free admission to state parks sometimes for all veterans but typically only for disabled veterans
- free copies of vital records for veterans making application for benefits
- free drivers licenses for disabled veterans
- free recording of discharge papers by County recorders
- free copies of certified discharge papers by County recorders
- tuition assistance for veterans, National Guard and dependents
- property tax exemptions for certain disabled veterans as well as for their widows
- partial property tax exemptions sometimes for any veteran but generally for those who are disabled
- one time grants and stipends for certain veterans or any veteran up to $3,000 in one state
- archiving of discharge records
- state income tax exemption for certain veterans or veterans recently discharged
- disability parking placards for disabled veterans
- honorary high school diplomas for World War II or Korean veterans
- in some states disabled veterans are exempt from payment of occupational taxes, administration fees, and regulatory fees imposed by local governments for peddling, conducting a business, or practicing a profession or semi profession.

Locating Specific Benefits in Each State
These are the most current links to state Departments of Veterans Affairs. State benefits are always changing and a check on the state website will indicate what benefits are available currently.

Alaska http://www.dmva.alaska.gov/
Alabama http://www.va.state.al.us/
Arkansas http://www.veterans.arkansas.gov/
Arizona http://www.azdvs.gov/
California http://www.calvet.ca.gov/
Colorado http://www.colorado.gov/dmva/
Connecticut http://www.ct.gov/ctva/site/default.asp
Delaware http://veteransaffairs.delaware.gov/
District of Columbia http://ova.dc.gov/
Florida http://www.floridavets.org/
Georgia http://veterans.georgia.gov/
Hawaii http://dod.hawaii.gov/

Idaho http://www.veterans.idaho.gov/
Illinois http://www.illinois.gov/veterans
Indiana http://www.in.gov/dva/index.htm
Iowa http://va.iowa.gov/
Kansas http://kcva.ks.gov/
Kentucky http://veterans.ky.gov
Louisiana http://vetaffairs.la.gov/
Maine http://www.maine.gov/dvem/bvs/
Maryland http://veterans.maryland.gov/
Massachusetts http://www.mass.gov/veterans/
Michigan http://www.michigan.gov/dmva
Minnesota http://mn.gov/mdva/
Mississippi http://www.vab.ms.gov/
Missouri http://mvc.dps.mo.gov/
Montana http://dma.mt.gov/
Nebraska http://www.vets.state.ne.us/
Nevada http://www.veterans.nv.gov/
New Hampshire http://www.nh.gov/nhveterans/
New Jersey http://www.state.nj.us/military/
New Mexico http://www.dvs.state.nm.us/
New York http://veterans.ny.gov/
North Carolina http://www.milvets.nc.gov/
North Dakota http://www.nd.gov/veterans/
Ohio http://ohio.gov/
Oklahoma https://www.ok.gov/odva/
Oregon http://www.oregon.gov/ODVA/
Pennsylvania http://www.dmva.pa.gov
Rhode Island http://www.va.gov/directory/guide/state.asp?STATE=RI&dnum=ALL
South Carolina http://www.va.gov/directory/guide/state.asp?State=SC&dnum=ALL
South Dakota http://military.sd.gov/
Tennessee http://www.tn.gov/
Texas http://www.tvc.state.tx.us/
Utah http://veterans.utah.gov/
Vermont http://veterans.vermont.gov/ova
Virginia http://www.dvs.virginia.gov/
Washington http://www.dva.wa.gov/
West Virginia http://www.veterans.wv.gov
Wisconsin http://dva.state.wi.us/
Wyoming http://www.va.gov/directory/guide/state.asp?dnum=ALL&STATE=WY

About State Veterans Homes

State veterans homes fill an important need for veterans with low income and veterans who desire to spend their last years with "comrades" from former active-duty. The predominant service offered is nursing home care. VA nursing homes must be licensed for their particular state and conform with skilled or intermediate nursing services offered in private sector nursing homes in that state. State homes may also offer assisted living or domiciliary care which is a form of supported independent living.

Every state has at least one veterans home and some states like Oklahoma have six or seven of them. There is great demand for the services of these homes but lack of federal and state funding has created a backlog of well over 70 major renovations to existing homes and approximately 22 new homes that are waiting to be built. We will discuss this problem in the section entitled "Challenges Facing the Construction of New Homes".

Unlike private sector nursing homes where the family can walk in the front door and possibly that same day make arrangements for a bed for their loved one, state veterans homes have an application process that could take a number of weeks or months. Many state homes have waiting lists especially for their Alzheimer's long term care units.

No facilities are entirely free to any veteran with an income. The veteran must pay his or her share of the cost. In some states the veterans contribution rates are set and if there's not enough income the family may have to make up the difference. Federal legislation, effective 2007, also allows the federal government to substantially subsidize the cost of veterans with service-connected disabilities in state veterans homes.

We have provided a current list of state veterans homes in the Appendix of this book.

The Appeal of Living in a State Veterans Home

We believe most veterans or their families seek out residency in a state veterans nursing home because they believe this service is one more VA entitlement that should be available to them.

But there is also a similar entitlement available to anyone in most private sector nursing homes -- facilities that may be geographically closer to the family than the nearest veterans home. This is Medicaid. Veterans seeking long term care from VA programs generally don't have the funds for private pay in a nursing home; however, Medicaid will also cover these same people in a private sector Medicaid certified facility. Most families who are seeking help for their loved ones, who are veterans, generally look to VA first before considering Medicaid. Or they are simply not aware of Medicaid. In many cases, Medicaid may be the better choice.

Aside from seeking long term care because of an expectation of entitlement are there any other reasons that veterans would prefer a State home? We asked this question of ourselves because we have noticed that in some states veterans homes are in distant rural areas. The fact that some of these homes are hundreds of miles from urban areas where the majority of veterans would tend to live, made us wonder why some veterans would move long distances to reside in these facilities.

To answer this question we contacted a number of rural state veterans homes on the phone and asked them why a veteran or his or her family would seek out their services as opposed to seeking services in a closer non-veterans facility under Medicaid. Almost unanimously the answer we got was that some veterans like the idea of sharing their living arrangement with other veterans. The facilities almost always referred to this as "camaraderie" -- a band of brotherhood.

Statistically, private sector nursing homes are mostly populated by older women who are generally in poor health. Some men may not feel comfortable in an environment where the activities and the social atmosphere are centered around women. In contrast, veterans homes are almost exclusively populated by men. In addition, based on our observation, we suspect the population of state homes is younger and healthier than that of private sector facilities.

These demographics would suggest that activities and the social atmosphere revolve around the needs of men not women. A younger, healthier population would also suggest veterans homes would offer more opportunity in the form of transportation or scheduled outings for the residents to be out in the community. One veterans home reported to us that they regularly scheduled fishing trips and outings to sporting events for their residents. These would be unheard-of activities for the typical private nursing home.

The second most common reason reported to us why veterans seek out state homes is for financial reasons. In many states the cost of the home is subsidized for veterans who meet an income test. The vet's income is considered sufficient to cover the cost. These veterans may own a home or other assets that they wish to protect from Medicaid and leave to their family. The state veterans home will allow them to give these assets to the family without penalty. Medicaid would require a spend down of those assets or impose a penalty for gifting.

Another reason related to finances may be there are no available Medicaid beds in the veteran's area. The veteran may be paying out of pocket for a nursing facility but have his name on a waiting list for a State Home where the out-of-pocket cost would be much less. When his name comes up he will move to the State home.

A financial incentive for the veteran is that all state veterans homes will apply for the pension benefit for those residents who are eligible. Federal law prohibits VA from paying any more than $90 a month to single veterans who are eligible for Medicaid in a non-veteran nursing home. State veterans homes are exempt from this rule and the single veteran can keep the entire pension amount although most of it will have to apply to the cost of care. For those state veterans homes that also accept Medicaid, pension represents additional disposable income.

Challenges for State Veterans Homes

The following is quoted from the Armed Forces Veterans Homes Foundation:

> "The demand for quality long term veteran care is growing at an astounding rate. Our nation faces the largest aging veteran population in its history. Today, roughly 10 million veterans are aged 65 and over, about 39 percent of all the veterans in America. This proportion will remain unchanged for the next 20 years. The number of veterans aged 85 and over will have increased by 600 percent from 1990 to 2010 and will total nearly two million in all."
>
> "The U.S. Department of Veterans Affairs has now designated the state veterans homes system as its primary provider of long term care service. One hundred new homes are slated to be built in the next 10 years, but even with such aggressive expansion, the demands for service will continue to far exceed the supply."
>
> "America's veterans homes face serious resource shortfalls. Ideally, home costs are shared equally by the Department of Veterans Affairs, state governments and residents. The reality is that 11 states currently provide little or no funding for their veterans home. And the others now face the worst fiscal crisis in 20 years, with two thirds of the states now reporting substantial cuts in programs serving low-income residents, including veterans."
>
> "In addition, nearly every home relies on support from its local veterans community to supplement its resources. Homes commonly log thousands of hours of veteran volunteer time each year, the equivalent of a significant number of full-time paid staff. But these veterans who contribute so generously of their time are dying at an alarming rate. An estimated 700,000 will die this year, and far fewer veterans will be there to follow in their footsteps."
>
> "State Veterans Homes are one of the largest long term care providers in the United States. During 2005, State Veterans Homes furnished 6,852,875 days of nursing home care and 1,477,885 days of domiciliary (assisted living) care. As of February 13, 2006, there were 133 State Veterans Homes in 50 states and Puerto Rico with 30,255 total beds."

History of State Veterans Homes

Our nation was faced with a staggering number of soldiers and sailors in critical need of medical care following the Civil War, and although the national homes were in operation at the time, their capacity was inadequate to meet the demand. At that time, several states established veterans homes, at their own expense, to provide for those residents who had served so honorably in the military.

In 1888, the U.S. Congress authorized federal cost-sharing for state veterans homes--about 30 cents per resident per day. Since the creation of the Veterans Administration in 1930, the program's per diem payments for 2010 have increased to $77.53 per day.

Challenges Facing the Construction of New Homes

The State Veterans Home Program is a partnership between the U.S. Department of Veterans Affairs and the States to construct or acquire nursing home, domiciliary or adult day health care facilities. A State nursing home, domiciliary or adult day care is owned and operated by the State.

The Veterans Administration may participate in up to 65 percent of the cost of construction or acquisition of State nursing homes or domiciliaries or for renovations to existing State homes.

Over the last five years, VA has awarded over $424 million in grants to the States for construction of or renovations to State veteran's homes. That is 34 percent of all grants awarded since 1964.

The Veterans Administration Secretary approved the 2011 Priority List on September 8, 2010. The Priority List contained 94 projects from the various States and was valued at over $567 million. There were 49 projects, valued at $296 million, with the required 35% state matching funds -- meaning legislators have set aside the money -- and are eligible for immediate VA grant awards. These are priority #1 grants and should be built as soon as possible. Unfortunately, there is not enough money to build these priority #1 grant facilities. For the year 2010, 17 projects were approved which included the construction of 6 new homes for a total value of $212 million. This amount included not only new appropriations for the year, but existing funds from prior committed years.

The VA will commit to as many projects as funds are available but funding is woefully inadequate. The State Home Construction Grant Program 2011 budget was funded at $100 million. The President's 2012 budget request is $85 million in grants for state construction programs. The 2012 budget proposal only represents about 15% of the projects on the priority list. At that amount, needed new projects on the priority list may not get constructed until 4 to 6 years from now.

Nursing Home Daily Rates

Standard Per Diem Program

The Veterans Administration pays the state veterans homes an annually adjusted rate per day for each veteran in the home. This is called the per diem. The 2015 nursing per diem amount is $102.38 and for domiciliary care rate is $44.19. Adult Day Health Care is $81.56 per day for 2015.

The per diem program and construction subsidies mean that State veterans homes can charge less money for their services than private facilities. Some states have a set rate, as an example $1,600 a month, and they may be relying on the pension benefit with aid and attendance plus the per diem to cover their actual costs. Other states may charge a percentage of the veterans income but be relying on other subsidies to cover the rest of the cost. Still, in other states, the rate may simply be the difference between all of the subsidies and the actual monthly cost of operation.

Most of the states with income-determined rates are selective about the veterans they accept. These states may rely on a variety of private and public sources to help fund the cost of care.

Example of Subsidy from the VA and the State.

Actual per Veteran Monthly Cost of Operation	$7,000
Per Diem Monthly to Subsidize the Veteran's Cost	$3,071
Possible State or Other Subsidies	$1,000
Possible VA Aid and Attendance Benefit	$1,789
Available to Pay for Care from All Sources above	$5,860
Veterans Out-of-Pocket Cost	$1,140

States without set rate subsidies may charge 50% to 70% of the rate of private facilities based on private or semi private room occupancy and if the veteran does not have enough income, these homes accept Medicaid or Medicare to make up the difference. In these states the veterans homes are Medicaid and possibly Medicare certified. Approximately 30% of all state veterans homes are CMS certified.

Alternate Per Diem Program

Alternatively, VA will pay a facility, recognized as a State home for nursing home care, a different per diem for the following veteran under VA Disability Compensation:

1. who is in need of nursing home care for a VA adjudicated service-connected disability, or

2. who has a singular or combined rating of 70 percent or more based on one or more service-connected disabilities or a rating of total disability based on individual un-employability and is in need of nursing home care.

Payment for care under this second option constitutes payment in full for all routine nursing home care provided to the veteran in the state nursing home. As a condition for receiving this per diem, the veteran must receive medications through the state nursing home rather than from VA. The veteran must also utilize the VA for any services not provided by the nursing home, such as hospital care, hearing aids, and eyeglasses. If the veteran chooses to utilize other service providers, the veteran will be responsible for payment for those services.

Medication Subsidy

In addition to the per diem payments discussed above, VA will also furnish drugs and medicines to a facility recognized as a state veterans home that are ordered by a duly licensed physician as specific therapy in the treatment of illness of injury for a veteran receiving care in a state home if the veteran:

1. has a singular or combined rating of less than 50 percent based on one or more service-connected disabilities and is in need of such drugs and medicines for a service-connected disability and is in need of nursing home care for reasons that do not include care for a VA adjudicated service-connected disability; or

2. has a singular or combined rating of 50 or 60 percent based on one or more service-connected disabilities and is in need of such drugs and medicines and is in need of nursing home care for reasons that do not include care for a VA adjudicated service-connected disability.

The drug or medicine must be included in VA's national formulary unless VA determines a non-formulary drug or medicine is medically necessary.

Per Diem Reimbursement Rates

	Nursing Home	Yearly Increase	Domiciliary	Adult Day Health Care
2000	$46.49		$20.36	N/A
2001	$51.38	9.52%	$22.03	N/A
2002	$53.17	3.37%	$23.74	N/A
2003	$56.24	5.46%	$26.95	N/A
2004	$57.78	2.67%	$27.19	N/A
2005	$59.36	2.66%	$27.44	N/A
2006	$63.40	6.37%	$29.31	$37.91
2007	$67.71	6.37%	$31.30	$40.48
2008	$71.42	5.19%	$33.01	$64.13
2009	$74.42	4.03%	$34.40	$66.82
2010	$77.53	4.01%	$35.84	$69.63
2011	$94.59	18.04%	$38.90	$73.51
2012	$95.82	1.30%	$39.90	$75.40
2013	$97.07	1.30%	$41.90	$77.33
2014	$100.37	3.40%	$43.32	$79.96
2015	$102.38	2.00%	$44.19	$81.56
Average		5.05%		

Type of Care Provided

Some state facilities offer assisted living or domiciliary care in addition to nursing care. Some states even build facilities devoted entirely for domiciliary. According to the Veterans Administration the definition of domiciliary care is as follows: "To provide the least intensive level of VA inpatient care for ambulatory veterans disabled by age or illness who are not in need of more acute hospitalization and who do not need the skilled nursing services provided in nursing homes. To rehabilitate the veteran in anticipation of his/her return to the community in a self-sustaining and independent or semi-independent living situation, or to assist the veteran to reach his/her optimal level of functioning in a protective environment."

A domiciliary is a living arrangement similar to assisted living without substantial assistance but is not intended as a permanent residence. Domiciliary rooms in veterans medical centers are designed around this concept and are used for rehabilitation recovery from surgery or accident, alcohol abuse, drug abuse, mental illness or depression.

The domiciliary concept does not work well in a state veterans home setting and in that context domiciliary is simply another name for assisted living without the assistance. This represents a form of independent retirement living with a little more support where the veteran can stay as long as he or she needs to. As far as state veterans homes go you should think of domiciliary as a substitute for supported independent retirement living.

Many state veterans facilities have set aside a wing for Alzheimer's patients. In some states this is the most popular service sought by veterans or their families and waiting lists could require a number of years before a bed opens up. A small number of facilities offer adult day care.

It appears that in most of the states, facilities are run by state employees through their State departments. Some states may contract with third-party administrators to run their programs.

Eligibility and Application Requirements for State Veterans Homes

From state to state, facilities vary in their rules for eligible veterans. And even in the same state it is common, where there is more than one state home, for some homes to have very stringent eligibility rules and others to be more lenient. These differing rules are probably based on the demand for care and the available beds in that particular geographic area.

Some homes require the veteran to be totally disabled and unable to earn an income. Some evaluate on the basis of medical need or age. Some evaluate entirely on income -- meaning applicants above a certain level will not be accepted. Some accept only former active-duty veterans, while others accept all who were in the military whether active duty or reserve. Still others accept only veterans who served during a period of war. Some homes accept the spouses or surviving spouses of veterans and some will accept the parents of veterans but restrict that to the parents of veterans who died while in service (Goldstar parents).

Federal regulations allow that 25% of the bed occupants at any one time may be veteran-related family members, i.e., spouses, surviving spouses, and/or gold star parents who are not entitled to payment of VA aid. When a State Home accepts grant assistance for a construction project, 75% of the bed occupants at the facility must be veterans.

Domicile residency requirements vary from state to state. The most stringent seems to be a three-year prior residency in the state whereas other homes may only require 90 days of residency. All states require an application process to get into a home. Typically a committee or board will approve or disapprove each application. Many states have waiting lists for beds.

Department Of Veterans Affairs Statistics and Funding for Veterans Care Programs

Long-Term Services and Supports (Geriatrics and Extended Care)

		2014			2016	2014-2015	2015-2016
	2013 Actual	Budget Estimate	Current Estimate	2015 Estimate	Advance Approp.	Increase / Decrease	Increase / Decrease
Institutional:							
Obligations ($000)							
VA Community Living Centers	$3,429,567	$4,022,694	3,499,576	3,558,288	3,729,201	$58,712	$170,913
Community Nursing Home	$664,653	$725,545	713,000	752,800	776,600	$39,800	$23,800
State Home Nursing	$891,469	$1,012,740	926,600	963,100	1,001,000	$36,500	$37,900
Subtotal (VA CLC, CNH, SNH)	$4,985,689	$5,760,979	$5,139,176	$5,274,188	$5,506,801	$135,012	$232,613
State Home Domiciliary	$60,198	$61,571	$62,000	63,900	65,800	$1,900	$1,900
Total Institutional	$5,045,887	$5,822,550	$5,201,176	$5,338,088	$5,572,601	$136,912	$234,513
Average Daily Census							
VA Community Living Centers	9,667	9,527	9,367	9,079	8,779	(288)	(300)
Community Nursing Home	7,318	7,362	7,624	7,918	8,177	294	259
State Home Nursing	19,566	22,190	19,672	19,774	19,817	102	43
Subtotal	36,551	39,079	36,663	36,771	36,773	108	2
State Home Domiciliary	3,796	3,387	3,853	3,926	3,991	73	65
Total Institutional	40,347	42,466	40,516	40,697	40,764	181	67
Per Diem Costs							
VA Community Living Centers	$971.97	$1,156.83	$1,023.58	$1,073.77	$1,160.62	$50.19	$86.85
Community Nursing Home	$248.83	$270.01	$256.22	$260.48	$259.49	$4.26	($0.99)
State Home Nursing	$124.83	$125.04	$129.05	$133.44	$138.01	$4.39	$4.57
State Home Domiciliary	$43.45	$49.80	$44.09	$44.59	$45.05	$0.51	$0.45
Denominator							
VA Community Living Centers	365	365	365	365	366	0	1
Community Nursing Home	365	365	365	365	366	0	1
State Home Nursing	365	365	365	365	366	0	1
State Home Domiciliary	365	365	365	365	366	0	1

Per diems shown may vary from authorized per diems due to additional services that VA requests and pays for, as well as retroactive payments.

Selected Facilities by Type

(as of December 2013)

Type of Facility	Number
Domiciliary Rehabilitation Treatment Programs – As of September 30, 2013	102
Geriatric Research, Education, and Clinical Centers	19
Health Administration Management Center	1
Independent Outpatient Clinics	6
Insurance Center	1
Memorial Service Networks	5
Mobile Clinics	11
Nursing Home Units	133
Orthotic and Prosthetic Services on-site stations	78
Prosthetic and Sensory Aids Restoration Clinics	3
Regional Loan Centers	9
Appeals Management Center	1
Regional Offices	56
Regional Pension Management Centers	3
Regional Education Processing Offices	4
VA Hospitals	152
VA National Cemeteries	131
VA Outpatient Clinics – As of September 30, 2013	820
Vet Centers – As of September 30, 2013	300
Mobile Vet Centers – As of September 30, 2013	70
Veterans Benefits Administration Area Offices	4
Veterans Integrated Service Networks (VISNS)	21

Medical Care Budget Request

($ in billions)

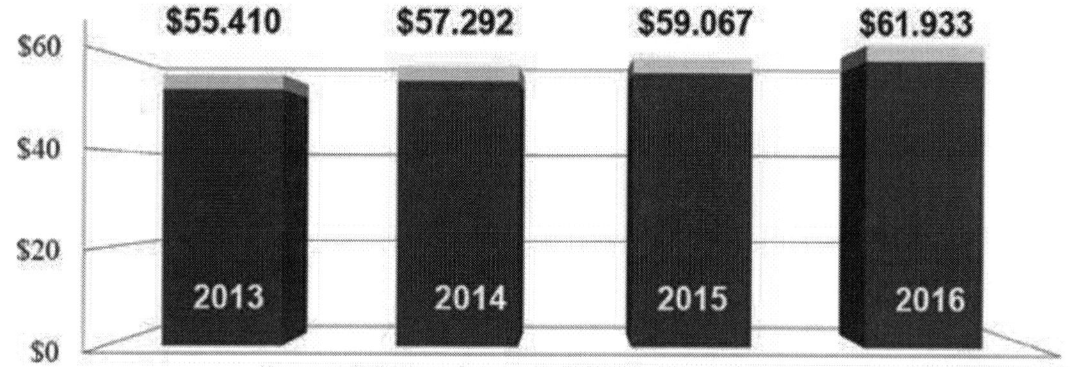

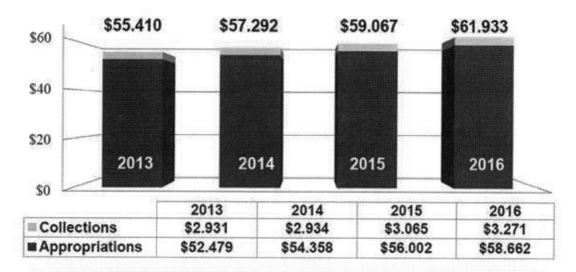

	2013	2014	2015	2016
Collections	$2.931	$2.934	$3.065	$3.271
Appropriations	$52.479	$54.358	$56.002	$58.662

Medical Care accounts for 87.7% of the VA Budget

FY 2015 President's Budget Request 12

Medical System Users

	2013 Actual	2014 Estimate	2015 Estimate	2016 Estimate	Change 2014-2015	Change 2009-2015
Priority 1-6	4,524,505	4,616,822	4,729,341	4,827,386	2.4%	22.0%
Priority 7-8	1,279,385	1,291,220	1,289,199	1,279,950	-0.2%	-4.3%
Subtotal Veterans	5,803,890	5,908,042	6,018,540	6,107,336	1.9%	15.3%
CHAMPVA / Non-Veterans	680,774	708,921	723,393	737,393	2.0%	38.3%
Total Unique Patients	**6,484,664**	**6,616,963**	**6,741,933**	**6,844,729**	**1.9%**	**17.4%**
OEF/OIF/OND (Incl. Above)	616,487	689,974	757,674	823,647	9.8%	127.6%

Overall increase in Unique Patients since 2009 is 17.4%

CHAPTER 6
Veterans Healthcare

The Best Health Care System in America

It comes as a surprise to some people who had experience with VA health care during the 1970s and 1980s, that this same system is now considered the best medical care in the United States. To illustrate this we quote below articles and comments from the several sources.

BusinessWeek, July 17, 2006 "The Best Medical Care in the Nation
How Veterans Affairs transformed itself -- and what it means for the rest of us"

> ". . . . Roemer seems to have stepped through the looking glass into an alternative universe, one where a nationwide health system that is run and financed by the federal government provides the best medical care in America. But it's true -- if you want to be sure of top-notch care, join the military."
>
> "The 154 hospitals and 875 clinics run by the Veterans Affairs Dept. have been ranked best-in-class by a number of independent groups on a broad range of measures, from chronic care to heart disease treatment to percentage of members who receive flu shots. It offers all the same services, and sometimes more, than private sector providers."
>
> "To much of the public, though, the VA's image is hobbled by its inglorious past. For decades the VA was the health-care system of last resort. The movies Coming Home (1978), Born on the Fourth of July (1989), and Article 99 (1992) immortalized VA hospitals as festering sinkholes of substandard care. The filmmakers didn't exaggerate. In an infamous incident in 1992, the bodies of two patients were found on the grounds of a VA hospital in Virginia months after they had gone missing. The huge system had deteriorated so badly by the early '90s that Congress considered disbanding it."
>
> "Instead, the VA was reinvented in every way possible. In the mid-1990s, Dr. Kenneth W. Kizer, then the VA's Health Under Secretary, installed the most extensive electronic medical-records system in the U.S. Kizer also decentralized decision-making, closed underused hospitals, reallocated resources, and most critically, instituted a culture of accountability and quality measurements. "Our whole motivation was to make the system work for the patient," says Kizer, now director of the National Quality Forum, a nonprofit dedicated to improving health care. "We did a top-to-bottom makeover with that goal always in mind.". . . .

Robert Bazell, Chief science and health correspondent, NBC News Updated: 6:33 p.m. MT March 15, 2006

"We report a story tonight that is going to turn a lot of heads. The Veterans Administration Health Care System, once famously known for horrendous medical care, now offers what many consider the best health care in the nation. I am sure we will hear from many of you who have had difficult times with care at the VA. That is understandable, because the improvement in the VA has occurred relatively recently and inevitably many people will be dissatisfied with their treatment at the hands of any medical provider."

"But here is the evidence. In a study two years ago a group of researchers from the RAND Corporation and several medical Centers found that 67 percent of patients in the VA system received "appropriate care" as defined by expert panels on medical practice. Two thirds sounds short of the mark, but in the current issue of the New England Journal of Medicine the same researchers report on a survey of the country that finds only 55 percent of Americans in general are getting appropriate health care. And that number does not vary much with the patients' level of education or income."

"In addition, a telephone survey last January from the University of Michigan found that VA patients rated their satisfaction with care at 83 out of a possible 100 points for inpatient care and 80 out of 100 for outpatient care. By comparison, the same survey found rates of 73 and 75 in the general population. Another indicator comes from the American Legion, which has been surveying its members and finding similar high levels of patient satisfaction."

"Indeed, the biggest complaint about the VA system these days is from people who want in. The VA provides unlimited care for service-related injuries and illnesses. but for other problems veterans must fall below a defined income level. As a result, patients at the VA tend to be poorer and sicker than the rest of the population, which makes the improvements all the more remarkable."

"What happened? The change began with Dr. Kenneth Kizer, who became undersecretary of health for Veterans Affairs in the Clinton administration and has continued in that role during the Bush administration. The VA changed its emphasis from hospital to outpatient care where possible. It also set up genuine prevention programs. As a result, people with conditions like diabetes get the simple measures that can save enormous misery and thousands of dollars in treatment costs. Every patient is assigned a personal physician and the mandate from headquarters is to treat veterans with the respect and dignity they deserve."

"The other big change was a massive shift to electronic medical records. At any VA facility in the country, a doctor or other health professional can access the records of any patient in the system, including lab tests, X-rays and chart notes that can be read easily. The electronic system challenges health providers who seem to be making mistakes, and it allows for a massive collection of data so the VA can know which treatments work and which don't."

"A big advantage for the VA is electronic medical records. The VA has the largest, and one of the most modern systems in the world. When a VA patient visits any facility in the country, the records are there. Indeed, after Hurricane Katrina, many VA patients received uninterrupted care even as they were forced to move."

"'All of the information I need about any of my patients, including their X-rays and their tests, are always available, always accurate, always there in a legible form,' says Gauge."

"The electronic records also allow the VA to track its performance — to quickly learn what works and what doesn't — providing what many say could be a model for health care nationwide."

A quote from Families USA

"A report released Tuesday (December 2006) by the consumer group Families USA says Medicare's prices for seniors' most frequently used drugs are about 58% higher than those provided by the Department of Veterans Affairs."

Percent distribution, by reasons, of veterans who never used VA health care

	Total
Uses other sources for health care	31.8
Did not need any care	23.7
Not aware of the VA health care benefits	21.6
Did not believe self entitled or eligible for health care benefits	20.4
VA care is inconvenient	13.3
Other	9.5
Did not need or want assistance from the VA	8.0
Never considered getting any health care from the VA	5.1
Didn't think VA health care would be as good as that available elsewhere	3.1
Applying for health care benefits too much trouble or red tape	3.0
Did not know how to apply for health care benefits	2.3
Number of veterans†	16,396,700

† Estimate of number of veterans is rounded to the nearest hundred; percent estimates will not sum to more than 100 because veterans could indicate more than one reason.

NOTE: This table only includes responses of those who indicated they had never used VA health care.

Why the VA Health Care System Works so Well

Actually it's not that VA is such a marvelous system, since any large-scale organization employing over 200,000 people is bound to have its inefficiencies. VA simply comes closer to the mark of providing excellent care than the rest of the health-care providers in the country. One big reason is the veteran system does not rely on insurance reimbursements so money saved through efficient operation remains in the system and does not transfer to insurance companies. This type of operational structure encourages innovation and change.

However, being a single-payer health plan alone would not necessarily result in a better system. The outstanding reawakening of VA health care is largely a result of the vision and leadership of Doctor Kizer and his successor. Here are some of the operational advantages that make VA health care so successful.

As a government entity, the agency cannot be sued by patients who have been mistreated. This obviously saves the time and money involved in lawsuits. However, in order to be responsive to medical errors, doctor Kizer instituted the "Sorry Now" program that holds staff accountable for their actions and provides damage awards to patients.

Veterans who are part of the system have the opportunity to remain with the system throughout their lives. This allows VA to practice preventative medicine by scheduling regular checkups, performing regular lab tests and intervening before a medical condition becomes too advanced. The provider/contractor insurance reimbursement model used in the United States typically does not allow for this type of preventative medicine.

An electronic records system provides the opportunity to practice outcome based medicine which has become the Holy Grail of all health-care systems. The computerized records allow tracking outcomes for various medical conditions and finding those that work best. This weeds out expensive procedures that are no more effective than other less expensive ones. Prescriptions for medications are also tracked on the computer and potential drug interactions are avoided. According to studies, VA has the lowest drug interaction incidents and deaths in the country

The electronic records also prevent duplication of expensive medical tests. Some surveys indicate that, 60% of the time, private sector providers order duplicates or triplicates of the same test. This is because paper records make it difficult or almost impossible to track tests between different care providers. Even in the same hospital, estimates are that one out of five tests are unnecessarily reordered.

Finally, electronic records help the veterans health system to maintain a more cost effective and smaller drug formulary. Fewer categories of drugs allow VA to negotiate with drug companies for larger quantities at a lower price. If an existing, less expensive drug is proven through electronic records computer data to be just as effective as newer more expensive medicines, then obviously the older medicine will be favored.

Proponents of the new Medicare drug plans criticize VA for limiting drug choice to only about 1,300 medications where some Medicare plans allow 4,500 different drugs or more. VA would probably argue that such a wide choice is unnecessary and that many newer more expensive drugs are simply analogues of less expensive versions that have been around for a long time.

Cost of overhead and administration is another issue that makes VA a better system. Our country's private insurance model results in insurers eating up a great deal of their premium income in unproductive overhead costs. It is estimated that private insurers spend anywhere from 20% to 30% of their premium income on advertising, agent commissions, insurance administrative oversight costs, expensive claims and records tracking systems, taxes, profit, and dividends for shareholders. VA has none of these additional cost burdens except for administrative costs associated with maintaining the system.

There is also evidence that the morale of employees in VA hospitals and outpatient clinics is especially high because of the pride those employees take in providing quality care. Motivated employees can be a major factor in providing care more effectively and more efficiently thus saving money.

What is Veterans Health Care?

The Veterans Health Administration is home to the United States' largest integrated health care system consisting of 152 medical centers, nearly 1,400 community-based outpatient clinics, community living centers, Vet Centers and Domiciliaries. Together these health care facilities and the more than 53,000 independent licensed health care practitioners who work within them provide comprehensive care to more than 8.3 million* Veterans each year. This system offers the following services.

- Hospital, outpatient medical, dental, pharmacy and prosthetic services
- Domiciliary, nursing home, and community-based residential care
- Sexual trauma counseling
- Specialized health care for women veterans
- Health and rehabilitation programs for homeless veterans
- Readjustment counseling
- Alcohol and drug dependency treatment
- Medical evaluation for disorders associated with military service in the Gulf War, or Treatment for exposure to Agent Orange, radiation, and other environmental hazards
- HISA grants
- Other special benefits

An example of one of VA's 22 regions is Region 19.-- geographically one of the largest in the system. Headquartered in Denver this region covers the states of Montana, Wyoming, Utah, Colorado and part of Nevada. Region 19 includes three health-care system hospitals and three satellite hospitals. There are also 33 outpatient clinics in urban centers scattered throughout the five states and 7 Vet Centers in urban areas that provide special services for veterans who served in combat.

The six hospitals in Region 19 offer a wide range of medical specialties and procedures and it is unlikely that any patient would have to be referred to the private care community for any services not offered by these hospitals. But if specialized services are not offered in the region, VA hospitals, region to region, share responsibilities for very specialized treatment and patients needing these specialties not offered in their region are referred to other VA facilities that do offer the care.

Hospitals in the VA system are typically associated with a local medical College where feasible. By acting as teaching hospitals the VA system has access to some of the best doctors and cutting edge medical treatments. In region 19, the Denver Medical Center is affiliated with the medical school, pharmacy, and nursing schools of the University of Colorado Health Sciences Center. The Fort Harrison facility near Helena, Montana is affiliated with nursing schools, pharmacy schools and physician-assistant schools in over 30 universities in the four adjoining states. The Salt Lake City Regional Medical Center is affiliated with the University of Utah Medical School which is located less than a mile away.

One of the disadvantages, in the past, of joining the health system was the difficulty of getting to a regional medical center for treatment. With the installation of outpatient clinics within easy driving distance for health-care beneficiaries, this challenge has become less of a problem in the past few years. The challenge still remains that major hospitalization, surgery and other specialized treatment must be obtained at a regional hospital. In the case of region 19 this could involve driving distances up to 600 miles one way to obtain the appropriate care.

VA is accommodating to certain low income patients who must drive long distances and the facilities offer, at no charge or reasonable charge, "hoptel" rooms in the hospital or nearby as an alternative to staying in a motel or hotel. Low income patients are also reimbursed at $0.285 per mile for travel to the nearest VA health care facility that can provide their needed care.

Other services are also available to certain qualifying veterans who may receive dental care, vision care and hearing aids. In addition, Vet Centers provide special counseling for active-duty veterans who served in combat zones. VA is also the most experienced healthcare provider in the country in services for rehabilitating patients with missing limbs, with burn injuries or with other complications due to combat injuries.

Regional VA hospitals often include associated nursing facilities or domiciliary rooms. They will also contract for home health care and hospice services if needed. For those hospitals that don't have nursing homes or domiciliary, contracts for these services are maintained with facilities in the local community.

Emergency Care in Non-VA facilities is provided as a safety net for veterans under specific conditions. If the non-VA emergency care is for a service-connected condition or, if the veteran has been enrolled with health services at least 24 months and has no other health care coverage then emergency care is covered. Also, it must be determined that VA health care facilities were not feasibly available; that a delay in medical attention would have endangered life or health, and that the veteran remains personally liable for the cost of the services in case of a dispute.

Outpatient Pharmacy Services

VA provides free outpatient pharmacy services to:

1. Veterans with a service-connected disability of 50 percent or more.
2. Veterans receiving medication for service-connected conditions.
3. Veterans whose annual income does not exceed the maximum annual rate of the VA pension.
4. Veterans enrolled in priority group 6 who receive medication for service-connected conditions.
5. Veterans receiving medication for conditions related to sexual trauma while serving on active duty.
6. Certain veterans receiving medication for treatment of cancer of the head or neck.
7. Veterans receiving medication for a VA-approved research project.
8. Former prisoners of war.

Veterans receiving pension can also have their prescriptions from doctors in the private sector provided by a VA pharmacy for free or with co-pay depending on their income.

A face-to-face interview with a pharmacy specialist must be conducted with any new prescription. This is part of the process that helps VA control unnecessary drug reactions or interactions with other drugs. Subsequent refills can be ordered on the phone and will be sent through the mail or picked up in person.

Veterans Health Administration Long Term Care Benefits

The following was taken from the Department of Veterans Affairs fact sheet dated January 2005 and distributed by the office of public affairs media relations

> *VA Long-Term Care*
> The Department of Veterans Affairs (VA) offers a spectrum of geriatric and extended care services to veterans enrolled in its health care system. More than 90 percent of VA's medical centers provide home- and community-based outpatient long-term care programs. This patient-focused approach supports the wishes of most patients to live at home in their own communities for as long as possible. In addition, nearly 65,000 veterans will receive inpatient long-term care this year through programs of VA or state veterans homes.
>
> *Non-Institutional Care*
> Veterans can receive home-based primary care, contract home health care, adult day health care, homemaker and home health aide services, home respite care, home hospice care and community residential care. In fiscal year 2003, 50 percent of VA's total extended care patient population received care in non-institutional settings, including:

Home-Based Primary Care
This program (formerly Hospital Based Home Care) began in 1970 and provides long-term primary medical care to chronically ill veterans in their own homes under the coordinated care of an interdisciplinary treatment team. This program has led to guidelines for medical education in home care, use of emerging technology in home care and improved care for veterans with dementia and their families who support them. In 2003, home-based primary care programs were located in 76 VA medical centers.

The Contract Home Health Care
Professional home care services, mostly nursing services, are purchased from private-sector providers at every VA medical center. The program is commonly called "fee basis" home care.

Adult Day Health Care (ADHC)
Adult Day Health Care programs provide health maintenance and rehabilitative services to veterans in a group setting during daytime hours. VA introduced this program in 1985. In 2004, VA operated 21 programs directly and provided contract ADHC services at 112 VA medical centers. Two state homes have received recognition from VA to provide ADHC, which has recently been authorized under the State Home Per Diem Program.

Homemaker and Home Health Aide (H/HHA)
VA began a program in 1993 of health-related services for service-connected veterans needing nursing home care. These services are provided in the community by public and private agencies under a system of case management provided directly by VA staff. VA purchased H/HHA services at 122 medical centers in 2004.

Community Residential Care
The community residential care program provides room, board, limited personal care and supervision to veterans who do not require hospital or nursing home care but are not able to live independently because of medical or psychiatric conditions, and who have no family to provide care. The veteran pays for the cost of this living arrangement. VA's contribution is limited to the cost of administration and clinical services, which include inspection of the home and periodic visits to the veteran by VA health care professionals. Medical care is provided to the veteran primarily on an outpatient basis at VA facilities. Primarily focused on psychiatric patients in the past, this program will be increasingly focused on older veterans with multiple chronic illnesses that can be managed in the home under proper care and supervision.

Respite Care
Respite care temporarily relieves the spouse or other caregiver from the burden of caring for a chronically ill or disabled veteran at home. In the past, respite care admission was limited to an institutional setting, typically a VA nursing home. The Veterans Millennium Health Care and Benefits Act expanded respite care to home and other community settings, and home respite care was provided at 15 VA medical centers in fiscal year 2003. Currently, respite care programs are operating in 136 VA medical centers, with each program typically providing care to approximately five veterans on any given day. Respite care is usually limited to 30 days per year.

Home Hospice Care
Home hospice care provides comfort-oriented and supportive services in the home for persons in the advanced stages of incurable disease. The goal is to achieve the best possible quality of life through relief of suffering, control of symptoms, and restoration or maintenance of functional capacity. Services are provided by an interdisciplinary team of health care providers and volunteers. Bereavement care is available to the family following the death of the patient. Hospice services are available 24 hours a day, seven days a week. VA provided home hospice care at 73 medical centers in fiscal year 2003, the first year the service was offered.

Domiciliary Care
Domiciliary care is a residential rehabilitation program that provides short-term rehabilitation and long-term health maintenance to veterans who require minimal medical care as they recover from medical, psychiatric or psychosocial problems. Most domiciliary patients return to the community after a period of rehabilitation.

Domiciliary care is provided by VA and state homes. VA currently operates 43 facilities. State homes operate 49 domiciliaries in 33 states. VA also provides a number of psychiatric residential rehabilitation programs, including ones for veterans coping with post-traumatic stress disorder and substance abuse, and compensated work therapy or transitional residences for homeless chronically mentally ill veterans and veterans recovering from substance abuse.

Telehealth
For most of VA's non-institutional care, telehealth communication technology can play a major role in coordinating veterans' total care with the goal of maintaining independence. Telehealth offers the possibility of treating chronic illnesses cost-effectively while contributing to the patient satisfaction generally found with care available at home.

Geriatric Evaluation and Management (GEM)
Older veterans with multiple medical, functional or psychosocial problems and those with particular geriatric problems receive assessment and treatment from an interdisciplinary team of VA health professionals. GEM services can be found on inpatient units, in outpatient clinics and in geriatric primary care clinics. In 2004, there were 57 inpatient GEM programs and more than 195,000 visits to GEM and geriatric primary care clinics.

Geriatric Research, Education and Clinical Centers (GRECC)
These centers increase the basic knowledge of aging for health care providers and improve the quality of care through the development of improved models of clinical services. Each GRECC has an identified focus of research in the basic biomedical, clinical and health services areas, such as the geriatric evaluation and management program. Medical and associated health students and staff in geriatrics and gerontology are trained at these centers. Begun in 1975, there are now 21 GRECCs in all but two of VA's health care networks.

Nursing Home Care
VA's nursing home programs include VA-operated nursing home care units, contract community nursing homes and state homes. VA contracts with approximately 2,500

community nursing homes. The state home program is growing and currently encompasses 114 nursing homes in 47 states and Puerto Rico. In fiscal year 2003, approximately 70 percent of VA's institutional nursing home care occurred in contract community and state home nursing homes.

Nursing home care units are located at VA hospitals where they are supported by an array of clinical specialties. The community nursing home program has the advantage of being offered in many local communities where veterans can receive care near their homes and families. VA contracts for the care of veterans in community nursing homes approved by VA. The state home program is based on a joint cost-sharing agreement between VA, the veteran and the state.

Who is Eligible for Nursing Home Care

- Any veteran who has a service-connected disability rating of 70 percent or more;
- A veteran who is rated 60 percent service-connected and is unemployable or has an official rating of "permanent and total disabled;"
- A veteran with combined disability ratings of 70 percent or more;
- A veteran whose service-connected disability is clinically determined to require nursing home care;
- Nonservice-connected veterans and those officially referred to as "zero percent, noncompensable, service-connected" veterans who require nursing home care for any nonservice-connected disability and who meet income and asset criteria; or
- If space and resources are available, other veterans on a case-by-case basis with priority given to service-connected veterans and those who need care for post-acute rehabilitation, respite, hospice, geriatric evaluation and management, or spinal cord injury.

HISA Grants
A local Regional Medical Center can pay veterans a grant to allow for home improvement and structural alterations -- HISA grants. These are necessary alterations in order to accommodate disability in the home. As a general rule these grants are typically provided to veterans who are receiving VA health care and who are service-connected disabled. Certain service-connected disabled veterans can receive a lifetime benefit of $6,800 for home improvement projects to aid with disability.

A clause in the eligibility statutes opens the door for veterans who are on Medicaid or receiving pension with aid and attendance or housebound ratings to also receive these grants. Also very low income -- means tested veterans -- may also receive the grant. For this class of veterans the grant is a lifetime payment of $2,000.

Although they are reluctant to provide these grants to veterans who are not in the health-care system, the medical center HISA committee will do so if adequate documentation is provided to justify the grant.

Millennium Act and VA's Efforts to Increase Long-Term Care Capacity
Public Law 106-117, the Veterans Millennium Health Care and Benefits Act, enacted in November 1999, requires VA to provide extended care services in its facilities, including

nursing home care, domiciliary, home-based primary care and adult day health care, with the goal of providing as much care as in 1998.

The budget for VA long-term care grew by more then $850 million between fiscal year 1998 and fiscal year 2003, and the number of full-time employees increased in nursing home care units and outpatient programs.

Enrolling in the Veterans Health Care System

Minimum Duty Requirements
Most Veterans who enlisted after September 7, 1980, or entered active duty after October 16, 1981, must have served 24 continuous months or the full period for which they were called to active duty in order to be eligible. This minimum duty requirement may not apply to Veterans who were discharged for a disability incurred or aggravated in the line of duty, for a hardship or "early out." Since there are a number of other exceptions to the minimum duty requirements, VA encourages all Veterans to apply in order to determine their enrollment eligibility.

Women Veterans Eligibility
Current estimates of the projected growth of women Veterans predict there will be 1.9 million by 2020, up from 1.1 million in 1980. Thus, women will continue to make up a larger share of the Veteran population, add to its diversity, and require Veteran services geared to their specific needs. Women Veterans may receive the full spectrum medical benefits package. They also receive the full continuum of comprehensive medical services, including health promotion and disease prevention, primary care, women's gender-specific health care, for example, hormone replacement therapy, breast and gynecological care, limited maternity and infertility (excluding in-vitro fertilization), acute medical/surgical, emergency and substance abuse treatment, mental health, domiciliary, rehabilitation and long-term care.

Readjustment Counseling Services
VA provides readjustment counseling and outreach services to all Veterans who served in any combat zone, through community based counseling centers called Vet Centers. Services are also available for their family members for military related issues. Veterans have earned these benefits through their service and all are provided at no cost to the Veteran or family. The Vet Centers are staffed by small multidisciplinary teams of dedicated personnel, many of whom are combat Veterans themselves. Vet Center staff are available toll-free during normal business hours at 1-800-905-4675 (Eastern) and 1-866-496-8838 (Pacific). For information online, visit www.vetcenter.va.gov .

Priority Group 8 Enrollment Relaxation
Regulations went into effect on June 15, 2009 which enabled the Department of Veterans Affairs (VA) to relax income restrictions on enrollment for health benefits. While this provision does not remove consideration of income, it does increase income thresholds. You may be eligible for enrollment under this provision. The VA National Income Thresholds can be found online at www.va.gov/healtheligibility/library/annualthresholds.asp .

An Enrollment Calculator is available to help Veterans determine their potential eligibility for VA health care services under the proposed regulation. Check to see if you qualify for VA health care at www.va.gov/healtheligibility/apps/ enrollmentcalculator .

Enrollment Restriction

Although the income relaxation regulation described above allows certain higher-income Veterans to be enrolled in the VA health care system, the previous Enrollment Restriction, effective January 17, 2003, by which VA suspended NEW enrollment of Veterans assigned to Priority Groups 8e and 8g is still in effect (VA's lowest priority group consisting of higher income Veterans). However, VA encourages Veterans in these priority groups to reapply for enrollment. They may now qualify if their current house- hold income exceeds the applicable income thresholds by the determined percentage or less, under current regulations. Veterans are assigned to Priority Groups 8e and 8g based on the following:

- The Veteran does not have any special qualifying eligibility, such as a compensable service-connected disability
- The Veteran's household income exceeds the current year VA income threshold and the geographic income threshold for the Veteran's residence
- New Veterans who decline to provide their financial information
- Veterans enrolled in Priority Groups 8a and 8c on or before January 16, 2003, remain enrolled and continue to be eligible

Initial Enrollment

Those seeking a VA benefit for the first time must submit a copy of their service discharge form (DD-214, DD-215, or for WWII veterans, a WD form), which documents service dates and type of discharge. The veteran's service discharge form should be kept in a safe location accessible to the veteran and next of kin or designated representative.

For most veterans, entry into the VA health care system begins by applying for enrollment. Application is submitted through VA Form 10-10EZ, Application for Health Benefits, which may be obtained from any VA health care facility or regional benefits office, or by calling 1-877-222-VETS (8387). Once enrolled, veterans can receive services at VA facilities anywhere in the country.
Veterans who are enrolled for VA health care are afforded privacy rights under federal law. VA's Notice of Privacy Practices is available at the VA health care Web site.

During enrollment, veterans are assigned to one of the priority groups VA uses to balance demand with resources. Changes in available resources may reduce the number of priority groups VA can enroll. If this occurs, VA will publicize the changes and notify affected enrollees. Veterans will be enrolled to the extent Congressional appropriations allow. If appropriations are limited, enrollment will occur based on the following priorities: (Please note that lower priority numbers generally mean no co-pays for medical services i.e. services are free)

Group 1: Veterans with service-connected disabilities rated 50 percent or more and/or veterans determined by VA to be unemployable due to service-connected conditions.

Group 2: Veterans with service-connected disabilities rated 30 or 40 percent.

Group 3: Veterans with service-connected disabilities rated 10 and 20 percent, veterans who are former Prisoners of War (POW) or were awarded a Purple Heart, veterans awarded special eligibility for disabilities incurred in treatment or participation in a VA Vocational Rehabilitation program, and veterans whose discharge was for a disability incurred or aggravated in the line of duty.

Group 4: Veterans receiving aid and attendance or housebound benefits and/or veterans determined by VA to be catastrophically disabled. Some veterans in this group may be responsible for co-pays.

Group 5: Veterans receiving VA pension benefits or eligible for Medicaid programs, and non service-connected veterans and non compensable, zero percent service-connected veterans whose annual income and net worth are below the established VA means test thresholds.

Group 6: Veterans of the Mexican border period or World War I; veterans seeking care solely for certain conditions associated with exposure to radiation or exposure to herbicides while serving inVietnam; for any illness associated with combat service in a war after the Gulf War or during a period of hostility after Nov. 11, 1998; for any illness associated with participation in tests conducted by the Defense Department as part of Project 112/Project SHAD; and veterans with zero percent service-connected disabilities who are receiving disability compensation benefits.

Group 7: Non service-connected veterans and non-compensable, zero percent service-connected veterans with income above VA's national means test threshold and below VA's geographic means test threshold, or with income below both the VA national threshold and the VA geographically based threshold, but whose net worth exceeds VA's ceiling (currently $80,000) who agree to pay co-pays.

Group 8: All other non service-connected veterans and zero percent, non-compensable service-connected veterans who agree to pay co-pays. (Note: Effective Jan. 17, 2003, VA no longer enrolls new veterans in priority group 8).

Percent distribution of veterans by health care enrollment priority groups

	Total
Priority group 1	2.9
Priority group 2	2.3
Priority group 3	5.7
Priority group 4	0.1
Priority group 5	21.1
Priority group 6	11.2
Priority group 7	56.1
Unknown	0.6
Total	100.0
Number of Veterans	25,196,000

Concurrent Enrollment in VA and Medicare
If you are eligible for Medicare Part D prescription drug coverage, you need to know that enrollment in the VA health care system is considered creditable coverage for Medicare Part D purposes. This means that VA prescription drug coverage is at least as good as the Medicare Part D coverage. Since only Veterans may enroll in the VA health care system, dependents and family members do not receive credible coverage under the Veteran's enrollment.

However, there is one significant area in which VA health care is NOT creditable coverage: Medicare Part B (outpatient health care, including doctors' fees). Creditable coverage for Medicare Part B can only be provided through an employer . As a result, VA health care benefits to Veterans are not creditable coverage for the Part B program. So although a Veteran may avoid the late enrollment penalty for Medicare Part D by citing VA health care enrollment, that enrollment would not help the Veteran avoid the late enrollment penalty for Part B.

VA does not recommend Veterans cancel or decline coverage in Medicare (or other health care or insurance programs) solely because they are enrolled in VA health care. Unlike Medicare, which offers the same benefits for all enrollees, VA assigns enrollees to priority levels, based on a variety of eligibility factors, such as service-connection and income. There is no guarantee that in subsequent years Congress will appropriate sufficient medical care funds for VA to provide care for all enrollment priority groups. This could leave Veterans, especially those enrolled in one of the lower-priority groups, with no access to VA health care coverage. For this reason, having a secondary source of coverage may be in the Veteran's best interest.

In addition, a Veteran may want to consider the flexibility afforded by enrolling in both VA and Medicare. For example, Veterans enrolled in both programs would have access to non-VA physicians (under Medicare Part A or Part B) or may obtain prescription drugs not on the VA formulary if prescribed by non-VA physicians and filled at their local retail pharmacies (under Medicare Part D).

Availability of the Other Services

Hearing Aids and Eyeglasses
Hearing aids and eyeglasses are listed as "limited" benefits. VA will provide hearing aids and eyeglasses to

1. Veterans who receive increased pension based on the need for regular aid and attendance or being permanently housebound,
2. receive compensation for a service-connected disability,
3. are a former POW or were awarded a Purple Heart.

Otherwise, hearing aids and eyeglasses are provided only in special circumstances, and not for normally occurring hearing or vision loss. For additional information, contact the prosthetic representative of your local VA health care facility.

Dental Benefits for Veterans

Dental benefits are provided by the Department of Veterans Affairs (VA) according to law. In some instances, VA is authorized to provide extensive dental care, while in other cases treatment may be limited. This Fact Sheet describes dental eligibility criteria and contains information to assist Veterans in understanding their eligibility for VA dental care.

The eligibility for outpatient dental care is not the same as for most other VA medical benefits and is categorized into classes. If you are eligible for VA dental care under Class I, IIC, or IV you are eligible for any necessary dental care to maintain or restore oral health and masticatory function, including repeat care. Other classes have time and/or service limitations.

Veterans receiving hospital, nursing home, or domiciliary care will be provided dental services that are professionally determined by a VA dentist, in consultation with the referring physician, to be essential to the management of the patient's medical condition under active treatment.

If you:	You are eligible for:	Through
Have a service-connected compensable dental disability or condition.	Any needed dental care	Class I
Are a former prisoner of war.	Any needed dental care.	Class IIC
Have service-connected disabilities rated 100% disabling, or are unemployable and paid at the 100% rate due to service-connected conditions.	Any needed dental care. [Please note: Veterans paid at the 100% rate based on a temporary rating, such as extended hospitalization for a service-connected disability, convalescence or pre-stabilization are not eligible for comprehensive outpatient dental services based on this temporary rating].	Class IV
Apply for dental care within 180 days of discharge or release (under conditions other than dishonorable) from a period of active duty of 90 days or more during the Persian Gulf War era.	One-time dental care if your DD214 certificate of discharge does not indicate that a complete dental examination and all appropriate dental treatment had been rendered prior to discharge.*	Class II

If you:	You are eligible for:	Through
Have a service-connected noncompensable dental condition or disability resulting from combat wounds or service trauma.	Needed care for the service-connected condition(s). A Dental Trauma Rating (VA Form 10-564-D) or VA Regional Office Rating Decision letter (VA Form 10-7131) identifies the tooth/teeth eligible for care.	Class IIA
Have a dental condition clinically determined by VA to be associated with and aggravating a service-connected medical condition.	Dental care to treat the oral conditions that are determined by a VA dental professional to have a direct and material detrimental effect to your service connected medical condition.	Class III
Are actively engaged in a 38 USC Chapter 31 vocational rehabilitation program.	Dental care to the extent necessary as determined by a VA dental professional to: • Make possible your entrance into a rehabilitation program • Achieve the goals of your vocational rehabilitation program • Prevent interruption of your rehabilitation program • Hasten the return to a rehabilitation program if you are in interrupted or leave status • Hasten the return to a rehabilitation program of a Veteran placed in discontinued status because of illness, injury or a dental condition, or • Secure and adjust to employment during the period of employment assistance, or enable you to achieve maximum independence in daily living.	Class V
Are receiving VA care or are scheduled for inpatient care and require dental care for a condition complicating a medical condition currently under treatment.	Dental care to treat the oral conditions that are determined by a VA dental professional to complicate your medical condition currently under treatment.	Class VI
Are an enrolled Veteran who may be homeless and receiving care under VHA Directive 2007-039.	A one-time course of dental care that is determined medically necessary to relieve pain, assist you to gain employment, or treat moderate, severe, or complicated and severe gingival and periodontal conditions.	Class IIB

Emergency Care at a Non-VA Facility
An eligible Veteran may receive emergency care at a non-VA health care facility at VA expense when a VA facility or other Federal health care facility with which VA has an agreement is unable to furnish economical care due to the Veteran's geographical inaccessibility to a VA medical facility, or when VA is unable to furnish the needed emergency services.

An emergency is defined as a condition of such a nature that a prudent layperson would have reasonably expected that delay in seeking immediate medical attention would have been hazardous to life or health. VA may directly refer or authorize the Veteran to receive emergency care at a non-VA facility at VA expense, or VA may pay for emergency care furnished certain Veterans by a non-VA facility without prior V A approval under certain conditions.

Emergency care must be pre-authorized by VA. When the emergency care is not authorized in advance by VA, it may be considered as preauthorized care when the nearest VA medical facility is notified within 72 hours of admission, the Veteran is eligible, and the care rendered is emergent in nature. Claims for non-VA emergency care not authorized by VA in advance of services being furnished must be timely filed; because timely filing requirements differ by type of claim, you should contact the nearest VA medical facility as soon as possible to avoid payment denial for an untimely filed claim.

Payment may not be approved for any period beyond the date on which the medical emergency ended, except when VA cannot accommodate transfer of the Veteran to a VA or other Federal facility. An emergency is deemed to have ended at that point when a VA physician has determined that, based on sound medical judgment, a Veteran who received emergency hospital care could have been transferred from the non-VA facility to a VA medical center for continuation of treatment.

VA has limited payment authority when emergency care at a non-VA facility is provided without authorization by VA in advance of services being furnished or notification to VA is not made within 72 hours of admission. VA may pay for unauthorized emergency care as indicated below. Since payment may be limited to the point your condition is stable for transportation to a VA facility, the nearest VA medical facility should be contacted as soon as possible for all care not authorized by VA in advance of the services being furnished.

VA may only pay for emergency care provided in a non-VA facility for treatment of a non-service-connected condition only if all of the following conditions are met:

- The episode of care cannot be paid as an unauthorized claim for service-connected Veterans
- The Veteran is enrolled in the VHA health care system and received VA medical care within a 24 month period preceding the furnishing of the emergency treatment
- The Veteran is personally liable to the health care provider for the emergency treatment
- The Veteran is not entitled to care or services under a health plan contract
- The Veteran has no other contractual or legal recourse against a third party that would, in whole or in part, extinguish the Veteran's liability

Copayments for Medical Services -- Veterans Means Testing

VA uses means testing to determine a veteran's level of copayments for medical services and in addition to accept or deny certain veterans applying for the first-time. Prior to 2003 VA allowed veterans to apply for medical coverage with any income level who were not required to meet means testing. These are veterans classified as priority 8. VA will no longer accept applications from these veterans. As the demand for services grows faster than funding, VA, in the future, may also exclude priority 7 veterans from enrolling in the system.

Although there are exceptions, as a general rule, veterans in priority categories 2 through 6 do not have to pay co-pays for the following services

- inpatient services,
- outpatient services or
- long term care services.

In other words these services are free.

Veterans in priority categories 7 and 8 generally do have to pay co-pays but there are some exceptions if the veteran meets VA's mean test or the geographic means test.

In some states VA's mean test for maximum income is less than the geographic means test and in other states it is just the opposite.

The most important thing to remember about co-pays is that a <u>veteran receiving VA pension</u> is classified a priority 5 veteran. Priority 5 veterans receive free; inpatient care, outpatient care and long term care. <u>They have no copayments for medical services.</u>

2014 VA National and Priority Group 8 Relaxation Income Thresholds

Income Thresholds for Cost-Free Health Care, Medications and/or Beneficiary Travel Eligibility

Based on Income Year 2013

VA HEALTH CARE | Defining EXCELLENCE in the 21st Century

VETERAN WITH:	VA NATIONAL INCOME THRESHOLD	VA PRIORITY GROUP 8 RELAXATION THRESHOLD	VA HOUSEBOUND THRESHOLD	VA PENSION WITH AID AND ATTENDANCE THRESHOLD	VA PENSION THRESHOLD	MEDICAL EXPENSE DEDUCTIBLE
0 dependents	$31,443 or less	$34,587 or less	$15,462	$21,107	$12,652 or less	$623
1 dependent	$37,733or less	$41,506 or less	$19,380	$25,022	$16,569 or less	$816
2 dependents	$39,894 or less	$43,883 or less	$21,541	$27,183	$18,730 or less	$923
3 dependents	$42,055 or less	$46,260 or less	$23.702	$29,344	$20,891 or less	$1,029
4 dependents	$44,216 or less	$48,637 or less	$25,863	$31,505	$23,052 or less	$1,136
For each additional dependent add:	$2,161	$2,161	$2,161	$2,161	$2,161	5% of the maximum allowable pension rate from the previous year
Child Earned Income Exclusion: $10,000				Income & Asset Net Worth Threshold: $80,000		

The GMT Income Threshold Test (geographic means test) could be higher or lower than the VA's means test. To obtain GMT income thresholds per state for purposes of qualifying under an enrollment priority go to

http://www.va.gov/healtheligibility/Library/pubs/GMTIncomeThresholds/

2014 Copay Rates

Outpatient Services *

Basic Care Services services provided by a primary care clinician	$15 / visit
Specialty Care Services services provided by a clinical specialist such as surgeon, radiologist, audiologist, optometrist, cardiologist, and specialty tests such as magnetic resonance imagery (MRI), computerized axial tomography (CAT) scan, and nuclear medicine studies	$50 / visit

* Copayment amount is limited to a single charge per visit regardless of the number of health care providers seen in a single day. The copayment amount is based on the highest level of service received. There is no copayment requirement for preventive care services such as screenings and immunizations.

Medications

Veterans in Priority Groups 2-6, for each 30-day or less supply of medication for treatment of nonservice-connected condition	$8

(Veterans in Priority Groups 2 through 6 are limited to $960 annual cap)

Veterans in Priority Groups 7-8, for each 30-day or less supply of medication for treatment of nonservice-connected condition	$9

(Veterans in Priority Groups 7-8 do not qualify for medication copay annual cap)

NOTE: Veterans in Priority Group 1 do not pay for medications

Inpatient Services

Priority Group 8

Inpatient Copay for first 90 days of care during a 365-day period	$1,216
Inpatient Copay for each additional 90 days of care during a 365-day period	$608
Per Diem Charge	$10/day

Priority Group 7

Inpatient Copay for first 90 days of care during a 365-day period	$243.20
Inpatient Copay for each additional 90 days of care during a 365-day period	$121.60
Per Diem Charge	$2/day

Long-Term Care **

Nursing Home Care/Inpatient Respite Care/Geriatric Evaluation	maximum of $97/day
Adult Day Health Care/Outpatient Geriatric Evaluation Outpatient Respite Care	maximum of $15/day
Domiciliary Care	maximum of $5/day
Spousal Resource Protection Amount	$117,240

** Copayments for Long-Term Care services start on the 22nd day of care during any 12-month period—there is no copayment requirement for the first 21 days. Actual copayment charges will vary from Veteran to Veteran depending upon financial information submitted on VA Form 10-10EC.

Health Care for Families of Veterans

Family Members of Veterans
Under certain circumstances, family members of Veterans are eligible for health benefits. Some of the programs offered include the Civilian Health and Medical Program of the Department of Veterans Affairs (CHAMPVA), Spina Bifida (SB), Children of Women Vietnam Veterans (CWVV), Foreign Medical Program (FMP) and Caregiver. Using these programs may reduce or eliminate your cost for medical supplies, office visits or prescriptions.

CHAMPVA
A health care benefits program that provides coverage to the spouse or widow(er) and to the dependent children of a qualifying sponsor who:

- is rated permanently and totally disabled due to a service-connected disability, or
- was rated permanently and totally disabled due to a service-connected condition at the time of death, or
- died of a service-connected disability, or
- died on active duty, and
- the dependents are not otherwise eligible for Department of Defense TRICARE benefits.

Under CHAMPVA, VA shares the cost of covered health care services and supplies with eligible beneficiaries.

Children of Women Vietnam Veterans (CWVV) Program
The CWVV Health Care Program is a Federal health benefits program administered by the Department of Veterans Affairs, for children with certain birth defects born to women Vietnam Veterans. The CWVV Program is a Fee for Service (indemnity plan) program. The CWVV Program provides reimbursement for medical care-related conditions associated with certain birth defects except spina bifida, which is covered under the VA's Spina Bifida Program.

Children whose biological mother is a Vietnam Veteran, who were conceived after the date on which the Veteran entered the Republic of Vietnam, during the period beginning on February 28, 1961, and ending May 7, 1975, and who have one of the covered birth defects, as determined by the Veterans Benefits Administration (VBA) are eligible for the program.

Spina Bifida Healthcare Program
The Spina Bifida Health Care Program is a health benefit program administered by the Department of Veterans Affairs for Vietnam and certain Korean Veterans' birth children who have been diagnosed with spina bifida (except spina bifida occulta). The program provides reimbursement for medical services and supplies.

Caregiver Program
"Operation Enduring Freedom" (OEF) is the official name used by the U.S. government for the War in Afghanistan, together with a number of smaller military actions, under the umbrella of the global "War on Terror" Reports indicate that there are high rates of suicide in Operation Iraqi Freedom (OIF) and Enduring Freedom (OEF) veterans.

(GWOT).Primary caregivers of OEF/OIF Veterans may be eligible to receive a stipend and access to healthcare coverage if they are not already entitled to care or services under a health plan contract, including Medicare, Medicaid or worker's compensation. Mental health counseling, including marriage and family counseling, will also be provided. Caregivers may also be eligible for travel, lodging and per diem when they accompany the Veteran for care or attend training. Caregivers need to complete VA Form 10-10CG, Application for Comprehensive Assistance for Family Caregivers Program to apply for VA's Comprehensive Assistance Family Caregivers Program. VA will use the information on this form to determine your eligibility for this program.

The VA believes that caring and supporting family caregivers improves the lives of Veterans. Learn more about how the VA supports family caregivers at www.caregiver.va.gov.
Read More

Non-VA Medical Care Program
Non-VA medical care is care provided to eligible Veterans outside of the VA when VA facilities are not feasibly available. All VA Medical Centers (VAMCs) can use this program when needed. The use of non-VA medical care is governed by federal laws containing eligibility criteria and other policies specifying when and why it can be used. A preapproval for treatment in the community is required for non-VA medical care – unless the medical event is an emergency. Emergency events may be reimbursed on behalf of the Veteran in certain cases.

Emergency Care Services
There may be a time when a Veteran requires emergency care. When it is not possible to go to a VA Medical Center, a Veteran may have to seek treatment at the nearest hospital with an emergency room. The Department of Veterans Affairs (VA) is authorized under Title 38 United States Code (U.S.C.) to make payment or reimbursement to a claimant for emergency treatment provided to Veterans meeting specific eligibility criteria.
Visit our Emergency Care page for more information.

Prior Approval for Veteran Care
The Non-VA Medical Care Program Office provides payment authorization for eligible Veterans to obtain routine outpatient medical services, and certain inpatient services, through community providers. This authorization may be granted when it has been determined that direct VA services are either geographically inaccessible or VA facilities are not available to meet a Veteran's needs. All community services must be preapproved before a Veteran receives treatment.

Patient-Centered Community Care (PC3)
Patient-Centered Community Care (PC3) is a program that contracts with vendors to develop a network of health care providers to deliver covered care to Veterans. The covered care includes primary care, inpatient specialty care, outpatient specialty care, mental health care, limited emergency care, limited newborn care for enrolled female Veterans following delivery, skilled home health care, and home infusion therapy. Care is available through PC3 when local VA Medical Centers cannot readily provide the needed care to Veterans due to demand exceeding capacity, geographic inaccessibility or other limiting factors.

Project ARCH (Access Received Closer to Home)
Project ARCH was originally a 3-year pilot program to provide specific non-VA medical care services through contractual agreements to eligible Veterans in Veteran Integrated Service Networks (VISNs) 1, 6, 15, 18 and 19. With the adoption of the Veterans Access, Choice and Accountably Act of 2014 (Public Law 113-146), the Project ARCH pilot program has been extended for two additional years, now ending in August 2016. Project ARCH intends to improve access to health care services for eligible Veterans by connecting them to services closer to their home. Project ARCH is managed by a parent Veterans Affairs Medical Center (VAMC) in each of the five VISNs, located in Northern Maine; Farmville, Va.; Pratt, Kan.; Flagstaff, Ariz.; and Billings, Mont.

State Veterans Home (SVH) Per Diem Program
VA's State Home program provides an economical alternative to constructing, maintaining and operating VA facilities for the provision of care to eligible Veterans. Under this program, the states provide quality care for eligible Veterans in three different types of programs: nursing home, domiciliary, and adult day health care. VA contributions to state home per diem expenses are projected to be $1.07 billion in FY 2014.

Indian Health Services (IHS)/Tribal Health Program (THP) Reimbursement Agreements Program
The Chief Business Office Purchased Care, Office of Tribal Government Relations (OTGR), and VA Medical Centers (VAMCs) work together to implement the Tribal Reimbursement Agreements Program. The Tribal Reimbursement Agreements Program provides a means for IHS and THP health facilities to receive reimbursement from the VA for direct care services provided to American Indian and Alaskan Native eligible Veterans. This program is part of a larger effort set forth in the VA and IHS Memorandum of Understanding signed in October 2010 to improve access to care and care coordination for our nation's Native Veterans.

CHAPTER 7
Burial Benefits

Where to Burial Benefit Claims – Claims Intake Center

Claimants should now send all burial and survivor benefit application directly to VA's Intake Center in Jainesville, Wisconsin with attention to the appropriate Pension Management Center (PMC). The intake center will scan and upload the digital images of the burial or survivor benefit application for processing. Please refer to the data disk for the appropriate Pension Center's PO Box in Jainesville, WI.

Folder #4 *Application for Burial Benefits*, found in the Data Disc, contains the following forms to help you apply:

SF 180 – Request Pertaining to Military Records
VA40-4970 – Request for Disinterment
VBA-21-530-ARE – Application for Burial Benefits
VBA-21-530a-ARE – State Application for Interment Allowance under 38 U.S.C. Chapter 23
VBA-21-8834-ARE – Application for Reimbursement of Headstone or Marker Expense
VBA-27-2008-ARE – Application for United States Flag for Burial Purposes

Burial Allowances

The information below was taken from the US department of Veterans Affairs web site

Burial, Headstone & Plot Rate Table 2015-16

SERVICE CONNECTED DEATH	*$2,000
NON-SERVICE CONNECTED DEATH (Reimbursement; veteran dies while hospitalized by VA)	$722.58
NON-SERVICE CONNECTED DEATH (Reimbursement for Veterans not hospitalized by VA)	$309.68
STATE CEMETERY (This amount will be paid to a state veterans cemetery for the plot/burial)	$722.58
PLOT ALLOWANCE (This amount will be paid to reimburse for a private-paid plot)	$722.58

Note 3: The PL 111-275 allows increase from $300 to $700 for Veterans who die while properly hospitalized by VA. For non-service-connected burial for indigent or Veterans not properly hospitalized by VA, the burial reimbursement remains $300. The increases from $300 to $700 will apply to deaths occurring on or after October 1, 2011. The first opportunity for an annual increase (i.e., cost-of-living adjustment) is October 1, 2012.

What Are VA Burial Allowances?

VA burial allowances are partial reimbursements of an eligible veteran's burial and funeral costs. When the cause of death is not service-related, the reimbursements are generally described as two payments: (1) a burial and funeral expense allowance, and (2) a plot interment allowance.

Who Is Eligible ?

You may be eligible for a VA burial allowance if:

- you paid for a veteran's burial or funeral AND
- you have not been reimbursed by another government agency or some other source, such as the deceased veteran's employer and
- the veteran was discharged under conditions other than dishonorable.

In addition, at least one of the following conditions must be met:

- the veteran died because of a service-related disability or
- the veteran was receiving VA pension or compensation at the time of death or
- the veteran was entitled to receive VA pension or compensation, but decided not to reduce his/her military retirement or disability pay or
- the veteran died in a VA hospital, in a nursing home under VA contract, or while in an approved state nursing home.

How Much Does VA Pay?

Service-Related Death. VA will pay up to $2,000 toward burial expenses for deaths on or after September 11, 2001. If the veteran is buried in a VA national cemetery, some or all of the cost of transporting the deceased may be reimbursed.

Nonservice-Related Death. VA will pay up to $309.68 toward burial and funeral expenses, and a $722.58 plot-interment allowance for deaths on or after October 1, 2011. If the death happened while the veteran was in a VA hospital or under VA contracted nursing home care, some or all of the costs for transporting the deceased's remains may be reimbursed.

The plot allowance may be paid to the state for the cost of a plot or interment in a state-owned cemetery reserved solely for Veteran burials if the Veteran is buried without charge. Burial expenses paid by the deceased's employer or a state agency will not be reimbursed.

Burial and Memorial benefits

Eligibility

1. Veterans discharged from active duty under conditions other than dishonorable and
2. service members who die while on active duty, active duty for training, or inactive duty training, as well as
3. spouses and dependent children of Veterans and active duty service-members, may be eligible for VA burial and memorial benefits. The Veteran does not have to die before a spouse or dependent child for them to be eligible.

With certain exceptions, active duty service beginning after Sept. 7, 1980, as an enlisted person, and after Oct. 16, 1981, as an officer, must be for a minimum of 24 consecutive months or the full period of active duty (as in the case of reservists or National Guard members called to active duty for a limited duration). Active duty for training, by itself, while serving in the reserves or National Guard, is not sufficient to confer eligibility. Reservists and National Guard members, as well as their spouses and dependent children, are eligible if they were entitled to retired pay at the time of death, or would have been upon reaching requisite age. See Chapter 8 for more information.

VA's National Cemetery Scheduling Office or local national cemetery directors verify eligibility for burial. A copy of the Veteran's discharge document that specifies the period(s) of active duty and character of discharge is usually sufficient to determine eligibility. In some instances, a copy of the deceased's death certificate and proof of relationship to the Veteran (for eligible family members) may be required.

Under Section 2411 of Title 38 of the United States Code, certain otherwise eligible individuals found to have committed federal or state capital crimes are barred from burial or memorialization in a VA national cemetery, and from receipt of government-furnished headstones, markers, medallions, burial flags, and Presidential Memorial Certificates.

Veterans and other claimants for VA burial benefits have the right to appeal decisions made by VA regarding eligibility for national cemetery burial or other memorial benefits.

Burial in VA National Cemeteries
Burial in a VA national cemetery is available for eligible Veterans, their spouses and dependents at no cost to the family and includes the gravesite, grave-liner, opening and closing of the grave, a headstone or marker, and perpetual care as part of a national shrine. For Veterans, benefits also include a burial flag (with case for active duty) and military funeral honors. Family members and other loved ones of deceased Veterans may request Presidential Memorial Certificates.

VA operates 131 national cemeteries, of which 72 are open for new casketed interments and 18 are open to accept only cremated remains. Burial options are limited to those available at a specific cemetery but may include in-ground casket, or interment of cremated remains in a columbarium, in ground or in a scatter garden. Contact the national cemetery directly, or visit our

Web site at: www.cem.va.gov to determine if a particular cemetery is open for new burials, and which other options are available.

The funeral director or the next of kin makes interment arrangements by contacting the National Cemetery Scheduling Office or, in some cases, the national cemetery in which burial is desired. VA normally does not conduct burials on weekends. Gravesites cannot be reserved; however, VA will honor reservations made under previous programs.

Surviving spouses of Veterans who died on or after Jan. 1, 2000, do not lose eligibility for burial in a national cemetery if they remarry. Burial of dependent children is limited to unmarried children under 21 years of age, or under 23 years of age if a full-time student at an approved educational institution. Unmarried adult children who become physically or mentally disabled and incapable of self-support before age 21, or age 23 if a full-time student, also are eligible for burial.

Burial in Arlington National Cemetery

Arlington National Cemetery is a national cemetery administered by the Department of the Army. The primary mission of Arlington National Cemetery is to serve as the final resting place for the men and women who honorably served in the Armed Forces and their immediate family members. The cemetery routinely performs 20 to 30 funeral services each day.

Vision:

1. America's premier military cemetery -
2. A national shrine -
3. A living history of freedom -
4. Where dignity and honor rest in solemn repose.

Mission: On behalf of the American people,

1. lay to rest those who have served our nation with dignity and honor,
2. treating their families with respect and compassion, and
3. connecting guests to the rich tapestry of the cemetery's living history, while maintaining these hallowed grounds befitting the sacrifice of all those who rest here in quiet repose.

The grounds of Arlington National Cemetery honor those who have served our nation by providing a sense of beauty and peace for our guests. The rolling green hills are dotted with trees that are hundreds of years in age and complement the gardens found throughout the 624 developed acres of the cemetery. This impressive landscape serves as a tribute to the service and sacrifice of every individual laid to rest within the hallowed grounds of Arlington National Cemetery.

Eligibility for interment at Arlington National Cemetery is verified at the time of need (at the time of death) and cannot be verified by the cemetery or accommodated before that time.

However, in accordance with the 1986 Title 32 Code of Federal Regulations Part 553, section 15, the following individuals are eligible for interment (ground burial) at Arlington National Cemetery:

(a) Any active duty member of the Armed Forces (except those members serving on active duty for training only).

(b) Any retired member of the Armed Forces. A retired member of the Armed Forces, in the context of this paragraph, is a retired member of the Army, Navy, Air Force, Marine Corps, Coast Guard, or a Reserve component who has served on active duty (other than for training), is carried on an official retired list, and is entitled to receive retired pay stemming from service in the Armed Forces. If, at the time of death, a retired member of the Armed Forces is not entitled to receive retired pay stemming from his service in the Armed Forces until some future date, the retired member will not be eligible for ground burial.

(c) Any former member of the Armed Forces separated for physical disability prior to 1 October 1949 who has served on active duty (other than for training) and who would have been eligible for retirement under the provisions of 10 United States Code (U.S.C.) 1201 had that statute been in effect on the date of his separation.

(d) Any former member of the Armed Forces whose last active duty (other than for training) military service terminated honorably and who has been awarded one of the following decorations:

(1) Medal of Honor.
(2) Distinguished Service Cross (Air Force Cross or Navy Cross).
(3) Distinguished Service Medal.
(4) Silver Star.
(5) Purple Heart.

(e) Persons who have held any of the following positions provided their last period of active duty (other than for training) as a member of the Armed Forces terminated honorably:

(1) An elective office of the United States Government.
(2) Office of the Chief Justice of the United States or of an Associate Justice of the Supreme Court of the United States.
(3) An office listed in 5 U.S.C. 5312 or 5 U.S.C. 5313.
(4) The Chief of a mission who was at any time during his/her tenure classified in class I under the provisions of Section 411 of the Act of 13 August 1946, 60 Stat. 1002, as amended (22 U.S.C. 866, 1964 ed.).

(f) Any former prisoner of war who, while a prisoner of war, served honorably in the active military, naval, or air service, whose last period of active military, naval, or air service terminated honorably and who died on or after November 30, 1993.

(1) The term "former prisoner of war" means a person who, while serving in the active military, naval, or air service, was forcibly detained or interned in line of duty—

(i) By an enemy government or its agents, or a hostile force, during a period of war; or

(ii) By a foreign government or its agents, or a hostile force, under circumstances which the Secretary of Veterans Affairs finds to have been comparable to the circumstances under which persons have generally been forcibly detained or interned by enemy governments during periods of war.

(2) The term "active military, naval, or air service" includes active duty, any period of active duty for training during which the individual concerned was disabled or died from a disease or injury incurred or aggravated in line of duty, and any period of inactive duty training during which the individual concerned was disabled or died from an injury incurred or aggravated in line of duty.

(g) The spouse, widow or widower, minor child and, at the discretion of the Secretary of the Army, unmarried adult child of any of the persons listed above.

(1) The term "spouse" refers to a widow or widower of an eligible member, including the widow or widower of a member of the Armed Forces who was lost or buried at sea or officially determined to be permanently absent in a status of missing or missing in action. A surviving spouse who has remarried and whose remarriage is void, terminated by death, or dissolved by annulment or divorce by a court with basic authority to render such decrees regains eligibility for burial in Arlington National Cemetery unless it is determined that the decree of annulment or divorce was secured through fraud or collusion.

(2) An unmarried adult child may be interred in the same gravesite in which the parent has been or will be interred, provided that child was incapable of self-support up to the time of death because of physical or mental condition. At the time of death of an adult child, a request for interment will be submitted to the Executive Director, Army National Cemeteries Program, Arlington National Cemetery. The request must be accompanied by a notarized statement from an individual who has direct knowledge as to the marital status, degree of dependency of the deceased child, the name of that child's parent, and the military service upon which the burial is being requested. A certificate of a physician who has attended the decedent as to the nature and duration of the physical and/or mental disability must also accompany the request for interment.

(h) Widows or widowers of service members who are interred in Arlington National Cemetery as part of a group burial may be interred/inurned in the cemetery, but not in the same gravesite as the group burial.

(i) The surviving spouse, minor child, and, at the discretion of the Secretary of the Army, unmarried adult child of any person already buried in Arlington.

(j) The parents of a minor child or unmarried adult child whose remains, based on the eligibility of a parent, are already buried in Arlington National Cemetery.

Certain Eligible Parents for VA Burial

A new federal law passed in 2010 (Public Law 111-275) extends burial benefits to certain parents of service-members who die as a result of hostile activity or from training-related injuries who are buried in a national cemetery in a gravesite with available space. The biological or adopted parents of a service-member who died in combat or while performing training in preparation for a combat mission, who leaves no surviving spouse or dependent child, may be buried with the deceased service-member if the Secretary of Veterans Affairs determines that there is available space. The law applies to service-members who died on or after Oct. 7, 2001 and to parents who died on or after Oct. 13, 2010.

Headstones, Markers and Medallions

Veterans, active duty service members, and retired Reservists and National Guard service members, are eligible for an inscribed headstone or marker for their grave at any cemetery – national, State Veterans, or private. VA will deliver a headstone or marker at no cost, anywhere in the world. For eligible Veterans whose deaths occurred on or after Nov. 1, 1990, VA may provide a government headstone or marker even if the grave is already marked with a private one, or VA may provide a medallion instead of a headstone or marker for Veterans' graves in private cemeteries when the grave is already marked with a privately-purchased headstone or marker. Spouses and dependent children are eligible for a government headstone or marker only if they are buried in a national or State Veterans cemetery.

Flat markers are available in bronze, granite or marble. Upright headstones come in granite or marble. In national cemeteries, the style provided will be consistent with existing monuments at the place of burial. Niche markers are available to mark columbaria used for inurnment of cremated remains. Medallions are made of bronze and are available in three sizes: 5-inch, 3-inch, and 1 ½-inches.

Headstones, markers and medallions previously provided by the government may be replaced at the government's expense if badly deteriorated, illegible, vandalized or stolen. To check the status of a claim for a headstone or marker for placement in a national or State Veterans cemetery, call the cemetery. To check the status of one being placed in a private cemetery, call 1-800-697-6947.

Inscription

Headstones and markers must be inscribed with the name of the deceased, branch of service, and year of birth and death. They also may be inscribed with other optional information, including an authorized emblem of belief and, space permitting, additional text including military rank; war service such as "World War II;" complete dates of birth and death; military awards; military organizations; civilian or Veteran affiliations; and personalized words of endearment.

Private Cemeteries
To submit a claim for a headstone, marker or medallion for a private cemetery, mail a completed VA Form 40-1330 (available at www4.va.gov/vaforms/va/pdf/VA40-1330.pdf), Application for Standard Government Headstone or Marker, and a copy of the Veteran's military discharge document to Memorial Programs Service (41A1), Department of Veterans Affairs, 5109 Russell Rd., Quantico, VA 22134-3903. The form and supporting documents may also be faxed toll free to 1-800-455-7143.

Before ordering, check with the cemetery to ensure that the Government-furnished headstone or marker will be accepted. All installation fees are the responsibility of the applicant.

"In Memory Of" Markers
VA provides memorial headstones and markers with "In Memory Of" as the first line of inscription, to memorialize those whose remains have not been recovered or identified, were buried at sea, donated to science or cremated and scattered. Eligibility is the same as for regular headstones and markers. There is no fee when the "In Memory Of" marker is placed in a national cemetery. All installation fees at private cemeteries are the responsibility of the applicant.

Medallions in Lieu of Government Headstone/Marker
Public Law 110-157 enacted December 26, 2007, expanded VA authority to provide a medallion instead of a headstone or marker for Veterans' graves in private cemeteries when the grave is already marked with a privately-purchased headstone or marker. Claimants will have the option to apply for either a traditional headstone or marker to place on the grave, or a medallion to affix to a privately-purchased headstone or marker. VA anticipates the medallion will be available during 2010. Current information regarding medallion availability is located at www.cem.va.gov.

Presidential Memorial Certificates
These are issued upon request to recognize the United States military service of honorably discharged deceased Veterans. Next of kin, relatives and other loved ones may apply for a certificate by mailing, e-mailing, or faxing a completed and signed VA Form 40-0247 along with a copy of the Veteran's military discharge documents or proof of honorable military service. The form and eligibility requirements can be found at www.cem.va.gov. All requests must be sent with supporting military documents or proof of honorable military service.

Burial Flag
A United States flag is provided, at no cost, to drape the casket or accompany the urn of a deceased veteran who served honorably in the U. S. Armed Forces. It is furnished to honor the memory of a veteran's military service to his or her country. VA will furnish a burial flag for memorialization for each other than dishonorable discharged

- veteran who served during wartime
- veteran who died on active duty after May 27, 1941
- veteran who served after January 31, 1955
- peacetime veteran who was discharged or released before June 27, 1950

- certain persons who served in the organized military forces of the Commonwealth of the Philippines while in service of the U.S Armed forces and who died on or after April 25, 1951
- certain former members of the Selected Reserves

Generally, the flag is given to the next-of-kin, as a keepsake, after its use during the funeral service. When there is no next-of-kin, VA will furnish the flag to a friend making request for it. For those VA national cemeteries with an Avenue of Flags, families of veterans buried in these national cemeteries may donate the burial flags of their loved ones to be flown on patriotic holidays.

You may apply for the flag by completing VA Form 21-2008, Application for United States Flag for Burial Purposes. You may get a flag at any VA regional office or U.S. Post Office. Generally, the funeral director will help you obtain the flag.

The law allows us to issue one flag for a veteran's funeral. We cannot replace it if it is lost, destroyed, or stolen. However, some veterans' organizations or other community groups may be able to help you get another flag.

The proper way to display the flag depends upon whether the casket is open or closed. VA Form 21-2008 does provide the correct method for displaying and folding the flag. The burial flag is not suitable for outside display because of its size and fabric. It is made of cotton and can easily be damaged by weather.

Military Funeral Honors
Upon request, DoD will provide military funeral honors consisting of folding and presentation of the United States flag and the playing of "Taps." A funeral honors detail consists of two or more uniformed members of the armed forces, with at least one member from the deceased's branch of service.

Family members should inform their funeral director if they want military funeral honors. DoD maintains a toll-free number (1-877-MIL-HONR) for use by funeral directors only to request honors. VA can help arrange honors for burials at VA national cemeteries. Veterans service organizations or volunteer groups may help provide honors. For more information, visit www.militaryfuneralhonors.osd.mil.

Veterans Cemeteries Administered by Other Agencies

Arlington National Cemetery
Administered by the Department of the Army. Eligibility is more restrictive than at VA national cemeteries. For information, call (703) 607-8000, write Superintendent, Arlington National Cemetery, Arlington, VA 22211, or visit www.arlingtoncemetery.mil.

Department of the Interior
Administers two active national cemeteries – Andersonville National Cemetery in Georgia and Andrew Johnson National Cemetery in Tennessee. Eligibility is similar to VA national cemeteries.

State Veterans Cemeteries
Seventy-nine State Veterans cemeteries offer burial options for Veterans and their families. These cemeteries have similar eligibility requirements but many require state residency. Some services, particularly for family members, may require a fee. Contact the State cemetery or State Veterans affairs office for information.

CHAPTER 8
Appeals

Where to File an Appeal for a Denied Compensation Claim

VBA encourages Veterans and Service-members to file compensation claims and appeals electronically through eBenefits. However, if you are filing a paper appeal for a compensation related claim, you should send notice to the address or fax number listed below:

Department of Veterans Affairs
Claims Intake Center
PO Box 5235
Janesville, WI 53547-5235
Toll Free Fax: 844-822-5246

If you received a letter from VA requesting additional evidence to support your or appeal, you can mail/fax to the following address or fax number:

Department of Veterans Affairs
Evidence Intake Center
PO Box 4444
Janesville, WI 53547-4444
Toll Free Fax: 844-822-5246

Where to File an Appeal for a Denied Pension / Survivor / Burial Claim

To file a pension related claim, submit notice and additional evidence to the Claims Intake Center with attention to the appropriate Pension Management Center. Please refer to the data disc for the Pension Center's PO Box in Jainesville, WI for your appeal.

The remaining information in this chapter was taken from the California Department of Veterans Affairs Training Manual for County Veterans Service Officers

Any unfavorable adjudicative decision by the department of veterans Affairs (VA) may be appealed to the Board of Veterans' Appeals, and if the denial continues, to the U.S. Court of Appeals for Veterans' Claims (previously called the Court of Veterans Appeals) and beyond. An adjudicative decision is one which establishes or denies eligibility to a VA benefit, such as service connection for a disability, eligibility for dental treatment, monthly rate of education assistance, waiver of overpayment, etc. A decision that a veteran should be given one type of medical treatment rather than some other is not an adjudicative decision, and is not appealable through these channels.

What Constitutes an Appeal? (Filing a Notice of Disagreement)
An appeal is defined as a timely filed written Notice of Disagreement (via VA Form 21-0958) from a VA decision and, after a Statement of the Case has been furnished, a timely filed written Substantive Appeal. A claimant generally has one year from the date of the letter notifying him or her of an adverse decision to submit a Notice of Disagreement; otherwise, that decision becomes final. The only requirements for a Notice of Disagreement are that it must be in writing, it must be addressed to the activity or operating element of VA which made the adverse decision, and it must be worded so it may reasonably be construed as a desire for appellate review. It is not required to say why the claimant is dissatisfied or to make any specific contentions on the Notice of Disagreement (although it is always helpful to do so).

If multiple issues were decided and the claimant disagrees with some but not all of the decisions, the Notice of Disagreement should specify which decisions are being contested. If the notice is ambiguous, i.e., does not reasonably indicate a desire to appeal or is not clear which decisions are being disagreed with, the claimant may be asked to clarify. If the claimant does not answer, or can not specify more clearly, the statement may be considered to not be a Notice of Disagreement.

There is a class of decisions which have a shorter appeal period than one year. These are called "simultaneously contested claims," and involve cases where there are two or more claimants for a single set of benefits; a grant of one claim necessarily means a denial of the other claim or a reduction in benefits for the other claimant. Examples would be two contending claimants, each claiming to be the veteran's legal surviving spouse; or when there is a claim by a dependent for an apportioned share of the veteran's (or other beneficiary's) award, and regardless of the outcome, the unsuccessful claimant contests the decision. In these cases, the unsuccessful claimant must submit a Notice of Disagreement within 60 days from the date of adverse notice; otherwise, that decision becomes final.

Decision Review Officer (DRO)

For certain Notices of Disagreement the claimant and/or representative may obtain a de novo review of the decision by a local Decision Review Officer (DRO) as a first step in the appeal process. This procedure is restricted to those issues governed by 38 CFR, Parts 3 and 4 (primarily Compensation and Pension claims, although issues governed by Part 3 which affect eligibility for other benefits, such as character of discharge, minimum active duty service requirements, recognition of dependents, etc., are also included).

To obtain a DRO review, the claimant and/or representative must request it. If a claimant or representative submits a Notice of Disagreement (via VA Form 21-0958) and does not specify if a DRO review is desired, VA is required to ask the claimant whether he or she wishes such review. The claimant is allowed 60 days to respond. This 60-day period may not be extended. If the claimant or representative does not request DRO review within 60 days after the date VA mails notice of eligibility for such review, the Notice of Disagreement will be processed in the traditional manner, as described below. Only one DRO review is allowed for each issue being contested.

If a DRO review is elected, the DRO will review the claim for correctness and reasonableness. If any additional development is indicated, the DRO will direct that it be done. If the claimant requests it, the DRO may also conduct either a formal hearing or an informal conference on the issue(s). When all development, hearings, etc., are completed, the DRO will then review the claim again, with no deference given to the contested decision. If there is no additional evidence, the DRO may modify or reverse an unfavorable decision based on either de novo review or on clear and unmistakable error.

The DRO may not issue a decision less favorable to the claimant than the original (contested) decision, unless the original decision was clearly erroneous. If the DRO review results in anything less than a full grant of all benefits being sought and the claimant or representative does not withdraw the Notice of Disagreement, the DRO will furnish a Statement of the Case (SOC) and regular appellate processing proceeds, as described below.

Statement of the Case (SOC)

For issues not subject to DRO review, or if the claimant does not wish DRO review (or does not answer the letter asking if a DRO review is wanted), when a valid Notice of Disagreement is received the responsible VA activity, called the Agency of Original Jurisdiction (AOJ), is obliged to review the decision for correctness and to determine if any further development is necessary, and if so, to do it. After this review, if the full benefit being sought is still not granted, VA will then furnish a SOC to the claimant and his or her representative (if any). If the disagreement was on a simultaneously contested claim, a copy of the SOC will be furnished to all parties and their representatives (if any).

If more than one VA element was involved in the unfavorable decision, the activity which notified the claimant of the decision has primary responsibility for the SOC. The SOC will contain a recitation of the evidence considered in the decision, a recitation of the laws and regulations applicable to the decision, a statement of the decision, and a discussion of the reasons and bases why the rules as applied to this evidence did not permit the benefit(s) being sought to be granted.

Substantive Appeal (VA Form 9)

The claimant then has 60 days or the remainder of the one-year appeal period, whichever is later, to submit a Substantive Appeal (VA Form 9, Appeal to the Board of Veterans' Appeals, or the equivalent written statement) on the issue(s) covered; otherwise, the decision becomes final. HOWEVER, if the appealed issue is a simultaneously contested claim, the appealing party must return the Substantive Appeal within 30 days from the date the Statement of the Case is furnished; if not, the appeal is not timely perfected and the decision becomes final.

A Supplemental Statement of the Case (SSOC) will be furnished if additional evidence is considered after the original SOC has been sent; if an amended decision has been made granting part but not all of the benefit(s) being sought; or if there was any material defect in the original SOC. The SSOC has the same elements as the original SOC. If the original appeal period had not expired when the additional evidence was considered, the claimant and representative (if any) will be furnished another VA Form 9 and allowed another 60 days (30 days for appeals on simultaneously contested claims) or to the end of the appeal period, whichever is later, for response.

If additional issues are raised which were not covered in the original SOC, a new SOC (with another VA Form 9) will be furnished regarding those additional issues. Return of this additional VA Form 9 is subject to the same time limits as the original Substantive Appeal.

In contrast to the Notice of Disagreement, the Substantive Appeal must make specific contentions relating to errors of fact or law made by VA in reaching the decision(s) being appealed; however, it does not need to be, and should not be, couched in legalistic jargon or terminology. To the extent feasible, it should relate to specific points in the Statement(s) of the Case. The Board of Veterans' Appeals (BVA) may dismiss any appeal that does not make specific contentions; however, they will construe the record in a liberal manner to determine if this requirement has been met. Once the Substantive Appeal has been returned, the appeal has been "perfected," and the appellant is not required to take any further actions except to cooperate with any additional development as is deemed to be necessary.

Final Review and Forward to BVA by the Office of Original Jurisdiction

The AOJ will again review the evidentiary record for completeness and to make sure that all due process requirements have been observed. If these reviews result in a SSOC, the appellant and representative (if any) will be given an additional 60 days to make any further response desired. However, once a Substantive Appeal on each issue has been submitted, any further response is optional and is not required to continue the appeal. If there is a representative, the representative will be invited to make a final argument. The AOJ will then certify that the appeal is ready for BVA review, and forward the complete record to them.

The appellant and representative (if any) will be notified when BVA receives the appeal, and will be allowed a period of up to 90 days to submit any additional evidence desired or to request a personal hearing (if not already done), or to request a change in representation. (Note that most veterans' service organizations have strict rules against accepting appointment as representative during an ongoing appeal.)

Board of Veterans Appeals (BVA)

BVA considers appeals in the order of receipt; however, an appeal may be moved to the head of the pending queue (advanced on the docket) if sufficient cause is shown. "Sufficient cause" would include terminal or serious illness of the appellant; advanced age of the appellant (over age 75); extreme financial hardship on the appellant, etc. Advancement on the docket must be requested in writing by either the appellant or the representative, and must state the reason(s) for the request.

If BVA determines that the appeal is not yet ready for review, they will remand it for additional development, observance of due process requirements, etc., as instructed. Under certain circumstances and depending on the specific evidence required, BVA may accomplish some additional development themselves without remanding the appeal: if BVA determines that the case requires special expertise or involves complex legal issues, they may request an independent (from outside VA) expert medical opinion, or a legal opinion from VA General Counsel. Otherwise, the appeal must generally be remanded. Because of the large number of remanded appeals and the length of time many have been pending because of other workload issues, a separate Appeals Management Center (AMC) has been established for the sole purpose of handling remanded appeals.

When BVA determines that the appeal is ready for review, they will proceed. BVA reviews all appeals under the de novo standard. Whether BVA's final decision grants the appeal or affirms the denial, the appellant and representative (if any) will be advised in writing of the decision. The notice will include a listing of the issue(s) considered; findings of fact and law; a recitation of the evidence considered; and the reasons and bases for the decision as to each issue. The decision will also include a notice of appeal rights to the Court of Appeals for Veterans' Claims. This will include instructions on how to file an appeal to the court, where to send it, and the time limit for filing the appeal.

Additional Evidence

Additional evidence may be submitted by or for the appellant at any point between the time VA first notifies the claimant of its decision and the time BVA notifies the appellant of its decision. Remember, however, that submission of additional evidence does NOT extend the time limits for initiating or completing an appeal. VA is required by law to review all decisions for correctness and completeness before proceeding with appellate processing when the claimant has disagreed with a decision. It is always in the claimant's best interests to word a request for reconsideration as a Notice of Disagreement with intent to appeal if the denial is continued; this will also avoid the problem of an "ambiguous" Notice of Disagreement..

After the appeal has been forwarded to BVA and the 90-day period has elapsed, any additional evidence submitted may not be reviewed by BVA until it has been first reviewed by the AOJ or AMC, unless the appellant or representative specifically waives such review. The waiver must be in writing and must accompany the evidence being submitted. If no waiver is given, BVA will remand the appeal for review of the additional evidence and preparation of a SSOC if the claim remains denied or if less than all the benefits being sought are granted and the appellant does not withdraw the appeal.

Personal Hearing

An appellant may request a personal hearing before BVA at any point in the appeal up to the time BVA issues its decision. The hearing may be held before the Board sitting in Washington, DC; before a traveling section of the Board at the VA Regional Office; or by video teleconference, with the claimant at a designated VA station and the Board member in Washington, DC. As described above, the DRO may also conduct a personal hearing for appellants at the Regional Office. Generally, an appellant will only be scheduled once for a hearing on appeal, unless good cause is shown why the hearing should be rescheduled or another hearing is required.

Further Defining a Notice of Disagreement and a Substantive Appeal

A Notice of Disagreement and a Substantive Appeal may be filed by the claimant or representative, by the claimant's next friend, or, if the claimant is under a disability by a court, by a fiduciary. Even if the claimant is under such disability, VA will still honor and act upon a Notice of Disagreement filed by the claimant if it is otherwise valid.

A Notice of Disagreement may be withdrawn in writing at any time prior to filing the Substantive Appeal, and a Substantive Appeal may be withdrawn in writing at any time before BVA promulgates its decision. Either the claimant or the representative may make the withdrawal. Withdrawal of a Notice of Disagreement or appeal as to any issue(s) does not preclude submitting another Notice of Disagreement on the same issue(s), provided the original time limit to appeal the decision has not expired.

Grounds for Request for Reconsideration

An appellant or representative may request reconsideration of a final BVA decision at any time upon allegation of clear and unmistakable error of fact or law (CUE); discovery of new and material evidence in the form of relevant service records; or allegation of fraud or misrepresentation of evidence which materially influenced the Board's decision. BVA may also on its own initiative (without request from the appellant or representative) reconsider its decision under the same circumstances. However, if an appeal is pending before the CAVC, BVA may not reconsider its decision unless the court gives it specific permission to do so.

Further Appeal to the Court Of Appeals for Veterans Claims (CAVC)

An appellant has 120 days from the date of an unfavorable BVA final decision to file an appeal to the U.S. Court of Appeals for Veterans' Claims (CAVC). This appeal must be sent directly to the court, NOT to BVA or to any VA office. The time limit for filing may not be extended or waived.

There is a filing fee, which may be waived. Only the appellant or representative may appeal a BVA decision to the court; the agency may not appeal.

The court may only consider the issues, evidence and arguments that BVA reviewed in its decision—no new evidence may be submitted and no new arguments or issues may be raised. The court will uphold BVA if there is any reasonable basis for its decision, unless the court finds an error of fact or law, or finds that BVA's decision was arbitrary and capricious. Either the appellant or VA may appeal the CAVC's decision to the U.S. Court of Appeals for the Federal Circuit, and if still unsuccessful, to the U.S. Supreme Court.

Hiring a Representative for Appeal

Although a claimant is entitled to representation by the representative of his or her choice (including an attorney or claims agent) throughout the entire claim and appeal process, no fee may be charged by the attorney, agent, or other representative for such representation until after the AOJ has notified the claimant of a decision denying the claim. At this point, if the claimant submits a Notice of Disagreement to begin appeal of the denial to BVA, he or she may now also enter into a contingency fee agreement with an attorney or claims agent for up to 20% of any retroactive benefits initially payable in the event of a favorable decision by either BVA or, if necessary, the court. This is a change from previous practice, which did not allow for charging of fees until after BVA had made a final decision denying the appeal. Public Law 109-461 allows this additional practice beginning in June 2007.

This fee agreement is subject to review for correctness and compliance with the law both by BVA and by the CAVC. If the appellant wins on appeal, the AOJ is responsible for withholding the amount payable to the attorney or other representative from the appellant's initial retroactive award. In no event may the payment for this purpose be withheld from any portion of any other benefits payable for any period after the date of the decision authorizing such award.

CHAPTER 9
Using the Claim Support Data Disk

Introduction and Contents

The Claim Support Data Disk contains four folders which in turn contain over 340 worksheets and claim forms. You will never use anywhere near this number of pieces of paper to prepare a claim, but these are most of the forms available from the Department of Veterans Affairs for:

1. Pension and Death (Survivors) Pension
2. Disability Compensation and DIC
3. Health Care Benefits
4. Burial Benefits

In addition, we have provided 4 Word files for you at the root level of this data disk that can be useful and 1 PDF file which will show you where to file claims and appeals.

- CENTRALIZED MAIL PROCESSING - Where to Send Claims, PDF
- 38 CFR Part 3 – Adjudication of Compensation, Pension, DIC and Burial Benefits.doc
- 38 CFR Part 4 – Schedule for Rating Disabilities.doc
- 38 CFR Part 19 – Board of Veterans Appeals Regulations.doc
- 38 CFR Part 20 – Board of Veterans Appeals Rules of Practice

FOLDERS AND SUBFOLDERS

1 Application for Pension and Death Pension

FV Forms
Intent to File – VA Form 21-0966 (formerly - Informal Claim)
VBA Forms
Checklists, Rates, Proposed Rule Changes, and Pension Center Info

2 Application for Compensation and DIC

Compensation and DIC Forms
Compensation and Pension Examination Worksheets
Disability Benefits Questionnaires
Step-By-Step Checklist Elements of the Fully Developed Claim for Compensation.pdf **(Your Master Checklist)**

3 Application for Health Care Benefits

4 Application for Burial Benefits

APPLICATION FOR PENSION AND DEATH PENSION – CONTAINS 3 SUBFOLDERS WITH THE FOLLOWING FORMS

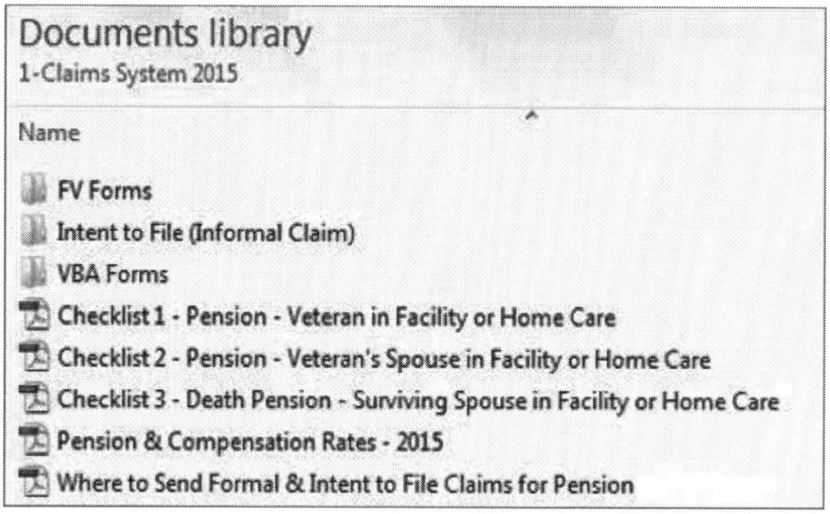

- Checklist 1 – Pension
- Checklist 2 – Pension, when the veteran's spouse is unhealthy
- Checklist 3 – Survivors Pension
- Pension Rates for 2015-16
- Where to Send Formal and Intent to File Claims (addresses of pension management centers)

Forms included in the Sub Folders:

Forms Used for an Initial Application

- FV 11 – Cover Letter for Submission

Form Used to Obtain DD 214 or equivalent discharge record

- SF 180 – Request Pertaining to Military Records

Initial Application Forms

- VBA-21-534EZ-ARE – Application for DIC, Death Pension, and/or Accrued Benefits
- VBA-21-527EZ-ARE – Application for Pension

Forms Used with Initial Application if filing with an Accredited Agent

- VBA-21-22A-ARE – Appointment of Individual as Claimant's Representative
- VBA-21-0845-ARE – Authorization to Disclose Personal Information to a Third Party
- FV18 - CERTIFICATION OF PROVIDED INFORMATION & ACKNOWLEDGEMENT OF UNDERSTANDING

Forms Used for Ratings and Medical Deductions

- VBA-21-2680-ARE – Exam for Housebound Status or Permanent Need for Regular Aid and Attendance
- VBA-21-0779-ARE – Request for Nursing Home Information in Connection with Claim for Aid and Attendance
- FV 12 – Doctor Report Addendum
- FV13 – Care Provider Certification of Services
- FV 16 – Claimants Certification of Out of Pocket Expenses
- FV 22 – Independent Living Community Certification of Services

VA General-Purpose Communication Form

- VBA-21-4138-ARE – Statement in Support of Claim

Forms for Intent to File

- VBA-21-0966 INTENT TO FILE

Forms Used If Claimant Dies before the Claim Is Approved or Back-pay released

- VBA-21-4138-ARE – Statement in Support of Claim
- VBA-21-0847-ARE Request for Substitution of Claimant upon Death of Claimant
- VBA-21-534EZ-ARE – Application for DIC, Death Pension, and/or Accrued Benefits
- VBA-21-601-ARE Application for Accrued Amounts due a Deceased Beneficiary

Other Forms

- VBA-21-8049 – Request for Details of Expenses
- VBA-21-8416 – Medical Expense Report
- VBA-21-0792 – Fiduciary Statement in Support of Claim

Forms not included in the Sub Folders (easily downloaded online if necessary):

Forms Used to Notify VA of Any Change in Income, Assets or Medical Expenses

- VBA-21-0510-ARE – Eligibility Verification Report Instructions
- VBA-21-0518-1-ARE – Improved Pension Eligibility Verification Report, Surviving Spouse with No Children

- VBA-21-0516-1-ARE – Improved Pension Eligibility Verification Report, Veteran with No Children

Forms Used to Verify Relationships Such As Marriage

- VBA-21-4138-ARE – Statement in Support of Claim
- VBA-21-1775-ARE – Statement of Disappearance
- VBA-21-4170-ARE – Statement of Marital Relationship
- VBA-21-4171-ARE – Supporting Statement Regarding Marriage
- VBA-21-686c-ARE – Declaration of Status of Dependents

Other Support Forms That Could Be Used in Special Situations but Are Not That Important

- VBA-21-4709-ARE – Certificate as to Assets
- VBA-21-527-ARE – Income, Net Worth and Employment Statement
- VBA-21-4103-ARE – Information From Remarried Widower
- VBA-21-4165-ARE – Pension Claim Questionnaire for Farm Income
- VBA-21-4176-ARE – Report of Accidental Injury in Support of Claim for Compensation or Pension Statement of Witness to Accident
- VBA-21-4185-ARE – Report of Income from Property or Business
- VBA-21-8416b-ARE – Report of Medical, Legal, and Other Expenses Incident to Recovery for Injury or Death
- FV78-VBA-21-4138 – Driving Statement

APPLICATION FOR COMPENSATION AND DIC – CONTAINS 3 SUBFOLDERS

Compensation and DIC Claim Forms – Contains the Following Forms

Intent to file for New Benefits, Obtaining Records and Communication with VA

- VA Form 21-0966 INTENT TO FILE
- VBA-21-4138-ARE – Statement in Support of Claim
- FV1 Standard Form 180

Initial Application for Disability Compensation or SMC Benefits

- VBA-21-526EZ-ARE – Application for Disability Compensation and Related Compensation Benefits
- VBA-21-0781a-ARE – Statement in Support of Claim for Service Connection for PTSD Secondary to Personal Assault
- VBA-21-0781-ARE – Statement in Support of Claim for Service Connection for PTSD
- VBA-21-686c-ARE – Declaration of Status of Dependents
- VBA-21-4192-ARE – Request for Employment Information in Connection With Claim for Disability Benefits

- VBA-21-4176-ARE – Report of Accidental Injury in Support of Claim for Compensation or Pension Statement of Witness to Accident
- VBA-21-4142-ARE – Authorization and Consent to Release Information to the Department of Veterans Affairs

Forms for Representation for Assistance

- VBA-21-22A-ARE – Appointment of Individual a Claimant's Representative
- VBA-21-0845-ARE – Authorization to Disclose Personal Information to a Third Party

Initial Application for Other Benefits Associated with Compensation

- VHA-10-0103 – Assistance in Acquiring Home Improvement and Structural Alterations (HISA Grant)
- VBA-21-4502-ARE – Application for Automobile or Other Conveyance and Adaptive Equipment
- VBA-26-4555-ARE – Application in Acquiring Special Housing Adaptations
- VBA-21-4142-ARE – Authorization and Consent to Release Information to the Department of Veterans Affairs

Application for Reevaluation or Change in Benefits for Existing Compensation Award

- VBA-21-526EZ-ARE – Veteran's Supplemental Claim for Compensation
- VBA-21-8940-ARE – Veteran's Application for Increased Compensation Based on Unemployability
- VBA-21-4192-ARE – Request for Employment Information in Connection With Claim for Disability Benefits
- VBA-21-4142-ARE – Authorization and Consent to Release Information to the Department of Veterans Affairs

Initial Application for Dependency and Indemnity Compensation (DIC)

- VBA-21-534EZ-ARE – Application for DIC, Death Pension, and or Accrued Benefits
- VBA-21-4170-ARE – Statement of Marital Relationship
- VBA-21-4171-ARE – Supporting Statement Regarding Marriage
- VBA-21-4103-ARE – Information from Remarried Widow
- VBA-21-1775-ARE – Statement of Disappearance
- VBA-21-601-ARE – Application for Accrued Amounts Due a Deceased Beneficiary
- VBA-21-8416b-ARE – Report of Medical, Legal, and Other Expenses Incident to Recovery for Injury or Death
- VBA-21-4142-ARE – Authorization and Consent to Release Information to the Department of Veterans Affairs

Forms for Representation for Assistance

- VBA-21-22A-ARE – Appointment of Individual a Claimant's Representative

- VBA-21-0845-ARE – Authorization to Disclose Personal Information to a Third Party

Application for Aid and Attendance or Housebound Benefits w/ Compensation or DIC

- VBA-21-2680-ARE – Exam for Housebound Status or Permanent Need for Regular A&A
- FV13 – Care Provider Certification of Services
- VBA-21-0779-ARE – Request for Nursing Home Info in Connection with Claim for Aid and Attendance
- VBA-21-4142-ARE – Authorization and Consent to Release Information to the Department of Veterans Affairs

Post Application Issues

- VBA-21-0790-ARE – Your Rights to Representation and a Hearing (Possible Overpayment)
- VBA-21-0847-ARE – Request for Substitution of Claimant upon Death of Claimant
- VBA-21-651-ARE – Election of Compensation In Lieu Of Retired Pay
- VBA-21-8951-2-ARE-1 – Notice of Waiver of VA Compensation to Receive Military Pay and Allowances

Compensation and Pension Examination Worksheets

ACROMEGALY
ARRHYTHMIAS
ARTERIES, VEINS, AND MISCELLANEOUS
AUDIO
BONES (FRACTURES AND BONE DISEASE)
BRAIN AND SPINAL CORD
CHRONIC FATIGUE SYNDROME
COLD INJURY PROTOCOL EXAMINATION
CRANIAL NERVES
CUSHING'S SYNDROME
DENTAL AND ORAL
DIABETES MELLITUS
DIGESTIVE CONDITIONS, MISCELLANEOUS
EAR DISEASE
EATING DISORDERS (Mental Disorders)
ENDOCRINE DISEASES, MISCELLANEOUS
EPILEPSY AND NARCOLEPSY
ESOPHAGUS AND HIATAL HERNIA
EYE EXAMINATION
FEET
FIBROMYALGIA
GENERAL MEDICAL EXAMINATION
GENITOURINARY EXAMINATION
GYNECOLOGICAL CONDITIONS AND DISORDERS OF THE BREAST

HAND, THUMB, AND FINGERS
HEART
HEMIC DISORDERS
HIV-RELATED ILLNESS
HYPERTENSION
INFECTIOUS, IMMUNE, AND NUTRITIONAL DISABILITIES
INITIAL EVALUATION FOR POST-TRAUMATIC STRESS DISORDER (PTSD)
INTESTINES (LARGE AND SMALL)
JOINTS (SHOULDER, ELBOW, WRIST, HIP, KNEE, AND ANKLE)
LIVER, GALL BLADDER, AND PANCREAS
LYMPHATIC DISORDERS
MENTAL DISORDERS (except PTSD and Eating Disorders)
MOUTH, LIPS, AND TONGUE
MUSCLES
NEUROLOGICAL DISORDERS, MISCELLANEOUS
NOSE, SINUS, LARYNX, AND PHARYNX
PERIPHERAL NERVES
PULMONARY TUBERCULOSIS AND MYCOBACTERIAL DISEASES
RECTUM AND ANUS
RESIDUALS OF AMPUTATIONS
RESPIRATORY (OBSTRUCTIVE, RESTRICTIVE, AND INTERSTITIAL)
RESPIRATORY DISEASES, MISCELLANEOUS
REVIEW EXAMINATION FOR POST-TRAUMATIC STRESS DISORDER (PTSD)
SCARS
SENSE OF SMELL AND TASTE
SKIN DISEASES (Other Than Scars)
SPINE (CERVICAL, THORACIC, AND LUMBAR)
STOMACH, DUODENUM, AND PERITONEAL ADHESIONS
THYROID AND PARATHYROID DISEASES

Disability Benefits Questionnaires

- VBA-21-0960A-1-ARE Ischemic Heart Disease (IHD) Questionnaire
- VBA-21-0960A-2-ARE Artery and Vein Conditions (Vascular Diseases Including Varicose Veins) Questionnaire
- VBA-21-0960A-3-ARE Hypertension Questionnaire
- VBA-21-0960A-4-ARE Heart Conditions (Including Ischemic and Non-Ischemic Heart Disease, Arrhythmias, Valvular Disease and Cardiac Surgery) Questionnaire
- VBA-21-0960B-1-ARE Hairy Cell and Other B-Cell Leukemias Questionnaire
- VBA-21-0960B-2-ARE Hematologic and Lymphatic Conditions, Including Leukemia Questionnaire
- VBA-21-0960C-1-ARE Parkinson's Disease Questionnaire
- VBA-21-0960C-10-ARE Peripheral Nerves Conditions (Not Including Diabetic Sensory-Motor Peripheral Neuropathy) Questionnaire
- VBA-21-0960C-11-ARE Seizure Disorders (Epilepsy) Questionnaire

- VBA-21-0960C-2-ARE Amyotrophic Lateral Sclerosis (Lou Gehrig's Disease) Questionnaire
- VBA-21-0960C-3-ARE Cranial Nerve Conditions Questionnaire
- VBA-21-0960C-4-ARE Diabetic Sensory-Motor Peripheral Neuropathy Questionnaire
- VBA-21-0960C-5-ARE Central Nervous System and Neuromuscular Diseases (Except Trau. Brain Injury, etc.) Questionnaire
- VBA-21-0960C-6-ARE Narcolepsy Questionnaire
- VBA-21-0960C-7-ARE Fibromyalgia Questionnaire
- VBA-21-0960C-8-ARE Headaches (Including Migraine Headaches) Questionnaire
- VBA-21-0960C-9-ARE Multiple Sclerosis (MS) Questionnaire
- VBA-21-0960D-1-ARE Oral and Dental Conditions Including Mouth, Lips and Tongue (Other Than Temporomandibular Joint Conditions) Questionnaire
- VBA-21-0960E-1-ARE Diabetes Mellitus Questionnaire
- VBA-21-0960E-2-ARE Endocrine Diseases (Other than Thyroid, Parathyroid or Diabetes Mellitus) Questionnaire
- VBA-21-0960E-3-ARE Thyroid and Parathyroid Conditions Questionnaire
- VBA-21-0960F-1-ARE Scars Disfigurement Questionnaire
- VBA-21-0960F-2-ARE Skin Diseases Questionnaire
- VBA-21-0960G-1-ARE Esophageal Conditions (Including gastroesophageal reflux disease (GERD), hiatal hernia and other esophageal disorders) Questionnaire
- VBA-21-0960G-2-ARE Gallbladder and Pancreas Conditions Questionnaire
- VBA-21-0960G-3-ARE Intestinal Conditions (Other that Surgical or Infections) (Including Irritable Bowel Syndrome, Crohn's Disease, Ulcerative Colitis, and Diverticulitis) Questionnaire
- VBA-21-0960G-4-ARE Intestinal Surgery (Bowel Resection, Colostomy, Ileostomy) Questionnaire
- VBA-21-0960G-5-ARE Hepatitis, Cirrhosis and Other Liver Conditions Questionnaire
- VBA-21-0960G-6-ARE Peritoneal Adhesions Questionnaire
- VBA-21-0960G-7-ARE Stomach and Duodenal Conditions (Not Including Gerd or Esophageal Disorders) Benefits Questionnaire
- VBA-21-0960G-8-ARE Infectious Intestinal Disorders, Including Bacterial and Parasitic Infections Questionnaire
- VBA-21-0960H-1-ARE Hernias (Including Abdominal, Inguinal and Femoral Hernias) Questionnaire
- VBA-21-0960H-2-ARE Rectum and Anus Conditions IIncluding Hemorrhoids) Benefits Questionnaire
- VBA-21-0960I-1-ARE Persian Gulf and Afghanistan Infectious Diseases Questionnaire
- VBA-21-0960I-2-ARE HIV - Related Illnesses Questionnaire
- VBA-21-0960I-3-ARE Infectious Diseases (Other than HIV-Related Illness, Chronic Fatigue Syndrome, or Tuberculosis) Questionnaire
- VBA-21-0960I-4-ARE Systemic Lupus Erythematosus (SLE) and Other Autoimmune Diseases Questionnaire
- VBA-21-0960I-5-ARE Nutritional Deficiencies Questionnaire
- VBA-21-0960I-6-ARE Tuberculosis Questionnaire
- VBA-21-0960J-1-ARE Kidney Conditions (Nephrology) Questionnaire

- VBA-21-0960J-2-ARE Male Reproductive Organ Conditions Questionnaire
- VBA-21-0960J-3-ARE Prostate Cancer Questionnaire
- VBA-21-0960J-4-ARE Urinary Tract (Including Bladder and Urethra) Conditions (Excluding Male Reproductive System) Questionnaire
- VBA-21-0960K-1-ARE Breast Conditions and Disorders Questionnaire
- VBA-21-0960K-2-ARE Gynecological Conditions Questionnaire
- VBA-21-0960L-1-ARE Respiratory Conditions (Other than Tuberculosis and Sleep Apnea) Questionnaire
- VBA-21-0960L-2-ARE Sleep Apnea Questionnaire
- VBA-21-0960M-1-ARE Amputations Questionnaire
- VBA-21-0960M-10-ARE Muscle Injuries Questionnaire
- VBA-21-0960M-11-ARE Osteomyelitis Questionnaire
- VBA-21-0960M-12-ARE Shoulder and Arm Conditions Questionnaire
- VBA-21-0960M-13-ARE Neck (Cervical Spine) Questionnaire
- VBA-21-0960M-14-ARE Back (Thoracolumbar Spine) Conditions Questionnaire
- VBA-21-0960M-15-ARE Temporomandibular Joint (TMJ) Conditions Questionnaire
- VBA-21-0960M-16-ARE Wrist Conditions Questionnaire
- VBA-21-0960M-2-ARE Ankle Conditions Questionnaire
- VBA-21-0960M-3-ARE Non-Degenerative Arthritis (Including Inflammatory, Autoimmune, Crystalline and Infectious Arthritis) and Dysbaric Osteonecrosis Questionnaire
- VBA-21-0960M-4-ARE Elbow and Forearm Conditions Questionnaire
- VBA-21-0960M-5-ARE Flatfoot (Pes Planus) Questionnaire
- VBA-21-0960M-6-ARE Foot Miscellaneous (Other Than Flatfoot PES Planus) Questionnaire
- VBA-21-0960M-7-ARE Hand and Finger Conditions Questionnaire
- VBA-21-0960M-8-ARE Hip and Thigh Conditions Questionnaire
- VBA-21-0960M-9-ARE Knee and Lower Leg Conditions Questionnaire
- VBA-21-0960N-1-ARE Ear Conditions (Including Vestibular and Infectious Conditions) Questionnaire
- VBA-21-0960N-2-ARE Eye Conditions Questionnaire
- VBA-21-0960N-3-ARE Loss of Sense of Smell andor Taste Questionnaire
- VBA-21-0960N-4-ARE Sinusitis Rhinitis and Other Conditions of the Nose, Throat, Larynx and Pharynx Questionnaire
- VBA-21-0960P-1-ARE Eating Disorders Questionnaire
- VBA-21-0960P-2-ARE Mental Disorders (Other Than PTSD and Eating Disorders) Questionnaire
- VBA-21-0960P-3-ARE Review Post Traumatic Stress Disorder (PTSD) Questionnaire
- VBA-21-0960Q-1-ARE Chronic Fatigue Syndrome Questionnaire

APPLICATION FOR HEALTH CARE BENEFITS

- VHA-10-10 – Health Benefits Renewal Form
- VHA-10-10CG – Instructions for Completing Application for Comprehensive Assistance for Family Caregivers Program
- VHA-10-10ez – Application for Health Care Benefits
- VHA-10-10HS – Request for Hardship Determination
- VHA-10-0103 – Assistance in Acquiring Home Improvement and Structural Alterations (HISA)
- VHA-10-5345 – Request to Release VA Medical Records to Someone Else
- VHA-10-5345a – Individuals' Request for a Copy of Their Own Health Information
- VHA-10-7959a – CHAMPVA Claim Form
- VHA-10-7959c – CHAMPVA - Other Health Insurance (OHI) Certificate
- VHA-10-7959d-form CHAMPVA Potential Liability Claim
- VHA-10-8678 – Application for Annual Clothing Allowance

APPLICATIONS FOR BURIAL AND ACCRUED BENEFITS

- SF 180 - Request Pertaining to Military Records
- VA40-4970 - Request for Disinterment
- VBA-21-530a-ARE - State Application for Interment Allowance under 38 U.S.C. Chapter 23
- VBA-21-530-ARE - Application for Burial Benefits
- VBA-21-601-ARE - Application for Accrued Amounts Due a Deceased Beneficiary
- VBA-21-0847 Request for Substitution of Claimant upon Death of Claimant
- VBA-21-8834-ARE - Application for Reimbursement of Headstone or Marker Expense
- VBA-27-2008-ARE - Application for United States Flag for Burial Purposes

APPENDIX

Contents

Appendix Section 1
List of VA Regional Offices

State	Regional Office	Street Address	City, State and Zip
Alabama	Montgomery Regional Office (Montgomery, AL)	345 Perry Hill Rd	Montgomery, AL 36109
Alaska	Anchorage Regional Office (Anchorage, AK)	1201 North Muldoon Road	Anchorage, AK 99504
Arizona	Phoenix Regional Office (Phoenix, AZ)	3333 North Central Avenue	Phoenix, AZ 85012-2436
Arkansas	North Little Rock Regional Office (North Little Rock, AR)	2200 Fort Roots Drive, Building 65	North Little Rock, AR 72114-1756
California	Los Angeles Regional Office (Los Angeles, CA)	Federal Building, 11000 Wilshire Boulevard	Los Angeles, CA 90024
California	Oakland Regional Office (Oakland, CA)	1301 Clay Street	Oakland, CA 94612
California	San Diego Regional Office (San Diego, CA)	8810 Rio San Diego Drive	San Diego, CA 92108
Colorado	Denver Regional Office (Lakewood, CO)	155 Van Gordon St.	Lakewood, CO 80228
Connecticut	Hartford Regional Office (Newington, CT)	555 Willard Avenue, Building 2E	Newington, CT. 06111
Delaware	Wilmington Regional Office (Wilmington, DE)	1601 Kirkwood Highway	Wilmington, DE 19805
Florida	St. Petersburg Regional Office (St. Petersburg, FL)	9500 Bay Pines Blvd	St Petersburg, FL 33708
Georgia	Atlanta VA Regional Office (Decatur, GA)	1700 Clairmont Road	Decatur, GA 30033
Hawaii	Honolulu Regional Office (Honolulu, HI)	459 Patterson Road, E-Wing	Honolulu , HI 96819-1522
Idaho	Boise Regional Office (Boise, ID)	444 W. Fort Street	Boise, ID 83702-4531
Illinois	Chicago Regional Office (Chicago, IL)	2122 W Taylor Street	Chicago, IL 60612

Indiana	Indianapolis Regional Office (Indianapolis, IN)	575 N Pennsylvania St.	Indianapolis, IN 46204
Iowa	Des Moines VA Regional Office (Des Moines, IA)	210 Walnut Street	Des Moines, IA 50309
Kansas	Wichita Regional Office (Wichita, KS)	5500 East Kellogg	Wichita, KS 67218
Kentucky	Louisville Regional Office (Louisville, KY)	321 West Main Street, Suite 390	Louisville, KY 40202
Louisiana	New Orleans Regional Office (New Orleans, LA)	1250 Poydras Street	New Orleans, LA 70113
Maine	Togus VA Medical/Regional Office Center (Augusta, ME)	1 VA Center	Augusta ME 04330-6795
Maryland	Baltimore Regional Office (Baltimore, MD)	31 Hopkins Plaza	Baltimore, MD 21201
Massachusetts	Boston VA Regional Office (Boston, MA)	JFK Federal Building, 15 New Sudbury Street	Boston, MA 02203-9928
Michigan	Detroit Regional Office (Detroit, MI)	477 Michigan Avenue	Detroit, MI 48226-2523
Minnesota	St. Paul Regional Office (St. Paul, MN)	1 Federal Drive, Fort Snelling	St. Paul, MN 55111-4050
Mississippi	Jackson Regional Office (Jackson, MS)	1600 E. Woodrow Wilson Ave	Jackson, MS 39216
Missouri	St. Louis Regional Office (St. Louis, MO)	400 South, 18th Street	St. Louis, MO 63103
Montana	Fort Harrison Regional Office (Fort Harrison, MT)	3633 Veterans Drive	Fort Harrison, MT 59636-0188
Nebraska	Lincoln Regional Office (Lincoln, NE)	3800 Village Drive	Lincoln, NE 68516
Nevada	Reno Regional Office (Reno, NV)	5460 Reno Corporate Drive,	Reno, NV 89511
New Hampshire	Manchester Regional Office (Manchester, NH)	Norris Cotton Federal Bldg., 275 Chestnut St.	Manchester, NH 03101
New Jersey	Newark Regional Office (Newark, NJ)	20 Washington Place	Newark, New Jersey 07102-3174

New Mexico	Albuquerque Regional Office (Albuquerque, NM)	Dennis Chavez Federal Building, 500 Gold Avenue, S.W.	Albuquerque, NM 87102
New York	Buffalo Regional Office (Buffalo, NY)	130 South Elmwood Avenue	Buffalo, NY 14202
New York	New York Regional Office (New York, NY)	245 West Houston Street	New York, New York 10014-4085
North Carolina	Winston-Salem Regional Office (Winston-Salem, NC)	Federal Building, 251N. Main Street	Winston-Salem, NC 27155
North Dakota	Fargo Regional Office (Fargo, ND)	2101 Elm Street	Fargo, ND 58102-2417
Ohio	Cleveland Regional Office (Cleveland, OH)	1240 East Ninth Street	Cleveland, OH 44199
Oklahoma	Muskogee Regional Office (Muskogee, OK)	125 South Main Street	Muskogee, OK 74401
Oregon	Portland Regional Office (Portland, OR)	100 SW Main Street, Floor 2	Portland, OR 97204
Pennsylvania	Philadelphia Regional Office and Insurance Center (Philadelphia, PA)	5000 Wissahickon Ave	Philadelphia, PA, 19144
Pennsylvania	Pittsburgh Regional Office (Pittsburgh, PA)	1000 Liberty Avenue	Pittsburgh, PA 15222
Philippines	Manila Regional Office (Pasay City, PI)	1501 Roxas Boulevard	Pasay City, PI 1302
Puerto Rico	San Juan Regional Office (Guaynabo, PR)	50 Carr 165	Guaynabo, PR 00968-8024
Rhode Island	Providence Regional Office (Providence, RI)	380 Westminster Street	Providence, RI 02903
South Carolina	Columbia Regional Office (Columbia, SC)	6437 Garners Ferry Road	Columbia, SC 29209
South Dakota	Sioux Falls Regional Office (Sioux Falls, SD)	2501 W 22nd St.	Sioux Falls, SD 57105
Tennessee	Nashville Regional Office (Nashville, TN)	110 9th Ave South	Nashville, TN 37203
Texas	Houston Regional Office (Houston, TX)	6900 Almeda Road	Houston, TX 77030

Texas	Waco Regional Office (Waco, TX)	1 Veterans Plaza, 701 Clay Av.	Waco, TX 76799
Utah	Salt Lake City Regional Office (Salt Lake City, UT)	550 Foothill Drive	Salt Lake City, UT 84158
Vermont	White River Junction Regional Office (White River Junction, VT)	215 North Main Street	White River Junction, VT 05009
Virginia	Roanoke Regional Office (Roanoke, VA)	116 N. Jefferson Street	Roanoke, VA 24016
Washington	Seattle Regional Office (Seattle, WA)	915 2nd Avenue	Seattle, WA 98174
Washington DC	Washington D.C. Regional Office (Washington D.C., DC)	1722 I Street N.W.	Washington D.C., DC 20421
West Virginia	Huntington Regional Office (Huntington, WV)	640 Fourth Ave	Huntington, WV 25701
Wisconsin	Milwaukee Regional Office (Milwaukee, WI)	5400 W National Ave	Milwaukee, WI 53214
Wyoming	Cheyenne VA Medical / Regional Office Center (Cheyenne, WY)	2360 E. Pershing Blvd.	Cheyenne, WY 82001

Appendix Section 2
List of VA State Veterans Homes

State	VA Nursing Home	Address	Phone
Alabama	Bill Nichols State Veterans Home	1784 Elkahatchee Road Alexander City, AL 35010	(256) 329-3311
Alabama	William F. Green State Veterans Home	300 Faulkner Drive Bay Minette, AL 36507	(251) 937-8049
Alabama	Floyd E. Tut Fann State Veterans Home	2701 Meridian Street Huntsville, AL 35811	(256) 851-2807
Alabama	Colonel Robert L. Howard State Veterans Home	7054 Veterans Parkway Pell City, AL 35125	(205) 338-6487
Alaska	State Veterans And Pioneers Home	250 East Fireweed Palmer, AK 99645	(907) 745-4241
Arizona	The Arizona State Veteran Home	4141 North S. Herra Way Phoenix, AZ 85012	(602) 248-1550
Arizona	Arizona State Veteran Home - Tucson	555 East Ajo Way Tucson, AZ 85713	(520) 638-2159
Arkansas	Little Rock Veterans Home	4701 West 20Th Street Little Rock, AR 72204	(501) 296-1885
Arkansas	Fayetteville Veterans Home	1179 North College Fayetteville, AR 72703	(479) 444-7001
California	Veterans Home Of California - Barstow	100 East Veterans Parkway Barstow, CA 92311	(760) 252-6281
California	Veterans Home Of California - Chula Vista	700 East Naples Court Chula Vista, CA 91911	(619) 482-6010
California	Veterans Home Of California - Yountville	260 California Drive Yountville, CA 94599	(707) 944-4601
California	Veterans Home of California - Lancaster	45221 30th Street West Lancaster, CA 93536	(661) 974-7035
California	Veterans Home of California - Fresno	2811 West California Avenue Fresno, CA 93706	(559) 493-4400
California	Veterans Home of California - Ventura	10900 Telephone Road Ventura, CA 93004	(805) 659-7502
California	Veterans Home of California - Redding	3400 Knighton Rd Redding, CA 96002	(530) 224-3300
California	Veterans Home of California - West Los Angeles	11500 Nimitz Ave Los Angeles, CA 90049	(424) 832-8200
Colorado	Colorado State Veterans Home At Fitzimons	1919 Quentin Street Aurora, CO 80045	(720) 857-6400
Colorado	Colorado State Veterans Center at Homelake	3749 Sherman Ave. Monte Vista, CO 81144	(719) 852-5118
Colorado	Bruce McCandless State Veterans Home at Florence	903 Moore Drive Florence, CO 81226	(719) 784-6331

Colorado	Colorado State Veterans Home at Rifle	851 East 5th Street Rifle, CO 81650	(970) 625-0842
Colorado	Colorado State Veterans Home at Walsenburg	23500 U.S. Highway 160 Walsenburg, CO 81089	(719) 738-5000
Connecticut	Sgt. John L. Levitow Veteran's Health Center at the Connecticut State Veterans Home	287 West Street Rocky Hill, CT 06067	(860) 616-3600
Delaware	Wilmington VA Medical Center, Nursing Home Care Unit	1601 Kirkwood Highway Wilmington, DE 19805	(302) 994-2511
Florida	Ardie R. Copas State Veterans' Nursing Home in Port St. Lucie	Port St. Lucie	(727) 518-3202 ext 5562
Florida	Robert H. Jenkins Jr. Veterans' Domiciliary Home in Lake City	751 SE Sycamore Terrace, Lake City, FL 32025	(386) 758-0600
Florida	Clifford C. Sims State Veterans' Nursing Home in Panama City	4419 Tram Road Panama City, FL 32404	(850) 747-5401
Florida	Douglas T. Jacobson State Veterans' Nursing Home in Port Charlotte	21281 Grayton Terrace Port Charlotte, FL 33954	(941) 613-0919
Florida	Emory L. Bennett State Veterans' Nursing Home in Daytona Beach	1920 Mason Avenue Daytona Beach, FL 32117	(386) 274-3460
Florida	Baldomero Lopez State Veterans' Nursing Home in Land O' Lakes	6919 Parkway Blvd Land-O-Lakes, FL 34639	(813) 558-5000
Florida	Alexander "Sandy" Nininger Veterans' Nursing Home in Pembroke Pines	8401 West Cypress Drive Pembroke Pines, FL 33025	(954) 985-4824
Florida	Clyde E. Lassen State Veterans' Nursing Home in St. Augustine	4650 State Road 16 St Augustine, FL 32092	(904) 940-2193
Georgia	Georgia War Veterans Nursing Home	1101 15Th Street Augusta, GA 30901	(706) 721-2824
Georgia	Georgia War Veterans Home	2249 Vinson Highway Milledgeville, GA 31061	(478) 445-6826
Hawaii	Yukio Okutsu State Veterans Home	1180 Waianuenue Avenue Hilo, HI 96720	(808) 961-1500
Idaho	Boise Veterans Home	320 Collins Road Boise, ID 83702	(208) 780-1600
Idaho	Lewiston Veterans Home	821 21St Avenue Lewiston, ID 83501	(208) 750-3600
Idaho	Pocatello Veterans Home	1957 Alvin Ricken Drive Pocatello, ID 83201	(208) 235-7800
Illinois (NEW)	Anna Veteran's Home	792 N. Main Street Anna, Illinois 62906	(618) 833-6302
Illinois	LaSalle Veterans' Home	1015 O'conor Avenue Lasalle, IL 61301	(815) 223-0303, ext. 222

Illinois	Manteno Veterans' Home	1 Veterans Drive Manteno, IL 60950	(815) 468-6581
Illinois	Quincy Veterans' Home	1707 N. 12Th Street Quincy, IL 62301	(217) 222-8641
Indiana	Indiana Veterans Home	3851 N. River Rd West Lafayette, IN 47906	(765) 463-1502
Iowa	Iowa Veterans Home	1301 Summit St Marshalltown, IA 50158	(641) 752-1501
Kansas	Kansas Veterans' Home	1220 World War II Memorial Drive Winfield, KS 67156	(620) 221-9479, ext. 201
Kansas	Kansas Soldiers' Home	714 Sheridan Fort Dodge, KS 67801	(620) 227-2121 ext 112
Kentucky	Thomson-Hood Veterans Center	100 Veterans Drive Wilmore, KY 40390	(859) 858-2814
Kentucky	Eastern Kentucky Veterans Center	200 Veterans Drive Hazard, KY 41701	(606) 435-6196
Kentucky	Radcliff Veterans Center	Radcliff, KY	Pending 2016
Kentucky	Joseph "Eddie" Ballard Western Kentucky Veterans Center	926 Veterans Drive Hanson, KY 42413	(270) 322-9087
Louisiana	SE Louisiana War Veterans Home	4080 W Airline Hwy Reserve, LA 70084	(985) 479-4080
Louisiana	Jackson War Veterans Home	4739 Highway 10 Jackson, LA 70748	(225) 634-5265
Louisiana	NE Louisiana War Veterans Home	6700 Highway 165 N. Monroe, LA 71203	(318) 362-4206
Louisiana	NW Louisiana War Veterans Home	3130 Arthur Ray Teague Parkway Bossier City, LA 71112	(318) 741-2763
Louisiana	South West Louisiana War Veterans' Home	1610 Evangeline Road Jennings, LA 70546	(337) 824-2829
Maine	Maine Veterans' Home	32 Veterans Drive Machias, ME 04654	(207) 255-0162
Maine	Maine Veterans' Home	310 Cony Road Augusta, ME 04330	(207) 622-2454
Maine	Maine Veterans' Home	44 Hogan Road Bangor, ME 04401	(207) 942-2333
Maine	Maine Veterans' Home	163 Van Buren Road Caribou, ME 04736	(207) 498-6074
Maine	Maine Veterans' Home	290 U.S. Route 1 Scarborough, ME 04074	(207) 883-7184
Maine	Maine Veterans' Home	477 High St. South Paris, ME 04281	(207) 743-6300
Maryland	Charlotte Hall Veterans Home	29449 Charlotte Hall Road Charlotte Hall, MD 20622	(301) 884-8171
Massachusetts	Massachusetts Soldiers' Home	110 Cherry Street Holyoke, MA 01041	(413) 532-9475
Massachusetts	Massachusetts Soldiers' Home	91 Crest Avenue Chelsea, MA 02150	(617) 884-5660

Michigan	Grand Rapids Home For Veterans	3000 Monroe Ave. N.E. Grand Rapids, MI 49505	(616) 364-5389
Michigan	D.J. Jacobetti Home For Veterans	425 Fisher St Marquette, MI 49855	(906) 226-3576
Minnesota	Minnesota Veterans Home - Minneapolis	5101 Minnehaha Avenue Minneapolis, MN 55417	(612) 548-5700
Minnesota	Minnesota Veterans Home - Hastings	1200 E. 18Th St Hastings, MN 55033	(651) 539-2400
Minnesota	Minnesota Veterans Home - Silver Bay	45 Banks Boulevard Silver Bay, MN 55614	(218) 353-8700
Minnesota	Minnesota Veterans Home - Luverne	1300 N. Kniss Ave. P.O. Box 539 Luverne, MN 56156	(507) 283-6200
Minnesota	Minnesota Veterans Home - Fergus Falls	1821 North Park Street Fergus Falls, MN 56537	(218) 736-0400
Mississippi	Mississippi Veterans Home	3466 Hwy. 80 East P.O. Box 5949 Pearl, MS 39288	(601) 576-4850
Mississippi	Armed Forces Retirement Home	1800 Beach Drive Gulfport, MS 39507	(800) 422-9988
Mississippi	Collins Veterans Home	3261 Hwy 49 Collins, MS 39428	(601) 765-0519
Mississippi	Jackson Veterans Home	4607 Lindbergh Dr. Jackson, MS 39209	(601) 353-6142
Mississippi	The Mississippi State Veterans Home	310 Autumn Ridge Dr. Kosciusko, MS 39090	(662) 289-7809
Mississippi	Oxford Veterans Home	120 Veterans Drive Oxford, MS 38655	(662) 236-1218
Missouri	Missouri Veterans Home Mexico	#1 Veterans Drive Mexico, MO 65265	(573) 581-1088
Missouri	Missouri Veterans Home Cape Girardeau	2400 Veterans Memorial Drive Cape Girardeau, MO 63701	(573) 290-5870
Missouri	Missouri Veterans Home St. Louis	10600 Lewis & Clark Blvd. St. Louis, MO 63136	(314) 340-6389
Missouri	Missouri Veterans Home Cameron	1111 Euclid Cameron, MO 64429	(816) 632-6010
Missouri	Missouri Veterans Home Warrensburg	1300 Veterans Road Warrensburg, MO 64093	(660) 543-5064
Missouri	Missouri Veterans Home Mt. Vernon	1600 S. Hickory Mt. Vernon, MO 65712	(417) 466-7103
Missouri	Missouri Veterans Home St. James	620 North Jefferson St. James, MO 65559	(573) 265-3271
Montana	Montana Veterans Home - Columbia Falls	400 Veterans Drive Columbia Falls, MT 59912	(406) 892-3256
Montana	Eastern Montana Veterans Home	2000 Montana Ave Glendive, MT 59330	(406) 345-8855
Nebraska	Grand Island Veterans' Home	2300 Capital Ave. Grand Island, NE 68803	(308) 385-6252 ext 452
Nebraska	Norfolk Veterans' Home	600 E. Benjamin Ave. Norfolk, NE 68701	(402) 370-3330

Nebraska	Eastern Nebraska Veterans' Home	12505 South 40th Street Bellevue, NE 68123	(402) 595-2180
Nebraska	Western Nebraska Veterans' Home	1102 W. 42Nd St. Scottsbluff, NE 69361	(308) 632-0300
Nevada	Nevada Veterans' Nursing Home	100 Veterans Memorial Drive Boulder City, NV 89005	(702) 332-6717
Hampshire	Hampshire Veterans Home	139 Winter Street Tilton, NH 03276	(603) 527-4400
Jersey	Veterans Memorial Home Vineland	524 North West Boulevard Vineland, NJ 08360	(856) 405-4200
Jersey	Veterans Memorial Home Menlo Park	132 Evergreen Road Edison, NJ 08818	(732) 452-4100
Jersey	Veterans Memorial Home Paramus	1 Veterans Drive Paramus, NJ 07652	(201) 634-8435
Mexico	Mexico Veterans Home	992 South Broadway Truth Or Consequences, NM 87901	(575) 894-4200
Mexico	Ft. Bayard Veterans Home	41 Fort Bayard Road Santa Clara, NM 88026	(575) 537-8600
York	NY State Veterans' Home at Batavia	220 Richmond Ave. Batavia, NY 14020	(585) 345-2000
York	NY State Veterans' Home at Oxford	4207 State Hwy. 220 Oxford, NY 13830	(607) 843-3100
York	Long Island State Veterans Home	100 Patriots Road Stonybrook, NY 11790	(631) 444-Vets
York	NY State Veterans' Home at St. Albans	17850 Linden Blvd Jamaica, NY 11437	(718) 481-6994
York	NY State Veterans' Home at Montrose	2090 Albany Post Road Montrose, NY 10548	(914) 788-6000
North Carolina	NC State Veterans Home Fayetteville	214 Cochran Ave. Fayetteville, NC 28301	(910) 482-4131
North Carolina	NC State Veterans Home Salisbury	W. G. Hefner Medical Center, 1601 Brenner Ave. Building #10 Salisbury, NC 28145	(704) 638-4200, ext. 204
North Carolina	NC State Veterans Home Kinston	2150 Hull Road Kinston, NC 28504	(252) 939-8000
North Carolina	NC State Veterans Home Black Mountain	62 Lake Eden Road Black Mtn., NC 28711	(828) 257-6800
North Carolina	Asheville VA Medical Center	1100 Tunnel Road Asheville, NC 28805	(828) 298-7911
North Dakota	North Dakota Veterans Home	1600 Veterans Drive Lisbon, ND 58054	(701) 683-6500
Ohio	Ohio Veterans Home - Sandusky Home	3416 Columbus Avenue Sandusky, OH 44870	(419) 625-2454
Ohio	Southern Ohio Veterans Home - Georgetown Home	2003 Veterans Blvd Georgetown, OH 45121	(937) 378-2900
Oklahoma	Lawton/Ft. Sill Veterans Center	501 SE Flower Mound Road Lawton, OK 73501	(580) 351-6511

Oklahoma	The Ardmore Veterans Center	1015 S. Commerce Ardmore, OK 73402	(580) 223-2266
Oklahoma	The Claremore Veterans Center	3001 W. Blue Starr Drive Claremore, OK 74018	(918) 342-5432
Oklahoma	The Clinton Veterans Center	1701 South 4th Clinton, OK 73601	(580) 331-2200
Oklahoma	The Norman Veterans Center	1776 East Robinson Street Norman, OK 73070	(405) 360-5600
Oklahoma	The Sulphur Veterans Center	304 E. Fairlane Sulphur, OK 73086	(580) 622-2144
Oklahoma	The Talihina Veterans Center	10014 SE 1138th Ave. Talihina, OK 74571	(918) 567-2251
Oregon	Oregon Veterans Home	700 Veterans Drive The Dalles, OR 97058	(541) 296-7190
Pennsylvania	Hollidaysburg Veterans Home	P.O. Box 319 Hollidaysburg, PA 16648	(814) 696-5201
Pennsylvania	Pennsylvania Soldiers' And Sailors' Home	560 East Third Street Erie, PA 16507	(814) 871-4531
Pennsylvania	Southeastern Veterans Center	1 Veterans Drive Spring City, PA 19475	(610) 948-2400
Pennsylvania	Gino J. Merli Veterans Center	401 Penn Avenue Scranton, PA 18503	(570) 961-4300
Pennsylvania	Southwestern Veterans Center	7060 Highland Drive Pittsburgh, PA 15206	(412) 665-6706
Pennsylvania	Delaware Valley Veterans Home	2701 Southampton Road Philadelphia, PA 19154	(215) 865-2700
Puerto Rico	Casa Del Veterano Carr	592,Km.5.6 Bo. Amuelas Juan Diaz, Pr 00795	(787) 837-6574
Rhode Island	Rhode Island Veterans Home	480 Metacom Ave. Bristol, RI 02809	(401) 253-8000
South Carolina	E. Roy Stone, Jr., Pavilion	2200 Harden Street Columbia, SC 29203	(803) 737-5301
South Carolina	Richard Michael Campbell Veterans Nursing Home	4605 Belton Highway Anderson, SC 29621	(864) 261-6734
South Carolina	Veterans Victory House Nursing Home	2461 Sidneys Road Walterboro, SC 29488	(803) 737-5282
South Dakota	Michael J. Fitzmaurice Veterans Home	2500 Minnekahta Ave. Hot Springs, SD 57747	(605) 745-5127
Tennessee	Tennessee State Veterans Home - Humboldt	2865 Main Street Humboldt, TN 38343	(731) 784-8405
Tennessee	Tennessee State Veterans Home -Murfreesboro	345 Compton Road Murfreesboro, TN 37130	(615) 895-8850
Tennessee	Tennessee State Veterans Home - Knoxville	1 Veterans Way Knoxville, TN 37931	(865) 862-8152
Tennessee	Tennessee State Veterans Home	Montgomery County, TN	Pending 2016
Tennessee	Brigadier General Wendell H. Gilbert Tennessee State Veterans' Home	250 Arrowood Drive Clarksville, TX 37042	931-245-4700

Texas	William R. Courtney Texas State Veterans Home	1424 MLK Jr. Lane Temple, TX 76504	(254) 791-8280
Texas	Frank M. Tejeda Texas State Veterans Home	200 Veterans Drive Floresville, TX 78114	(830) 216-9456
Texas	Ambrosio Guillen Texas State Veterans Home	9650 Kenworthy Street El Paso, TX 79924	(915) 751-0967
Texas	Ussery-Roan Texas State Veterans Home	1020 Tascosa Road Amarillo, TX 79124	(806) 322-8387
Texas	Alfredo Gonzalez Texas State Veterans Home	301 E. Yuma Avenue McAllen, TX 78503	(956) 682-4224
Texas	Lamun-Lusk-Sanchez Texas State Veterans Home	1809 North Highway 87 Big Spring, TX 79720	(432) 268-8387
Texas	Clyde W. Cosper Texas State Veterans Home	1300 Seven Oaks Road Bonham, TX 75418	(903) 640-8387
Texas	Watkins-Logan-Garrison Texas State Veterans Home	11466 Honor Lane Tyler, TX 75708	(903) 617-6150
Utah	William E. Christofferson Salt Lake City Veterans Home	700 Foothill Drive Salt Lake City, UT 84113	(801) 584-1900
Utah	George E Wahlen Ogden Veterans Home	1102 N 1200 W Ogden, UT 84113	(801) 334-4315
Utah	Central Utah Veterans Home Payson	1551 North Main Street Payson, UT 84651	(801) 465-5400
Utah	Southern Utah Veterans Home in Ivins	160 N. 200 E Street Ivins, UT 84738	(435) 634-5220
Vermont	Vermont Veterans Home	325 North Street Bennington, VT 05201	(802) 447-6523
Virginia	Sitter & Barfoot Veterans Care Center	1601 Broad Rock Blvd Richmond, VA 23224	(804) 371-8000
Virginia	Virginia Veterans Care Center	4550 Shenandoah Ave. Roanoke, VA 24017	(540) 982-2860 EXT 4107
Virginia	Virginia State Veterans Home	100 Emancipation Drive Hampton, VA 23667	(757) 722-9961
Washington	Washington Veterans Home	1141 Beach Dr. Retsil, WA 98378	(360) 895-4700
Washington	Washington Soldiers Home And Colony	1301 Orting-Kapowsin Hwy. Orting, WA 98360	(360) 893-4515
Washington	Spokane Veterans' Home	225 E. 5Th Ave. Spokane, WA 99202	(509) 344-5770
Washington	Walla Walla Veterans Home	Pending 2016	Pending 2016
Washington, D.C.	Armed Forces Retirement Home	UPDATE 140 Rock Creek Church Road NW Washington, DC 20011-8400	(800) 422-9988
West Virginia	West Virginia Veterans Home	512 Water St. Barboursville, WV 25504	(304) 736-1027
West Virginia	West Virginia State Veterans Home	One Freedoms Way Clarksburg, WV 26301	(304) 626-1602
Wisconsin	Wisconsin Veterans Home At King	N2665 County Road QQ King, WI 54946	(715) 258-5586

Wisconsin	Wisconsin Veterans Home At Union Grove	21425 G Spring St. Union Grove, WI 53182	(262) 878-6700
Wisconsin	Wisconsin State Veterans Home At Chippewa Falls	2175 E. Park Avenue Chippewa Falls, WI 54729	(715) 720-6775
Wyoming	Veterans' Home Of Wyoming	700 Veterans Lane Buffalo, WY 82834	(307) 684-5511

Appendix Section 3
Evidence of Marriage and Death

Surviving Spouse

Criteria for a Surviving Spouse
There are three requirements that must be met for a surviving spouse to receive death pension or DIC and certain other benefits applicable to surviving spouses and their children. **All 3 together must be met.** There are, however, specific exceptions to these requirements that are discussed further below.

38 CFR § 3.50 Spouse and surviving spouse.

1. "Surviving spouse" means a person of the opposite sex whose marriage to the veteran meets the requirements of §3.1(j) and who was the spouse of the veteran at the time of the veteran's death and:

2. Who lived with the veteran continuously from the date of marriage to the date of the veteran's death except where there was a separation which was due to the misconduct of, or procured by, the veteran without the fault of the spouse; and

3. Except as provided in §3.55, has not remarried or has not since the death of the veteran and after September 19, 1962, lived with another person of the opposite sex and held himself or herself out openly to the public to be the spouse of such other person.

Marriage Deemed Valid
A claimant filing for death benefits as the surviving spouse of a veteran must establish that the claimant and the veteran had a valid marriage. In most cases, this is accomplished by proving the existence of a legal marriage under State law. However, it is also possible under certain circumstances to "deem valid" for Department of Veterans Affairs (VA) purposes a marriage which is not valid under State law.

The fact that benefits were paid for a person as the spouse of the veteran during the veteran's lifetime does not automatically establish that person's status as the surviving spouse after the veteran's death.

The surviving spouse claimant must submit satisfactory evidence of his/her status as the surviving spouse of the veteran based on a marriage that is either legal or deemed valid and must meet the other requirements set forth in this topic.

Remarriage
Generally, remarriage of the surviving spouse after the death of the veteran will void any benefits that were available to the surviving spouse including death pension and DIC. Here are some exceptions to this rule

38 CFR § 3.55 Marriage void, terminated or annulled

Marriage Was Void or Annulled
Remarriage of a surviving spouse shall not bar the furnishing of benefits to such surviving spouse if the marriage:

- Was void, or
- Has been annulled by a court having basic authority to render annulment decrees, unless it is determined by the Department of Veterans Affairs that the annulment was obtained through fraud by either party or by collusion.

Marriage Terminated Prior to November 1, 1990
On or after January 1, 1971, remarriage of a surviving spouse terminated prior to November 1, 1990, or terminated by legal proceedings commenced prior to November 1, 1990, by an individual who, but for the remarriage, would be considered the surviving spouse, shall not bar the furnishing of benefits to such surviving spouse provided that the marriage:

- Has been terminated by death, or
- Has been dissolved by a court with basic authority to render divorce decrees unless the Department of Veterans Affairs determines that the divorce was secured through fraud by the surviving spouse or by collusion.

DIC Benefits for Terminated Remarriage
On or after October 1, 1998, remarriage of a surviving spouse terminated by death, divorce, or annulment, will not bar the furnishing of dependency and indemnity compensation (DIC), unless the Secretary determines that the divorce or annulment was secured through fraud or collusion.

Non--Married Relationship

- On or after January 1, 1971, the fact that a surviving spouse has lived with another person and has held himself or herself out openly to the public as the spouse of such other person shall not bar the furnishing of benefits to him or her after he or she terminates the relationship, if the relationship terminated prior to November 1, 1990.

- On or after October 1, 1998, the fact that a surviving spouse has lived with another person and has held himself or herself out openly to the public as the spouse of such other person will not bar the furnishing of dependency and indemnity compensation (DIC) to the surviving spouse if he or she ceases living with such other person and holding himself or herself out openly to the public as such other person's spouse.

Benefits for a surviving spouse who remarries after age 57 (presumed currently married)
On or after January 1, 2004, the remarriage of a surviving spouse after the age of 57 shall not bar the furnishing of benefits relating to

- DIC -- dependency and indemnity compensation under 38 U.S.C. 1311,
- medical care for survivors and dependents under 38 U.S.C. 1781,
- educational assistance under 38 U.S.C. chapter 35, or
- housing loans under 38 U.S.C. chapter 37, subject to the limitation in paragraph (a)(10)(ii) of this section.

Divorce or Annulment
Documentary proof of dissolution of all prior marriages of both parties is required if dissolution of prior marriages cannot be established based on the claimant's certified statement. This means that the statement in the application attesting to the dates and places of the divorces or annulments will be sufficient evidence for proof unless those facts are not furnished.

Acceptable documentary evidence for termination of a prior marriage through annulment is a copy or abstract of the annulment decree.

The only acceptable documentary evidence for termination of a prior marriage through divorce (other than the original divorce decree) is a copy or abstract of a final decree of divorce.

Some jurisdictions provide a two-step process for dissolving a marriage:

- first: an interlocutory decree of divorce is granted, and
- second: after a passage of a specified period of time, a final divorce decree is entered.

Notes:
- The parties continue to be married until the final divorce decree is granted.
- An interlocutory decree of divorce does not dissolve a marriage.

Certain "marriages" have no legal effect even though the parties may have gone through a marriage ceremony, and registered the marriage. Such marriages are legally void because the parties did not satisfy the legal requirements for entering into a marriage at the time of the alleged marriage. Not all legally defective marriages are void. For example, in most jurisdictions marriage by underage individuals is not automatically void.

Generally, a marriage is considered void only if the defect is fundamental. Grounds for voiding a marriage vary from state to state, but in most States a marriage is void if either party is already married at the time of the marriage, or if the parties are closely related.

If a marriage is determined to have been void, there is no need to dissolve it through divorce or annulment before entering into a subsequent marriage. Likewise, a remarried surviving spouse whose subsequent marriage is annulled or declared void may reestablish entitlement as a surviving spouse.

When a claimant who was divorced from the veteran at the time of the veteran's death attempts to establish entitlement as the veteran's surviving spouse based on a court decree setting aside or vacating the divorce, obtain all relevant documents, such as the court decree that set aside the divorce, and refer the case to Regional Counsel for an opinion on the issue of the validity of the order setting aside the divorce.

A determination by Regional Counsel that the decree setting aside the divorce is valid means that the claimant was the legal surviving spouse of the veteran (assuming the marriage can be established in the first place).

38 CFR § 3.53 Continuous cohabitation.
(a) General. The requirement that there must be continuous cohabitation from the date of marriage to the date of death of the veteran will be considered as having been met when the evidence shows that any separation was due to the misconduct of, or procured by, the veteran without the fault of the surviving spouse. Temporary separations which ordinarily occur, including those caused for the time being through fault of either party, will not break the continuity of the cohabitation.

(b) Findings of fact. The statement of the surviving spouse as to the reason for the separation will be accepted in the absence of contradictory information. If the evidence establishes that the separation was by mutual consent and that the parties lived apart for purposes of convenience, health, business, or any other reason which did not show an intent on the part of the surviving spouse to desert the veteran, the continuity of the cohabitation will not be considered as having been broken. State laws will not control in determining questions of desertion; however, due weight will be given to findings of fact in court decisions made during the life of the veteran on issues subsequently involved in the application of this section.

The claimant must meet the continuous cohabitation requirement of 38 CFR 3.50(b)(1) to qualify as the surviving spouse of a veteran for VA purposes. This requirement is most commonly met by virtue of the surviving spouse having lived continuously with the veteran from the date of marriage to the date of the veteran's death; however, the requirement is also met in any of the following occurred.

1. The veteran and claimant were living apart at the time of the veteran's death due to marital discord, but the claimant was not materially at fault for the separation, or any fault on the part of the claimant was insignificant.

2. Fault or the absence of fault is determined based on an analysis of conduct at the time of the separation. This means that the conduct of the spouse after the separation is not a factor in determining continuous cohabitation and may not be used as a basis for denying benefits.

Separations occurring during the course of the marriage, regardless of fault, are irrelevant if the parties are no longer estranged at the time of the veteran's death.

The spouse of a deceased veteran who was separated from the veteran due to the fault of the veteran has no affirmative obligation to attempt to reconcile with the veteran. As long as the spouse is not materially at fault in the separation, the continuous cohabitation requirement is met. Note: It is irrelevant that the parties lived apart for many years prior to the veteran's death, as long as the spouse was not at fault for the separation.

Evidence for the Marriage

Successful development of a marital relationship for VA purposes requires knowledge of where the claimed marriage took place, and the requirements for establishing a legal marriage in the jurisdiction where the marriage took place.

VA accepts the oral, written, or faxed statement of a claimant as proof of marriage provided the statement contains the

1. date of marriage (month and year), and
2. location of the event (city and state.)

Before a marriage may be established for VA purposes, it is always necessary to have the claimant's statement of marital history. The statement of marital history must

1. show all prior marriages of both parties, and
2. include the following information:
    a. the first and last name of prior marriage partners
    b. the current spouse's Social Security number (SSN)
    c. how the prior marriages terminated (death, divorce, annulment)
    d. the date the prior marriages terminated (month and year, at a minimum), and
    e. the place where the prior marriages terminated (city and state).

Documentary evidence of marriage is required if

- the claimant does not reside within a State (outside of the United States)
- the claimant's statement raises a question as to its validity
- the claimant's statement conflicts with other evidence of record, or
- there is a reasonable indication of fraud or misrepresentation.

In all jurisdictions in the U.S. and most other places in the world, a marriage cannot be contracted if either party is already married. Establishment of a legal marriage always implies a finding that the parties to the marriage were free to marry at the time of the alleged marriage. If either party was married previously, the current marriage may not be established unless the prior marriage is

1. terminated by
    a. death
    b. divorce
    c. annulment, or
2. determined to be void under State law.

Documentary proof of dissolution of all prior marriages of both parties is required if dissolution of prior marriages cannot be established based on the claimant's certified statement.

Request documentary evidence of a marriage when the claimant's statement is not sufficient to establish the marriage.

Primary evidence consists of a copy or abstract of the public record of a marriage, or a copy of the church record of marriage, containing sufficient data to identify the

1. parties involved
2. date and place of the marriage, and
3. number of prior marriages, if shown on the official record.

Note: Telephone the claimant, use the MARRIAGE CERTIFICATE field on the BDN 204 screen, or send a locally-generated letter via MAP-D to request a marriage certificate.

If primary evidence is unavailable, the marriage may still be established by submission of the following evidence in the order of preference listed:

- an official report from the service department as to a marriage that occurred while the veteran was in service
- an affidavit of the clergyman or magistrate who officiated
- the original certificate of marriage, if VA is satisfied that it is genuine and free from alteration
- affidavits or certified statements signed by two or more witnesses to the ceremony, or
- any other secondary evidence that reasonably supports a belief by the adjudicating activity that a valid marriage actually occurred.

Evidence for Death
The fact of death may be established on the basis of any one of the following forms of primary evidence:

- an official death certificate
- a copy of a coroner's report of death or a verdict of a coroner's jury
- a death certificate signed by a medical officer if death occurred in a hospital or institution under the control of the U.S. Government
- a clinical summary or other report showing the fact and date of death signed by a medical officer if death occurred in a hospital or institution under the control of the U.S. Government
- an official report of death of a member of a uniformed service from the Secretary of the department concerned if death occurred while the deceased was
    - on the retired list
    - in an inactive duty status, or
    - on active duty
- a U.S. consular report of death bearing the signature and seal of the U.S. consul if death occurred abroad, or

- an official report of death from the head of the department concerned if the
    - deceased was, at the time of death, a civilian employee of a U.S. Government agency, and
    - death occurred abroad.

When primary evidence cannot be furnished, the claimant must state the reason why. Once the claimant explains the reason for the lack of primary evidence, the fact of death may be established on the basis of the following secondary evidence:

- a finding of the fact of death made by another Federal agency in the absence of evidence to the contrary, or
- affidavits from persons who have
    - personal knowledge of the fact of death, and
    - viewed the body and know it to be the body of the person whose death is being established

Note: Affidavits must set forth all the facts and circumstances concerning the death such as the date, place, time, and cause thereof.

In the absence of the primary or secondary evidence outlined in M21-1MR, Part III, Subpart iii, 5.B.8. b and c, VA may make a finding of death if the fact of death is shown by a preponderance of competent evidence. An administrative decision is required.

Death Determined by a Seven-Year Absence
No State law providing for presumption of death shall be applicable to claims for benefits under laws administered by VA. If evidence is submitted, establishing the continued and unexplained absence of any individual from home and family for a 7-year period, death shall be considered sufficiently proved. Except in a suit brought pursuant to section 784, Government insurance, the finding of death by VA shall be final and conclusive. See VA Form 21-1775, Statement of Disappearance.

Appendix Section 4
Information on Individual Unemployability

DEPARTMENT OF VETERANS AFFAIRS
Veterans Benefits Administration
Washington, D.C. 20420

September 14, 2010

Director (00/21)
All VA Regional Offices

In Reply Refer To: 211B
Training Letter 10-07

SUBJ: Adjudication of Claims for Total Disability Based on Individual Unemployability (TDIU)

PURPOSE

Our purpose in issuing this training letter is to revise and clarify our policies and procedures concerning the adjudication of TDIU decisions in order to restore the original intention of the TDIU evaluation – accurately, timely, and adequately compensating our Veterans who are unable to be gainfully employed due to service-connected disabilities.

BACKGROUND

VA has a longstanding and well-established policy of granting total disability ratings to Veterans who, due to service-connected disability(ies), are unable to secure and maintain substantially gainful employment even if a Veteran's combined disability evaluation does not result in a total schedular evaluation. The provisions of 38 C.F.R. § 4.16(a) provide the minimal schedular standards for TDIU consideration: if there is one disability, this disability shall be ratable at 60 percent or more; and, if there are two or more disabilities, there must be at least one disability ratable at 40 percent or more and additional disability to bring the combined rating to 70 percent or more. Alternatively, if these schedular requirements are not met, but the evidence shows the Veteran is unemployable due to service-connected disabilities, 38 C.F.R. § 4.16(b) authorizes VA to grant a TDIU evaluation on an extra-schedular basis upon approval by the Director, Compensation and Pension Service.

In recent years, several factors, including internal inconsistencies in developing and adjudicating TDIU decisions and changing policies and procedures issued in response to court decisions addressing the TDIU issue, have led to a conclusion that the TDIU issue requires new guidance. A review of TDIU grants has also revealed that the benefit is, at times, granted on a quasi-automatic basis when the Veteran attains a certain age and/or schedular rating. This practice is not supported by VA regulation or policy.

History of TDIU Evaluations

The regulatory history does not provide an explanation for the creation of TDIU ratings. VA's 1933 Schedule for Rating Disabilities (VASRD) provided the first definition of total disability as existing "when there is (or are) present any impairment (or impairments) of mind or body which is (or are) sufficient to render it impossible for the average person to follow a substantially gainful occupation." A 1934 revision of the VASRD provided the first authorization of a TDIU rating, sanctioned total disability ratings "without regard to the specific provisions of the rating schedule if a Veteran with disabilities is unable to secure or follow a substantially gainful occupation as a result of his disabilities."

In 1941, the Administrator of Veterans Affairs issued an extension of the 1933 VASRD, which provided that total disability ratings may be assigned without regard to the specific provisions of the rating schedule when the disabled person is, in the judgment of the rating agency, unable to secure or follow a substantially gainful occupation as a result of his/her disabilities. The 1941 regulation also provided the current TDIU rating criteria.

The 1945 Schedule for Rating Disabilities established that age may not be considered a factor in evaluating service-connected disability, and that service-connected unemployability could not be based on advancing age or additional (nonservice-connected) disability. (Paragraph 16, General Policy in Rating Disability)

38 C.F.R. § 4.16(a) became effective in March 1963. The regulation was amended in September 1975 to include subsection (b), which authorized a TDIU evaluation on an extra-schedular basis. In March 1989, subsection (c) was added to § 4.16, which directed that if a Veteran was rated 70 percent for a mental disorder that precluded gainful employment, 38 C.F.R. § 4.16(a) was not for application and such Veteran was to be assigned a 100-percent schedular evaluation.

In August 1990, 38 C.F.R. § 4.16(a) was revised to include language that marginal employment would not be considered gainful employment and also provided a definition of what constituted marginal employment. Following VA's adoption of the fourth edition of the *Diagnostic and Statistical Manual for Mental Disorders*, 38 C.F.R. § 4.16(c) was rescinded in October 1996. The provision was now viewed as being extraneous, as a Veteran with a service-connected mental disorder would not be disadvantaged with the application of the other subsections of 38 C.F.R. § 4.16.

Case Law

The Court of Appeals for Veterans Claims (CAVC) and the Court of Appeals for the Federal Circuit (Federal Circuit) have issued many precedent opinions that have substantively affected Veterans' rights associated with TDIU evaluations, as well as how VA adjudicates the issue. Below are some of the most pertinent holdings in decisions concerning TDIU from both courts.

Moore v. Derwinski, 1 Vet.App. 83 (1991) The term "substantially gainful occupation" refers to, at a minimum, the ability to earn a living wage.

Wood (Clarence) v. Derwinski, 1 Vet.App. 367 (1991) An application for unemployability compensation is an application for increased compensation within the meaning of 38 U.S.C. § 5110(b)(2).

Blackburn v. Brown, 4 Vet.App. 395 (1993) Entitlement to TDIU compensation must be established solely on the basis of impairment arising from service-connected disabilities.

Hattlestad v. Brown, 5 Vet.App. 524 (1993) In determining entitlement to TDIU evaluations, a clear explanation requires analysis of the current degree of unemployability attributable to the service-connected condition as compared to the degree of unemployability attributable to the non-service connected condition.

Norris v. West, 12 Vet.App. 413 (1999) When VA is considering a rating increase claim from a claimant whose schedular rating meets the minimum criteria of § 4.16(a) and there is evidence of current service-connected unemployability in the claims file or under VA control, evaluation of that rating increase must also include an evaluation of a reasonably raised claim for TDIU.

Faust v. West, 13 Vet.App. 342 (2000) In determining entitlement to a TDIU rating, VA must consider the amount established by the U.S. Department of Commerce, Bureau of the Census, as the poverty threshold for one person. A determination of whether a person is capable of engaging in a substantially gainful occupation must consider both that person's abilities and employment history.

Hurd v. West, 13 Vet.App. 449 (2000) A TDIU claim is a claim for increased compensation, and the effective date rules for increased compensation apply to a TDIU claim.

Roberson v. Principi, 251 F.3d 1378 (2001) Once a Veteran submits evidence of a medical disability, makes a claim for the highest rating possible, and submits evidence of unemployability, the requirement in 38 C.F.R. § 3.155(a) that an informal claim "identify the benefit sought" has been satisfied and VA must consider whether the Veteran is entitled to TDIU.

Bradley v. Peake, 22 Vet.App. 280 (2008) The provisions of 38 U.S.C. § 1114(s) do not limit a "service-connected disability rated as total" to only a schedular 100-percent rating. A TDIU rating may serve as the "total" service-connected disability, if the TDIU entitlement was solely predicated upon a single disability for the purpose of considering entitlement to SMC at the (s) rate.

Comer v. Peake, 552 F.3d 1362, 1367 (Fed. Cir. 2009) A claim for a total disability evaluation due to individual unemployability (TDIU) is implicitly raised whenever a pro se Veteran (unrepresented), who presents cogent evidence of unemployability, seeks to obtain a higher disability rating, regardless of whether the Veteran specifically states that he is seeking TDIU benefits.

Rice v. Shinseki, 22 Vet.App. 447 (2009) A request for a total disability evaluation on the basis of individual unemployability (TDIU), whether expressly raised by the Veteran or reasonably raised by the record, is not a separate claim for benefits, but involves an attempt to obtain an appropriate rating for a disability or disabilities, either as part of the initial adjudication of a claim or as part of a claim for increased compensation, if entitlement to the disability upon which TDIU is based has already been found to be service connected. There is no freestanding TDIU claim.

Processing

VA has historically handled TDIU claims as freestanding claims that were adjudicated separately from other compensation issues in its decisions. However, as a result of the *Rice* decision, a request for TDIU, whether specifically raised by the Veteran or reasonably raised by the evidence of record, is no longer to be considered as a separate claim but will be adjudicated as part of the initial disability rating or as part of a claim for increased compensation.

The current Veterans Claims Assistance Act (VCAA) notice letters used for original disability compensation claims or claims for increased evaluation are sufficient if a request for a TDIU evaluation is introduced. A separate notice letter for a TDIU evaluation is no longer required. If a VA Form 21-8940, *Veteran's Application for Increased Compensation based on Unemployability,* or other submission expressly requests TDIU, this will be considered a claim for increased evaluation in all service-connected disabilities unless TDIU is expressly claimed as being due to one or more specific disabilities. The initial notice letter will provide VCAA compliant information for all service-connected disabilities that are not currently evaluated at the schedular maximum evaluation for that condition.

The principle of staged ratings may be applied in considering the effective date for a TDIU evaluation as either part of the initial disability evaluation or as part of a claim for increase. *See Fenderson v. West*, 12 Vet.App. 119 (1999); *Hart v. Mansfield,* 21 Vet.App. 505 (2007).

VA Forms 21-8940 and 21-4192

Notwithstanding any favorable medical evidence or opinion indicating that the Veteran is unemployable due to service-connected disabilities, a TDIU evaluation may not be granted if the evidence otherwise shows that the Veteran is engaged in, or capable of being engaged in, gainful employment. Accordingly, a VA Form 21-8940, *Veteran's Application for Increased Compensation based on Unemployability*, should still be forwarded to the

Veteran if a request for a TDIU evaluation is expressly raised by the Veteran or reasonably raised by the evidence of record.

The VA Form 21-8940 remains an important vehicle for developing the claim and determining entitlement to a TDIU evaluation. However, the determination of an effective date for the establishment of a TDIU evaluation is no longer primarily based upon the date of receipt of the VAF 21-8940, but upon consideration of other factors such as the date of the original claim or claim for increase and the date that the evidence establishes inability to maintain substantially gainful employment due to service-connected disability(ies). Once the VA Form 21-8940 is received and former employers are identified, then VA Form 21-4192, *Request for Employment Information in Connection with Claim for Disability Benefit*, will be forwarded to the former employers listed on the form. The VA Form 21-4192 requests that the employer provide information about the Veteran's job duties, on-the-job concessions, date of and reason for job termination, etc. A TDIU evaluation should not be denied solely because an employer failed to return a completed VA Form 21-4192.

The VA Form 21-8940, while still important as a development tool, is not required to render a decision concerning whether or not to assign a TDIU evaluation. A decision concerning entitlement to a TDIU evaluation may be rendered without a completed VA Form 21-8940 of record, based on the entire body of evidence available.

<u>Examinations</u>

VA examinations are generally undertaken in conjunction with original disability compensation claims and claims for increase in accordance with VA's statutory duty to assist a Veteran in developing his/her claim. See 38 U.S.C. § 5103A(d); 38 C.F.R. § 3.159(c)(4). In such claims, if a request for a TDIU evaluation is expressly raised by the Veteran or reasonably raised by the evidence of record, a general medical examination is to be scheduled. Specialty examinations (Eye, Audio, Mental, Traumatic Brain Injury, and Dental) may also need to be scheduled. These specialty examinations are only to be ordered when the Veteran is service connected for an eye, audio, mental, or dental condition that is not already at the schedular maximum, even if this condition is not one that the Veteran is claiming as causing his or her unemployability. Additionally, the examiner should be requested to provide an opinion as to whether or not the Veteran's service-connected disability(ies) render him or her unable to secure and maintain substantially gainful employment, to include describing the disabilities' functional impairment and how that impairment impacts on physical and sedentary employment.

In applying the Court's holding in *Bradley*, if the medical evidence is insufficient to render an adjudicative determination as to whether the Veteran's TDIU entitlement solely originates from a single service-connected disability, and there is potential entitlement to SMC at the (s) rate, the VA examination should also include an opinion as to what disability or disabilities render the Veteran unable to secure and maintain substantially gainful employment.

Other TDIU Development Considerations

If the evidence indicates that the Veteran has been seen by the Vocational Rehabilitation and Employment Service (VR&E) or has applied for disability benefits from the Social Security Administration (SSA), these records, to include any decisions and supporting documentation, must be obtained.

The Rating Decision

Although TDIU is no longer a freestanding claim, the determination of entitlement to a TDIU evaluation, raised as part of an original claim or claim for increased evaluation, must still be disposed of as a separate issue in the rating decision.

In assigning the effective date for a TDIU evaluation, the regulations concerning effective dates for original claims and claims for increase – 38 C.F.R. §§ 3.400(b)(2) or (o) – will be applied. Also, when a TDIU evaluation is assigned, the evidentiary record should be carefully reviewed to determine the applicability of 38 C.F.R. § 3.156(b), whether as part of an initial disability rating or as part of a claim for increase. 38 C.F.R. § 3.157 may be applicable in claims for increased evaluation that also raise a request for a TDIU evaluation. (For further guidance, see our Decision Assessment Document in *Rice v. Shinseki*, May 6, 2009).

In compliance with the *Bradley* holding, if TDIU is granted, a determination must also be rendered as to what specific service-connected disability(ies) render the Veteran unemployable. Generally, there would have to be clear and substantial evidence to show that unemployability is caused by a single disability when there are multiple service-connected disabilities. In original disability claims, where service connection is not established for any disability, the issue of entitlement to a TDIU evaluation is rendered moot, unless specifically claimed.

When establishing an end product for TDIU, it will be adjudicated as part of the initial disability rating or as part of a claim for increase. If a claim for TDIU is received after development has been initiated, to include VCAA notification, and a determination of entitlement to service connection for the disability upon which TDIU is based is still pending or has not been found, adjudicate the TDIU issue under the existing end product.

In situations where TDIU is inferred and additional evidence is needed, rate all other claimed issues that can be decided before rending a decision on TDIU entitlement. Show the issue of potential TDIU entitlement as deferred in the rating decision. Develop the inferred TDIU issue under the existing or appropriate end product, which will remain pending. Send the Veteran a VA Form 21-8940 to complete and return. Every inferred TDIU request that is deferred for additional evidence must be resolved by a formal rating decision after the evidence is received or the notification period expires. See Fast Letter 08-06 (February 27, 2008).

Whenever a rating decision grants TDIU and establishes permanency, it must include the statement, "Basic eligibility under 38 U.S.C. Chapter 35 is established from [date]." This statement is required regardless of whether or not there are potential dependents.

Continuing Requirements for the TDIU Award

As inability to maintain substantially gainful employment constitutes the basic criteria that must be satisfied for a TDIU evaluation, after the initial TDIU grant is awarded, VA must continue to ensure that the Veteran is unemployable.

Therefore, the Veteran must complete and return a VA Form 21-4140, *Employment Questionnaire*, annually for as long as the TDIU evaluation is in effect. Yearly submission of the form is required unless the Veteran is 70 years of age or older, or has been in receipt of a TDIU evaluation for a period of 20 or more consecutive years (See 38 C.F.R. § 3.951(b)), or has been granted a 100-percent schedular evaluation. The form is sent out annually to the Veteran from the Hines Information Technology Center and must be returned to the regional office. It requests that the Veteran report any employment for the past twelve months or certify that no employment has occurred during this period. The VA Form 21-4140 must be returned within 60 days or the Veteran's benefits may be reduced. If the form is returned in a timely manner and shows no employment, then the TDIU evaluation will continue uninterrupted. The VA Form 21-4140 must be returned with the Veteran's signature certifying employment status. A telephone call to the Veteran is not acceptable to certify employment status for TDIU claims.

If the VA Form 21-4140 is timely returned and shows that the Veteran has engaged in employment, VA must determine if the employment is marginal or substantially gainful employment. If the employment is marginal, then TDIU benefits will continue uninterrupted. If the employment is substantially gainful, then VA must consider discontinuing the TDIU evaluation. 38 C.F.R. § 3.343(c)(1) and (2) provide that actual employability must be shown by clear and convincing evidence before the benefit is discontinued. Neither vocational rehabilitation activities nor other therapeutic or rehabilitative pursuits will be considered evidence of renewed employability unless the Veteran's medical condition shows marked improvement. Additionally, if the evidence shows that the Veteran actually is engaged in a substantially gainful occupation, the TDIU evaluation cannot be discontinued unless the Veteran maintains the gainful occupation for a period of 12 consecutive months. See 38 C.F.R. § 3.343(c).

Once this period of sustained employment has been maintained, the Veteran must be provided with due process before the benefit is actually discontinued, as stated at 38 C.F.R. §§ 3.105(e) and 3.501(e)(2). This consists of providing the Veteran with a rating that

- Proposes to discontinue the IU benefit
- Explains the reason for the discontinuance
- States the effective date of the discontinuance, and
- States that the Veteran has 60 days to respond with evidence showing why the discontinuance should not take place.

If the TDIU evaluation is discontinued, the effective date of the discontinuance will be the last day of the month following 60 days from the date the Veteran is notified of the final rating decision. If the VA Form 21-4140 is not returned within the 60 days specified on the form, then the regional office must initiate action to discontinue the TDIU evaluation pursuant to 38 C.F.R. § 3.652(a). Due process must also be provided with a rating decision that proposes to discontinue the TDIU benefit for failure to return the form. If a response is not received within 60 days, then the TDIU evaluation will be discontinued and a rating decision will be sent to the Veteran providing notice of the discontinuance. date of discontinua nce will be the date specified in the rating decision which proposed discontinuance, as described above, or the day following the date of last payment of the TDIU benefit, as specified at § 3.501(f), whichever is later. The Veteran must also be notified that if the form is returned within one year and shows continued unemployability, then the TDIU evaluation may be restored from the date of discontinuance.

VA may also use the income verification match (IVM) to verify continued unemployability. The IVM is a method of comparing a TDIU recipient's earned income, as reported to VA by other federal agencies, with the earned income limits that define marginal employment. If income reports show significant earned income above the poverty threshold, the regional office must undertake development to determine if the Veteran is still unemployable. IVM information does not meet the requirements for a completed VA Form 21-4140 for the purpose of continuing TDIU benefits. A completed VA Form 21-4140 still must be provided by the Veteran for continuation of TDIU benefits.

Another method of monitoring unemployability status among TDIU recipients is through the VA Fiduciary Activity. This service conducts field examinations when it has been notified that a TDIU recipient might be pursuing a substantially gainful occupation. If the field examiner finds evidence of employment or if the Veteran is unwilling to cooperate with the examiner, then the examiner will forward this information to the Rating Activity. A decision must then be made as to whether the TDIU evaluation will be discontinued. The regulatory requirements listed above will be applied to the determination.

As an exception to the aforementioned procedures; if the veteran has certified no employment status in a VA Form 21-4140 and VA obtains credible information indicating that the veteran has engaged in gainful employment, continued entitlement to TDIU benefits may be terminated on the basis of fraud. The due process provisions of § 3.105(e) must still be followed. However, if a finding of fraud is confirmed, the effective date of termination of TDIU benefits will be the day preceding the date that VA received the veteran's VA Form 21-4140 that fraudulently certified continuation of no employment status. See 38 C.F.R. § 3.500(k).

Scenarios

Below are several factual scenarios intended to illustrate how claims involving requests for TDIU evaluations should be developed and rated, as well as the appropriate regulations to be applied in determining the effective date of the TDIU evaluation.

(1) A Veteran files a claim for service connection for PTSD in January 1999. The RO grants service connection in November 1999 with a 50-percent evaluation. The Veteran files a Notice of Disagreement (NOD) with the evaluation and submits a VAF 21-8940 in February 2000 indicating that he has been unable to work due to PTSD. The RO, in September 2000, grants a 70-percent evaluation for PTSD from January 1999 and also assigns a TDIU evaluation effective January 1999.

In this scenario, the TDIU evaluation is considered as part of the initial disability rating, not a freestanding TDIU claim. 38 C.F.R. § 3.156(b) is applicable as the Veteran had submitted evidence of unemployability within the appeal period and 38 C.F.R. § 3.400(b)(2) will be applied in determining the effective date of the TDIU evaluation.

(2) The Veteran has been service connected for several disabilities, to include migraine headaches, since 2001. In March 2006, he/she submits a claim for increased evaluation for migraine headaches, rated 10-percent disabling at the time, stating that the frequency and severity of his migraine headaches have worsened. The RO issues a decision in December 2006 granting a 50-percent evaluation from March 2006. His/her combined disability evaluation is also increased to 70 percent. The Veteran timely files an NOD in response to the evaluation assigned for migraine headaches and appears before a Decision Review Officer (DRO) in an informal conference. He/she submits a VAF 21-8940, additional medical evidence, and a letter from his/her employer indicating that the Veteran was unable to continue working because he/she missed too much time because of his/her migraine headaches and last worked in March 2006. The DRO, in February 2007, grants a TDIU evaluation effective March 2006.

In this scenario, the TDIU evaluation is considered as part of the claim for increased compensation. 38 C.F.R. § 3.156(b) is applicable as the Veteran had submitted evidence within the appeal period and 38 C.F.R. § 3.400(o) will be applied in determining the effective date. The effective date for the TDIU evaluation will be based upon the date it is factually ascertainable that the Veteran was unable to maintain substantially gainful employment due to his service-connected disability(ies), to include up to one year prior to the date of the March 2006 claim for increased evaluation under § 3.400(o)(2).

(3) The Veteran is service connected for post traumatic stress disorder (PTSD), rated 50-percent disabling; arthritis of the knees, each rated 10-percent disabling; and several other disabilities that have been assigned noncompensable evaluations. He files a claim for increased evaluation for PTSD, stating that the condition has worsened and that he had to discontinue working due to problems associated with the condition. He submits medical evidence and identifies VA medical records that only concern treatment for PTSD and show difficulty in maintaining employment due to the mental disorder.

A VCAA notice for the PTSD evaluation and TDIU and a VA Form 21-8940 should be forwarded to the Veteran. The notice should not refer to the other service-connected disabilities, as the Veteran specifically indicated that only PTSD has rendered him unemployable. A general medical examination with a special psychiatric examination for PTSD is to be requested. The VA examiner should be requested to render an opinion concerning the effect of PTSD on employability as a request for a TDIU evaluation has been reasonably raised by the Veteran and the evidence of record.

(4) The Veteran has been service connected for ankylosing spondylitis, rated 60-percent disabling; eczema, rated 30-percent disabling; and hiatal hernia, rated 10-percent disabling, since 2003. In January 2007, he submits a statement indicating that he cannot work due to his service-connected disabilities.

In this scenario, the correct course of action is to send the Veteran a VCAA notice for claims for increased evaluation that pertain to all service-connected disabilities not currently at the schedular maximum evaluation, as the Veteran did not specifically state what service-connected disability(ies) affects his employability.

The Veteran should be scheduled for a general medical examination that also includes an opinion as to whether or not the service-connected disability(ies) render the Veteran unable to secure and maintain substantially gainful employment.

This Training Letter rescinds Training Letter 07-01 (February 21, 2007). M21-MR, IV.ii.2.F will be revised in accordance with this Training Letter.

WHO TO CONTACT FOR HELP

Questions should be e-mailed to VAVBAWAS/CO/21Q&A.

/S/
Thomas J. Murphy
Director
Compensation and Pension Service

Training Letter 07-01

Total Disability Ratings Based on Individual Unemployability (IU)

Benefits granted under the VA rating schedule are intended to compensate veterans for the average impairment in earning capacity that results from service-connected disease or injury. IU is a special additional benefit to address the truly unique disability picture of a veteran who is unemployable due to service-connected disability, but for whom the application of the rating schedule does not fully reflect the veteran's level of impairment. An award of IU allows the veteran to receive compensation at a rate equivalent to that of a 100 percent schedular award. However, this benefit is not intended, by regulation or policy, to be a quasi-automatic benefit granted whenever a veteran has met a qualifying schedular evaluation or reached an advanced age.

When raised as an issue, IU is appropriate only in exceptional cases. First determine if the veteran's disability(ies) warrant a 100 percent schedular evaluation before considering whether to assign a total disability rating under either 38 CFR 4.16 or 3.321.

1. General Requirements for Entitlement to IU Entitlement to IU requires that the veteran meet certain initial criteria listed at 38 CFR 4.16 as well as continuing criteria as explained below. The IU benefit continues only as long as the veteran remains unemployable. VA monitors the employment status of IU beneficiaries and requires that they submit an annual certification of unemployability.

Consideration for IU requires that:

The veteran has service-connected disability(ies) as described in 38 CFR 4.16(a) or 4.16(b), and

The evidence shows unemployability due to a service-connected disability.

1.a. Schedular Requirements

The qualifying schedular evaluations are provided at § 4.16(a). The veteran must be service connected for a single disability evaluated at least 60 percent disabling or service connected for multiple disabilities evaluated at least 70 percent disabling, with one of the multiple disabilities rated at least 40 percent disabling. This section also provides a list of circumstances where the requirement for a single 60 or 40 percent disability may be met by a combination of disabilities that can be considered a single disability (such as those arising from common etiology or a single accident, or those affecting a single body system, etc.).

Careful consideration must also be given to the cause of the veteran's unemployability. Unemployability must result from one or more service-connected disabilities. Disabilities for which service connection has not been granted do not qualify for consideration as a source of unemployability.

If the veteran does not meet the requirements of 38 CFR 4.16(a) but there is evidence of unemployability due to a service-connected disability, then the case should be submitted to the Director of Compensation and Pension Service for a determination of eligibility, as provided at 38 CFR 3.321(b) and 4.16(b).

1.b. Unemployability

Unemployability means the inability of a veteran to secure or follow a substantially gainful occupation. A finding of unemployability cannot be made if the evidence shows that the veteran is engaged in, or is capable of being engaged in, a substantially gainful occupation. However, a finding could be made if the evidence shows marginal employment. Marginal employment is defined in terms of a veteran's earned annual income. This income should generally not exceed the government's established poverty threshold for one person. Exceeding this threshold may indicate a substantially gainful occupation, as noted by the Court of Appeals for Veteran's Claims (CAVC) in Faust v. West, 13 Vet.App. 342 (2000), where a substantially gainful occupation was defined as "one that provides annual income that exceeds the poverty threshold for one person."

In addition to the income criterion, evidence showing that employment is marginal rather than substantially gainful may also exist on a "facts found" basis. Examples of this marginal status include employment in the protected environment of a family business or sheltered workshop. Such fact-based marginal employment is consistent with a finding of unemployability.

1.c. Age Factor

It is clear from 38 CFR 4.19 that consideration of a veteran's age is appropriate when evaluating disabilities for pension claims, but not for awarding IU benefits. The regulation states that unemployability associated with advancing age may not be used as a basis for a total disability rating in service-connected claims. This provision is echoed at 38 CFR 3.341, which states that the service-connected disability must be sufficient to produce unemployability without regard to advancing age.

Advancing age in this context may relate to voluntary retirement or removal from the work force based on tenure or longevity rather than disability. Voluntary retirement does not necessarily show unemployability and should not be used as the only evidence of unemployability. Therefore, when evaluating a claim for IU received from a retired veteran of advanced age, careful consideration must be given to distinguishing a worsened disability that would have caused unemployability from unemployment due to retirement. When an IU claim is received from a veteran of advanced age, the rating should discuss the factor of age and provide an explanation of how the available evidence was evaluated to arrive at the decision to grant or deny IU.

2. Claims for IU

Claims for IU are generally submitted by the veteran but may also be reasonably raised by the evidence of record, including statements or evidence submitted by the veteran indicating unemployability. IU claims filed by the veteran can be considered as claims for an increased evaluation when associated with evidence of a worsened service-connected condition. Claims for an increased evaluation, even without a specific IU claim from the veteran, may give rise to a claim for IU that must be considered.

2.a. Reasonably Raised or Informal Claims

In Norris v. West, 12 Vet.App. 413 (1999), the Court held that where the rating activity is considering a claim for increased evaluation from a veteran who meets the qualifying schedular disability percentage requirements and there is evidence in the claims folder, or under VA control, which shows unemployability due to service-connected disability, then a rating for the claimed increase must also include a rating of a reasonably raised claim for IU. Thus, under the proper circumstances, a claim for IU exists, even though the veteran did not specifically make the claim.

The issue of a reasonably raised claim for IU was also addressed in the Federal Circuit case of Roberson v. Principi, 251 F.3d 1378 (Fed. Cir. 2001). In that case, the Court held that once a veteran submits evidence of a medical disability, makes a claim for the highest possible rating, and submits evidence of unemployability, the requirement of 38 CFR 3.155(a) that a claimant must "identify the benefit sought" is met. In such cases, VA must consider total disability based upon IU. The Court noted that, under these circumstances, the IU benefit being sought has been identified in conformity with the informal claim requirements of § 3.155(a). (See also, Servello v. Derwinski, 3 Vet.App. 196, 199 (1992) (veteran must provide evidence of entitlement to IU rating by virtue of unemployability)). The Court further stated that VA is obligated to develop a claim "to its optimum," which means considering all potential claims raised by the evidence and applying all relevant laws and regulations, regardless of whether the claim is specifically labeled as a claim for IU. Under circumstances where these conditions apply, but where the veteran does not meet the schedular requirements of § 4.16(a), the case should be referred for extra-schedular consideration as specified at § 4.16(b).

When the veteran has already been awarded a 100 percent total evaluation for one disability, an award of IU for a separate disability or disabilities should not be considered. The VA Office of General Counsel held in VAOPGCPREC 6-99, that when a schedular total disability grant has already been made, no additional monetary benefit would be available to a veteran based on unemployability and any such claim would be moot.

2.b. Claim for IU Defined
A formal claim for IU on VA Form 21-8940.
Any written communication indicating that the veteran is unable to work because of his or her service-connected disability(ies).

To raise an informal IU claim, the veteran must claim an increased evaluation for his or her service-connected disability(ies), submit medical evidence or be shown on VA examination to meet the requirements of § 4.16, and claim the inability to work due to his or her service-connected disability.

Although a claimant who seeks an increased rating is presumed to be seeking the highest rating possible, a claim for IU cannot reasonably be raised unless the veteran claims to be unable to maintain substantially gainful employment due to service-connected disability.

3. IU Claim Development
3.a. VA Forms 21-8940 and 21-4192
Claims for IU require that a VA Form (VAF) 21-8940, Veteran's Application for Increased Evaluation Based on Unemployability, be completed and submitted to the VA regional office by the veteran. If an IU claim has been reasonably raised by the evidence of record, a VAF 21-8940 must be sent to the veteran for completion and return before an award can be considered. The

VAF 21-8940 requires that the veteran list all employment for the five years prior to becoming too disabled to work and provide an accounting of current income. If the VAF 21-8940 is not returned by the veteran within 60 days, a formal rating decision will be made on the basis of the evidence of record, which considers, among other factors, that necessary evidence was not furnished by the claimant. If the VAF 21-8940 is returned after the rating decision is issued, but within one year of the date sent, the claim should be re-rated. See also section 4.d., Effective Dates for Reasonably Raised IU Claims.

Once the regional office receives VAF 21-8940 and former employers are identified, then VAF 21-4192, Request for Employment Information in Connection with Claim for Disability Benefit, will be forwarded to the former employers listed on the form. The VAF 21-4192 requests that the employer provide information about the veteran's job duties, on-the-job concessions, date of and reason for job termination, etc. Information given on both VAF 21-8940 and VAF 21-4192 is essential to a fair evaluation of the IU claim. However, IU benefits should not be denied solely because an employer failed to respond to VAF 21-4192.

3.b. Medical Evidence

The available medical evidence must show that a service-connected physical or mental condition is currently so severe and disabling that it prevents the veteran from securing or following a substantially gainful occupation. Any relevant medical evidence must be obtained from both VA and private sources as part of the development and evaluation process. These documents may contain descriptions of physical limitations caused by a service-connected disability or may contain opinions by medical professionals regarding the veteran's ability or inability to engage in work-related activity. If the evidence obtained is incomplete or inconsistent and does not provide a basis for assessing unemployability, then a VA examination should be scheduled, as provided under 38 CFR 3.326 and 3.159(c)(4). The medical examiner should be requested to provide an opinion regarding the effect of the service-connected disabilities on the veteran's ability to engage in substantially gainful employment. Further, because it is preferable to rate a veteran as 100 percent disabled on a schedular basis as opposed to awarding IU, order an examination for each service-connected condition that is not at the maximum schedular evaluation.

3.c. Vocational Rehabilitation and Employment Service (VR&E) Records

When the veteran's claims folder indicates that he or she has been seen by VR&E Service, any records related to this contact must be obtained and evaluated. The records may document the veteran's participation in a training program or may show that training was not feasible or was unsuccessful. The VR&E records provide important evidence for evaluating current unemployability. VA recognizes the importance of fostering a return-to-work attitude among veterans awarded IU and has implemented the use of a "motivational letter" encouraging new IU recipients to contact VR&E for assistance in returning to work.

3.d. Social Security Administration (SSA) Records

When the claims folder indicates that the veteran has been examined or awarded disability benefits by SSA, any relevant records must be obtained and evaluated. The CAVC held in Murincsak v. Derwinski, 2 Vet.App. 362 (1992), that VA's duty to assist includes requesting both the SSA decision granting or denying benefits and any supporting medical records. Although VA is not obligated to follow a determination made by SSA, these records may be relevant to the issue of the level of impairment of the veteran's service-connected disability. However, remember that SSA benefits may be awarded for any disability, whereas IU benefits must be based on service-connected disability. Therefore, careful attention must be paid to determining what disability resulted in a SSA benefit award and whether that disability is one for which service connection has been granted.

4. Rating Considerations
Rating decisions granting or denying entitlement to IU must provide enough explanation so that the claimant and representative can understand the reasons and bases for the decision. As with any decision, the rating must list the evidence considered, a clear explanation of the basis of the decision, and an explanation of the effective date of entitlement.

4.a. Date of Claim
A veteran's initial claim for IU may be received from any source indicating the benefit being sought, including a VAF 21-4138, Statement in Support of Claim. If the veteran files an informal claim, the regional office must send the veteran a VAF 21-8940 with instructions to complete and return it within one year in order to preserve date of receipt of the earlier communication as the date of claim. If the VAF 21-8940 is received after the one-year period has expired, the date of claim will be the date of receipt of the VAF 21-8940 as provided in § 3.159(b)(1). If the veteran submits a VAF 21-8940 as the initial IU claim, receipt of this form will represent a claim for IU and will establish the date of claim.

4.b. Effective Dates for IU Awards - Application of 38 CFR 3.400(o)(2)
When an IU claim is associated with a veteran's worsened service-connected disability, it is considered a claim for increase and the effective date of entitlement must be in accordance with § 3.400(o)(2). That section specifies that the effective date for an increase will be the earliest date that it is "factually ascertainable" that an increase occurred, provided this date is within one year preceding receipt of the claim. Otherwise, the effective date is the date of receipt of the claim.

Claims for an increased rating are considered claims for IU if any of the following conditions apply:

The IU claim is submitted on VAF 21-8940, or

In addition to a formal or informal claim for an increased rating, the veteran alleges that he or she is unemployable or VA receives evidence of unemployability, or

In the course of developing a claim for an increased rating, VA obtains evidence of unemployability and VA grants the veteran a rating that makes the veteran eligible for IU. When a veteran claims entitlement to IU without claiming increased disability, but increased disability is shown on VA examination or other medical evidence, the effective date of both grants is controlled by 38 CFR 3.400(o)(2).

4.c. Application of 38 CFR 3.400(o)

There are cases, however, where a claim for IU is not associated with a claim for increased disability. In these situations, the effective date is governed by § 3.400(o), which provides that the effective date will be the date of receipt of claim or the date entitlement arose, whichever is later. A case such as this might occur where a veteran has been unemployable due to service-connected disability meeting the schedular requirements for IU, but has never applied for IU. When the veteran files a claim for IU, and there is no associated worsened disability, it is not a claim for an increased disability. Therefore, the date of claim would generally be the effective date, unless evidence indicated a date of entitlement later than the date of claim.

4.d. Effective Dates for Reasonably Raised IU Claims
Reasonably raised claims for IU may arise in a veteran's original claim or claim for an increased rating. In original claims, IU must be considered when there is evidence of unemployability due to the claimed service-connected disability or disabilities. In claims for an increased evaluation, the CAVC holding in Norris requires that VA must consider a claim for IU when a veteran:

has submitted a claim for an increased evaluation, and
meets the minimum schedular requirements for IU, and
there is evidence of unemployability resulting from service-connected disability.

In addition, if VA receives, or is in possession of, evidence showing a worsened service-connected disability based on a report of medical examination or hospitalization, that evidence may establish an informal claim for increased evaluation, as provided in 38 CFR 3.157. In that event, if the schedular requirements for IU are met, evaluation of the informal claim for increase must also include an evaluation of a reasonably raised claim for IU.

When a claim for IU is reasonably raised, VAF 21-8940 must be sent to the veteran for completion and return. Because this type of IU claim arises when there is an associated claim for increase, the effective date of a grant of IU is governed by § 3.400(o)(2). This means that evidence of a factually ascertainable date of unemployability within the year preceding the date of claim may establish the effective date. In many cases, this may be the same date as that for the increase.

If the reasonably raised IU claim is received at the same time as other claims from the veteran and a rating decision is issued on the other claims, defer the IU claim and send the veteran VAF 21-8940. When the form is returned, it can be evaluated along with other evidence and a decision can be made regarding IU.

If the form is not returned within 60 days of mailing, issue a formal rating decision based on the evidence of record. If the VAF 21-8940 is returned after the rating decision is promulgated but within one year of the date the VAF 21-8940 was requested, re-rate the claim using the date of mailing of the form to the veteran as the date of claim. If IU is granted, the effective date of the award would be the date of receipt of the informal claim. If the form is not returned within one year of the date sent, benefits cannot be paid prior to date of receipt of the VAF 21-8940.

4.e. Chapter 35 Benefits: Survivors' and Dependents' Educational Assistance

38 U.S.C. Chapter 35 and regulations at 38 CFR 3.807 establish that educational benefits are available for dependents of a veteran who has been awarded a permanent and total service-connected disability. Although the disabling conditions that lead to an award of IU are considered to be total based on unemployability, they are not always permanent.

Unemployability may be temporary: for example, where the veteran undergoes VR&E training and is subsequently able to engage in a substantially gainful occupation. The VA Office of General Counsel has acknowledged that an IU award may be temporary. In VAOPGPREC 5-05, it was determined that § 4.16(b) "permits the award of a total disability rating based on temporary (i.e., non-permanent) inability to follow a substantially gainful occupation." Because IU is

acknowledged as a benefit that is not necessarily permanent, careful consideration must be given to granting the Chapter 35 educational benefit in association with the IU award. Substantial evidence must show that the veteran's unemployability status is permanent before the Chapter 35 grant is appropriate.

5. Continuing Requirements for IU Award

5.a. VA Form 21-4140

After the initial IU award has been made, the veteran must submit a VAF 21-4140, Employment Questionnaire, on a yearly basis to certify continuing unemployability. The VAF 21-4140 is required unless the veteran is 70 years of age or older, has been in receipt of IU for a period of 20 or more consecutive years (as provided at 38 CFR 3.951(b)), or has been granted a 100 percent schedular evaluation. The form is sent out annually to the veteran from the Hines Information Technology Center and must be returned to the regional office. It requests that the veteran report any employment for the past 12 months or certify that no employment has occurred during this period. The VAF 21-4140 includes a statement that it must be returned within 60 days or the veteran's benefits may be reduced. Completion of this form has a major impact on IU benefits in one of three ways, as described below.

VAF 21-4140 returned with no change

If VAF 21-4140 is returned in a timely manner and shows no employment, then IU benefits will continue uninterrupted.

VAF 21-4140 returned showing employment

If VAF 21-4140 is returned in a timely manner and shows that the veteran has engaged in employment, VA must determine if the employment is marginal or substantially gainful employment. If the employment is marginal, then IU benefits will continue uninterrupted. If the employment is substantially gainful, then VA must consider discontinuing the IU benefit. VA regulations at 38 CFR 3.343(c)(1) and (2) provide that actual employability must be shown by clear and convincing evidence before the benefit is discontinued. Neither vocational rehabilitation activities nor other therapeutic or rehabilitative pursuits will be considered evidence of renewed employability unless the veteran's medical condition shows marked improvement. Additionally, if the evidence shows that the veteran actually is engaged in a substantially gainful occupation, IU cannot be discontinued unless the veteran maintains the gainful occupation for a period of 12 consecutive months.

Once this period of sustained employment has been maintained, the veteran must be provided with due process before the benefit is actually discontinued, as stated at 38 CFR 3.105(e) and 3.501(e)(2). This consists of providing the veteran with a rating which:

Proposes to discontinue the IU benefit
Explains the reason for the discontinuance
States the effective date of the discontinuance, and
States that the veteran has 60 days to respond with evidence showing why the discontinuance should not take place.

If the veteran responds with evidence, it must be evaluated. If the evidence is insufficient or the veteran does not respond, then the regional office will discontinue the IU benefit and provide the veteran with a final rating decision explaining the decision. The effective date of the discontinuance will be the last day of the month following an additional period of 60 days, which begins from the date the veteran is notified of the final rating decision.

VAF 21-4140 not returned
If VAF 21-4140 is not returned within the 60 days specified on the form, then the regional office must initiate action to discontinue the IU benefit pursuant to 38 CFR 3.652(a). Due process must be provided with a rating decision that proposes to discontinue the IU benefit for failure to return the VAF 21-4140. If a response is not received within 60 days, then the IU benefit will be discontinued and a rating decision will be sent to the veteran providing notice of the discontinuance. The effective date of discontinuance will be the date specified in the rating decision which proposed discontinuance, as described above, or the day following the date of last payment of the IU benefit, as specified at § 3.501(f), whichever is later. The veteran must also be notified that if the form is returned within one year and shows continued unemployability, then the IU benefit may be restored from the date of discontinuance.

5.b. Income Verification Match (IVM) and Field Examinations
The IVM is a method of comparing an IU recipient's earned income, as reported to VA by other federal agencies, with the earned income limits that define marginal employment. If income reports show significant earned income above the poverty threshold, the regional office must undertake development to determine if the veteran is still unemployable.

Another method of monitoring unemployability status among IU recipients is through the VA Fiduciary Activity. This service conducts field examinations when it has been notified that an IU recipient might be pursuing a substantially gainful occupation. If the field examiner finds evidence of employment or if the veteran is unwilling to cooperate with the examiner, then the examiner will forward this information to the Rating Activity. A decision must then be made as to whether the IU benefit will be discontinued. This determination must take into account the regulatory requirements listed above, including: (1) whether there is actual employability by clear and convincing evidence and (2) whether there has been substantially gainful employment for 12 continuous months. If termination of the IU benefit is appropriate, a rating decision proposing discontinuance must be completed, with notice to the veteran that he or she has 60 days in which to contest the discontinuance. If no evidence or insufficient evidence is received within this period, then a final rating decision must be promulgated with notice to the veteran that the IU benefit will be discontinued on the last day of the month in which the additional 60-day due process period expires. This 60-day period will begin from the date of the notice of the final rating decision, as provided in § 3.105(e).

Ratings under SMC(s) are also available if the veteran is permanently housebound. The VA defines "permanently housebound" as being substantially (as opposed to completely) confined to a dwelling as the result of service-connected disability and it is reasonably certain that that such disability will continue throughout the veteran's lifetime. These kinds of determinations should be made by a physician, whose written opinions or reports in this respect would serve as the best evidence to submit in support of a claim for "s" SMC benefits. SMC S can also be awarded to veterans rated 100 percent if they are housebound but do not meet the required level of assistance for SMC L.

For purposes of SMC (s) many websites and books equate 100% disabled with being Totally Disabled due to Individual Unemployability (TDIU). Both ratings pay out at the same dollar amount. But both ratings are not entirely equivalent. The rules are confusing. TDIU is acceptable under certain limiting conditions for getting the special benefit in this section. Under Bradley vs Peake the court ruled that TDIU can be used in lieu of a 100% rating under certain conditions. The Court's holding allows a TDIU rating to serve as the "total" service-connected disability, if the TDIU entitlement was solely predicated upon a single disability for the purpose of considering entitlement to SMC at the (s) rate.

> *"The Court held that the requirement for a single "service-connected disability rated as total" cannot be satisfied by a combination of disabilities. Multiple service-connected disabilities that combine to 70 percent or more and establish entitlement to TDIU under 38 C.F.R. § 4.16(a) cannot be treated as a single "service-connected disability rated as total" for purposes of entitlement to SMC at the (s) rate."*

Here is what another court ruled if Bradley vs Peake does not apply

> *April 29, 2011, Federal Circuit, Guerra v. Shinseki, No. 2010-7080, TDIU, Subsection 1114(s), Special Monthly Compensation*
>
> *"In addition to having a schedular rating of 100%, a veteran can also be rated as totally disabled, and thus entitled to benefits at the statutory level for total disability, if the veteran is unable to maintain gainful employment as a result of service-connected disability. In that case, even if the veteran does not qualify for a schedular rating of 100%, the Secretary can rate the veteran as "totally disabled based on individual unemployability," – a rating referred to as TDIU. 38 C.F.R. § 4.16(b). If the veteran's claim for a total disability rating predicated on TDIU is based on "one . . . disability," that disability must be ratable at 60% or more under the rating schedule. For the purpose of TDIU, "one disability" includes multiple disabilities resulting from a single accident and multiple disabilities affecting a single bodily system. Id. § 4.16(a).*

Appellant Lionel Guerra served on active duty in the United States Marine Corps from 1966 to 1968 and suffered service-connected injuries. Most of his injuries resulted from a single combat incident. The regional office awarded Mr. Guerra a 70% rating for an upper-extremity gunshot wound, a 70% rating for post-traumatic stress disorder, a 40% rating for injuries to his left leg and thigh, a 40% rating for injuries to his right leg and thigh, and a 30% rating for neuropathy. None of his disabilities is individually rated at 100%, but his individually rated disabilities combine to a rating of 100%, i.e., total disability. His rating of total disability is not based on TDIU, however.

The Veterans Court held that Mr. Guerra did not meet the threshold requirement for special monthly compensation under subsection 1114(s) because none of his disabilities is independently rated as total. In construing the statute, the court followed its earlier decision in Bradley v. Peake, 22 Vet. App. 280, 289-90 (2008), in which the court held that a veteran with a scheduler rating of total disability must have a single disability rated at 100% in order to qualify for benefits under subsection 1114(s). The court rejected the argument that a veteran is entitled to benefits under subsection 1114(s) if the veteran suffers from several disabilities, no one of which is rated at 100%, even if the veteran's combined disability rating is 100%.

In sum, we conclude that subsection 1114(s) requires that a disabled veteran whose disability level is determined by the ratings schedule must have at least one disability that is rated at 100% in order to qualify for the special monthly compensation provided by that statute. Because no one of Mr. Guerra's disabilities carries a disability rating of 100%, he is not eligible for that statutory benefit. We therefore affirm the decision of the Veterans Court."

We include these two court decisions to caution you that you must be careful about what you are told for qualifying for SMC (s) by the many websites and books that are out there.

Appendix Section 5
Information on Posttraumatic Stress Disorder – PTSD

Information in this section was taken from the Department of Veterans Affairs "National Center for PTSD" website.

DSM Criteria for PTSD

Criterion A: stressor

The person has been exposed to a traumatic event in which both of the following have been present:

1. The person has experienced, witnessed, or been confronted with an event or events that involve actual or threatened death or serious injury, or a threat to the physical integrity of oneself or others.
2. The person's response involved intense fear,helplessness, or horror. Note: in children, it may be expressed instead by disorganized or agitated behavior.

Criterion B: intrusive recollection

The traumatic event is persistently re-experienced in at least one of the following ways:

1. Recurrent and intrusive distressing recollections of the event, including images, thoughts, or perceptions. Note: in young children, repetitive play may occur in which themes or aspects of the trauma are expressed.
2. Recurrent distressing dreams of the event. Note: in children, there may be frightening dreams without recognizable content
3. Acting or feeling as if the traumatic event were recurring (includes a sense of reliving the experience, illusions, hallucinations, and dissociative flashback episodes,including those that occur upon awakening or when intoxicated). Note: in children, trauma-specific reenactment may occur.
4. Intense psychological distress at exposure to internal or external cues that symbolize or resemble an aspect of the traumatic event.
5. Physiologic reactivity upon exposure to internal or external cues that symbolize or resemble an aspect of the traumatic event

Criterion C: avoidant/numbing

Persistent avoidance of stimuli associated with the trauma and numbing of general responsiveness (not present before the trauma), as indicated by at least three of the following:

1. Efforts to avoid thoughts, feelings, or conversations associated with the trauma
2. Efforts to avoid activities, places, or people that arouse recollections of the trauma
3. Inability to recall an important aspect of the trauma
4. Markedly diminished interest or participation in significant activities
5. Feeling of detachment or estrangement from others
6. Restricted range of affect (e.g., unable to have loving feelings)
7. Sense of foreshortened future (e.g., does not expect to have a career, marriage, children, or a normal life span)

Criterion D: hyper-arousal

Persistent symptoms of increasing arousal (not present before the trauma), indicated by at least two of the following:

1. Difficulty falling or staying asleep
2. Irritability or outbursts of anger
3. Difficulty concentrating
4. Hyper-vigilance
5. Exaggerated startle response

Criterion E: duration

Duration of the disturbance (symptoms in B, C, and D) is more than one month.

Criterion F: functional significance

The disturbance causes clinically significant distress or impairment in social, occupational, or other important areas of functioning.

Specify if:

Acute: if duration of symptoms is less than three months

Chronic: if duration of symptoms is three months or more

Specify if:

With or Without delay onset: Onset of symptoms at least six months after the stressor

References

1. American Psychiatric Association. (2000). Diagnostic and statistical manual of mental disorders (Revised 4th ed.). Washington, DC: Author.

New Diagnostic Criteria for PTSD to Be Released: DSM-5

The Diagnostic and Statistical Manual of Mental Disorders provides standard criteria and common language for the classification of mental disorders. It is published by the American Psychiatric Association. The fifth revision (DSM-5) is scheduled to release in May 2013: This will include changes to the diagnostic criteria for PTSD and Acute Stress Disorder.

The reason the PTSD criteria are being revised is to take into account the things we have learned from scientific research and clinical experience.

What can we tell you now about those revisions?

- Based on the proposed DSM-5 criteria, the prevalence of PTSD will be similar to what it is currently in DSM-IV.
- Symptoms are mostly the same. The 3 clusters of DSM-IV symptoms will be divided into 4 clusters in DSM-5: intrusion symptoms, avoidance symptoms, arousal/reactivity symptoms and negative mood and cognitions. It is proposed that a few symptoms will be added and some revised.
- Criterion A2 (requiring fear, helplessness or horror happen right after the trauma) will be removed.
- The diagnosis is proposed to move from the class of anxiety disorders into a new class of "trauma and stressor-related disorders."
- PTSD assessment measures, such as the CAPS and the PCL, are being revised by the National Center for PTSD to be made available upon the release of DSM-5.

PTSD History and Overview

Matthew J. Friedman, MD, PhD

A brief history of the PTSD diagnosis

The risk of exposure to trauma has been a part of the human condition since we evolved as a species. Attacks by saber tooth tigers or twenty-first century terrorists have probably produced similar psychological sequelae in the survivors of such violence. Shakespeare's Henry IV appears to meet many, if not all, of the diagnostic criteria for Posttraumatic Stress Disorder (PTSD), as have other heroes and heroines throughout the world's literature. The history of the development of the PTSD concept is described by Trimble (1).

In 1980, the American Psychiatric Association added PTSD to the third edition of its Diagnostic and Statistical Manual of Mental Disorders (DSM-III) nosologic classification scheme. Although controversial when first introduced, the PTSD diagnosis has filled an important gap in psychiatric theory and practice. From an historical perspective, the significant change ushered in by the PTSD concept was the stipulation that the etiological agent was outside the individual (i.e., a traumatic event) rather than an inherent individual weakness (i.e., a traumatic neurosis). The key to understanding the scientific basis and clinical expression of PTSD is the concept of "trauma."

In its initial DSM-III formulation, a traumatic event was conceptualized as a catastrophic stressor that was outside the range of usual human experience. The framers of the original PTSD diagnosis had in mind events such as war, torture, rape, the Nazi Holocaust, the atomic bombings of Hiroshima and Nagasaki, natural disasters (such as earthquakes, hurricanes, and volcano eruptions), and human-made disasters (such as factory explosions, airplane crashes, and automobile accidents). They considered traumatic events to be clearly different from the very painful stressors that constitute the normal vicissitudes of life such as divorce, failure, rejection, serious illness, financial reverses, and the like. (By this logic, adverse psychological responses to such "ordinary stressors" would, in DSM-III terms, be characterized as Adjustment Disorders rather than PTSD.) This dichotomization between traumatic and other stressors was based on the assumption that, although most individuals have the ability to cope with ordinary stress, their adaptive capacities are likely to be overwhelmed when confronted by a traumatic stressor.

PTSD is unique among psychiatric diagnoses because of the great importance placed upon the etiological agent, the traumatic stressor. In fact, one cannot make a PTSD diagnosis unless the patient has actually met the "stressor criterion," which means that he or she has been exposed to an historical event that is considered traumatic. Clinical experience with the PTSD diagnosis has shown, however, that there are individual differences regarding the capacity to cope with catastrophic stress. Therefore, while some people exposed to traumatic events do not develop PTSD, others go on to develop the full-blown syndrome. Such observations have prompted the recognition that trauma, like pain, is not an external phenomenon that can be completely objectified. Like pain, the traumatic experience is filtered through cognitive and emotional processes before it can be appraised as an extreme threat. Because of individual differences in this appraisal process, different people appear to have different trauma thresholds, some more protected from and some more vulnerable to developing clinical symptoms after exposure to extremely stressful situations. Although there is currently a renewed interest in subjective aspects of traumatic exposure, it must be emphasized that events such as rape, torture, genocide, and severe war zone stress are experienced as traumatic events by nearly everyone.

The DSM-III diagnostic criteria for PTSD were revised in DSM-III-R (1987), DSM-IV (1994), and DSM-IV-TR (2000). A very similar syndrome is classified in ICD-10 (The ICD-10 Classification of Mental and Behavioural Disorders: Clinical Descriptions and Diagnostic Guidelines). Diagnostic criteria for PTSD include a history of exposure to a traumatic event and symptoms from each of three symptom clusters: intrusive recollections, avoidant/numbing symptoms, and hyper-arousal symptoms. A fifth criterion concerns duration of symptoms. One important finding, which was not apparent when PTSD was first proposed as a diagnosis in 1980, is that it is relatively common. Recent data from the National Comorbidity Survey indicates PTSD prevalence rates are 5% and 10% respectively among American men and women (2). Rates of PTSD are much higher in postconflict settings such as Algeria (37%), Cambodia (28%), Ethiopia (16%), and Gaza (18%) (3).

Criteria for a PTSD diagnosis

As noted above, the "A" stressor criterion specifies that a person has been exposed to a catastrophic event involving actual or threatened death or injury, or a threat to the physical integrity of him/herself or others. During this traumatic exposure, the survivor's subjective response was marked by intense fear, helplessness, or horror.

The "B", or intrusive recollection, criterion includes symptoms that are perhaps the most distinctive and readily identifiable symptoms of PTSD. For individuals with PTSD, the traumatic event remains, sometimes for decades or a lifetime, a dominating psychological experience that retains its power to evoke panic, terror, dread, grief, or despair. These emotions manifest in daytime fantasies, traumatic nightmares, and psychotic reenactments known as PTSD flashbacks. Furthermore, trauma-related stimuli that trigger recollections of the original event have the power to evoke mental images, emotional responses, and psychological reactions associated with the trauma. Researchers can use this phenomenon to reproduce PTSD symptoms in the laboratory by exposing affected individuals to auditory or visual trauma-related stimuli (4).

The "C", or avoidant/numbing, criterion consists of symptoms that reflect behavioral, cognitive, or emotional strategies PTSD patients use in an attempt to reduce the likelihood that they will expose themselves to trauma-related stimuli. PTSD patients also use these strategies in an attempt to minimize the intensity of their psychological response if they are exposed to such stimuli. Behavioral strategies include avoiding any situation in which they perceive a risk of confronting trauma-related stimuli. In its extreme manifestation, avoidant behavior may superficially resemble agoraphobia because the PTSD individual is afraid to leave the house for fear of confronting reminders of the traumatic event(s). Dissociation and psychogenic amnesia are included among the avoidant/numbing symptoms and involve the individuals cutting off the conscious experience of trauma-based memories and feelings. Finally, since individuals with PTSD cannot tolerate strong emotions, especially those associated with the traumatic experience, they separate the cognitive from the emotional aspects of psychological experience and perceive only the former. Such "psychic numbing" is an emotional anesthesia that makes it extremely difficult for people with PTSD to participate in meaningful interpersonal relationships.

Symptoms included in the "D", or hyper-arousal, criterion most closely resemble those seen in panic and generalized anxiety disorders. While symptoms such as insomnia and irritability are generic anxiety symptoms, hyper-vigilance and startle are more characteristic of PTSD. The hyper-vigilance in PTSD may sometimes become so intense as to appear like frank paranoia. The startle response has a unique neurobiological substrate and may actually be the most pathognomonic PTSD symptom.

The "E", or duration, criterion specifies how long symptoms must persist in order to qualify for the (chronic or delayed) PTSD diagnosis. In DSM-III, the mandatory duration was six months. In DSM-III-R, the duration was shortened to one month, which it has remained.

The "F", or functional significance, criterion specifies that the survivor must experience significant social, occupational, or other distress as a result of these symptoms.

Assessing PTSD

Since 1980, there has been a great deal of attention devoted to the development of instruments for assessing PTSD. Keane and associates (4), working with Vietnam war-zone Veterans, have developed both psychometric and psychophysiologic assessment techniques that have proven to be both valid and reliable. Other investigators have modified such assessment instruments and used them with natural disaster survivors, rape/incest survivors, and other traumatized individuals. These assessment techniques have been used in the epidemiological studies mentioned above and in other research protocols.

Neurobiological research indicates that PTSD may be associated with stable neurobiological alterations in both the central and autonomic nervous systems. Psychophysiological alterations associated with PTSD include hyper-arousal of the sympathetic nervous system, increased sensitivity and augmentation of the acoustic-startle eye blink reflex, and sleep abnormalities. Neuropharmacologic and neuroendocrine abnormalities have been detected in most brain mechanisms that have evolved for coping, adaptation, and preservation of the species. These include the noradrenergic, hypothalamic-pituitary-adrenocortical, serotonergic, glutamatergic, thyroid, endogenous opioid, and other systems. Structural brain imaging suggests reduced volume of the hippocampus and anterior cingulated. Functional brain imaging suggests excessive amygdala activity and reduced activation of the prefrontal cortex. This information is reviewed extensively elsewhere (5).

Longitudinal research has shown that PTSD can become a chronic psychiatric disorder and can persist for decades and sometimes for a lifetime. Patients with chronic PTSD often exhibit a longitudinal course marked by remissions and relapses. There is also a delayed variant of PTSD in which individuals exposed to a traumatic event do not exhibit the PTSD syndrome until months or years afterward. Usually, the immediate precipitant is a situation that resembles the original trauma in a significant way (for example, a war Veteran whose child is deployed to a war zone or a rape survivor who is sexually harassed or assaulted years later).

If an individual meets diagnostic criteria for PTSD, it is likely that he or she will meet DSM-IV-TR criteria for one or more additional diagnoses (6-7). Most often, these comorbid diagnoses include major affective disorders, dysthymia, alcohol or substance abuse disorders, anxiety disorders, or personality disorders. There is a legitimate question whether the high rate of diagnostic comorbidity seen with PTSD is an artifact of our current decision-making rules for the PTSD diagnosis since there are not exclusionary criteria in DSM-III-R. In any case, high rates of comorbidity complicate treatment decisions concerning patients with PTSD since the clinician must decide whether to treat the comorbid disorders concurrently or sequentially.

Although PTSD continues to be classified as an Anxiety Disorder, areas of disagreement about its nosology and phenomenology remain. Questions about the syndrome itself include: what is the clinical course of untreated PTSD; are there different subtypes of PTSD; what is the distinction between traumatic simple phobia and PTSD; and what is the clinical phenomenology of prolonged and repeated trauma? With regard to the latter, Herman (8) has argued that the current PTSD formulation fails to characterize the major symptoms of PTSD commonly seen in victims of prolonged, repeated interpersonal violence such as domestic or sexual abuse and political torture. She has proposed an alternative diagnostic formulation that emphasizes multiple symptoms, excessive somatization, dissociation, changes in affect, pathological changes in relationships, and pathological changes in identity.

PTSD has also been criticized from the perspective of cross-cultural psychology and medical anthropology, especially with respect to refugees, asylum seekers, and political torture victims from non-Western regions. Clinicians and researchers working with such survivors argue that since PTSD has usually been diagnosed by clinicians from Western industrialized nations working with patients from a similar background, the diagnosis does not accurately reflect the clinical picture of traumatized individuals from non-Western traditional societies and cultures. Major gaps remain in our understanding of the effects of ethnicity and culture on the clinical phenomenology of posttraumatic syndromes. We have only just begun to apply vigorous ethnocultural research strategies to delineate possible differences between Western and non-Western societies regarding the psychological impact of traumatic exposure and the clinical manifestations of such exposure (9).

Treatment for PTSD

The many therapeutic approaches offered to PTSD patients are presented in Foa, Keane, Friedman and Cohen's (10) comprehensive book on treatment. The most successful interventions are cognitive-behavioral therapy (CBT) and medication. Excellent results have been obtained with some CBT combinations of exposure therapy and cognitive restructuring, especially with female victims of childhood or adult sexual trauma. Sertraline (Zoloft) and paroxetine (Paxil) are selective serotonin reuptake inhibitors (SSRI) that are the first medications to have received FDA approval as indicated treatments for PTSD. Success has also been reported with Eye Movement Desensitization and Reprocessing (EMDR), although rigorous scientific data are lacking and it is unclear whether this approach is as effective as CBT.

A frequent therapeutic option for mildly to moderately affected PTSD patients is group therapy, although empirical support for this is sparse. In such a setting, the PTSD patient can discuss traumatic memories, PTSD symptoms, and functional deficits with others who have had similar experiences. This approach has been most successful with war Veterans, rape/incest victims, and natural disaster survivors. It is important that therapeutic goals be realistic because, in some cases, PTSD is a chronic and severely debilitating psychiatric disorder that is refractory to current available treatments. The hope remains, however, that our growing knowledge about PTSD will enable us to design interventions that are more effective for all patients afflicted with this disorder.

There is great interest in rapid interventions for acutely traumatized individuals, especially with respect to civilian disasters, military deployments, and emergency personnel (medical personnel, police, and firefighters). This has become a major policy and public health issue since the massive traumatization caused by the September 11 terrorist attacks on the World Trade Center, Hurricane Katrina, the Asian tsunami, the Hatian eathquake, and the current wars in Iraq and Afghanistan. Currently, there is controversy about which interventions work best during the immediate aftermath of a trauma. Research on critical incident stress debriefing (CISD), an intervention used widely, has brought disappointing results with respect to its efficacy to attenuate posttraumatic distress or to forestall the later development of PTSD. The National Center for PTSD and the National Center for Child Traumatic Stress have developed an alternative early intervention, Psychological First Aid, that is available online. Promising results have also been shown with brief cognitive-behavioral therapy.

References

1. Trimble, M.D. (1985). Post-traumatic Stress Disorder: History of a concept. In C.R. Figley (Ed.), Trauma and its wake: The study and treatment of Post-Traumatic Stress Disorder. New York: Brunner/Mazel. Revised from Encyclopedia of Psychology, R. Corsini, Ed. (New York: Wiley, 1984, 1994)
2. Kessler, R.C., Sonnega, A., Bromet, E., Hughes, M. & Nelson, C.B. (1996). Posttraumatic Stress Disorder in the National Comorbidity Survey. Archives of General Psychiatry, 52, 1048-1060.
3. De Jong, J., Komproe, T.V.M., Ivan, H., von Ommeren, M., El Masri, M., Araya, M., Khaled, N.,van de Put, W., & Somasundarem, D.J. (2001). Lifetime events and Posttraumatic Stress Disorder in 4 postconflict settings. Journal of the American Medical Association, 286 (5), 555-562.
4. Keane, T.M., Wolfe, J., & Taylor, K.I. (1987). Post-traumatic Stress Disorder: Evidence for diagnostic validity and methods of psychological assessment. Journal of Clinical Psychology, 43, 32-43.
5. Friedman, M.J., Charney, D.S. & Deutch, A.Y. (1995) Neurobiological and clinical consequences of stress: From normal adaptation to PTSD. Philadelphia: Lippincott-Raven.
6. Kulka, R.A., Schlenger, W.E., Fairbank, J.A., Hough, R.L., Jordan, B.K., Marmar, C.R., & Weiss, D.S. (1990). Trauma and the Vietnam War generation. New York:Brunner/Mazel.

Complex PTSD

Many traumatic events (e.g. car accidents, natural disasters, etc.) are of time-limited duration. However, in some cases people experience chronic trauma that continues or repeats for months or years at a time. The current PTSD diagnosis often does not fully capture the severe psychological harm that occurs with prolonged, repeated trauma. People who experience chronic trauma often report additional symptoms alongside formal PTSD symptoms, such as changes in their self-concept and the way they adapt to stressful events.

Dr. Judith Herman of Harvard University suggests that a new diagnosis, Complex PTSD, is needed to describe the symptoms of long-term trauma (1). Another name sometimes used to describe the cluster of symptoms referred to as Complex PTSD is Disorders of Extreme Stress Not Otherwise Specified (DESNOS)(2). A work group has also proposed a diagnosis of Developmental Trauma Disorder (DTD) for children and adolescents who experience chronic traumatic events (3).

Because results from the DSM-IV Field Trials indicated that 92% of individuals with Complex PTSD/DESNOS also met diagnostic criteria for PTSD, Complex PTSD was not added as a separate diagnosis classification (4). However, cases that involve prolonged, repeated trauma may indicate a need for special treatment considerations.

What types of trauma are associated with Complex PTSD?

During long-term traumas, the victim is generally held in a state of captivity, physically or emotionally, according to Dr. Herman (1). In these situations the victim is under the control of the perpetrator and unable to get away from the danger.

Examples of such traumatic situations include:

- Concentration camps
- Prisoner of War camps
- Prostitution brothels
- Long-term domestic violence
- Long-term child physical abuse
- Long-term child sexual abuse
- Organized child exploitation rings

What additional symptoms are seen in Complex PTSD?

An individual who experienced a prolonged period (months to years) of chronic victimization and total control by another may also experience the following difficulties:

- Emotional Regulation. May include persistent sadness, suicidal thoughts, explosive anger, or inhibited anger.

- Consciousness. Includes forgetting traumatic events, reliving traumatic events, or having episodes in which one feels detached from one's mental processes or body (dissociation).
- Self-Perception. May include helplessness, shame, guilt, stigma, and a sense of being completely different from other human beings.
- Distorted Perceptions of the Perpetrator. Examples include attributing total power to the perpetrator, becoming preoccupied with the relationship to the perpetrator, or preoccupied with revenge.
- Relations with Others. Examples include isolation, distrust, or a repeated search for a rescuer.
- One's System of Meanings. May include a loss of sustaining faith or a sense of hopelessness and despair.

What other difficulties are faced by those who experienced chronic trauma?

Because people who experience chronic trauma often have additional symptoms not included in the PTSD diagnosis, clinicians may misdiagnose PTSD or only diagnose a personality disorder consistent with some symptoms, such as Borderline, Dependent, or Masochistic Personality Disorder.

Care should be taken during assessment to understand whether symptoms are characteristic of PTSD or if the survivor has co-occurring PTSD and personality disorder. Clinicians should assess for PTSD specifically, keeping in mind that chronic trauma survivors may experience any of the following difficulties:

- Survivors may avoid thinking and talking about trauma-related topics because the feelings associated with the trauma are often overwhelming.
- Survivors may use alcohol or other substances as a way to avoid and numb feelings and thoughts related to the trauma.
- Survivors may engage in self-mutilation and other forms of self-harm.
- Survivors who have been abused repeatedly are sometimes mistaken as having a "weak character" or are unjustly blamed for the symptoms they experience as a result of victimization.

Treatment for Complex PTSD

Standard evidence-based treatments for PTSD are effective for treating PTSD that occurs following chronic trauma. At the same time, treating Complex PTSD often involves addressing interpersonal difficulties and the specific symptoms mentioned above. Dr. Herman contends that recovery from Complex PTSD requires restoration of control and power for the traumatized person. Survivors can become empowered by healing relationships which create safety, allow for remembrance and mourning, and promote reconnection with everyday life (1).

References

1. Herman, J. (1997). Trauma and recovery: The aftermath of violence from domestic abuse to political terror. New York: Basic Books.
2. Ford, J. D. (1999). Disorders of extreme stress following war-zone military trauma: Associated features of Posttraumatic Stress Disorder or comorbid but distinct syndromes? Journal of Consulting and Clinical Psychology, 67, 3-12.
3. van der Kolk, B. (2005). Developmental trauma disorder. Psychiatric Annals, 35(5), 401-408.
4. Roth, S., Newman, E., Pelcovitz, D., van der Kolk, B., & Mandel, F. S. (1997). Complex PTSD in victims exposed to sexual and physical abuse: Results from the DSM-IV field trial for Posttraumatic Stress Disorder. Journal of Traumatic Stress, 10, 539-555.

Epidemiology of PTSD

Jaimie L. Gradus, DSc, MPH

What is epidemiology?

Epidemiology is the study of the distribution and determinants of disease in a population. Numerous studies have been conducted to assess the prevalence of PTSD across different populations. Below is a brief review of some of the major studies that have assessed the prevalence of PTSD in nationally representative samples as well as in samples of Veterans.

What is prevalence?

Prevalence is the proportion of people in a population that have a given disorder at a given time. It represents the existing cases of a disorder in a population or group. Prevalence estimates can be influenced by many factors including disorder occurrence (if new disorder occurrences increase, prevalence will increase) and the duration of the disorder (the longer people live with a disorder, the higher the prevalence). These estimates can also differ by demographic factors such as age and gender. It is important to qualify prevalence estimates with the time at which they were measured, as prevalence estimates can shift over time. Similarly, when interpreting prevalence estimates, it is important to keep in mind that prevalence is dynamic - it can change over people, places, and time.

Often prevalence is discussed in terms of lifetime prevalence. Other times, statistics will be given on current prevalence of PTSD in a given time frame, usually one year. At the end of this fact sheet you will find descriptions of other terms commonly used in epidemiology.

Prevalence of PTSD

U.S. National Comorbidity Survey Replication

The National Comorbidity Survey Replication (NCS-R), conducted between February 2001 and April 2003, comprised interviews of a nationally representative sample of 9,282 Americans aged 18 years and older. PTSD was assessed among 5,692 participants, using DSM-IV criteria. The NCS-R estimated the lifetime prevalence of PTSD among adult Americans to be 6.8% (1). Current past year PTSD prevalence was estimated at 3.5% (2).The lifetime prevalence of PTSD among men was 3.6% and among women was 9.7%. The twelve month prevalence was 1.8% among men and 5.2% among women (3).

These findings are very similar to those of the first National Comorbidity Survey. The original survey was conducted in the early 1990's and comprised interviews of a representative national sample of 8,098 Americans aged 15 to 54 years. In this earlier sample, the estimated prevalence of lifetime PTSD was 7.8% in the general population. Women (10.4%) were more than twice as likely as men (5%) to have PTSD at some point in their lives (4).

PTSD among children and adolescents

To date, no population-based epidemiological study has examined the prevalence of PTSD among children. However, studies have examined the prevalence of PTSD among high-risk children who have experienced specific traumatic events, such as abuse or natural disasters. Prevalence estimates from studies of this type vary greatly; however, research indicates that children exposed to traumatic events may have a higher prevalence of PTSD than adults in the general population (5).

Kilpatrick and colleagues (2003) assessed the prevalence of PTSD among adolescents based on data from the National Survey of Adolescents, which included a household probability sample of 4,023 adolescents between the ages of 12 and 17. Using DSM-IV criteria for PTSD, the six-month prevalence was estimated to be 3.7% for boys and 6.3% for girls (6).

PTSD in other countries

In the late 1990s the World Health Organization (WHO) began collecting epidemiological information on mental health disorders around the world. As of 2008, the research consortium had collected data from nearly 200,000 respondents in 27 countries (7). Published estimates are available of PTSD lifetime prevalence in most of the first 17 countries to complete the World Mental Health Surveys. In general, the estimates for lifetime PTSD prevalence range from a low of 0.3% in China to 6.1% in New Zealand. However, statistics reported from various countries are not directly comparable due to methodological differences in survey administration and sampling strategies.

National Vietnam Veterans Readjustment Study

The National Vietnam Veterans Readjustment Study (NVVRS) , conducted between November 1986 and February 1988, comprised interviews of 3,016 American Veterans selected to provide a representative sample of those who served in the armed forces during the Vietnam era. The estimated lifetime prevalence of PTSD among these Veterans was 30.9% for men and 26.9% for women. Of Vietnam theater Veterans, 15.2% of males and 8.1% of females were currently diagnosed with PTSD at the time the study was conducted (8).

Gulf War Veterans

Kang and others conducted a study to estimate the prevalence of PTSD in a population-based sample of 11,441 Gulf War Veterans from 1995 to 1997. PTSD was assessed using the PTSD Checklist (PCL;9) rather than interviews, with those scoring 50 or higher considered to have met criteria for PTSD. The prevalence of current PTSD in this sample of Gulf War Veterans was 12.1%. Further, the authors estimated the prevalence of PTSD among the total Gulf War Veteran population to be 10.1% (10).

Operation Enduring Freedom/Operation Iraqi Freedom

In 2008, the RAND Corporation, Center for Military Health Policy Research, published a population-based study that examined the prevalence of PTSD among previously deployed Operation Enduring Freedom and Operation Iraqi Freedom (Afghanistan and Iraq) service members (11). PTSD was assessed using the PCL, as in the Gulf War Veterans study. Among the 1,938 participants, the prevalence of current PTSD was 13.8%.

Commonly-used epidemiologic terms (12)

What is cumulative incidence?

Cumulative incidence (sometimes called "risk") is the proportion of people that develop a disorder over time among only the population at risk for that disorder. It represents the occurrence of new cases of a disorder in a population or group.

Like prevalence, it is important to qualify cumulative incidence estimates with the length of time over which they are measured (e.g. over 5 years). This is because a large cumulative incidence (or a large amount of new disorder occurrence) occurring over a short period of time has different intervention implications than a large cumulative incidence occurring over a very long period of time.

What is a cumulative incidence ratio?

A cumulative incidence ratio (sometimes called a risk ratio or a relative risk) is a relative measure of the cumulative incidence of disorder in a group exposed to a certain factor compared to the cumulative incidence of a disorder in a group that is unexposed to that factor.

What is the incidence rate?

An incidence rate is the proportion of people who develop a disorder over a period of time among the population at risk for that disorder. It represents the rate at which new cases of a disorder are occurring in a population or group. Incidence rates are expressed as the number of new cases of a disorder per person-time.

What is an incidence rate ratio?

A rate ratio (sometimes called relative risk), is a relative measure of incidence rate of disorder in a group exposed to a certain factor compared to the incidence rate of a disorder in a group that is unexposed to that factor.

What is an odds ratio?

An odds ratio (sometimes called a relative risk) is a relative measure of the odds of a disorder in a group exposed to a certain factor compared to the odds of a disorder in a group unexposed to that factor.

References

1. Kessler, R.C., Berglund, P., Delmer, O., Jin, R., Merikangas, K.R., & Walters, E.E. (2005). Lifetime prevalence and age-of-onset distributions of DSM-IV disorders in the National Comorbidity Survey Replication. Archives of General Psychiatry, 62(6): 593-602.
2. Kessler, R.C., Chiu, W.T., Demler, O., Merikangas, K.R., & Walters, E.E. (2005). Prevalence, severity, and comorbidity of 12-month DSM-IV disorders in the National Comorbidity Survey Replication. Archives of General Psychiatry, 62(6): 617-627.
3. National Comorbidity Survey. (2005). NCS-R appendix tables: Table 1. Lifetime prevalence of DSM-IV/WMH-CIDI disorders by sex and cohort. Table 2. Twelve-month prevalence of DSM-IV/WMH-CIDI disorders by sex and cohort. Accessed at: http://www.hcp.med.harvard.edu/ncs/publications.php
4. Kessler, R.C., Sonnega, A., Bromet, E. Hughes, M., & Nelson, C.B. (1995). Posttraumatic stress disorder in the National Comorbidity Survey. Archives of General Psychiatry, 52(12), 1048-1060.
5. Gabbay, V., Oatis, M.D., Silva, R.R., & Hirsch, G. (2004). Epidemiological aspects of PTSD in children and adolescents. In Raul R. Silva (Ed.), Posttraumatic Stress Disorder in Children and Adolescents: Handbook (1-17). New York: Norton.
6. Kilpatrick, D.G., Ruggiero, K.J., Acierno, R., Saunders, B.E., Resnick, H.S., & Best, C.L. (2003). Violence and risk of PTSD, major depression, substance abuse/dependence, and comorbidity: results from the National Survey of Adolescents. Journal of Consulting and Clinical Psychology, 71(4), 692-700.
7. Kessler, R.C., & ÃœstÃ¼n, T. B. (Eds.). (2008).The WHO World Mental Health Surveys: global perspectives on the epidemiology of mental disorders. New York: Cambridge University Press, 1-580.
8. Kulka, R.A., Schlenger, W.A., Fairbanks, J.A., Hough, R.L., Jordan, B.K., Marmar, C.R.,... Cranston, A.S. (1990). Trauma and the Vietnam War generation: Report of findings from the National Vietnam Veterans Readjustment Study. New York: Brunner/Mazel.
9. Weathers, F., Litz, B., Herman, D., Huska, J., & Keane, T. (October 1993). The PTSD Checklist (PCL): Reliability, Validity, and Diagnostic Utility. Paper presented at the Annual Convention of the International Society for Traumatic Stress Studies, San Antonio, TX.

Overview of Psychotherapy for PTSD

Hamblen, PhD, Schnurr, PhD, Rosenberg, MA, & Eftekhari, PhD

Several clinical practice guidelines offer recommendations for the treatment of PTSD, for example see the VA/DoD PTSD Clinical Practice Guideline (2010). These guidelines come from different federal agencies, professional organizations, and countries (1-5). The Institute of Medicine (IOM) also published a report in 2007 evaluating the evidence on PTSD treatment (6). The guidelines unanimously recommend cognitive behavioral therapies as the most effective treatment for PTSD, and the majority of guidelines recommend Eye Movement Desensitization and Reprocessing (EMDR) as well.

Cognitive behavioral treatments typically include a number of components, including psychoeducation, anxiety management, exposure, and cognitive restructuring. Exposure and cognitive restructuring are thought to be the most effective components.

Exposure-based treatments

The greatest number of studies has been conducted on exposure-based treatments, which involve having survivors repeatedly re-experience their traumatic event. There is strong evidence for exposure therapy (7-12), and of the various approaches, Prolonged Exposure (PE) has received the most attention. PE (8) includes both imaginal exposure and in vivo exposure to safe situations that have been avoided because they elicit traumatic reminders.

In a multisite randomized controlled trial of PE in female Veterans and active-duty personnel with PTSD, those who received PE experienced greater reduction of PTSD symptoms relative to women who received present-centered therapy and were less likely to meet PTSD diagnostic criteria (13). Moreover, PE was more effective than the combination of PE plus stress inoculation training (SIT), SIT alone, or a waitlist control in female sexual assault survivors (10). In addition, PE alone and PE plus cognitive restructuring reduced PTSD and depression relative to a waitlist control in intention-to-treat and completer samples (11).

Cognitive approaches

Cognitive interventions also are widely supported in treatment guidelines (12, 15-17). Cognitive Processing Therapy (CPT; 18), one of the most well-researched cognitive approaches, has a primary focus on challenging and modifying maladaptive beliefs related to the trauma, but also includes a written exposure component.

Veterans with chronic military-related PTSD who received CPT showed better improvements in PTSD and comorbid symptoms than the waitlist control group (19). A dismantling study of CPT then examined the relative utility of the full protocol compared with its components: cognitive therapy alone and written exposure alone (20). Results indicated significant improvement in PTSD and depression for participants in all three treatments. However, the cognitive therapy alone resulted in faster improvement than the written exposure alone, with the effects of the full protocol of CPT falling in-between (20). Both CPT and PE have shown great success in outcome research; thus, one logical research question involves whether one is more effective than the other. In a head-to-head comparison, CPT and PE were equally effective in treating PTSD and depression in female sexual assault survivors (7).

Ehlers and Clark have also developed a cognitive therapy for PTSD that involves three goals: modifying excessively negative appraisals, correcting autobiographical memory disturbances, and removing problematic behavioral and cognitive strategies (21). Elements unique to Ehlers and Clark's cognitive therapy include performing actions that are incompatible with the memory or engaging in behavioral experiments. Two randomized controlled trials have compared cognitive therapy to a waitlist, both with positive results (15, 16).

Adding components

Some investigators have added a novel component to an effective treatment in hopes of further optimizing outcomes (22-27). Three groups of investigators compared an enhanced treatment to a waitlist control group: Cloitre and colleagues (23) sequenced skills training in affect and interpersonal regulation before PE; Falsetti and colleagues (24) developed Multiple Channel Exposure Therapy, a combination of PE, CPT, and interoceptive exposure techniques for panic disorder; and Lindauer and colleagues (27) developed Brief Eclectic Therapy, a combination of psychodynamic and cognitive behavioral therapy. These studies showed that the combined treatments were effective, but not whether the additional components enhanced the standard treatments.

Glynn and colleagues (25) compared exposure therapy alone with exposure therapy followed by behavioral family therapy, and Arntz and colleagues (22) compared imaginal exposure alone with imaginal exposure plus imagery rescripting. In both studies, the combined treatment did not result in a greater reduction of PTSD severity, which suggests that the novel component was not necessary. However, statistical power may have been too low to compare the active treatments adequately.

EMDR

In addition to cognitive behavioral therapies, EMDR is recommended in most practice guidelines. Patients receiving EMDR engage in imaginal exposure to a trauma while simultaneously performing saccadic eye movements. There is good evidence that EMDR is more effective than waitlist and nonspecific comparison conditions (28-30). Further, two well-controlled studies compared EMDR to PE. One study found equivalent results (29) while the other found PE to be superior (30). Additional research has investigated the mechanism of action in EMDR, and there is growing evidence that the theorized eye movements are an unnecessary component (31), suggesting that perhaps the mechanism of action is exposure.

Other approaches

Other treatments in addition to cognitive behavioral therapy and EMDR may be effective; however, at this time we do not have enough evidence to confidently indicate that they are effective. For example, despite the appeal of group treatments, results of the few randomized controlled trials of group therapy have been mixed (32-36). In addition, psychodynamic therapy, hypnotherapy, and trauma desensitization were more effective than a waitlist control group in one trial (40). Rogerian supportive therapy was less effective in treating symptoms of PTSD and anxiety than cognitive behavioral therapy in one study (41).

Acceptance and Commitment Therapy (ACT), which is considered a third wave behavioral therapy, focuses on reducing experiential avoidance and engagement with maladaptive thoughts and encourages clients to approach activities consistent with their personal values. Several case studies have documented support for ACT in the treatment of PTSD (37, 38). However, no trials of ACT for PTSD have been published to date. Finally, there is also interest in alternative medicine treatments. For example, acupuncture was as effective as group cognitive behavioral treatment, and both were more effective than the waitlist condition (39).

Conclusion

Overall, cognitive behavioral therapies such as Prolonged Exposure and Cognitive Processing Therapy, as well as Eye Movement Desensitization Reprocessing, are considered first-line treatments for PTSD and have strong evidence bases. Components of these treatments have been combined with other interventions, with no support for improved benefits over the standard treatments alone. Other interventions, such as group treatment, show promise; however, more research is needed before drawing firm conclusions about their effectiveness.

References

1. Australian Centre for Posttraumatic Mental Health. (2007). Australian guidelines for the treatment of adults with acute stress disorder and posttraumatic stress disorder. Melbourne, Victoria: Author.
2. Foa, E. B., Keane, T.M., & Friedman, M.J. (2009). Effective treatments for PTSD: Practice guidelines from the International Society for Traumatic Stress Studies (1-388). New York: Guilford.
3. National Collaborating Centre for Mental Health. (2005). Post-traumatic stress disorder: The management of PTSD in adults and children in primary and secondary care (1-167). London: Gaskell and the British Psychological Society.
4. Ursano, R. J., Bell, C., Eth, S., Friedman, M. J., Norwood, A. E., & Pfefferbaum, B. (2004). Practice guideline for the treatment of patients with acute stress disorder and posttraumatic stress disorder [Special issue]. American Journal of Psychiatry, (Suppl), 161.
5. VA/DoD Clinical Practice Guideline Working Group. (December 2003). Management of post-traumatic stress. Washington, DC: Veterans Health Administration, Department of

Veterans Affairs and Health Affairs; Department of Defense; Office of Quality and Performance, publication 10Q-CPG/PTSD-03.
6. Institute of Medicine (2008). Treatment of posttraumatic stress disorder: An assessment of the evidence. Washington, DC: The National Academies Press.
7. Resick, P. A., Nishith, P., Weaver, T. L., Astin, M. C., & Feuer, C. A. (2002). A comparison of cognitive-processing therapy with prolonged exposure and a waiting condition for the treatment of chronic posttraumatic stress disorder in female rape victims. Journal of Consulting and Clinical Psychology, 70, 867-879.
8. Foa, E. B., & Rothbaum, B. O. (1998). Treating the trauma of rape: Cognitive behavioral therapy for PTSD (1-266). New York: Guilford.
9. Bryant, R. A., Moulds, M. L., Guthrie, R. M., Dang, S. T., & Nixon, R. D. V. (2003). Imaginal exposure alone and imaginal exposure with cognitive restructuring in treatment of posttraumatic stress disorder. Journal of Consulting and Clinical Psychology, 71, 706-712.
10. Foa, E. B., Dancu, C.V., Hembree, E. A., Jaycox, L.H., Meadows, E. A., & Street, G.P. (1999). A comparison of exposure therapy, stress inoculation training, and their combination for reducing posttraumatic stress disorder in female assault victims. Journal of Consulting and Clinical Psychology, 67, 194-200.
11. Foa, E. B., Hembree, E. A., Cahill, S. P., Rauch, S. A. M., Riggs, D. S., & Feeny, N. C. (2005). Randomized trial of prolonged exposure for posttraumatic stress disorder with and without cognitive restructuring: Outcome at academic and community clinics. Journal of Consulting and Clinical Psychology, 73, 953-964.
12. Marks, I., Lovell, K., Noshirvani, H., Livanou, M., & Thrasher, S. (1998). Treatment of posttraumatic stress disorder by exposure and/or cognitive restructuring. Archives of General Psychiatry, 55, 317-324.
13. Schnurr, P. P., Friedman, M. J., Engel, C. C., Foa, E. B., Shea, M. T., Chow, B. K., ...Bernardy, N. (2007). Cognitive behavioral therapy for posttraumatic stress disorder in women: A randomized controlled trial. Journal of the American Medical Association, 297, 820-830.
14. Tarrier, N., Pilgrim, H., Sommerfield, C., Faragher, B., Reynolds, M., & Graham, E. (1999). A randomized trial of cognitive therapy and imaginal exposure in the treatment of chronic posttraumatic stress disorder. Journal of Consulting and Clinical Psychology, 67, 13-18.
15. Ehlers, A., Clark, D. M., Hackmann, A., McManus F., & Fennell, M. J. V. (2005). Cognitive therapy for post-traumatic stress disorder: Development and evaluation. Behavioral Research and Therapy, 43, 413-431.
16. Duffy, M., Gillespie, K., & Clark, D. M. (2007). Post-traumatic stress disorder in the context of terrorism and other civil conflict in Northern Ireland: Randomised controlled trial. British Medical Journal, 334, 1147-1150.
17. Mueser, K. T., Rosenberg, S. D., Xie, H., Jankowski. J. K., Bolton, E. E., & Lu, W. (2008). A randomized controlled trial of cognitive-behavioral treatment of Posttraumatic Stress Disorder in severe mental illness. Journal of Consulting and Clinical Psychology, 76, 259-271.
18. Resick, P.A., & Schnicke, M. K. (1996). Cognitive processing therapy for rape victims: A treatment manual. Newbury Park, CA: Sage Publications.

19. Monson, C. M., Schnurr, P. P., Resick, P. A., Friedman, M. J., Young-Xu, Y., & Stevens, S. P. (2006). Cognitive processing therapy for veterans with military-related posttraumatic stress disorder. Journal of Consulting and Clinical Psychology, 74, 898-907.
20. Resick, P. A., Galovski, T. E., Uhlmansiek, M. O., Scher, C. D., Clum, G. A., & Young-Xu, Y. (2008). A randomized clinical trial to dismantle components of cognitive processing therapy for posttraumatic stress disorder in female victims of interpersonal violence. Journal of Consulting and Clinical Psychology, 76, 243-258.
21. Ehlers, A., & Clark, D. M. (2000). A cognitive model of posttraumatic stress disorder. Behavioral Research and Therapy, 38, 319-345.
22. Arntz, A., Tiesema, M., & Kindt, M. (2007). Treatment of PTSD: A comparison of imaginal exposure with and without imagery rescripting. Journal of Behavioral Therapy and Experimental Psychiatry, 38, 345-370.
23. Cloitre, M., Koenen, K. C., Cohen, L.R., & Han, H. (2002). Skills training in affective and interpersonal regulation followed by exposure: A phase-based treatment for PTSD related to childhood abuse. Journal of Consulting and Clinical Psychology, 70, 1067-1074.
24. Falsetti, S.A., Resnick, H. S., & Davis, J. L. (2008). Multiple channel exposure therapy for women with PTSD and comorbid panic attacks. Cognitive Behaviour Therapy, 37, 117-130.
25. Glynn, S. M., Eth, S., Randolph, E.T., Foy, D. W., Urbaitis, M., & Boxer, L. (1999). A test of behavioral family therapy to augment exposure for combat-related posttraumatic stress disorder. Journal of Consulting and Clinical Psychology, 67, 243-251.
26. Hogberg, G., Pagani, M., Sundin, O., Soares, J. J. F., Averg-Wistedt, A., & Tarnell, B. (2008). Treatment with eye movement desensitization and reprocessing of chronic post-traumatic stress disorder in public transportation workers: Outcome is stable in 35-month follow-up. Psychiatric Research, 159, 101-108.
27. Lindauer, R. J. L., Gersons, B. P. R., van Meijel, E. P. M., Els, P. M., Blom, K., & Carlier, I. V. E. (2005). Effects of brief eclectic psychotherapy in patients with posttraumatic stress disorder: Randomized clinical trial. Journal of Traumatic Stress, 18, 205-212.
28. Chemtob, C. M., Tolin, D. F., van der Kolk, B., & Pitman, R. K. (2000). Eye movement desensitization and reprocessing. In E. Foa, T. M. Keane, & M. J. Friedman (Eds.), Effective treatments for PTSD (139-154). New York: Guilford.
29. Rothbaum, B. O., Astin, M. C., & Marsteller, F. (2005). Prolonged exposure versus eye movement desensitization and reprocessing (EMDR) for PTSD rape victims. Journal of Traumatic Stress, 18, 607-616.
30. Taylor, S., Thordarson, D. S., Maxfield, L., Fedoroff, I.C., Lovell, K., & Ogrodniczuk, J.S. (2003). Comparative efficacy, speed, and adverse effects of three PTSD treatments: Exposure therapy, EMDR, and relaxation training. Journal of Consulting and Clinical Psychology, 71, 330-338.
31. Davidson, P. R., & Parker, K. C. H. (2001). Eye movement desensitization and reprocessing (EMDR): A meta-analysis. Journal of Consulting and Clinical Psychology, 69, 305-316.

32. Alexander, P. C., Neimeyer, R. A., Follette, V. M., Moore, M. K., & Harter, S. L. (1989). A comparison of group treatments of women sexually abused as children. Journal of Consulting and Clinical Psychology, 57, 479-483.
33. Chard, K. M. (2005). An evaluation of cognitive processing therapy for the treatment of posttraumatic stress disorder related to childhood sexual abuse. Journal of Consulting and Clinical Psychology, 75, 965-971.
34. Krupnik, J. L., Green, B. L., Stockton, P., Miranda, J., Krause, E. D., & Mete, M. (2008). Group interpersonal psychotherapy for low-income women with posttraumatic stress disorder. Psychotherapy Research, 18, 497-507.
35. Schnurr, P. P., Friedman, M. J., Foy, D. W., Shea, M. T., Hsieh, F. Y., & Lavori, P. W. (2003). Randomized trial of trauma-focused group therapy for posttraumatic stress disorder: Results from a Department of Veterans Affairs Cooperative Study. Archives of General Psychiatry, 60, 481-489.
36. Zlotnick, C., Shea, M. T., Rosen, K. H., Simpson, E., Mulrenin, K., Begin, A., & Pearlstein, T. (1997). An affect-management group for women with posttraumatic stress disorder and histories of childhood sexual abuse. Journal of Traumatic Stress, 10, 425-436.
37. Batten, S. V., & Hayes, S. C. (2005). Acceptance and commitment therapy in the treatment of comorbid substance abuse and post-traumatic stress disorder: A case study. Clinical Case Studies, 4, 246-262.
38. Orsillo, S. M., & Batten, S. V. (2008). Acceptance and commitment therapy in the treatment of posttraumatic stress disorder. Behavior Modification, 29, 95-129.
39. Hollifield, M., Sinclair-Lian, N., Warner, T. D., & Hammerschlag, R. (2007). Acupuncture for posttraumatic stress disorder: A randomized controlled pilot trial. Journal of Nervous and Mental Disorders, 195, 504-513.
40. Brom, D., Kleber, R. J., & Defares, P. B. (1989). Brief psychotherapy for posttraumatic stress disorders. Journal of Consulting and Clinical Psychology, 57, 607-612.
41. Cottraux, J., Note, B., & Chen, Y. (2008). Randomized controlled comparison of cognitive behavior therapy with Rogerian supportive therapy in chronic post-traumatic stress disorder: A 2-year follow-up. Psychotherapy and Psychosomatics, 77, 101-110.

Clinician's Guide to Medications for PTSD

Matt Jeffreys, MD

Overview

Posttraumatic Stress Disorder (PTSD) has biological, psychological, and social components. Medications can be used in treatment to address the biological basis for PTSD symptoms and co-morbid Axis I diagnoses. Medications may benefit psychological and social symptoms as well. While studies suggest that cognitive behavioral therapies such as prolonged exposure (PE) and cognitive processing therapy (CPT) have greater effects in improving PTSD symptoms than medications, some people may prefer medications or may benefit from receiving a medication in addition to psychotherapy.

Placebo-controlled double-blind randomized controlled trials are the gold standard for pharmacotherapy. Less strongly supported evidence includes open trials and case reports. It is important for the clinician to question the level of evidence supporting the medications prescribed in PTSD treatment. There are a variety of factors influencing prescribing, including marketing, patient preferences, and clinical custom, all of which can be inconsistent with the evidence base.

Currently, the evidence base is strongest for the selective serotonin reuptake inhibitors (SSRIs). The only two FDA approved medications for the treatment of PTSD are sertraline (Zoloft) and paroxetine (Paxil) (1, 2). All other medication uses are off label, though there are differing levels of evidence supporting their use. In addition to sertraline and paroxetine, there is strong evidence for the SSRI fluoxetine (Prozac) and for the serotonin norepinephrine reuptake inhibitor (SNRI) venlafaxine (Effexor) which are considered first-line treatments in the VA/DoD Clinical Practice Guideline for PTSD. There are a number of biological changes which have been associated with PTSD, and medications can be used to modify the resultant PTSD symptoms. Veterans whose PTSD symptoms have been present for many years pose a special challenge. Studies indicate they are more refractory to the beneficial effects of medications for PTSD symptoms (3).

What core PTSD symptoms are we trying to treat?

The three main PTSD symptom clusters are listed below:

- Re-experiencing. Examples include nightmares, unwanted thoughts of the traumatic events, and flashbacks.
- Avoidance. Examples include avoiding triggers for traumatic memories including places, conversations, or other reminders. The avoidance may generalize to other previously enjoyable activities.
- Hyperarousal. Examples include sleep problems, concentration problems, irritability, increased startle response, and hypervigilance.

What are some of the biological disturbances found in PTSD?

Some of the main biological disturbances in PTSD can be conceptualized as dysregulation of the naturally occurring stress hormones in the body and increased sensitivity of the stress and anxiety circuits in the brain. There is dysregulation of adrenergic mechanisms that mediate the classical fight-flight or freeze response. Yehuda and others have found that patients with PTSD have hypersensitivity of the hypothalamic-pituitary-adrenal axis (HPA) as compared to patients without PTSD (4). Patients have a much greater variation in their levels of adrenocorticoids than patients without PTSD. Other researchers have found differences in both brain structures and brain circuits that process threatening input between patients with PTSD and those without.

It is not known for certain whether these changes were present before the traumatic event and predisposed the person to developing PTSD or whether these changes were the result of the PTSD. One way to think of this is the fear circuitry no longer being integrated with the executive centers of the brain located in the prefrontal cortex (5). Even minor stresses may then set off the "fight or flight" response in patients with PTSD which leads to increased heart rate, sweating, rapid breathing, tremors, and other symptoms of hyperarousal listed above.

How do medications help regulate these responses?

The medications prescribed for treating PTSD symptoms act upon neurotransmitters related to the fear and anxiety circuitry of the brain including serotonin, norepinephrine, GABA, and dopamine among many others. There is great interest in developing newer, more specific agents than are currently available to target the PTSD symptoms described earlier while also minimizing potential side effects of medications.

Studies show that a number of medications are helpful in minimizing the three symptom clusters of PTSD. Most of the time, medications do not entirely eliminate symptoms but provide a symptom reduction and are best used in conjunction with an ongoing program of trauma specific psychotherapy for patients such as PE or CPT.

How do we measure the effects of treatment?

There are a number of self-rating scales and structured clinical interviews to monitor the effects of treatment. Two examples include the Post-Traumatic Stress Disorder Checklist (PCL) and the Clinician Administered PTSD Scale (CAPS). The PCL military or civilian version is an example of a patient self-rating form without stressor information, while the CAPS is an example of a structured clinical interview including stressor information.

There is literature supportive of a strong correlation between the two measures, and the PCL has the advantage of being quick and easy to administer. Both the PCL and the CAPS provide a quantitative measure of the patient's PTSD symptoms and response to treatment over time. This information enhances the clinical assessment and interview with the patient.

What is the evidence base for the specific groups of medications used for PTSD treatment?

Selective Serotonin Reuptake Inhibitors (SSRIs)

These medications are the only FDA approved medications for PTSD. SSRIs primarily affect the neurotransmitter serotonin which is important in regulating mood, anxiety, appetite, and sleep and other bodily functions. This class of medication has the strongest empirical evidence with well designed randomized controlled trials (RCTs) and is the preferred initial class of medications used in PTSD treatment (1, 2). Exceptions may occur for patients based upon their individual histories of side effects, response, and comorbidities.

- An example of an exception would be a PTSD patient with comorbid Bipolar Disorder. In this patient, there is a risk of precipitating a manic episode with the SSRIs. Each patient varies in their response and ability to tolerate a specific medication and dosage, so medications must be tailored to individual needs.

Research has suggested that maximum benefit from SSRI treatment depends upon adequate dosages and duration of treatment. Treatment adherence is key to successful pharmacotherapy treatment for PTSD. Examples of the SSRIs and some typical dosage ranges are listed below:

- Sertraline (Zoloft) 50 mg to 200 mg daily
- Paroxetine (Paxil) 20 to 60 mg daily
- Fluoxetine (Prozac) 20 mg to 60 mg daily

Note: : Only sertraline and paroxetine have been approved for PTSD treatment by the FDA. All other medications described in this guide are being used "off label" and may have empirical support but have not been through the FDA approval process for PTSD.

Other newer antidepressants for PTSD

Antidepressants that work through other neurotransmitter combinations or through different mechanisms for altering serotonin neurotransmission are also helpful in PTSD. Venlafaxine acts primarily as a serotonin reuptake inhibitor at lower dosages and as a combined serotonin and norepinephrine reuptake inhibitor at higher dosages. It is now a recommended first-line treatment for PTSD in the revised VA/DoD Clinical Practice Guideline for PTSD based upon large multi-site RCTs (6).

There have been smaller RCTs with mirtazapine as well as open trials (7). Mirtazapine may be particularly helpful for treatment of insomnia in PTSD. Trazodone is also commonly used for insomnia in PTSD even though there is little empirical evidence available for its use. Nefazodone is still available in a generic form but carries a black box warning regarding liver failure, so liver function tests need to be monitored and precautions taken as recommended in the medication's prescribing information (8, 9).

Examples of the newer antidepressants for PTSD and some typical dosage ranges are listed below:

- Mirtazapine (Remeron) 7.5 mg to 45 mg daily
- Venlafaxine (Effexor) 75 mg to 300 mg daily
- Nefazodone (Serzone) 200 mg to 600 mg daily

All of the antidepressants described above are also effective in treating comorbid Major Depressive Disorder (MDD) which often accompanies PTSD. While bupropion is useful in treating comorbid MDD, it has not been shown effective for PTSD in controlled trials (10). A recent trial showed superior outcomes on MDD when mirtazapine was combined initially with antidepressants versus patients being randomized to monotherapy with fluoxetine (11). This raises important questions regarding costs, side effects, and patient preferences which merit further study.

Mood stabilizers for PTSD

These medications, also known as anticonvulsants or anti-epileptic drugs, either block glutamate or potentiate GABA or do both. Topiramate has demonstrated promising results in randomized controlled trials with civilians and Veterans with PTSD, but currently is listed as having no demonstrated benefit in the VA/DoD Clinical Practice Guideline for PTSD.

There are two double-blind, placebo-controlled trials evaluating topiramate as monotherapy in civilians with PTSD (12,13). The trial published in 2007 included 38 participants and found no significant difference in total CAPS scores between topiramate and placebo. The 2010 trial included 38 participants and demonstrated a significant decrease in total CAPS scores. There are also two published double-blind, placebo-controlled trials evaluating topiramate as adjunctive treatment for PTSD in Veterans (14,15). The trial published in 2004 included 67 participants and found a significant decrease in the total CAPS score. The 2007 trial included 40 participants and showed no significant decrease in total CAPS scores.

Based upon the current studies, topiramate could provide a useful option for clinicians in treatment of PTSD symptoms in patients who fail first line pharmacotherapy. Further studies and meta-analyses are needed regarding the place of topiramate in PTSD treatment (16).

Otherwise, despite some promising open label studies, other RCTs have been negative for this group of medications in treating PTSD (17). As a group, this class of medications is helpful in the treatment of comorbid Bipolar Disorder and PTSD. Patients who have Bipolar Disorder and PTSD often benefit from these medications since SSRIs and other antidepressants sometimes precipitate a manic episode. Most require some regular lab work to monitor side effects. Neither lamotrigine nor topiramate require lab work but must be titrated slowly according to package insert directions to avoid potentially serious side effects. Examples are given below:

- Carbamazepine (Tegretol). Requires monitoring of white blood cell counts due to risk of agranulocytosis. Will self-induce its own metabolism and increase the metabolism of other medications including oral contraceptives.

- Divalproex (Depakote). Requires monitoring of liver function tests due to risk of hepatotoxicity and platelet levels due to risk of thrombocytopenia. Target dosage is 10 times the patient's weight in pounds.
- Lamotrigine (Lamictal). Requires slow titration according to the package insert due to risk of serious rash.
- Topiramate (Topimax). Requires clinical monitoring for glaucoma, sedation, dizziness and ataxia.

Atypical antipsychotics for PTSD

While originally developed for patients with a psychotic disorder, this class of medications is being applied to patients with many other psychiatric disorders including PTSD. They act primarily on the dopaminergic and serotonergic systems. They can be used when a person with PTSD has a psychotic disorder. There is some evidence that they are useful in ameliorating psychotic symptoms in PTSD patients. The real question is whether these medications are useful in PTSD when psychotic disorder or symptoms are not present.

Previously, a number of small single-site studies suggested that atypical antipsychotic agents were effective adjunctive treatment for PTSD patients who had poor responses to first-line SSRIs or SNRIs (18). A recent large-scale multi-site trial of risperidone as an adjunctive agent for SSRI poor/partial responders showed that there was no benefit (in comparison with a placebo group) for adjunctive use of this agent. As a result the recent VA/DoD PTSD Clinical Practice Guideline has been revised as follows:

- Atypical antipsychotics are not recommended as mono-therapy for PTSD.
- Risperidone (Risperdal) is contraindicated for use as an adjunctive agent - potential harm (side effects) exceeds benefits.
- There is insufficient evidence to recommend any other atypical antipsychotic as an adjunctive agent for PTSD.

Other medications for PTSD

There are a number of other medications that can be helpful for specific PTSD symptoms or that have been used as second line agents including the following:

- Prazosin (Minipress)
- Tricyclic Antidepressants (such as Imipramine)
- Monoamine Oxidase Inhibitors (MAOIs) (such as Phenelzine)

Prazosin has been found to be effective in RCTs in decreasing nightmares in PTSD. It blocks the noradrenergic stimulation of the alpha 1 receptor. Its effectiveness for PTSD symptoms other than nightmares has not been determined at this time (19, 20).

The tricyclic antidepressants and MAOIs act on a number of neurotransmitters. While there are RCTs supporting their use, these medications are not used as first line agents due to their safety and side effect profiles (21, 22). The tricyclics have quinidine like effects on the heart and can cause ventricular arrhythmias especially in overdose.

The MAOI phenezine has been shown to be effective in PTSD. Careful management of the MAOIs and strict dietary controls are important because they can cause potentially fatal hypertensive reactions when taken with other medications or certain foods rich in tyramine. MAOIs can also provoke the potentially fatal serotonin syndrome when used concurrently with SSRIs.

Buspirone and beta blockers are sometimes used adjunctively in treatment of hyperarousal symptoms, though there is little empirical evidence in support of this. Buspirone acts on serotonin and might reduce anxiety in PTSD without sedation or addiction. There are some case reports supporting its use. Beta blockers block the effects of adrenalin (epinephrine) on organs such as the heart, sweat glands, and muscles. There is interest in using beta blockers to prevent PTSD, though the evidence at the current time does not support this. Beta blockers reduce the peripheral manifestations of hyperarousal and may reduce aggression as well. They may be used for comorbid conditions such as performance anxiety in the context of social phobia for example.

Benzodiazepines and PTSD

Benzodiazepines act directly on the GABA system which produces a calming effect on the nervous system. This is the only potentially addictive group of medications discussed. Studies have not shown them to be useful in PTSD treatment as they do not work on the core PTSD symptoms (23, 24). There are several other concerns with the benzodiazepines including potential disinhibition, difficulty integrating the traumatic experience, interfering with the mental processes needed to benefit from psychotherapy, and addiction. Because of their potential for addiction and disinhibition, they must be used with great caution in PTSD. Examples are listed below:

- Lorazepam (Ativan)
- Clonazepam (Klonopin)
- Alprazolam (Xanax)

Developing new medications for PTSD

The pathophysiological mechanism of PTSD in the nervous system is unknown, but there are several interesting areas that could lead to new drug development for the treatment or the prevention of PTSD. There are competing hypotheses about the role of glucocorticoids following trauma and their effects on the brain. It might be possible to intervene at some level in the hypothalamic-pituitary-adrenal axis or at the level of the glucocorticoid receptors in the brain to modulate the effects of stress and the development of PTSD. Neuropeptides such as Substance P and Neuropeptide Y (NPY) have been implicated in PTSD as well (25). Combat troops exposed to stress have been found to have lower levels of NPY. Perhaps altering this neuromodulator could improve the resiliency of the brain to the effects of trauma. One challenge with this new focus research is dealing with the blood-brain barrier for introducing neuropeptides into the brain.

D-cycloserine (DCS) has been used in panic disorder, specifically phobia and social phobia, to enhance the effects of exposure therapy (26). It is a partial agonist of the glutamatergic N-methyl-D-aspartate (NMDA) receptor. Based upon animal research supporting the use of DCS to facilitate extinction of conditioned fear, it is hypothesized that use of DCS in conjunction with exposure therapy may reduce the number of psychotherapy sessions required (27). This line of research recognizes a paradigm shift in the use of pharmacotherapy to assist learning during psychotherapy as opposed to directly affecting PTSD symptoms (28).

Memantine (Namenda) is a drug of much interest in preventing neurodegeneration by protecting against glutamatergic destruction of neurons. It has been approved for use in certain neurodegenerative conditions such as Alzheimer's disease. This drug could be potentially useful in preventing hypothesized neurodegneration in the hypothalamus and memory loss in PTSD.

Current research is looking towards the possibility of one day intervening early in the course of PTSD with a combination of psychotherapy and pharmacotherapy that would prevent the development of the pathophysiology of PTSD in the brain.

Common barriers to effective medication treatment in PTSD

There are several common barriers to effective medication treatment for PTSD which are listed below. These need to be addressed with patients in an ongoing dialogue with their prescribing clinician. Side effects need to be examined and discussed, weighing the risks and the benefits of continued medication treatment. Patient education about the side effects, necessary dosages, duration of treatment, and taking the medications consistently can improve adherence. A simple intervention of setting up a pill organizer weekly can go a long way to improve adherence.

- Fear of possible medication side effects including sexual side effects
- Feeling medication is a "crutch" and that taking it is a weakness
- Fear of becoming addicted to medications
- Taking the medication only occasionally when symptoms get severe
- Not being sure how to take the medication
- Keeping several pill bottles and not remembering when the last dosage was taken
- Using "self medication" with alcohol or drugs with prescribed medications

A final word regarding medications and treatment for PTSD

A more comprehensive discussion of pharmacotherapy can be found online in the VA/DoD PTSD Clinical Practice Guidelines. Based upon current knowledge, most prescribing clinicians view pharmacotherapy as an important adjunct to the evidenced based psychotherapies for PTSD. While there are few direct comparisons of pharmacotherapy and psychotherapy, the greatest benefits of treatment appear to come from evidenced based therapies such as CPT, PE, and patients need to be informed of the risks and benefits of the differing treatment options. When using a combined approach of medication and therapy, it is important to keep several practices in mind.

If treatment is being provided by a therapist and a prescriber, it is important for the clinicians to discuss treatment response and to coordinate efforts. It is important for the prescribing clinician to have an ongoing dialogue with the patient about their medications and side effects. It is important for the patient to take an active role in his or her treatment rather than feeling they are a passive recipient of medications to alleviate their symptoms. There is emerging evidence that when given a choice, most patients will select psychotherapy treatment for their PTSD symptoms rather than medications.

Important Considerations

- Patients with anxiety disorders including PTSD may be very aware of their somatic reactions, and it is important to start low and go slow often on dosage adjustments to improve patient adherence.
- Be sure to ask female patients of childbearing age about contraception when prescribing medication.
- Be sure to ask all patients about substance abuse as well.
- Once mediations are started, it is crucial that the provider remember to discontinue medications which are not proving efficacious and to simplify the number and types of medications used whenever possible.

References

1. Brady K, Pearlstein T, Asnis GM, Baker D, Rothbaum B, Sikes CR, Farfel GM. Efficacy and safety of sertraline treatment of posttraumatic stress disorder: a randomized controlled trial. JAMA. 2000 Apr 12;283(14):1837-44.
2. Marshall RD, Beebe KL, Oldham M, Zaninelli R. Efficacy and safety of paroxetine treatment for chronic PTSD: a fixed-dose, placebo-controlled study. Am J Psychiatry. 2001 Dec;158(12):1982-8.
3. Randomized, double blind comparison of sertraline and placebo for posttraumatic stress disorder in Department of Veterans Affairs setting. Friedman MJ, Marmar CR, Baker DG, Sikes CR, Farfel GM. J Clin Psychiatry. 2007 May; 68(5):711-20.
4. Yehuda R, Bierer LM. Transgenerational transmission of cortisol and PTSD risk. Prog Brain Res. 2008; 167:121-35.
5. Lanius RA, Vermetten E, Loewenstein RJ, Brand B, Schmahl C, Bremner JD, Spiegel D. Emotion modulation in PTSD: Clinical and neurobiological evidence for a dissociative subtype. Am J Psychiatry. 2010 Jun; 167(6):640-7.
6. Davidson J, Baldwin D, Stein DJ, Kuper E, Benattia I, Ahmed S, Pedersen R, Musgnung J. Treatment of posttraumatic stress disorder with venlafaxine extended release: a 6-month randomized controlled trial. Arch Gen Psychiatry. 2006 Oct;63(10):1158-65.
7. Chung MY, Min KH, Jun YJ, Kim SS, Kim WC, Jun EM. Efficacy and tolerability of mirtazapine and sertraline in Korean veterans with posttraumatic stress disorder: a randomized open label trial. Hum Psychopharmacol. 2004 Oct;19(7):489-94.
8. Davis LL, Jewell ME, Ambrose S, Farley J, English B, Bartolucci A, Petty F. A placebo-controlled study of nefazodone for the treatment of chronic posttraumatic stress disorder: a preliminary study. J Clin Psychopharmacol. 2004 Jun;24(3):291-7.

9. McRae AL, Brady KT, Mellman TA, Sonne SC, Killeen TK, Timmerman MA, Bayles-Dazet W. Comparison of nefazodone and sertraline for the treatment of posttraumatic stress disorder. Depress Anxiety. 2004;19(3):190-6.
10. Becker ME, Hertzberg MA, Moore SD, Dennis MF, Bukenya DS, Beckham JC. A placebo-controlled trial of bupropion SR in the treatment of chronic posttraumatic stress disorder. J Clin Psychopharmacol. 2007 Apr; 27(2):193-7.
11. Blier P, Ward HE, Tremblay P, Laberge L, Hérbert C, Bergeron R. Combination of antidepressant medications from treatment initiation for major depressive disorder: a double-blind randomized study. Am J Psychiatry. 2010 Mar; 167(3):281-8.
12. Tucker P, Trautman RP, Wyatt DB, Thompson J, We SC, Capece JA, Rosenthal NR. Efficacy and safety of topiramate monotherapy in civilian posttraumatic stress disorder: a randomized, double-blind, placebo-controlled study. J Clin Psychiatry. 2007;68:201-6.
13. Yeh MS, Mari JJ, Costa MC, Andreoli SB, Bressan RA, Mello MF. A double-blind randomized controlled trial to study the efficacy of topiramate in a vivilian sample of PTSD. CNS Neurosci Ther. 2011 Oct;17(5):305-10.
14. Akuchekian S, Amant S. The comparison of topiramate and placebo in the treatment of posttraumatic stress disorder: a randomized, double-blind study. J Res Med Sci. 2004;9(5):240-4.
15. Lindley SE, Carlson EB, Hill K. A randomized, double-blind, placebo-controlled trial of augmentation topiramate for chronic combat-related posttraumatic stress disorder. J Clin Psychopharmacol. 2007;27: 677-81.
16. Andrus MR, Gilbert E. Treatment of civilian and combat-related posttraumatic stress disorder with topiramate. Ann Pharmacother. 2010 Nov;44: 1810-6.
17. Davis LL, Davidson JR, Ward LC, Bartolucci A, Bowden CL, Petty F. Divalproex in the treatment of posttraumatic stress disorder: a randomized, double-blind, placebo-controlled trial in a veteran population. J Clin Psychopharmacol. 2008 Feb;28(1):84-8.
18. Pae CU, Lim HK, Peindl K, Ajwani N, Serretti A, Patkar AA, Lee C. The atypical antipsychotics olanzapine and risperidone in the treatment of posttraumatic stress disorder: a meta-analysis of randomized, double-blind, placebo-controlled clinical trials. Int Clin Psychopharmacol. 2008 Jan;23(1):1-8.
19. Krystal JH, Rosenheck RA, Cramer JA, Vessicchio JC, Jones KM, Vertrees JE, Horney RA, Huang GD, Stock C. Adjunctive risperidone treatment for antidepressant-resistant symptoms of chronic military service-related PTSD. JAMA. 2011;306(5):493-502.
20. Raskind MA, Peskind ER, Hoff DJ, Hart KL, Holmes HA, Warren D, Shofer J, O'Connell J, Taylor F, Gross C, Rohde K, McFall ME. A parallel group placebo controlled study of prazosin for trauma nightmares and sleep disturbance in combat veterans with post-traumatic stress disorder. Biol Psychiatry. 2007 Apr 15;61(8):928-34.
21. Davidson J, Kudler H, Smith R, Mahorney SL, Lipper S, Hammett E, Saunders WB, Cavenar JO Jr. Treatment of posttraumatic stress disorder with amitriptyline and placebo. Arch Gen Psychiatry. 1990 Mar;47(3):259-66.
22. Frank JB, Kosten TR, Giller EL Jr, Dan E. A randomized clinical trial of phenelzine and imipramine for posttraumatic stress disorder. Am J Psychiatry. 1988 Oct;145(10):1289-91.
23. Braun P, Greenberg D, Dasberg H, Lerer B. Core symptoms of posttraumatic stress disorder unimproved by alprazolam treatment. J Clin Psychiatry. 1990 Jun;51(6):236-8.

24. Gelpin E, Bonne O, Peri T, Brandes D, Shalev AY. Treatment of recent trauma survivors with benzodiazepines: a prospective study. J Clin Psychiatry. 1996 Sep;57(9):390-4.
25. Morales-Medina JC, Dumont Y, Quirion R. A possible role of neuropeptide Y in depression and stress. Brain Res. 2010 Feb 16; 1314:194-205.
26. Otto MW, Tolin DF, Simon NM, Pearlson GD, Basden S, Meunier SA, Hofmann SG, Eisenmenger K, Krystal JH, Pollack MH. Efficacy of d-cycloserine for enhancing response to cognitive-behavior therapy for panic disorder. Biol Psychiatry. 2010 Feb 15;67(4):365-70.
27. Ressler KJ, Rothbaum BO, Tannenbaum L, Anderson P, Graap K, Zimand E, Hodges L, Davis M. Cognitive enhancers as adjuncts to psychotherapy: Use of D-cycloserine in phobic individuals to facilitate extinction of fear.Arch Gen Psychiatry. 2004; 61: 1136-1144.
28. Rothbaum BO, Gerardi M, Bradley B, and Friedman MJ. Evidence-based treatments for posttraumatic stress disorder in Operation Enduring Freedom and Operation Iraqi Freedom military personnel. In JI Ruzek, PP Schnurr, JJ Vasterling, & MJ Friedman (Eds.), Caring for Veterans with Deployment-Related Stress Disorders (pp. 215-239) Washington DC: American Psychological Association.

ARMY ENLISTED MILITARY OCCUPATIONAL SPECIALTIES

MOS	JOB TITLE	HIGHLY PROBABLE	MODERATE	LOW
35T	MILITARY INTELLIGENCE SYSTEMS MAINTAINER/INTEGRATOR			X
35X	INTELLIGENCE SENIOR SERGEANT/CHIEF INTELLIGENCE SERGEANT			X
35Y	CHIEF COUNTER INTELLIGENCE/HUMAN INTELLIGENCE SERGEANT			X
35Z	SIGNALS INTELLIGENCE (ELECTRONIC WARFARE) / SENIOR SERGEANT / CHIEF		X	
36B	FINANCIAL MANAGEMENT TECHNICIAN			X
37F	PSYCHOLOGICAL OPERATIONS SPECIALIST			X
38B	CIVIL AFFAIRS SPECIALIST			X
42A	HUMAN RESOURCES SPECIALIST			X
42F	HUMAN RESOURCES INFORMATION SYSTEMS MANAGEMENT SPECIALIST			
42R	ARMY BANDPERSON	X		
42S	SPECIAL BAND MEMBER	X		
43F	HUMAN RESOURCES INFORMATION SYSTEMS MANAGEMENT SPEC			X
46Q	PUBLIC AFFAIRS SPECIALIST			X
46R	PUBLIC AFFAIRS BROADCAST SPECIALIST		X	
46Z	CHIEF PUBLIC AFFAIRS NCO			X
51C	AQUISITION, LOGISTICS & TECHNOLOGY (AL&t) CONTRACTING NCO			X
56M	CHAPLAIN ASSISTANT			X
68A	BIOMEDICAL EQUIPMENT SPECIALIST			X
68D	OPERATING ROOM SPECIALIST			X
68E	DENTAL SPECIALIST		X	
68G	PATIENT ADMINISTRATION SPECIALIST			X
68H	OPTICAL LABORATORY SPECIALIST			X
68J	MEDICAL LOGISTICS SPECIALIST			X
68K	MEDICAL LABORATORY SPECIALIST			X
68M	NUTRITION CARE SPECIALIST			X
68P	RADIOLOGY SPECIALIST			X
68Q	PHARMACY SPECIALIST			X
68R	VETERINARY FOOD INSPECTION SPECIALIST			X
68S	PREVENTIVE MEDICINE SPECIALIST			X
68T	ANIMAL CARE SPECIALIST			X
68V	RESPIRATORY SPECIALIST			X
68W	HEALTH CARE SPECIALIST			X
68X	BEHAVIORAL HEALTH SPECIALIST			X
68Z	CHIEF MEDICAL NCO			X
74D	CHEMICAL, BIOLOGICAL, RADIOLOGICAL AND NUCLEAR (CBRN) SPECIALIST		X	
79R	RECRUITER NCO			X
79S	CAREER COUNSELOR			X
79T	RECRUITING & RETENTION NCO (ARMY NATIONAL GUARD OF THE UNITED STATES)			X
79V	RETENTION & TRANSITION NCO, USAR			X

C.Robeson

All entries were approved by the Service Department,
and all entries in Red were provided by the Service Department

MOS	JOB TITLE	HIGHLY PROBABLE	MODERATE	LOW
14Z	AIR DEFENSE ARTILLERY SENIOR SERGEANT	X		
15B	AIRCRAFT POWERPLANT REPAIRER	X		
15D	AIRCRAFT POWERTRAIN REPAIRER	X		
15F	AIRCRAFT ELECTRICIAN	X		
15G	AIRCRAFT STRUCTURAL REPAIRER	X		
15H	AIRCRAFT PNEUDRAULICS REPAIRER	X		
15J	OH-58D/ARH ARMAMENT/ELECTRICAL/AVIONICS SYSTEMS REPAIRER	X		
15K	AIRCRAFT COMPONENTS REPAIR SUPERVISOR	X		
15M	UH-1 HELICOPTER REPAIRER (RC)	X		
15N	AVIONICS MECHANIC	X		
15P	AVIATION OPERATIONS SPECIALIST	X		
15Q	AIR TRAFFIC CONTROL OPERATOR	X		
15R	AH-64 ATTACK HELICOPTER REPAIRER	X		
15S	OH-58D/ARH HELICOPTER REPAIRER	X		
15T	UH-60 HELICOPTER REPAIRER	X		
15U	CH-47 HELICOPTER REPAIRER	X		
15V	OBSERVATION/SCOUT HELICOPTER REPAIRER (RC)	X		
15W	UNMANNED AERIAL VEHICLE OPERATOR		X	
15X	AH-64A ARMAMENT/ELECTRICAL/AVIONICS SYSTEMS REPAIRER	X		
15Y	AH-64D ARMAMENT/ELECTRICAL/AVIONICS SYSTEMS REPAIRER	X		
15Z	AIRCRAFT MAINTENANCE SENIOR SERGEANT	X		
18B	SPECIAL FORCES WEAPONS SERGEANT	X		
18C	SPECIAL FORCES ENGINEER SERGEANT	X		
18D	SPECIAL FORCES MEDICAL SERGEANT	X		
18E	SPECIAL FORCES COMMUNICATIONS SERGEANT	X		
18F	SPECIAL FORCES ASSISTANT OPERATIONS & INTELLIGENCE SERGEANT	X		
18Z	SPECIAL FORCES SENIOR SERGEANT	X		
19D	CAVALRY SCOUT	X		
19K	M1 ARMOR CREWMAN	X		
19Z	ARMOR SENIOR SERGEANT	X		
21B	COMBAT ENGINEER (conversion to 12B 1 Oct 10)	X		
21C	BRIDGE CREWMEMBER (conversion to 12C 1 Oct 10)	X		
21D	DIVER (conversion to 12D 1 Oct 10)		X	
21E	CONSTRUCTION EQUIPMENT OPERATOR (conversion to 12N 1 Oct 10)	X		
21G	QUARRYING SPECIALIST (RC) (conversion to 12G 1 Oct 10)	X		
21H	CONSTRUCTION ENGINEERING SUPERVISOR (conversion to 12H 1 Oct 10)	X		
21K	PLUMBER (conversion to 12K 1 Oct 10)		X	
21M	FIREFIGHTER (conversion to 12M 1 Oct 10)	X		
21N	HORIZONTAL CONSTRUCTION ENGINEER (conversion to 12N 1 Oct 10)	X		

C.Robeson

MOS	JOB TITLE	HIGHLY PROBABLE	MODERATE	LOW
88H	CARGO SPECIALIST		X	
88K	WATERCRAFT OPERATOR		X	
88L	WATERCRAFT ENGINEER		X	
88M	MOTOR TRANSPORT OPERATOR		X	
88N	TRANSPORTATION MANAGEMENT COORDINATOR			X
88P	RAILWAY EQUIPMENT REPAIRER (RC)	X		
88T	RAILWAY SECTION REPAIRER (RC)	X		
88U	RAILWAY OPERATIONS CREWMEMBER (RC)	X		
88Z	TRANSPORTATION SENIOR SERGEANT	X		
89A	AMMUNITION STOCK CONTROL & ACCOUNTING SPECIALIST			X
89B	AMMUNITION SPECIALIST			X
89D	EXPLOSIVE ORDNANCE DISPOSAL SPECIALIST	X		
91A	M1 ABRAHMS TANK SYSTEM MAINTAINER (FORMERLY 63A)	X		
91B	WHEELED VEHICLE MECHANIC (FORMERLY 63B)	X		
91C	UTILITIES EQUIPMENT REPAIRER (FORMERLY 52C)	X		
91D	POWER-GENERATION EQUIPMENT REPAIRER (FORMERLY 52D)	X		
91E	ALLIED TRADES SPECIALIST (FORMERLY 44E)	X		
91F	SMALL ARMS/ARTILLERY REPAIRER (FORMERLY 45B)		X	
91G	FIRE CONTROL REPAIRER (FORMERLY 45G)	X		
91H	TRACK VEHICLE REPAIRER (FORMERLY 63H)	X		
91J	QUARTERMASTER & CHEMICAL EQUIPMENT REPAIRER (FORMERLY 63J)		X	
91K	ARMAMENT REPAIRER (FORMERLY 45K)		X	
91L	CONSTRUCTION EQUIPMENT REPAIRER (FORMERLY 62B)	X		
91M	BRADLEY FIGHTING VEHICLE SYSTEM MAINTAINER (FORMERLY 63M)	X		
91P	ARTILLERY MECHANIC (FORMERLY 63D)	X		
91W	METAL WORKER (FORMERLY 44B)	X		
91X	MAINTENANCE SUPERVISOR (FORMERLY 63X)	X		
91Z	MECHANICAL MAINTENANCE SUPERVISOR (FORMERLY 63Z)	X		
92A	AUTOMATED LOGISTICAL SPECIALIST			X
92F	PETROLEUM SUPPLY SPECIALIST			X
92G	FOOD SERVICE SPECIALIST (FORMERLY 94B)			X
92L	PETROLEUM LABORATORY SPECIALIST			X
92M	MORTUARY AFFAIRS SPECIALIST			X
92R	PARACHUTE RIGGER			X
92S	SHOWER/LAUNDRY & CLOTHING REPAIR SPECIALIST			X
92W	WATER TREATMENT SPECIALIST		X	
92Y	UNIT SUPPLY SPECIALIST			X
92Z	SENIOR NONCOMISSIONED LOGISTICIAN			X
94A	LAND COMBAT ELECTRONIC MISSILE SYSTEM REPAIRER		X	

C.Robeson

Appendix Section 7
Agent Orange

AGENT ORANGE STORED IN THE US

Arizona

Location: Pinal Mountains near Globe, AZ
Dates: 1965, 1966, 1968, and 1969
Project Description: In 1965, the USFS began a land improvement program in the Pinal Mountains. The program called for spraying an area of chaparral with herbicides to accomplish the objectives of multiple land use.
Agents: 2,4-D isooctyl-ester, 2,4,5-t isooctyl-ester, silvex, propyleneglycolbutylether ester, 2,4,5-T butyl ester, 2,4,5-T 2-e-h e
DoD Involvement: No

Arkansas

Location: Fort Chaffee, AR
Dates: 5/16/1967 - 5/18/1967, 7/22/1967 - 7/23/1967, 8/23/1967 - 8/24/1967
Project Description: During the period of 12/1966 - 10/1967, a comprehensive short-term evaluation was conducted by personnel from Fort Derrick's Plant Science Lab in coordination with contract research on formulations by chemical industry and field tests by USDA and U of HI.
Agents: Basic, in-house, improved desiccants and Orange, Blue
DoD Involvement: Yes

California

Location: Brawley, CA
Dates: 1950-51
Project Description: The purpose was to determine means of accomplishing defoliation of tropical forest vegetation by application of a chemical agent. Here, irrigation water studies were done with the agent. H.F. Arle worked here.
Agents: 2,4-D
DoD Involvement: Undetermined

Florida

Location: Orlando, FL; Cocoa, FL
Dates: 1944
Project Description: Tests were conducted in 1944 by the Army in Orlando and Cocoa areas of Florida to determine the value of ammonium thiocyanate and chloride as marking and defoliation agents. They were conducted initially at ground level and later from aircraft.
Agents: Ammonium thiocyanate and zinc chloride
DoD Involvement: Yes

Location: Near Lake George, FL
Dates: Spring 1944
Project Description: The purpose was to determine means of accomplishing defoliation of tropical forest vegetation by application of a chemical agent. Spraying here.
Agents: Zinc chloride
DoD Involvement: Yes

Location: Orlando, FL at Army Grove Air Force's Tactical Center
Dates: 3/14/1944, 4/12/1944
Project Description: The purpose was to determine means of accomplishing defoliation of tropical forest vegetation by application of a chemical agent.
Agents: Ammonium thiocynate, zinc chloride, sodium nitrate, sodium arsenate, sodium fluoride
DoD Involvement: Yes

Location: Marathon, FL
Dates: 3/21/1944 - 3/23/1944
Project Description: The purpose was to determine means of accomplishing defoliation of tropical forest vegetation by application of a chemical agent. Spraying was done here.
Agents: Zinc chloride, ammonium sulphamate, ammonium thiocynate
DoD Involvement: Yes

Location: Bushnell Army Air Field, FL
Dates: 2/1945
Project Description: Small plot experiments were commenced to test the effectiveness of LN agents. Various trials were done under contract with the USDA, aided by personnel at Camp Detrick. Here, it was aerial spray experiments on potted plants.
Agents: LN *phenoxy
DoD Involvement: Yes

Location: Bushnell Army Air Field, FL
Dates: 2/1945 - 4/1945
Project Description: Trials, performed by C.W.S. personnel from Camp Detrick, MD, tested the practicability of severely injuring or destroying crop plants sprayed from smoke tanks mounted on tactical aircraft.
Agents: 2,4-D and its ammonium salt
DoD Involvement: Yes

Location: Avon Air Force Base, FL
Dates: 2/1951 - 4/1951
Project Description: Trials were conducted at Avon Air Force Base, FL by Chemical Corps with personnel of the Air Force and Navy to determine the practical effectiveness of spraying pure anticrop agents from at low volume from aircraft. C-47 and Navy XBT2D-1 aircraft with various nozzles were used.
Agents: Butyl 2,4 D
DoD Involvement: Yes

Location: Englin Air Force Base, FL
Dates: 11/1952 - 12/1952
Project Description: Two trials: Chemical Corps- concerned with basic fundamental work, using 2,4-D, Air Force-concerned with evaluating prototype large capacity spray system for aircraft installation using 2,4,5-T, primarily. Used 3 atomizing nozzles: Bete Fog Nozzles, Whirljet Spray Nozzles, and Fogjet 1.5F50.
Agents: 2,4-D, 2,4,5-T: 143 and 974, respectively
DoD Involvement: Yes

Location: Avon Park Air Force Base, FL
Dates: Spring 1954
Project Description: Series of tests were conducted at Avon Park AFB during the spring of 1954 to study the behavior of chemical anticrop aerial sprays when released from high-speed jet aircraft. The Navy F3D jet fighter was used with Aero 14A Airborne Spray Tanks to disperse the anticrop agents.
Agents: Butyl 2,4-D, butyl 2,4,5-T, Isopropyl 2,4-D
DoD Involvement: Yes

Location: Jacksonville, FL
Dates: 7/18/1962 - 7/21/1962
Project Description: The HIDAL was used successfully on an H-34 helicopter to spray herbicidal materials. Therefore, it had not been calibrated previously. Spray tests were performed to do so. This was done under order by OSD/ARPA.
Agents: Purple, Fuel Oil, Mix
DoD Involvement: Yes

Location: Eglin AFB, FL, C-52A test area
Dates: 1962-70
Project Description: CPT John Hunter discussed vegetation changes and ecological studies of the 2 square mile test area which had been sprayed with herbicides over the period 1962-70.
Agents: Orange (1962-68), Purple (1962-68), White (1967-70), Blue (1968-70)
DoD Involvement: Yes

Location: Apalachicola National Forest near Sophoppy, FL
Dates: 5/3/1967 - 5/8/1967
Project Description: During the period of 12/1966 - 10/1967, a comprehensive short-term evaluation was conducted by personnel from Fort Detrick's Plant Science Lab in coordination

with contract research on formulations by chemical industry and field tests by USDA and U of HI.
Agents: Basic desiccants and Orange/Blue
DoD Involvement: Yes

Location: Eglin AFB, FL
Dates: 6/11/1968-9/12/1968
Project Description: A spread factor study was performed by the Army to correlate the spherical drop sizes of both Orange and Stull Bifluid defoliants. It involved development of new techniques to determine spread factors over an extended range of drop sizes. A spinning cup drop generator was used.
Agents: Orange, Bifluid #1, Bifluid#2, Stull Bifluid
DoD Involvement: Yes

Location: 2 areas in FL, 2 areas in GA, and 1 in TN
Dates: 1968
Project Description: In 1968, emphasis was given to soil applied herbicides for grass control. Applications were made by a jeep-mounted sprayer on small plots or by helicopter on larger plots.
Agents: Bromacil, Tandex, monuron, diuron, and fenuron
DoD Involvement: Undetermined

Georgia

Location: Georgia and Tennessee
Dates: 1964
Project Description: In 1964, helicopter spray tests were conducted on transmission line rights-of-way by the Georgia Power Company and Tennessee Valley Authority in collaboration with Fort Detrick to evaluate effectiveness of several commercially available herbicides.
Agents: Diquat and Tordon 101, various
DoD Involvement: Yes

Location: Fort Gordon, GA
Dates: 7/15/1967 - 7/17/1967
Project Description: During the period of 12/1966 - 10/1967, a comprehensive short-term evaluation was conducted by personnel from Fort Detrick's Plant Science Lab in coordination with contract research on formulations by chemical industry and field tests by USDA and U of HI.
Agents: In-house desiccants mixtures and formulations, Orange and Blue
DoD Involvement: Yes

Location: 2 areas in GA, 2 areas in FL, and 1 in TN
Dates: 1968
Project Description: In 1968, emphasis was given to soil applied herbicides for grass control. Applications were made by a jeep-mounted sprayer on small plots or by helicopter on larger plots.

Agents: Bromacil, Tandex, monuron, diuron, and fenuron
DoD Involvement: Undetermined

Hawaii

Location: Hilo, HI
Dates: 12/1966
Project Description: Field tests of defoliants were designed to evaluate such variables as rates, volume of application, season, and vegetation. Data from aerial application tests at several CONUS and OCONUS locations are provided in tables. There were Fort Detrick personnel there.
Agents: Orange
DoD Involvement: Yes

Location: State Forest area, 3500 ft.elevation on slope of Mauna Loa, near Hilo, HI
Dates: 12/2/1966, 12/4/1966, 1/12/1967
Project Description: The purpose of this project was to evaluate iso-octyl ester of picloram (TORDON) in mixtures with ORANGE, as a candidate defoliant agent, using ORANGE as standard. There were personnel from Fort Detrick there.
Agents: Orange, M-3140, TORDON ester, 2,4-D ester, 2,4,5-T ester
DoD Involvement: Undetermined

Location: Kauai, HI
Dates: 1967
Project Description: Field tests of defoliants were designed to evaluate such variables as rates, volume of application, season, and vegetation. Data from aerial application tests at several CONUS and OCONUS locations are provided in tables.
Agents: Orange
DoD Involvement: Yes

Location: Kauai Branch Station near Kapaa, Kawai, HI
Dates: 6/1967, 10/1967, 12/1967, 2/1968
Project Description: During the period of 12/1966 - 10/1967, a comprehensive short-term evaluation was conducted by personnel from Fort Detrick's Plant Science Lab in coordination with contract research on formulations by chemical industry and field tests by USDA and U of HI.
Agents: Blue,diquat,paraquat, Orange, PCP, Picloram, White, HCA, 2,4,5T, Endothall
DoD Involvement: Yes

Indiana

Location: Vigo Plant CWS, Terre Haute, IN
Dates: 5/1945 - 9/1945
Project Description: Small plot experiments were commenced to test the effectiveness of LN agents. Various trials were done under contract with the USDA, aided by personnel at Camp

Detrick. Here, it was aerial trials spraying field grown plants.
Agents: LN *phenoxy
DoD Involvement: Yes

Location: Jefferson Proving Grounds, Madison, IN
Dates: Summer 1945
Project Description: Small plot experiments were commenced to test the effectiveness of LN agents. Various trials were done under contract with the USDA, aided by personnel at Camp Detrick. Here, it was dropping trials.
Agents: LN *phenoxy
DoD Involvement: Yes

Kansas

Location: Hays, KS; Langdon, ND
Dates: 1960
Project Description: Two studies on the stem rust of wheat were conducted during 1960 to obtain data on the establishment, development, and destructiveness of artificially induced stem rust epiphytotics.
Agents: Stem rust of wheat
DoD Involvement: Undetermined

Kentucky

Location: Fort Knox, KY
Dates: 1945
Project Description: In 1945, a special project known as Sphinx was conducted jointly by CWS and the ARML to investigate the use of chemical agents for increasing the flammability of vegetation prior to flame attack.
Agents: Various
DoD Involvement: Yes

Maryland

Location: Camp Detrick, MD - Fields A, B, and C
Dates: 1946-47
Project Description: The experiments were directed mainly towards the investigation of plant inhibitors applied as sprays or to the soil in the solid form to be taken up by the roots.
Agents: 2,4,5-T, 2,4,5-T triethanolamine, tributylphosphate, ethyl 2,4-D, butyl 2,4,5-Ttriet 2,4-D
DoD Involvement: Yes

Location: Camp Detrick, MD - Fields C, D, and E
Dates: 1948
Project Description: The experiments were directed mainly towards the investigation of plant inhibitors applied as sprays or to the soil in the solid form to be taken up by the roots.

Agents: 2,4,5-T, isopropyl phenol carbamate, LN-2426, 2,4-D
DoD Involvement: Yes

Location: Camp Detrick, MD - Fields C, D, and E
Dates: 1949
Project Description: The experiments were directed mainly towards the investigation of plant inhibitors applied as sprays or to the soil in the solid form to be taken up by the roots. Experiments were done by Ennis, DeRose, Newman, Williamson, DeRigo, and Thomas.
Agents: Triethelyne. 2,4,5-T, carbamates
DoD Involvement: Yes

Location: Camp Detrick, MD - Fields A, B, D, and E
Dates: 1950
Project Description: The experiments were directed mainly towards the investigation of plant inhibitors applied as sprays or to the soil in the solid form to be taken up by the roots. Experiments were done by Ennis, DeRose, Acker, Newman, Williamson, and Zimmerly.
Agents: 2464, butyl 2,4-D, 974, butyl 2,4,5-T, q:q 143 and 974
DoD Involvement: Yes

Location: Camp Detrick, MD - Field F
Dates: 1950-51
Project Description: The experiments were directed mainly towards the investigation of plant inhibitors applied as sprays or to the soil in the solid form to be taken up by the roots. Experiments were done by Acker, DeRose, McLane, Newman, Williamson, Baker, Dean, Johnson, Taylor, Walker, and Zimmerly.
Agents: 2464, carbamate, butyl 2,4-D, 143 and 974 (orange?),2,4,5-T, 2,4-D, Orange
DoD Involvement: Yes

Location: Area B, Camp Detrick, MD
Dates: Spring/Summer 1953
Project Description: Personnel at Camp Detrick tested the feasibility of using an experimental spray tower for applying a mixture of chemical anticrop agents to broad-leaf crops.
Agents: 3:1 mixture 2, 4-D and 2, 4, 5-T
DoD Involvement: Yes

Location: Fort Detrick, MD; Fort Ritchie, MD
Dates: 1956-57
Project Description: In 1956 And 1957, defoliation and desiccation were carried out at Fort Detrick and Fort Ritchie, Maryland by the Chemical Corps and Biological Warfare Research. These were bench tests.
Agents: Various, 577 compounds
DoD Involvement: Yes

Location: Fort Detrick, MD
Dates: 8/1961 - 6/1963
Project Description: From 8/1961 to 6/1963, compounds were spray-tested in the greenhouse to

evaluate them as effective defoliants, desiccants, and herbicides.
Agents: 1410 compounds
DoD Involvement: Yes

Location: Fort Ritchie, MD
Dates: 1963
Project Description: Various studies were done to explore the effectiveness of different herbicides. They were all field trials. These studies were done by personnel from the US Army Biological Laboratories.
Agents: Tordon, 2,4-D, Orange, diquat, endothal, and combinations of each with Tordon
DoD Involvement: Yes

Location: Fort Meade, MD
Dates: 1963
Project Description: Various studies were done to explore the effectiveness of different herbicides. They were all field trials. These studies were done by personnel from the US Army Biological Laboratories.
Agents: Cacodylic acid, Dowco 173, butyediol
DoD Involvement: Yes

Location: Poole's Island, Aberdeen Proving Ground, MD
Dates: 7/14/1969 -
Project Description: During the week of 7/14/1969, personnel from Naval Applied Science Laboratory in conjunction with personnel from Limited War Laboratory conducted a defoliation test along the shoreline.
Agents: Orange, Orange plus foam, Orange plus foam Orange, Foam
DoD Involvement: Yes

Mississippi

Location: Near Wayside, MS, Wilcox Road, Greenville, MS
Dates: 9/19/1967
Project Description: In 1967, the Dow Chemical Company was awarded a DoD research contract. The objective was to prepare as pellets mixtures of various herbicides and to test them on varying vegetation situations for the control of a range of plant species.
Agents: Picloram, bromacil, pyriclor, and terbacil, Orange, cacodylic acid
DoD Involvement: Undetermined

Location: Fulcher Ranch, Greenville, MS
Dates: 4/15/1968
Project Description: In 1967, the Dow Chemical Company was awarded a DoD research contract. The objective was to prepare as pellets mixtures of various herbicides and to test them on varying vegetation situations for the control of a range of plant species.
Agents: Picloram and bromicil
DoD Involvement: Undetermined

Location: Gulfport, MS
Dates: 1968-70
Project Description: While discussing the mandatory disposal of Orange, it was mentioned that 15,161 drums were being stored at Gulfport, Mississippi.
Agents: Orange
DoD Involvement: Yes

Montana

Location: Galatin Valley near Bozeman, MT
Dates: 7/3/1953, 7/6/1953, 7/14/1953
Project Description: A preliminary series of field evaluations ofchemical agents for attacking wheat using a miniature spraying system mounted on light aircraft were performed by USDA.
Agents: 4- fluorophenoxy-acetic acid and 2 of its esters, 3:1 butyl 2,4-D and butyl 2,4,5-T
DoD Involvement: No

New York

Location: Fort Drum, NY
Dates: 1959
Project Description: The Commanding General, 1st US Army, requested that Fort Detrick assist with defoliation efforts at Fort Drum. Thirteen drums were sprayed there on 4 square miles from a helicopter spray device.
Agents: Orange
DoD Involvement: Yes

North Dakota

Location: Langdon, ND; Hays, KS
Dates: 1960
Project Description: Two studies on the stem rust of wheat were conducted during 1960 to obtain data on the establishment, development, and destructiveness of artificially induced stem rust epiphytotics.
Agents: Stem rust of wheat
DoD Involvement: Undetermined

Pennsylvania

Location: Stone Valley Experimental Forest in Huntington County and near State College in Centre County, PA
Dates: 3/1969 - 10/1970
Project Description: Soil- applied herbicides were studied by the U of Pa with Ft Detrick for 18 months for their effectiveness, rapidity of action, and duration of response in native stands of central PA grasses, broadleaf weeds and woody plants. These herbicides were spread or sprayed.

Agents: Bromacil, diuron, tandex, fenuron, picloram
DoD Involvement: Undetermined

Rhode Island

Location: Kingston, RI
Dates: 7/26/1949, 1950-51
Project Description: The experiments were directed mainly towards the investigation of plant inhibitors applied as sprays or to the soil in the solid form to be taken up by the roots. Experiments were carried out under supervision of T.E. Odland if RI State College. H.T. DeRigo was also there.
Agents: Trieth.2,4,5-T, butyl 2,4,5-T,974
DoD Involvement: Yes

Tennessee

Location: Tennessee and Georgia
Dates: 1964
Project Description: In 1964, helicopter spray tests were conducted on transmission line rights-of-way by the Georgia Power Company and Tennessee Valley Authority in collaboration with Fort Detrick to evaluate effectiveness of several commercially available herbicides.
Agents: Diquat and Tordon 101, various
DoD Involvement: Yes

Location: 1 in TN, 2 areas in FL, 2 areas in GA
Dates: 1968
Project Description: In 1968, emphasis was given to soil applied herbicides for grass control. Applications were made by a jeep-mounted sprayer on small plots or by helicopter on larger plots.
Agents: Bromacil, Tandex, monuron, diuron, and fenuron
DoD Involvement: Undetermined

Texas

Location: Beaumont, TX
Dates: 6/1944
Project Description: Small plot experiments were commenced to test the effectiveness of LN agents. Various trials were done under contract with the USDA, aided by personnel at Camp Detrick. Here, they were testing on rice crops.
Agents: LN *phenoxy
DoD Involvement: No

Location: Beaumont, TX
Dates: 1950-51
Project Description: The purpose was to determine means of accomplishing defoliation of

tropical forest vegetation by application of a chemical agent. Here, irrigation water studies were done with the agent. Coghill, Hasse, and Yeatner worked here.
Agents: 2,4-D
DoD Involvement: Undetermined

Location: Weslaco, TX
Dates: 5/1967 - 1/1969
Project Description: 71 new arsenic compounds were tested in primary screening against 6 plant species in greenhouse tests. Then, 5 of the most active compounds were tested in field trials against Red Maple and compared to formulations of cacodylic acid and a 50:50 blend of orange and sodium cacodylate. The Ansul Co. for DoD.
Agents: Arsenic compounds, Orange, cacodylic acid, sodium cacodylate
DoD Involvement: Yes

Utah

Location: Granite Peak, UT
Dates: Summer 1945
Project Description: Small plot experiments were commenced to test the effectiveness of LN agents. Various trials were done under contract with the USDA, aided by personnel at Camp Detrick. Here, it was dropping trials.
Agents: LN *phenoxy
DoD Involvement: Yes

Washington

Location: Prosser, WA
Dates: 1950-51
Project Description: The purpose was to determine means of accomplishing defoliation of tropical forest vegetation by application of a chemical agent. Here, irrigation water studies were done with the agent. V.F. Burns worked here.
Agents: 2,4-D
DoD Involvement: Undetermined

Wisconsin

Location: Marinette, WI
Dates: 5/1967 - 1/1969
Project Description: 71 new arsenic compounds were tested in primary screening against 6 plant species in greenhouse tests. Then, 5 of the most active compounds were tested in field trials against Red Maple and compared to formulations of cacodylic acid and a 50:50 blend of orange and sodium cacodylate. The Ansul Co. for DoD.
Agents: Arsenic compounds, Orange, cacodylic acid, sodium cacodylate
DoD Involvement: Yes

AGENT ORANGE STORED INTERNATIONALLY

Cambodia

Location: Southeastern part of Kompong Cham Province and Dar and Prek Clong plantations, Cambodia
Dates: 6/1969
Project Description: In 6/1969, the U.S. government received notice of charge by Cambodian government that major defoliation damage to the Cambodian rubber plantation near the RVN border had occurred as a result of U.S. defoliation activity. This was confirmed by a team of experts.
Agents: Orange
DoD Involvement: Yes

Canada

Location: Base Gagetown near Fredericton, New Brunswick, Canada
Dates: 6/20/1967 - 6/24/1967
Project Description: During the period of 12/1966 - 10/1967, a comprehensive short-term evaluation was conducted by personnel from Fort Detrick's Plant Science Lab in coordination with contract research on formulations by chemical industry and field tests by USDA and University of Hawaii.
Agents: Basic desiccants and Orange, Blue, various
DoD Involvement: Yes

India

Location: Kumbla, South India
Dates: 1945-1946
Project Description: The main objective of the experiments was to determine the feasibility of accomplishing severe injury or destruction of tropical food crops by the application of growth-inhibiting (LN*) compounds in static trials. Field plantings were treated with various agents at different rates in different forms.
Agents: LN compounds *phenoxy
DoD Involvement: Yes

Korea

Location: Korea, third Brigade, 2nd Division area
Dates: 7/23/1968 - 7/24/1968
Project Description: In 1968, chemicals were sent from the Plant Sciences Lab, Ft Detrick, MD, to the Republic of Korea for the purpose of testing their effectiveness in the control of vegetation.
Agents: Hyvar XWS, tandex, Urox B, Urox Oil concentrate (liquids) bromacil, tandex, Urox 22

(solids)
DoD Involvement: Yes

Location: Korea, 2nd and 4th Brigades, 2nd Division area
Dates: 8/1968
Project Description: In 1968, chemicals were sent from the Plant Sciences Lab, Ft Detrick, MD, to the Republic of Korea for the purpose of testing their effectiveness in the control of vegetation.
Agents: Hyvar XWS, tandex, Urox B, Urox Oil concentrate (liquids) bromacil, tandex, Urox 22 (solids)
DoD Involvement: Yes

Location: Korea, third Brigade, 2nd Division area
Dates: 10/3/1968
Project Description: In 1968, chemicals were sent from the Plant Sciences Lab, Ft Detrick, MD, to the Republic of Korea for the purpose of testing their effectiveness in the control of vegetation.
Agents: Hyvar XWS, tandex, Urox B, Urox Oil concentrate (liquids) bromacil, tandex, Urox 22 (solids)
DoD Involvement: Yes

Laos

Location: Laos
Dates: 12/1965 - 1967
Project Description: In December 1965, herbicide operations were begun in Laos, with sorties being flown from Tan Son Nhut and Da Nang. The purpose was the exposure of foot trails, dirt roads and other LOCs that crossed into SVN. This network leads from NVN, through the eastern panhandle, to Cambodian border.
Agents: Orange
DoD Involvement: Yes

Puerto Rico

Location: Las Mesas and La Jagua experimental areas at Mayaguez, Puerto Rico
Dates: 2/1956 - 6/1956
Project Description: During February to June, 9 chemicals were evaluated in PR on 16 genera tropical woody plants. The chemicals were applied in highly concentrated solutions with a microsprayer to the leaves.
Agents: 2,4,5-T, 2,4-D, pentachlorophenol, ammate, weedazol, endothal Harvestaid, Butyne - 1,4-diol
DoD Involvement: Yes

Location: Guanica and Joyuda, Puerto Rico
Dates: 6/1956 - 9/1956

Project Description: 9 chemicals were evaluated on 16 genera of tropical woody between June and September. The chemicals were sprayed to duplicate small branches, using a microsprayer.
Agents: 2,4,5-T, potassium cyanate, amiendo, F-2, 6-Ca-4, Y-F Tree and Brush Kiler, ACP M-118, ShedA-Leaf
DoD Involvement: Yes

Location: Las Mesas and La Jagua, Mayaguez, Joyuda at Cabo Rojo, and Guanica Insular Forest at Guanica, Puerto Rico
Dates: 9/1956-12/1956
Project Description: 16 compounds with defoliating properties were evaluated using 28 different tropical woody plants, each representing a separate genus. The chemicals were applied to duplicate small branches with a microsprayer and to single larger branches or whole trees with a 2-gallon knapsack sprayer.
Agents: 6-Ca-4,Liojn Oil,2,4,5-T, B-1613, B-1638, Ammate, V-C1-186, endothal, shed-a-leaf, M-118, Y-F,esteron 2,4-D,F3,F4,F5,F6
DoD Involvement: Yes

Location: Las Mesas and La Jagua, Mayaguez, Guanica Beach, Puerto Rico
Dates: 1/1957 - 3/1957
Project Description: 7 compounds were evaluated on 29 different woody plants to determine their effectiveness as defoliants, desiccants, and as killing agents. They were applied with a microsprayer to the upper leaf surfaces of duplicate small branches.
Agents: V-C 3-105, V-C 1-21, V-C 1-443, F-7, TBP, Phillips 713, V-C 3-173
DoD Involvement: Yes

Location: Las Mesas and La Jagua, Mayaguez, Guanica Beach, Puerto Rico
Dates: 4/1957 - 6/1957
Project Description: 7 compounds were sprayed on 25 different plants in order to evaluate their effectiveness as defoliants, desiccants, and killing agents. The compounds were applied with a microsprayer to the upper and lower leaf surfaces of duplicate small branches.
Agents: B-1676, B-1638, NP 1098, SD 1369, Ammate, Shed-a-leaf
DoD Involvement: Yes

Location: Las Mesas and La Jagua, Mayaguez, Puerto Rico
Dates: 7/1957 - 12/1957
Project Description: 8 different spray formulations were applied to 16 different tropical trees and shrubs in order to evaluate their effectiveness as defoliants, desiccants, and killing agents.
Agents: MgClO3, Golden Harvest Defoliant, Dow-M562, F-8, F9, F-10, F-11, F-12
DoD Involvement: Yes

Location: Loquillo, Puerto Rico
Dates: 4/1966, 10/1966
Project Description: Field tests of defoliants were designed to evaluate such variables as rates, volume of application, season, and vegetation. Data from aerial application tests at several CONUS and OCONUS locations are provided in tables.

Agents: Orange
DoD Involvement: Yes

Location: Las Marias, Puerto Rico
Dates: 2/1967 - 12/1967
Project Description: During the period of 12/1966 - 10/1967, a comprehensive short-term evaluation was conducted by personnel from Fort Detrick's Plant Science Lab in coordination with contract research on formulations by chemical industry and field tests by USDA and U of HI.
Agents: Various, including Orange
DoD Involvement: Yes

Location: Near Rio Grande, on the northeast coast of Puerto Rico
Dates: 8/23/1967, 10/18/1967, 12/21/1967-12/26/1967
Project Description: In 1967, the Dow Chemical Company was awarded a DoD research contract. The objective was to prepare as pellets mixtures of various herbicides and to test them on varying vegetation situations for the control of a range of plant species.
Agents: Picloram, bromacil, pyriclor, and terbacil
DoD Involvement: Undetermined

Location: Las Mesas Cerros, Mayaguez, Puerto Rico
Dates: 5/24/1968, 5/26/1968, 5/27/1968
Project Description: In 1967, the Dow Chemical Company was awarded a DoD research contract. The objective was to prepare as pellets mixtures of various herbicides and to test them on varying vegetation situations for the control of a range of plant species.
Agents: Picloram, bromacil, pyriclor
DoD Involvement: Undetermined

At Sea

Location: At Sea
Dates: Summer 1977
Project Description: In 1977, the USAF incinerated 2.22 million gallons of Herbicide Orange at sea in an operation entitled PACER HO. Extensive industrial hygiene sampling efforts supporting the transfer operations at Gulfport, MS and Johnston Island indicated all exposures were inconsequential (2-3 orders of magnitude below the TLVs for 2,4-D and 2,4,5-T).
Agents: Orange
DoD Involvement: Yes (Gulfport, MS); No (Johnston Island)

Thailand

Location: Replacement Training Center of the Royal Thai Army near Pranburi, Thailand
Dates: 1964 and 1965
Project Description: An extensive series of tests were conducted by Fort Detrick during 1964 and 1965 in collaboration with the Military Research and Development Center of Thailand. The

objective was to perform onsite evaluation of phytotoxic chemicals on vegetation in SE Asia.
Agents: Orange, Purple
DoD Involvement: Yes

Location: Thailand
Dates: 1964-65
Project Description: Sponsored by ARPA; ARPA Order 423, Between the mentioned dates, there was a large-scale test program to determine effectiveness of mentioned agents in defoliation of upland forest or jungle vegetation representative of SEA.
Agents: Purple, Orange, Others
DoD Involvement: Yes

Location: Thailand
Dates: 1964-65
Project Description: Field tests of defoliants were designed to evaluate such variables as rates, volume of application, season, and vegetation. Data from aerial application tests at several CONUS and OCONUS locations are provided in tables.
Agents: Orange, Blue
DoD Involvement: Yes

VA AGENT ORANGE NEWSLETTERS

See the following 24 pages

VA HEALTH CARE | Defining EXCELLENCE in the 21st Century

Agent Orange Review

INFORMATION FOR VETERANS | Vol. 26 No. 1 | WINTER 2012

VA Expands Dates of Agent Orange Exposure in Korea from 1968-1969 to 1968-1971

FEATURES

Veterans who served along the demilitarized zone (DMZ) in Korea during the Vietnam War now have an easier path to access health care and benefits. The Department of Veterans Affairs (VA) expanded the dates when illnesses associated with exposure to Agent Orange can be presumed related to their military service.

Previously, VA recognized exposure for service between April 1968 and July 1969. VA now presumes exposure for service between April 1, 1968, and August 31, 1971, if a Veteran served in a unit determined by VA and the Department of Defense to have operated in an area of the DMZ where Agent Orange or other herbicides were applied. The expanded dates took effect on February 24, 2011 (see **www.publichealth.va.gov/exposures/agentorange/korea.asp**).

This presumption simplifies and speeds the application process for Veterans of the Korean DMZ. VA encourages Veterans who believe they have health problems related to Agent Orange to submit their applications for VA health care and disability compensation benefits.

- To apply for health care benefits, apply online at **www.1010ez.med.va.gov/sec/vha/1010ez**, or contact the nearest VA health care facility at **1-877-222-VETS (8387)**.
- To file a claim for disability benefits, apply online at **www.ebenefits.va.gov,** or contact the nearest VA regional office at **1-800-827-1000**.

Veterans who served along the Korean DMZ may also be eligible for a free Agent Orange Registry health evaluation (see page 7).

The regulation expanding the dates for eligible service in Korea is available on the Office of the Federal Register website at **www.regulations.gov/#!documentDetail;D=VA-2009-VBA-0021-0007.** ■

Also in this Issue

About the Agent Orange Review

VA's Office of Public Health publishes the **Agent Orange Review** to provide information on Agent Orange and related matters to Veterans, their families, and others with concerns about herbicides used in Vietnam or other locations.

This is the 49th Agent Orange Review that VA has published. This issue was completed in winter 2012 and does not include developments that occurred after that time. For past issues of the newsletter and other information, please visit our website at **www.publichealth.va.gov/exposures/agentorange**.

Questions, comments, and suggestions for future issues and topics are encouraged and can be sent to Editor, Agent Orange Review, Office of Public Health (10P3), Department of Veterans Affairs, 810 Vermont Avenue, NW., Washington, D.C. 20420.

Blue Water Navy Veterans and Agent Orange

The National Academy of Sciences' Institute of Medicine (IOM) released its report "Blue Water Navy Vietnam Veterans and Agent Orange Exposure" in May 2011. The report concluded that "there was not enough information for the IOM to determine whether Blue Water Navy personnel were or were not exposed to Agent Orange."

The IOM is an independent, nonprofit organization that provides unbiased and evidence-based recommendations to the government and other health and science policy makers. VA considers the IOM report findings in the presumptive disability decision-making process.

VA presumes that Veterans who served on the ground or on inland waterways in Vietnam ("Brown Water" Navy) were exposed to Agent Orange. VA has not granted this presumption to "Blue Water" Navy Veterans, who served on open sea ships off the shore of Vietnam. To be presumed exposed, Blue Water Veterans must show they set foot on the land of Vietnam or served on its inland waterways any time between January 9, 1962, and May 7, 1975. VA decides claims from Blue Water Veterans on a case-by-case basis.

For more information on Blue Water Navy, including the IOM report, go to **www.publichealth.va.gov/exposures/agentorange/bluewaterveterans.asp.** ■

Presumptions Available to Veterans with Agent Orange Exposure

www.publichealth.va.gov/exposures/agentorange/diseases.asp

Veterans may be eligible for disability compensation and health care benefits for diseases that VA has recognized as associated with exposure to Agent Orange and other herbicides. Surviving spouses, children and dependent parents of Veterans who were exposed to Agent Orange and died as the result of diseases associated with Agent Orange may be eligible for survivors' benefits.

- **AL Amyloidosis**
  A rare disease caused when an abnormal protein, amyloid, enters tissues or organs.
- **Chronic B-cell Leukemias** *(added October 30, 2010)*
  A type of cancer which affects white blood cells.
- **Chloracne (or similar acneform disease)**
  A skin condition that occurs soon after exposure to chemicals and looks like common forms of acne seen in teenagers. Under VA's rating regulations, chloracne (or other acneform disease similar to chloracne) must be at least 10 percent disabling within one year of exposure to herbicides.
- **Diabetes Mellitus Type 2**
  A disease characterized by high blood sugar levels resulting from the body's inability to respond properly to the hormone insulin.
- **Hodgkin's Disease**
  A malignant lymphoma (cancer) characterized by progressive enlargement of the lymph nodes, liver, and spleen, and by progressive anemia.
- **Ischemic Heart Disease** *(added October 30, 2010)*
  A disease characterized by a reduced supply of blood to the heart that leads to chest pain.
- **Multiple Myeloma**
  A cancer of plasma cells, a type of white blood cell in bone marrow.
- **Non-Hodgkin's Lymphoma**
  A group of cancers that affect the lymph glands and other lymphatic tissue.
- **Parkinson's Disease** *(added October 30, 2010)*
  A progressive disorder of the nervous system that affects muscle movement.
- **Peripheral Neuropathy, Acute and Subacute**
  A nervous system condition that causes numbness, tingling, and motor weakness. Currently it must be at least 10 percent disabling within one year of exposure to herbicides. VA proposed on August 10, 2012, to replace "acute and subacute" with "early-onset" and eliminate the requirement that symptoms resolve within two years.
- **Porphyria Cutanea Tarda**
  A disorder characterized by liver dysfunction and by thinning and blistering of the skin in sun-exposed areas. Under VA's rating regulations, it must be at least 10 percent disabling within one year of exposure to herbicides.
- **Prostate Cancer**
  Cancer of the prostate; one of the most common cancers among men.
- **Respiratory Cancers**
  Cancers of the lung, larynx, trachea, and bronchus.
- **Soft Tissue Sarcomas (other than osteosarcoma, chondrosarcoma, Kaposi's sarcoma, or mesothelioma)**
  A group of different types of cancers in body tissues such as muscle, fat, blood and lymph vessels, and connective tissues. ■

Presumptions Available to Children of Vietnam and of Korean DMZ Veterans

www.publichealth.va.gov/exposures/agentorange/birth_defects.asp

VA presumes that certain birth defects in children of Vietnam-era Veterans are associated with Veterans' qualifying military service:

- Spina bifida (except spina bifida occulta), a birth defect that occurs when the spine fails to close properly during pregnancy, is associated with Veterans' exposure to Agent Orange or other herbicides during qualifying service in Vietnam or Korea.
- At least 18 birth defects in children of women Veterans are linked to the mother's military service in Vietnam, but are not related to herbicide exposure. Some examples include cleft lip or palate, congenital heart defects, and hypospadias. ■

Presumption Available to All Vietnam Veterans

www.publichealth.va.gov/exposures/agentorange/conditions/nonhodgkinslymphoma.asp

VA presumes service connection for non-Hodgkin's Lymphoma occurring in Veterans who served in Vietnam as well as Blue Water Veterans who served on its offshore waters; these Veterans do not need to prove a connection between their disease and military service to be eligible to receive VA disability compensation.

Presumption Available to All Veterans

www.publichealth.va.gov/exposures/compensation.asp

VA presumes that Lou Gehrig's Disease (amyotrophic lateral sclerosis or ALS) diagnosed in a Veteran from any era is related to their military service, as long as they served on active duty for at least 90 continuous days. ■

Understanding Heart Disease and How to Reduce Your Risk

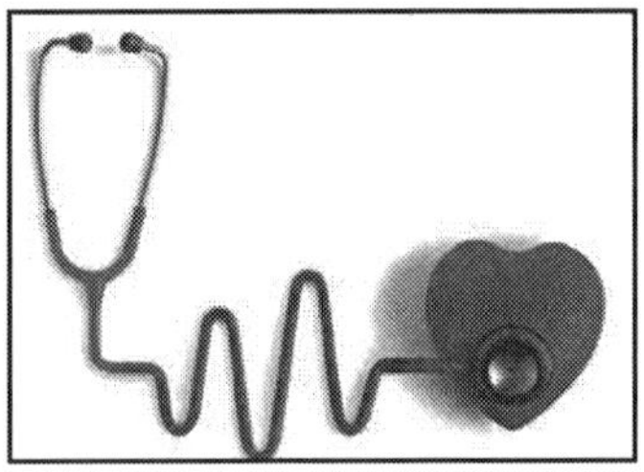

Ischemic heart disease is also known as coronary artery disease or "hardening of the arteries." Cholesterol plaque can build up in the arteries of the heart and cause "ischemia," which means the heart is not getting enough blood flow and oxygen. If the plaque blocks an artery, a heart attack can result.

Heart disease is the #1 killer of men and women in the U.S. Up to 90 percent of heart attacks are due to the following risk factors:

- Smoking
- High cholesterol
- High blood pressure
- Diabetes
- Abdominal obesity ("spare tire")
- Not eating enough fruits and vegetables
- Not being active/lack of exercise
- Drinking too much alcohol
- Stress

The good news is that you can do something about these risk factors and lower your risk of heart disease and heart attack:

- Get moving - walk/exercise at least 30 minutes a day
- Eat better - consume at least 5 fruits/veggies a day and 2 servings of fish a week
- Stop bad habits - get help to quit smoking or drinking too much
- Shed excess weight - lose even a few pounds and you will start to reap health benefits

VA presumes ischemic heart disease is associated with exposure to Agent Orange or other herbicides, regardless of other major risk factors that a Veteran may have. Veterans exposed to herbicides do not have to prove a connection between their heart disease and military service to be eligible for disability compensation, but the diagnosis must be ischemic heart disease.

Talk to your doctor to learn more about preventing or treating heart disease. You can also check out VA's prevention website for more tips on living healthier at **www.prevention.va.gov**. ■

Are You or a Fellow Veteran in Crisis? Make the Call: 1-800-273-TALK

The Veterans Crisis Line provides confidential help for Veterans and their families. VA started this nationwide suicide prevention hotline to give Veterans who need help free access to caring counselors 24 hours a day, 7 days a week, 365 days a year. Since its launch in 2007, the Veterans Crisis Line has answered more than half a million calls and made more than 21,000 life-saving rescues. In 2009, VA added an anonymous online chat that has since helped thousands of Veterans and family members.

Veterans and their loved ones now have three different ways to get help:

- Phone: talk with a counselor by calling **1-800-273-TALK(8255)**, and press "**1**".
- Text: send a text message to **838255**.
- Online: chat live 1-on-1 with a counselor at **www.veteranscrisisline.net.**

Self-Check Quiz: Answer some questions online to see if you might benefit from services at **www.veteranscrisisline.net**. (At any point you can connect live with a counselor.) ■

Do You Need Help to Quit Smoking or Quit Using Other Forms of Tobacco?

VA has partnered with the Department of Defense to make an online resource, *Quit Tobacco. Make Everyone Proud*, available to Veterans enrolled in VA health care. This website provides tools—such as quit plans, savings calculators, and 24/7 live chat-to help Veterans and service members quit tobacco (**www.ucanquit2.org**). From the homepage, Veterans who receive their health care in VA can access information tailored just for them by clicking on the section "VA Veterans."

VA is committed to helping Veterans quit smoking and prevent smoking-related diseases. VA offers free counseling to every Veteran through their primary care provider and through smoking cessation clinics. VA also provides medicines that have been proven to help people quit. Quitting smoking is not easy, but VA can help. See your primary care provider today to get help quitting. You can do it!

For more information on quitting smoking or tobacco, see **www.publichealth.va.gov/smoking** or call **1-877-222-8387.** ■

Check VA's "Ships List"

VA maintains a list of U.S. Navy and Coast Guard ships that operated in Vietnam during the war and could have been exposed to Agent Orange. Exposure is presumed for any Veteran with duty or visitation within the country of Vietnam or on its inland waterways. Veterans who served aboard a listed ship that operated on Vietnam's inland waterways will automatically receive the presumption of exposure. Veterans who served aboard open sea ships that did not enter inland waterways will only be presumed exposed if the ship docked to shore, sent small boats ashore, or otherwise sent crew members ashore. The Veteran must further provide a statement of personally going ashore. VA adds ships to this list after confirming service on inland waterways based on military records. As of press time, there were more than 200 ships on the list. To look up your ship, go to **www.publichealth.va.gov/exposures/agentorange/shiplist.** ■

VA Studies High Blood Pressure, Chronic Lung Disease Among Vietnam Veterans

VA researchers are studying U.S. Army Chemical Corps (ACC) Veterans who handled or sprayed herbicides in Vietnam to find out if they have higher rates of high blood pressure (hypertension) or lung disease than other Veterans. For lung disease, researchers will look at chronic obstructive pulmonary disease (COPD), which includes emphysema and chronic bronchitis.

Researchers are asking about 4,000 Veterans who served in the ACC during the Vietnam era (1964-1975) to participate. The study will compare ACC Veterans who served in Vietnam with those who did not. ACC personnel represent the largest group of Vietnam-era Veterans who had the greatest potential exposure to herbicides.

How this research helps Veterans: The study will help VA understand the relationship between herbicide exposure in Vietnam and a Veteran's risk of developing high blood pressure or COPD.

Background: VA researchers have been following this group of ACC Veterans since the 1990s. An earlier study found that those who sprayed Agent Orange or other herbicides were more likely to self-report having high blood pressure. Based on this and other studies, a 2008 Institute of Medicine (IOM) report added high blood pressure to the category of "limited or suggestive evidence of an association," meaning there could be a link with Agent Orange exposure, although only some of the studies show this. Researchers also noted a possible association between Veterans who reported spraying herbicides in Vietnam and those who had respiratory problems such as COPD.

Study Methods: VA is contacting ACC Veterans to ask if their physician has diagnosed them with high blood pressure or COPD. Researchers are also reviewing medical records and will measure the blood pressure and lung function of a smaller sample of these Veterans. Researchers cannot accept volunteers, but encourage Veterans who are contacted to participate.

To learn more about this latest study, go to **www.publichealth.va.gov/epidemiology/studies/vietnam-army-chemical-corps.asp.** ■

"Million Veteran Program" Seeks Volunteers

Why do some Veterans get diabetes, cancer, or post-traumatic stress disorder – and others do not? The answer could be in their genes.

VA launched the Million Veteran Program (MVP) to study how heredity (genetics) affects health and illness. To do this, MVP will build one of the world's largest databases with blood samples and medical histories from one million Veteran volunteers who sign up over the next 5 to 6 years. The data will be stored anonymously to ensure privacy and will be used to study chronic diseases and military-related illnesses. The results may lead to new ways of preventing and treating these conditions in Veterans.

Veterans can sign up at any of the 40 participating VA medical centers across the country. To learn more, please call **1-866-441-6075** or visit **http://www.research.va.gov/mvp.** ■

Institute of Medicine Issues Latest Report on Veterans and Agent Orange

The Institute of Medicine (IOM) released its latest report, "Veterans and Agent Orange: Update 2010," on September 29, 2010. This is the eighth IOM report to review the latest scientific evidence on health effects of exposure to Agent Orange and other herbicides used during the Vietnam War.

The report looked at studies of Veterans, industrial workers, and others exposed to dioxins or herbicides, as well as animal studies. Three new health outcomes were studied – hearing loss, eye problems, and osteoporosis. None were found to have enough evidence to show an association with Agent Orange.

Peripheral neuropathy, a condition where damage to nerves can cause numbness, tingling, or muscle weakness, remained in the category of "limited or suggestive evidence" for an association with Agent Orange exposure. However, the IOM noted new evidence showing that symptoms can persist longer than 2 years and do not always go away over time.

"Veterans and Agent Orange: Update 2010" and earlier IOM reports can be read or downloaded free at **www.publichealth.va.gov/exposures/agentorange/institute-of-medicine.asp**. The next IOM report on Veterans and Agent Orange is expected to be released in January 2014.

VA has recognized certain cancers and other health problems as "presumptive" diseases associated with exposure to Agent Orange or other herbicides during military service. Presumptive diseases are those that VA assumes can be related to a Veteran's military service. Veterans and their survivors may be eligible for disability compensation or survivors' benefits. For the current list, please see page 3 or visit our website at **www.publichealth.va.gov/exposures/agentorange/diseases.asp**. ■

Agent Orange Registry Health Evaluation for Eligible Veterans - Including Korea

VA started the Agent Orange Registry program in 1978 to respond to the health concerns of Vietnam Veterans. VA offers this evaluation to eligible Veterans free of charge. Veterans do not need to be enrolled in VA health care to get a registry evaluation.

What does a registry evaluation provide?

- A free, specialized health evaluation that includes a medical and military service history, and may include a physical exam and other evaluation as needed
- Answers to questions about environmental exposures
- Information about VA health care and other benefits

Who is eligible for an Agent Orange registry evaluation?

- Vietnam Veterans
- Korean demilitarized zone (DMZ) Veterans
- Veterans from certain locations in Thailand
- Veterans from other locations who were exposed during the spraying, testing, or transport of herbicides for military purposes

How do I get an appointment for a registry evaluation?

- Talk to an Environmental Health Coordinator at any VA medical facility. Call **1-877-222-VETS (8387)** to find the closest facility or visit **www.va.gov/directory**.
- Find contact information for Environmental Health Coordinators online at **www.publichealth.va.gov/exposures/coordinators.asp**.

NOTE: A registry evaluation is not a disability compensation exam. A Veteran can file a claim for VA benefits without having had a registry evaluation.

How many Veterans have received an Agent Orange registry evaluation?	
Initial evaluations	573,088
Follow-up evaluations	65,758
Total (initial + follow-up)	638,846
(as of September 30, 2012)	

For more information about the registry evaluation, see **www.publichealth.va.gov/exposures/agentorange/registry.asp**. ■

New Hotline for Homeless Veterans: 1-877-4AID VET

VA's National Call Center for Homeless Veterans launched a telephone hotline to provide support for homeless and at-risk Veterans. VA counselors answer the **1-877-4AID VET (1-877-424-3838)** hotline 24 hours a day, 7 days a week. Callers are linked directly to VA Homeless Program staff at VA medical centers across the country. Family members, workers at community agencies, and non-VA providers also may call the hotline to learn about the many programs and services available to help homeless and at-risk Veterans within the VA and their communities.

The homeless hotline is just one part of VA's "Homeless Veterans Initiatives" to prevent and end homelessness among Veterans. VA wants to make sure that all Veterans have access to the resources and support they have earned. For additional information, go to **www.va.gov/homeless.** ■

How to Apply for VA Benefits

Veterans can apply for health care benefits online (**www.1010ez.med.va.gov/sec/vha/1010ez**), or contact their nearest VA health care facility at **1-877-222-VETS (8387)**.

Veterans with service-connected illnesses or injuries may be eligible for monthly payments called disability compensation. The disability must have occurred or worsened during active military service. In addition, the Veteran must have been separated or discharged under conditions that were other than dishonorable. Information on monthly compensation amounts is available at **www.vba.va.gov/bln/21/Rates/index.htm.**

Veterans can file for compensation benefits online at **www.ebenefits.va.gov**, or contact their nearest VA regional office at **1-800-827-1000.** ■

Connect to VA Caregiver Support: 1-855-260-3274

If you are a family member taking care of a Veteran, VA knows your focus is to take care of your loved one. It can be an incredibly demanding job, and VA wants you to know you do not have to do it alone. VA makes it easier to find support with the new VA Caregiver Support Line. Caring professionals will tell you about help that is available to you or the Veteran, and can connect you to the Caregiver Support Coordinator at your nearest VA medical center. The Coordinator will match you with services available in your area, or they will just listen, if that is the support you need right now.

Help is just a quick phone call away. Reach the VA Caregiver Support Line by calling **1-855-260-3274.** Hours: Monday-Friday 8 a.m.-11 p.m. ET, and Saturday 10:30 a.m.-6 p.m. ET.

Learn more about the variety of services VA offers by visiting the new VA Caregiver Support website at **www.caregiver.va.gov.** ■

Where to Get Help and Information

Agent Orange Helpline	1-800-749-8387
VA Benefits Information	1-800-827-1000
Agent Orange Information	www.publichealth.va.gov/exposures/agentorange
Nearest VA Medical Center	1-877-222-8387 www.va.gov/directory

If you are concerned about Agent Orange exposure: Contact the nearest VA medical center to request an Agent Orange registry evaluation and get your questions answered. You can find the VA medical center nearest you by calling **1-877-222-VETS (8387)** or visiting **www.va.gov/directory.**

If you are a Vietnam Veteran and need medical treatment for conditions that may be related to Agent Orange: Contact the nearest VA medical center for eligibility information. You can find the nearest VA medical center at **www.va.gov/directory** or call toll-free **1-877-749-8387.**

If you need help resolving a problem related to your medical care: Contact the "patient advocate" or "patient representative" at that facility for assistance. Ask the VA medical center telephone operator for the patient advocate or patient representative.

Veterans with difficult-to-diagnose illnesses or other deployment health concerns: VA has the War Related Illness and Injury Study Center (WRIISC) with three locations to help Veterans who have difficult-to-diagnose illnesses or other deployment health concerns that require special expertise. A VA primary provider can refer a Veteran to a WRIISC.

For further questions:

- Visit **www.warrelatedillness.va.gov** or
- Call the National Referral Program Coordinator at the WRIISC nearest you:
  - WRIISC-California: **1-888-482-4376**
  - WRIISC-District of Columbia: **1-800-722-8340**
  - WRIISC-New Jersey: **1-800-248-8005**

Vietnam-era Veterans with children who have spina bifida: Contact VA's national hotline at **1-888-820-1756**, or the nearest VA regional office by calling **1-800-827-1000.** Additional information about spina bifida is available from the Spina Bifida Association of America at 4590 MacArthur Blvd, NW., Suite 250, Washington, DC 20007, by calling **1-800-621-3141**, or by email at **sbaa@sbaa.org**. The website is **www.sbaa.org.**

Vietnam-era Women Veterans with children who have birth defects: Contact VA's national hotline at **1-888-820-1756**, or the nearest VA regional office by calling **1-800-827-1000.**

For disability information: Contact a VA Veteran Service Representative at the nearest VA regional office or health care facility to talk with a counselor and apply for disability compensation. VA disability counselors have information about the wide range of benefit programs that VA offers. The national number is **1-800-827-1000.**

To start a disability claim online: Go to **http://www.ebenefits.va.gov.** You also can get information about disability compensation from VA's Special Issues Helpline at **1-800-749-8387.**

Support from Veterans Service Organizations: Many Veterans have been helped by Veterans Service Organizations, including Vietnam Veterans who are seeking benefits they earned through their service. VA does not endorse or recommend any specific group. State and County Veteran Service Officers are also good resources for Vietnam and other Veterans.

For additional benefits information, see VA's "Federal Benefits for Veterans, Dependents and Survivors" booklet. This booklet is updated every year to reflect changes in law and policies and can be downloaded free at **www.va.gov/opa/publications/benefits_book.asp.** It may be purchased from the U.S. Government Printing Office at their website (**bookstore.gpo.gov**) or by mail:
U.S. Government Printing Office Superintendent of Documents Washington, DC 20402. ■

Check Out New Feature on VA's Military Exposures Website

Veterans and the public can quickly search for military exposure topics on VA's newly designed Military Exposures website **www.publichealth.va.gov/exposures.**

The user-friendly "4 Ways to Find Exposures" serves as a virtual compass to point visitors to information on a range of chemical, physical and environmental hazards during military service. Visitors can search by: related health concerns, wars and operations, exposure categories, and exposure topics "A to Z." From the same page, visitors can get to information on VA health care, disability compensation, and registry evaluations. Other new navigation tools make it even easier for Veterans and others to find their way around the website and seek out information that is important to them. ■

Service in Camp Lejeune?

Before this issue went to press, the President signed Public Law 112-154, which requires VA to provide health care to Veterans and eligible family members for one or more of 15 specified illnesses or conditions. To be eligible for care, the Veteran or family member must have served on active duty or resided in Camp Lejeune (North Carolina) for not fewer than 30 days between January 1, 1957, and December 31, 1987. For more information, visit **www.publichealth.va.gov/exposures/camp-lejeune/**. ■

SUBSCRIBE TO WEB UPDATES ON AGENT ORANGE: www.publichealth.va.gov/exposures/agentorange.

Do you know a Vietnam Veteran who does not receive the Agent Orange Review?
Do you know a Gulf War Veteran who does not receive the Gulf War Review?
Do you know an OEF OIF Veteran who does not receive the OEF OIF Review?
Do you know an Atomic Veteran or other Veteran exposed to ionizing radiation during military service who does not receive the Ionizing Radiation Review?

Maybe it is you!

If you or a fellow Veteran want to read one of the Reviews on line, go to **www.publichealth.va.gov/exposures/resources.asp**. All of the publications may be found there.

Address Changes

If this newsletter has your old address, please use this form to update our mailing list.

Send the completed form to:

Agent Orange Review
Department of Veterans Affairs
AITC-ATTN: Mailing list update (32B)
1615 Woodward Street
Austin, TX 78772-0001

If you receive more than one copy of the Agent Orange Review, or prefer to read it online at **www.publichealth.va.gov/exposures/agentorange**, let us know by returning the form above to the address at left. Please provide your name, address, and last four digits of your Social Security number. You may use this or other paper. Thank you.

✂- -

Subscription or address change form for **Agent Orange Review Newsletter**: *Please print.*

Name First: ______ Middle: ______ Last: ______ Last 4 of SSN: ______

Address Street (Please indicate which APO/FPO, if applicable)

______ City: ______ State: ______ Zip Code: ______

New Address Street

______ City: ______ State: ______ Zip Code: ______

- ☐ My address has changed, and I would like to continue to receive the newsletter.
- ☐ I am receiving more than one copy, and only want to get a single copy.
- ☐ I don't need the newsletter by mail as I can read it at **www.publichealth.va.gov/exposures/agentorange**.

Department of
Veterans Affairs

Agent Orange Review
AITC (32B)
1615 Woodward Street
Austin, TX 78772-0001

OFFICIAL BUSINESS

Agent Orange Review

INFORMATION FOR VETERANS
WHO SERVED IN VIETNAM

WINTER 2012

Agent Orange Review

INFORMATION FOR VETERANS WHO SERVED IN VIETNAM | Vol. 25 No. 1 | July 2010

VA Extends Agent Orange Benefits to More Veterans

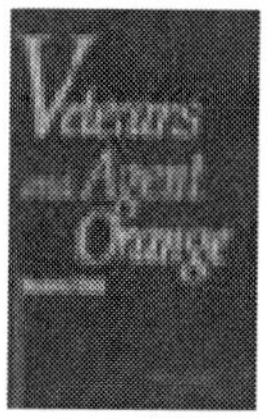

The Department of Veterans Affairs (VA) will add two new conditions to the list of "presumptive illnesses" related to Agent Orange exposure. These are Parkinson's disease and ischemic heart disease. In addition, VA will expand the presumption for chronic lymphocytic leukemia to include all chronic B-cell leukemias, such as hairy cell leukemia. These conditions will now be presumed to be service-connected to herbicide exposure in Vietnam.

Vietnam Veterans with these illnesses will be able to claim VA disability benefits and health care services without having to prove that their conditions are connected to Agent Orange exposure. The new policy, expected to take effect in late 2010, will apply to Veterans who served in Vietnam anytime during the period beginning January 9, 1962, and ending on May 7, 1975. It will not apply to Veterans who only served on "Blue Water" Navy ships in the region.

"We must do better reviews of illnesses that may be connected to service, and we will," said Secretary of Veterans Affairs Eric K. Shinseki. "Veterans who endure health problems deserve timely decisions based on solid evidence."

CONTINUED ON PAGE 3

A Message to Veterans from Secretary of Veterans Affairs, Eric "Ric" Shinseki

Fellow Veterans,

My name is Ric Shinseki, and I am a Veteran. For me, serving as Secretary of Veterans Affairs is a noble calling. It provides me the opportunity to give back to those who served with and for me during my 38 years in uniform and those on whose shoulders we all stood as we grew up in the profession of arms.

VA has a solemn responsibility to all of you, today and in the future, as more Veterans join our ranks and enroll to secure the benefits and services they have earned.

I am committed to transforming our Department so that it will be well-positioned to perform this duty even better during the 21st Century. We welcome the assistance and advice of our Veterans Service Organizations, other government departments and agencies, Congress, and all VA stakeholders as we move forward, ethically and transparently, so that Veterans and citizens can understand our efforts.

Creating that vision for transforming VA into a 21st Century organization requires a comprehensive review of our Department. We approach that review understanding that Veterans are central to everything VA does. We know that results count, that the Department will be measured

CONTINUED ON PAGE 4

"Blue Water" Update – Supreme Court Decision and New IOM Review

A Supreme Court decision, in response to a case filed in fall of 2008, has been announced regarding Blue Water Veterans. Blue Water Veterans are those that served during the Vietnam War on open sea ships, generally in the Navy or Coast Guard.

In January 2009, the Supreme Court effectively let stand an earlier court ruling that requires a Servicemember to have served on land or on the inland waterways of Vietnam in order to be presumed exposed to Agent Orange.

CONTINUED ON PAGE 4

FEATURES

Also in this Issue

About the Agent Orange Review

The **Agent Orange Review** is produced by VA's Environmental Agents Service (EAS). The Review is published to provide information on Agent Orange and related matters to Vietnam Veterans, their families, and others with concerns about herbicides used in Vietnam. This publication, including previous issues and other information, is available online at **www.publichealth.va.gov/exposures/agentorange.**

This issue is the 48th and was completed in July 2010. It does not include developments that occurred since that time.

Comments and questions about the content or design of the newsletter are encouraged. Suggestions and ideas for future issues should be sent to Editor, **Agent Orange Review**, Environmental Agents Service (131), U.S. Department of Veterans Affairs, 810 Vermont Avenue, NW, Washington, DC 20420.

VA updates The Review mailing address listing annually based on IRS records. Recipients who have not been filing Federal income tax returns annually and have moved to another residence are encouraged to provide updated mailing information using the form on the back page of this newsletter.

Questions about the **Agent Orange Registry Examination** program should be directed to the Environmental Health Clinician, previously known as the Registry Health Physician, or to the Environmental Health Coordinator (formerly called the Agent Orange Registry Coordinator) at any VA Medical Center. Questions regarding eligibility for health care should be directed to the hospital administration service at the nearest VA Medical Center. Information on enrolling for VA health care may be obtained by calling **1-877-222-8387.**

VA Simplifies Access to Health Care and Benefits for Veterans with PTSD

VA streamlined its process to provide health care and disability compensation for Veterans with post-traumatic stress disorder (PTSD), with the publication of a final regulation in the Federal Register in July 2010.

The new rule, which applies to Veterans of all eras, will simplify the process for a Veteran to establish service-connection for PTSD by reducing the evidence needed to support a claim.

While each claim will be evaluated and require confirmation by a VA psychiatrist or psychologist, the new process is expected to allow for faster and more accurate decisions to help connect Veterans to medical care and other benefits available through VA.

More than 400,000 Veterans with PTSD currently receive VA compensation benefits. PTSD is an anxiety disorder with symptoms that include recurrent thoughts of a traumatic event, emotional numbing, hyper-alertness, anxiety, and irritability.

For more information, go to **www.va.gov** or call **1-800-827-1000.** ■

VA Establishes ALS as a Presumptive Service-Connected Illness; Cites Association Between Military Service and Development of ALS

Veterans with amyotrophic lateral sclerosis (ALS) may receive urgently needed support for themselves and their families after VA announced that ALS is now presumed service-connected for all Veterans with 90 days or more of continuous active service in the military.

VA based the decision primarily on a November 2006 Institute of Medicine (IOM) report on the association between military service and ALS.

"We are extremely grateful to VA, Congressman Henry Brown and Senator Lindsey Graham for standing on the side of Veterans with ALS across the country," said Gary Leo, president and CEO of The ALS Association from 2004-2009.

"Thanks to their leadership, Veterans with ALS will receive the benefits and care they need, when they need them. Thanks to their efforts, no Veteran with ALS will ever be left behind."

The IOM report, titled *Amyotrophic Lateral Sclerosis in Veterans: Review of the Scientific Literature*, analyzed scientific and medical studies on the issue and concluded "there is limited and suggestive evidence of an association between military service and later development of ALS."

ALS is a disease that progresses rapidly. VA's decision makes those claims much easier to process, and for Veterans and their families to receive the compensation they have earned through their service to the Nation.

ALS, also called Lou Gehrig's disease—a neuromuscular disease that affects about 20,000 to 30,000 people of all races and ethnicities in the United States—is generally relentlessly progressive and is almost always fatal.

ALS causes degeneration of nerve cells in the brain and spinal cord that leads to muscle weakness, muscle atrophy, and spontaneous muscle activity. Currently, the cause of ALS is unknown, and there is no effective treatment.

In August 2009, VA contacted Veterans who may have been denied service-connection for ALS.

Veterans may also contact VA's disability compensation program, available online at **www.va.gov** or by phone at **1-800-827-1000.** ■

CONTINUED FROM PAGE 1 ***VA Extends Agent Orange Benefits to More Veterans***

Secretary Shinseki, a Vietnam Veteran, made the decision to add these conditions to the list of presumptive service-connected illnesses based on an independent study by the Institute of Medicine (IOM). The report, titled *Veterans and Agent Orange: Update 2008* (www.nap.edu/catalog.php?record_id=12662), found some evidence linking exposure to Agent Orange with increased risk for Parkinson's disease and ischemic heart disease, and a stronger link between the herbicide and chronic B-cell leukemias. VA's decision to include these conditions brings the total number of categories of presumed illnesses linked to Agent Orange to 14. The decision regarding chronic B-cell leukemias actually expands the presumptive determination of chronic lymphocytic leukemia to include all chronic B-cell leukemias.

John Rowan, National President of Vietnam Veterans of America, praised the Secretary's decision and said in a statement that Secretary Shinseki, "has taken significant strides toward 'doing the right thing' by the Veterans with whom he fought some 40 years ago."

For more information VA's services and programs for Veterans exposed to Agent Orange, go to **www.publichealth.va.gov/exposures/agentorange** or call VA at **1-800-749-8387.** ■

VA Seeks to Fast Track New Agent Orange Claims

In March 2010, VA announced a new initiative to "fast track" the claims process for presumptive service-connected illnesses due to Agent Orange exposure during the Vietnam War.

Over the next two years, about 100,000 Vietnam Veterans are expected to file disability compensation claims related to the recent expansion of presumptive illnesses announced by Secretary Shinseki.

VA will move the claims process a major step forward, using the latest technology to migrate the manual processing of claims to an automated process that meets the needs of today's Veterans in a more timely manner.

With this new approach, VA expects to shorten the time it takes to gather evidence, which now takes on average over 90 days. Once the claim is fully developed and all pertinent information is gathered, VA will be able to more quickly decide the claim and process the award, if granted.

The modernized claims process is expected to roll out in 2010.

For more information about disability compensation, go to **www.vba.va.gov/bln/21/compensation/index.htm.** ■

VA Helps Vets Address Mortgage Problems, Has a "Solid Record of Success"

Many homeowners have recently found it difficult to pay their mortgages, but quick intervention by loan counselors at VA has reduced the number of Veterans defaulting on their home loans.

VA is reaching out to Veterans to help keep people in their homes. VA has a solid record of success in helping Veterans and active-duty personnel deal with financial crises.

VA counselors, located at 10 VA offices nationwide, are available to assist those with VA-guaranteed home loans to avoid foreclosure through counseling and special financing arrangements. The counselors also can assist Veterans with non-VA loans. Since the year 2000, VA has helped about 91,000 Veterans, active-duty members, and survivors keep their homes, saving the government approximately $1.8 billion.

Depending on a Veteran's circumstances, VA can intercede on the Veteran's behalf to pursue options such as repayment plans, forbearance, and loan modifications that can allow a Veteran to keep a home.

To obtain help from a VA financial counselor, call **1-877-827-3702.** Information about VA's home loan guaranty program is available on the Internet at **www.homeloans.va.gov.** ■

CONTINUED FROM PAGE 1 ***A Message to Veterans from Secretary of Veterans Affairs, Eric "Ric" Shinseki***

by what we do, not what we promise, and that our best days as an organization supporting Veterans are ahead of us. We will fulfill President Lincoln's charge to care for Veterans and their families by redesigning and reengineering ourselves for the future.

Transforming any institution is supremely challenging; I know this from my own experience in leading large, proud, complex, and high-performing organizations through change. But the best organizations must be prepared to meet the challenging times, evolving technology and, most importantly, evolving needs of clients. Historically, organizations that are unwilling or unable to change soon find themselves irrelevant. You and your needs are not irrelevant.

Veterans are our clients, and delivering the highest quality care and services in a timely, consistent, and fair manner is a VA responsibility. I take that responsibility seriously and have charged all of the Department's employees for their best efforts and support everyday to meet our obligations to you. Our path forward is challenging, but the President and Congress support us. They have asked us to do this well—for you.

Veterans are our sole reason for existence and our number one priority—bar none. I look forward to working together with all VA employees to transform our Department into an organization that reflects the change and commitment our country expects and our Veterans deserve.

Thank you and God bless our military, our Veterans, and our Nation. ■

CONTINUED FROM PAGE 1 ***"Blue Water" Update – Supreme Court Decision and New IOM Review***

Blue Water Veterans continue to have the same access to health care as any Veteran.

VA has asked the Institute of Medicine (IOM) to review the medical and scientific evidence regarding Blue Water Veterans' possible exposure to Agent Orange. A report of the IOM findings is expected by summer 2011.

VA has notified Veterans with disability claims on file that are affected by the Supreme Court ruling. For questions regarding claim status, Veterans may contact their VA Regional Office (VARO). A list of VARO contacts is available at **www.va.gov/directory.**

In addition, all Veterans may be eligible for a full range of other benefits offered by VA, including education, training, home loan programs, pension, and more.

To learn more about VA's programs, Veterans can visit **www.vba.va.gov/VBA/benefits/factsheets** or call **1-800-827-1000.**

To learn more about the Agent Orange Registry exam, visit **www.publichealth.va.gov/exposures/agentorange/registry.asp** or call **1-800-749-8387**, then press 3. ■

VA to Bring Service Closer to Veterans: Rural Veterans Benefit from New Programs

The Department of Veterans Affairs is undertaking several initiatives to improve access and quality of care for enrolled rural Veterans. In addition, VA is part of a larger initiative to explore how communities, states, and the Federal government can work together to support rural America.

VA continually seeks innovative ways to improve quality of care for Veterans in rural areas.

Rural Mobile Health Care Clinics

VA has rolled out new mobile health clinics to bring primary care and mental health services closer to Veterans in rural counties across the nation. These mobile clinics help better serve patients living far from a VA Medical Center or outpatient clinic.

The mobile clinics are equipped to serve as primary care and mental health clinics. Rural areas in Colorado, Nebraska, and Wyoming share a single mobile van, while Maine, Washington State, and West Virginia each have a VA mobile van.

Veterans Rural Health Resource Centers (VRHRCs)

VA has opened three Veterans Rural Health Resource Centers to support and improve care to rural Veterans. With clinically trained health care providers and researchers leading each center, VRHRCs conduct clinical demonstration and pilot programs, and serve as regional experts to support VA's rural health efforts.

These centers reflect VA's commitment to provide the best quality care to Veterans everywhere.

The eastern center is located in Vermont at the White River Junction VA Medical Center, the central region in Iowa at the Iowa City VA Medical Center, and the western region at Utah's Salt Lake City VA Medical Center.

Mobile Counseling Centers across America

VA's Vet Center program has launched a fleet of new mobile counseling centers to reach rural and underserved Veterans with high-quality readjustment counseling services.

The 38-foot motor coaches, which have spaces for confidential counseling, carry Vet Center counselors and outreach workers to events and activities to reach Veterans in broad geographic areas. These mobile centers supplement the care provided at the 232 VA Vet Centers across the country. VA has plans to expand to a total of 299 authorized Vet Centers.

These vehicles are used to provide outreach and direct readjustment counseling at active-duty and Reserve and National Guard activities, including post-deployment health reassessments for returning combat Servicemembers.

The vehicles are also used to visit events typically staffed by local Vet Center staff, including homeless "stand downs," Veteran community events, county fairs, and unit reunions at sites ranging from Native American reservations to colleges.

While the primary focus is on readjustment counseling services, the local manager may arrange with VA hospitals or clinics in the region to provide support for health promotion activities such as health screenings.

Thirteen Named to Veterans' Rural Health Advisory Committee

A Veterans Rural Health Advisory Committee was established by former VA Secretary Dr. James B. Peake to advise on health care issues affecting Veterans in rural areas.

The 13-member group examines ways to enhance VA health care services for Veterans in rural areas by evaluating current programs and identifying barriers to health care.

The committee, chaired by Dr. James F. Ahrens, former head of the Montana Hospital Association, includes Veterans, rural health experts in academia, state and Federal professionals who focus on rural health, state-level Veterans affairs officials, and leaders of Veterans Service Organizations. ■

Comprehensive Health Care for Women Veterans: You Served, You Deserve the Best Care Anywhere

As the frontlines of battle and the rules of warfare have changed dramatically in the last 50 years, so has the face of the U.S. military and Veterans. Today's women soldiers are tomorrow's women Veterans.

VA now treats more women Veterans than ever, while getting ready for even more in the coming years. The number of women Veterans using VA care is expected to double over the next two to five years.

VA is committed to providing a comprehensive approach to women Veterans' health care needs, to include primary care, preventive care screenings for breast and cervical cancer, gender-specific mental health care, and beyond. In addition, VA strives for excellence in meeting the unique needs of women Veterans who are over age 55, and is prepared to address health issues such as high risk for heart disease, cancers, and obesity-related issues such as diabetes.

To better serve women Veterans' needs, VA is launching a number of programs to address provider education and has increased access through clinic enhancements and home tele-health, the development and improvement of diagnostic services including laboratory and mammography, and created a system-wide focus on continuity of care.

Meeting women's health care needs starts at the nearest VA Medical Center. VA knows women's health issues and each VA hospital has a Women Veterans Program Manager, who is there to help provide the quality care women Veterans need and deserve.

Contact the Women Veterans Program Manager at any VA Medical Center or call **1-877-222-8387** to find the nearest VA facility. Learn more about Women Veterans Health Care online at **www.publichealth.va.gov/womenshealth.** ■

Self Management: You Can Live a Better Life!

The New Jersey War Related Illness and Injury Study Center (WRIISC) sees many Veterans with chronic symptoms, such as muscle pain, fatigue, and headaches, which can be debilitating and difficult to cope with. The goal is to provide Veterans with a "roadmap" for managing these symptoms and ultimately give them tools to help them improve the quality of their lives.

Because there is often no cure for many chronic symptoms, it is important for Veterans to work at overcoming the physical and emotional problems these symptoms cause. Many Veterans and their relatives ask if this approach is realistic—it is, and one key is to practice self-management techniques. Several self-management strategies are effective for a variety of symptoms (for example, the same strategy might work for a person with pain or fatigue) because they not only reduce symptoms but help to reduce some of the normal but difficult emotions that result from symptoms. Some self-management strategies include: exercising, eating healthy, and practicing relaxation strategies such as deep breathing.

Self management is more than just trying new things on your own to make your symptoms better. The Veterans Health Administration (VHA) defines self management as "helping you to learn about your condition(s), learn how you and your family can help, learn what skills you need, learn what help and resources are available, improving access to your health care team, and helping you do what you want for you health and life."

Where to Start:

Select a self-management strategy that you want to try. Keep in mind that when trying something new it is important to set small goals that are attainable. For example, say you wish to practice deep breathing to relieve stress, you should start by saying you will do this for 5 minutes 3 out of 7 days a week versus everyday for a half-hour. You can accomplish your goals if they are realistic and change your life little by little as you go along.

While it can be hard to fully control chronic health problems, patients can control how well they live. Always do what is necessary to take care of an illness and ask for help when needed. Ultimately, adopting self-management strategies can help patients feel more in control and more confident in their ability to manage symptoms and conditions. Most importantly, self management helps to maintain and improve the current level of function regardless of symptoms.

For more information about self management or WRIISC medical services for Veterans, please contact the national WRIISC referral line at **202-461-1013** or go to **www.WarRelatedIllness.va.gov.** ■

Health Conditions* Recognized for Presumptive Service-Connection

The information below has been updated as of July 2010. For additional updates, visit **www.publichealth.va.gov/exposures/agentorange.**

Presumptive service-connection means that VA acknowledges that a condition is service-connected. Veterans who served in Vietnam who have one or more of these conditions do not have to show that their illness(es) is (are) related to their military service to get disability compensation. However, claims must still be filed by these Veterans to be considered for disability compensation.

Conditions* Recognized for Presumptive Service-Connection for In-Country Vietnam Veterans

Acute and Subacute Peripheral Neuropathy: A nervous system condition that causes numbness, tingling, and motor weakness. Under VA's rating regulations, it must be at least 10% disabling within 1 year of exposure to Agent Orange and resolve within 2 years after the date it began.

AL Amyloidosis: A rare disease caused when an abnormal protein, amyloid, enters tissues or organs.

Chloracne (or similar acneform disease): A skin condition that occurs soon after exposure to certain chemicals (those that contain chlorine, hence the term chloracne). Under VA's rating regulations, chloracne (or other acneform disease similar to chloracne) must be at least 10% disabling within 1 year of exposure to Agent Orange.

***All chronic B-Cell Leukemias (previously this category included only chronic lymphocytic leukemias. It is now expanded to include other chronic leukemias affecting B-cells such as hairy cell leukemia):** A type of cancer that affects white blood cells.

Diabetes Mellitus (Type 2): A disease characterized by high blood sugar levels resulting from the body's inability to respond properly to the hormone insulin.

Hodgkin's Disease: A malignant lymphoma (cancer) characterized by progressive enlargement of the lymph nodes, liver, and spleen, and by progressive anemia.

***Ischemic Heart Disease:** A disease characterized by a reduced supply of blood to the heart that leads to chest pain.

Multiple Myeloma: A disorder which causes an overproduction of certain proteins from white blood cells.

Non-Hodgkin's Lymphoma: A group of cancers that affect the lymph glands and other lymphatic tissue.

***Parkinson's Disease:** A motor system condition with symptoms that include a trembling of the hands, imbalance, and loss of facial expression.

Porphyria Cutanea Tarda: A disorder characterized by liver dysfunction and by thinning and blistering of the skin in sun-exposed areas. Under VA's rating regulations, it must be at least 10% disabling within 1 year of exposure to Agent Orange.

Prostate Cancer: Cancer of the prostate; one of the most common cancers among men.

Respiratory Cancers: Cancers of the lung, larynx, trachea, and bronchus.

Soft Tissue Sarcoma (other than Osteosarcoma, Chondrosarcoma, Kaposi's sarcoma, or Mesothelioma): A group of different types of cancers in body tissues such as muscle, fat, blood and lymph vessels, and connective tissues.

***On March 25, 2010, VA published a proposed regulation that will establish chronic B-cell leukemias (including chronic lymphocytic leukemia, hairy cell leukemia, and others), Parkinson's disease, and ischemic heart disease as associated with Agent Orange exposure. Eligible Vietnam Veterans who have filed claims may receive disability compensation for these diseases when the regulation is final.**

Conditions Recognized in Children of Vietnam Veterans

Spina bifida: A neural tube birth defect that results from the failure of the bony portion of the spine to close properly in the developing fetus during early pregnancy.

Disabilities other than spina bifida in the children of women Vietnam Veterans: Covered birth defects include a wide range of conditions. Eighteen defects are specifically included and others not specifically excluded are covered. For more information, contact a Veteran Service Representative at **1-800-827-1000.**

Covered birth defects include, but are not limited to, the following conditions:

1. achondroplasia,
2. cleft lip and cleft palate,
3. congenital heart disease,
4. congenital talipes equinovarus (clubfoot),
5. esophageal and intestinal atresia,
6. Hallerman-Streiff syndrome,
7. hip dysplasia,
8. Hirschsprung's disease (congenital megacolon),
9. hydrocephalus due to aqueductal stenosis,
10. hypospadias,

CONTINUED ON PAGE 8

VA Expands Suicide Prevention Efforts

VA has implemented a comprehensive strategy for suicide prevention that includes a number of initiatives and innovations that hold great promise for preventing suicide among Veterans.

VA's Suicide Prevention Lifeline program includes a Hotline, **1-800-273-TALK (8255)**. The lifeline is staffed by trained professionals 24 hours a day to assist Veterans in crisis. Nearly 33,000 Veterans, family members, or friends of Veterans called the Hotline in the first year of operation. Of those calls, there have been more than 1,600 rescues to prevent possible tragedy.

In July 2009, VA added an online "chat" component to the Lifeline program. This service, available at **www.suicidepreventionlifeline.org**, enables Veterans and their loved ones to chat online anonymously with a trained VA counselor and have their questions and concerns answered. When needed, the counselor can immediately connect users to the Hotline for crisis intervention or additional referral services.

Other initiatives include the hiring of suicide prevention coordinators at each of VA's 153 Medical Centers, the establishment of a Mental Health Center of Excellence in Canandaigua, NY, focusing on developing and testing clinical and public health intervention standards for suicide prevention, the creation of an additional research center on suicide prevention in Denver, CO, which focuses on research in the clinical and neurobiological conditions that can lead to increased suicide risk and a plus-up in staff making more than 400 mental health professionals entirely dedicated to suicide prevention.

New efforts are also underway, based on findings from a review of suicide prevention experts from VA, the Department of Defense, the Centers for Disease Control and Prevention, the National Institute of Health, and the Substance Abuse and Mental Health Services Administration.

Among the recommendations to further enhance VA programs, many of which are underway, include:

- Improve VA's screening for suicide among Veterans with depression or post-traumatic stress disorder (PTSD). VA is designing a new screening protocol, with pilot testing undertaken in 2009.
- Develop educational materials about suicide prevention for families and community groups. VA is examining the effectiveness of support groups and educational material for the families of suicidal Veterans, and producing a brochure for the families of Veterans with traumatic brain injury about suicide.
- Increase training for VA chaplains about the warning signs of suicide. VA offices responsible for chaplains and mental health professionals are studying ways to implement this recommendation.
- Ensure that evidence-based research is used to determine the appropriateness of medications for depression, PTSD and suicidal behavior. VA is providing written warnings to patients about side effects, and the Department's suicide prevention coordinators are contacting health care providers to advise them of the latest evidence-based research on medications.
- Devise a policy for protecting the confidential records of VA patients who may also be treated by the military's health care system. VA is developing a plan to clarify the privacy rights of patients who come to VA while serving in the military.
- Increase research about suicide prevention. VA has announced several funding opportunities for research on suicide prevention and is developing priorities for suicide prevention research.
- Design a study that will identify suicide risk among Veterans of different conflicts, ages, genders, military branches and other factors. VA has committed to work with other Federal agencies to design such a study.
- Develop a gun-safety program for Veterans with children in the home, both as a child-safety measure and a suicide prevention effort. ■

CONTINUED FROM PAGE 7 ***Conditions Recognized in Children of Vietnam Veterans***

11. imperforate anus,
12. neural tube defects,
13. Poland syndrome,
14. pyloric stenosis,
15. sundactyly (fused digits),
16. tracheoesophageal fistula,
17. undescended testicle, and
18. Williams syndrome.

These diseases are not tied to herbicides, including Agent Orange, or dioxin exposure, but rather to service in Vietnam. ■

National Suicide Prevention Resources: Hotline and Online Chat

VA has established national suicide prevention resources to ensure Veterans in emotional crisis have free, around-the-clock access to trained counselors.

Veterans can call **1-800-273-TALK (8255)**, and press "1" to be connected to the Veterans Hotline or visit **www.suicidepreventionlifeline.org** to connect with trained VA counselors on the Internet.

To operate the Veterans Hotline, VA partnered with the Substance Abuse and Mental Health Services Administration (SAMHSA) and the National Suicide Prevention Lifeline.

What to Look For: Suicide Warning Signs

If you or anyone you know shows any of the following signs, seek help as soon as possible :

- Threatening to hurt or kill oneself or talking about wanting to hurt or kill oneself
- Looking for ways to kill oneself by seeking access to firearms, available pills, or other means
- Talking or writing about death, dying, suicide when this is out of the ordinary for the person
- Feeling hopeless
- Feeling rage or uncontrolled anger or seeking revenge
- Acting reckless or engaging in risky activities
- Feeling trapped—like there's no way out
- Increasing use of alcohol or drugs
- Withdrawing from friends, family, and society
- Feeling anxious, agitated, or unable to sleep or sleeping all the time
- Experiencing dramatic mood changes
- Seeing no reason for living or having no sense of purpose in life ■

Q's & A's

The Review includes a questions-and-answers feature in response to questions sent by readers. Vietnam Veterans and their families and friends often have questions and concerns about health issues relating to military service in Vietnam. They want answers and knowledge about what VA and other Federal departments and agencies are doing to help these Veterans. Readers often ask about VA disability policy.

Q The October 2007 edition of The Review included information regarding the association between herbicide and dioxin exposure and AL amyloidosis. This condition was listed as having "limited or suggestive evidence of an association" with herbicide and dioxin exposure, which is the weakest positive category of association.

Has a determination been made regarding establishing presumptive service-connection for this disorder?

A In the Institute of Medicine (IOM) report "Veterans and Agent Orange: Update 2006," released on July 27, 2007, IOM concluded that "there is limited or suggestive evidence of an association between exposures to the compounds of interest [found in the herbicide Agent Orange] and AL amyloidosis."

The Secretary of Veterans Affairs, after considering all of the evidence, determined that there is a positive association between exposure to herbicide agents and the occurrence of AL amyloidosis.

On May 7, 2009, VA published a final rule in the Federal Register to establish AL amyloidosis as an Agent Orange/herbicide presumptive disability. This rule now establishes presumptive service-connection for AL amyloidosis based on herbicide exposure. ■

Disability Compensation from VA

Veterans with service-connected illnesses or injuries may be eligible for monthly payments, called disability compensation. The disability must have been incurred or aggravated during active military service. Furthermore, the military service of the Veteran must have been terminated through separation or discharge under conditions that were other than dishonorable.

Disability compensation varies according to the degree of disability and the number of dependents. Benefits are not subject to Federal or state income tax. Receipt of military retirement pay, disability severance pay, and separation incentive payments, known as SSB and VSI (Special Separation Benefits and Voluntary Separation Incentives), may affect the amount of VA compensation paid.

Disability ratings range from 0 to 100 percent (in increments of 10 percent). For example, in 2010, a Veteran with a disability rating of 10 percent receives $123 per month; a Veteran with disability rating of 50 percent gets $770 per month; and a Veteran with no dependents who is totally disabled and evaluated at 100 percent receives $2,673 monthly.

Veterans with disability ratings between 30 and 100 percent also may be eligible for monthly allowances for eligible dependents. (The amount depends on the disability rating).

A Veteran who is in need of regular aid and attendance of another person (including the Veteran's spouse), or who is permanently housebound may be entitled to additional benefits. VA must make that determination before the Veteran can receive these benefits.

Veterans can apply for VA disability benefits by completing and submitting VA Form 21-256, Veterans Application for Compensation and Pension. If you have any of the following materials, please attach them to the application:

- Discharge or separation papers (DD-214 or equivalent).
- Dependency records (marriage and children's birth certificates).
- Medical evidence (doctor and hospital reports).

You can also apply online at **http://vabenefits.vba.va.gov/vonapp.**

Other Benefits

In addition to the disability compensation program described above, individual Veterans may be eligible for the full range of other benefits offered by VA, including education and training, vocational rehabilitation, home loan guaranties, life insurance, pension, burial benefits, and more.

To learn more about VA's programs, Veterans and other interested parties can visit VA's home page at **www.va.gov** or call **1-800-827-1000.** For additional information on other benefits programs, please check online at **www.vba.va.gov/VBA/benefits/factsheets.** ■

Monthly Disability Rates for 2010

Percent Disabled	No Dependents	Veteran & Spouse
10	$123	———
20	$243	———
30	$376	$421
40	$541	$601
50	$770	$845
60	$974	$1,064
70	$1,228	$1,333
80	$1,427	$1,547
90	$1,604	$1,739
100	$2,673	$2,823

Agent Orange Registry Statistics: As of March 2010

The Agent Orange Registry began in mid-1978 to respond to the health-related concerns of Vietnam Veterans. The examinations are available free of charge to all eligible Veterans. If you would like to schedule a registry exam, contact an Environmental Health (EH) Coordinator at your local VA Medical Center. A listing of EH Coordinators is available online at **www.publichealth.va.gov/exposures/eh_coordinators.asp.**

Initial Examinations--------------------------------------502,056

Follow-up Examinations -----------------------------------57,353

Total (Initial & Follow-up) -----------------------------559,409

Fore more information about the Agent Orange Registry, go to **www.publichealth.va.gov/exposures/agentorange/registry.asp.**

Where to Get Help and Additional Information

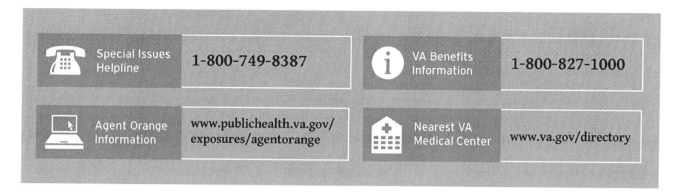

Special Issues Helpline	1-800-749-8387
VA Benefits Information	1-800-827-1000
Agent Orange Information	www.publichealth.va.gov/exposures/agentorange
Nearest VA Medical Center	www.va.gov/directory

Veterans with Questions about Agent Orange – Key contacts:

- VA's Special Issues Helpline at **1-800-749-8387**
- Your nearest VA Medical Center, which you can locate at: **www.va.gov/directory**
- VA benefits information **1-800-827-1000**

General questions about Agent Orange:

Contact VA's Special Issues Helpline at **1-800-749-8387.** You also can find information on our Web site at **www.publichealth.va.gov/exposures/agentorange.**

If you are concerned about Agent Orange exposure:

Contact the nearest VA Medical Center to request an Agent Orange registry examination. You can find the VA Medical Center nearest you at: **www.va.gov/directory.**

If you are a Vietnam Veteran and need medical treatment for conditions that may be related to herbicides used in Vietnam:

Contact the nearest VA Medical Center for eligibility information and possible medical treatment, or call VA's Special Issues Helpline at **1-800-749-8387.** You can find the VA Medical Center nearest you at **www.va.gov/directory.**

If you encounter difficulties at a VA Medical Center:

Contact the "patient advocate" or "patient representative" at that facility for assistance in resolving the problem. Ask the Medical Center telephone operator for the patient advocate or representative.

Vietnam Veterans with children with spina bifida:

Contact VA's national hotline at **1-888-820-1756,** or the nearest VA Regional Office by calling **1-800-827-1000.** Additional information about spina bifida is available from the Spina Bifida Association of America at 4590 MacArthur Blvd, NW, Suite 250, Washington, DC 20007, or by calling **1-800-621-3141,** or by email at **sbaa@sbaa.org.** The Web site is **www.sbaa.org.**

For disability information:

Contact a VA Veteran Service Representative at the nearest VA Regional Office or health care facility to talk with a counselor and apply for disability compensation. VA disability counselors have information about the wide range of benefit programs that VA administers.

The national number is **1-800-827-1000.** To start a disability claim online, go to **www.va.gov.** You also can get information about disability compensation from VA's Special Issues Helpline at **1-800-749-8387.**

Representatives of Veterans Service Organizations have been of great help to many military Veterans, including Vietnam Veterans who are seeking benefits they earned through their service to the Nation. VA does not endorse or recommend any specific group over another. State and County Veteran Service Officers are also good resources for Vietnam and other Veterans.

For additional benefits information, see VA's "Federal Benefits for Veterans, Dependents and Survivors" booklet. This booklet is updated annually to reflect changes in law and policies and is available at **www.va.gov/opa/Is1.** It also may be purchased from the U.S. Government Printing Office either at their Web site **http://bookstore.gpo.gov** or by mail:

U.S. Government Printing Office
Superintendent of Documents
Washington, DC 20402

VA's Web sites are updated throughout the year to provide the most current information. VA's home page **www.va.gov** contains links to selections on compensation and pension benefits, health care benefits and services, burial and memorial benefits, and more. ■

Subscription or address change form for **Agent Orange Review** Newsletter. Please print.

Name First: ______ Middle: ______ Last: ______ Last 4 of SSN: ______

Address Street (Please indicate which APO/FPO, if applicable) ______ City: ______ State: ______ Zip Code: ______

New Address Street ______ City: ______ State: ______ Zip Code: ______

- ☐ My address has changed, and I would like to continue to receive the newsletter.
- ☐ I am receiving more than one copy, and only want to get a single copy.
- ☐ I don't need the newsletter by mail as I can read it at **www.publichealth.va.gov/exposures/agentorange.**

Address Changes

If this newsletter has your old address, please use this form to update our mailing list.

Send the completed form to:

Agent Orange Review
Department of Veterans Affairs
AITC-ATTN: Mailing list update (32B)
1615 Woodward Street
Austin, TX 78772-0001

If you receive more than one copy of the Agent Orange Revie or prefer to read it online at **www.publichealth.va.gov/exposures/agentorange**, let us know by returning the fo above to the address at left. Please provide your name, address, and last four digits of your Social Security numbe You may use this or other paper. Thank you.

Department of Veterans Affairs
Agent Orange Review
AITC (32B)
1615 Woodward Street
Austin, TX 78772-0001

OFFICIAL BUSINESS

Agent Orange Review

INFORMATION FOR VETERANS
WHO SERVED IN VIETNAM

July 2010